"It is of inestimable benefit to our souls to be exposed to the godly comfort and exhortation from God's giants. In this well-selected collection we discover pastors in the trenches during Europe's worst plagues. This volume is a treasure."

—MICHAEL HORTON, J. Gresham Machen Professor of Theology and Apologetics, Westminster Seminary California

"*Faith in the Time of Plague: Selected Writings from the Reformation and Post-Reformation* could, I suppose, be read as a scholars' inquiry into classic Protestant writings. But that misses the real point: this is serious theology for serious times—for our times—tightly reasoned, and balm for the soul. All the great voices of classical Reformed thought are here: Beza, Voetius, Rivet's plea against recklessness, Ursinus on mortality, the prayers of the Reformed English Church. And there is even Luther, reminding everyone caught up in pandemics that 'God himself shall be his attendant and his physician, too.' Here is sane advice which, although hundreds of years old, we could wish some modern authorities had heeded. Bounty, indeed, in time of need, and a book for the bedside and chairside."

—ALLEN C. GUELZO, Senior Research Scholar in the Council of the Humanities at Princeton University, Director of the James Madison Program Initiative on Politics and Statesmanship

"When Christians face an outbreak of deadly disease, they wrestle with many questions about God's sovereignty and human responsibility, science and the Bible, faith and fear, grief and worship, and prudence and faithfulness. What we sometimes forget is that godly people have thought through these issues centuries before us, and we can learn much from them. This collection of writings on the plague by Reformers and Reformed orthodox theologians is full of wisdom and comfort for the crises of our modern era."

—JOEL R. BEEKE, President, Puritan Reformed Theological Seminary

"What a tremendous pastoral resource this is for the trying days in which we live. Our Christian forebears of the early modern era, who lived through times as grim and fearsome as ours—some might say that grimmer days were theirs—have much to teach us about living for God in times of fear and dread. Although our technological resources for dealing with pestilence and pandemic are far greater than theirs, the deep sensibilities of the

heart are the same and it is there, within those affections, that we need to heed their voices. Most welcome and highly recommended."
—MICHAEL A.G. HAYKIN, Chair and Professor of Church History,
The Southern Baptist Theological Seminary

"We are often told that the coronavirus pandemic has thrown us into unprecedented times. *Faith in the Time of Plague* shows that such a description is historically myopic: there is nothing new about pestilence and plague. By gathering rich reflections on contagious disease from great Protestant theologians like Beza, Voetius, and Luther—Christians who wrote theology against a backdrop of plague—this volume has given us a helpful resource with which to approach the challenges of our own (thoroughly precedented) times."
—JAMES EGLINTON, Meldrum Senior Lecturer in Reformed Theology,
University of Edinburgh

"The exercise of humility almost always leads to learning. So it is with these texts from church history. If we in the church today humble ourselves enough to ask if there is anything we can learn from the past regarding plagues and pandemics then we will be setting ourselves up to learn. We'll learn of faith and courage in the face of death and upheaval. We'll see examples of loving one's neighbor. We'll find guidance for gracious debate regarding our response. And, above all, we'll be reminded anew and afresh to look to our King, who is good and sovereign, and to look toward Heaven, our eternal home."
—STEPHEN J. NICHOLS, President, Reformation Bible College,
Chief Academic Officer, Ligonier Ministries

"As much as the COVID-19 pandemic feels 'unprecedented,' plague and pestilence are nothing new. Throughout church history Christians have faced similar circumstances and thought deeply about what it means to live faithfully amidst them. We might even speak of a 'plague theology' or 'theology of pandemic' that has developed in the church's historical reflection. It is astonishing how much we can benefit from listening to the wisdom of prior generations and encouraging to know we are not the first to face such challenges. Todd M. Rester and Stephen M. Coleman have provided the church with a wonderful and amazingly useful resource in this collection of previously untranslated writings."
—GAVIN ORTLUND, Senior Pastor, First Baptist Church of Ojai

"Times of plague throughout history have always elicited honest and challenging questions. Is pestilence a result of God's wrath and judgment? What is the Christian's duty as it concerns care for the sick and dying during a highly contagious pandemic? Should pastors always visit infected members of the flock or are there occasions to flee and seek safety? This rich compendium of Reformation and Post-Reformation era writings serve to answer these and many other complex and important questions from a biblical perspective. This remarkable volume is brimming with ageless wisdom and truth for today's believer."
—Jon D. Payne, Senior Pastor, Christ Church Presbyterian, Charleston, Executive Coordinator, Gospel Reformation Network

"In times of epidemic disease, how should pastors care, courageously and tenderly, for the fearful hearts of Christ's flock? I did not wrestle with that question as a seminary student, nor did I address it in the pastoral theology courses that I taught over the decades. We now know how vital that issue is. In order to navigate these perilous and—to us—uncharted waters, we need not only the divine wisdom of God's Word and Spirit but also the sage voices of our pastoral predecessors, who tended Jesus' lambs in times of widespread, deadly disease. In *Faith in the Time of Plague* we hear the biblical, theological, and pastoral wisdom of those whom God called, as he has called us, to minister to those who walk through the valley of the shadow of death. I thank God that this timely book has appeared at this particular moment."
—Dennis E. Johnson, Professor Emeritus of Practical Theology, Westminster Seminary California

Faith
in the Time of Plague

Faith

in the Time of Plague

Selected Writings from the Reformation and Post-Reformation

Edited by Stephen M. Coleman & Todd M. Rester
Foreword by Gregory A. Poland
Introduction by Peter A. Lillback

WESTMINSTER SEMINARY PRESS

Faith in the Time of Plague:
Selected Writings from the Reformation and Post-Reformation
Copyright © 2021 by Westminster Seminary Press

All Rights Reserved. No part of the copyrighted material may be reproduced without the written consent of the publisher, except for brief quotations for the purpose of review or comment. Every effort has been made to trace any remaining copyright holders and obtain permission to reproduce this material. For inquiries and information, contact Westminster Seminary Press: 2960 Church Road, Glenside, Pennsylvania 19038, or at wsp@wts.edu.

"Whether one may flee from a deadly plague" reprinted from *Luther's Works* (Vol. 43), copyright © Fortress Press. Used with permission.

Unless otherwise indicated, all English Scripture quotations are translated from the original work.

Partial funding for this book was provided by Framework: Public Theology from Westminster

Printed and Bound in the United States of America

Cover design by Jessica Hiatt
Cover image: "View of Bleaching Fields near Haarlem" by Jacob van Ruisdael
Typeset in Adobe Minion Pro by Angela Messinger

Hardcover ISBN: 978-1-7336272-5-2
Ebook ISBN: 978-1-7336272-7-6

Contents

Foreword by Gregory A. Poland xi

Introduction by Peter A. Lillback. xvii

Preface by Stephen M. Coleman and Todd M. Rester. xxiii

Acknowledgments xxxiii

Part I
Variorum tractatus theologici de peste

1. *A Learned Treatise on the Plague* 3
   Theodore Beza

2. *A Letter to a Friend* 31
   André Rivet

3. *A Treatise on the Plague, or a Spiritual Antidote to the Plague* 67
   Gisbertus Voetius

4. *A Theological Dissertation on the Plague*. 123
   Johannes Hoornbeeck

Part II
Reformation and Post-Reformation Plague Writings

5. *Pestlied (Plague Hymn)* 185
   Huldrych Zwingli

6. *Whether One May Flee from a Deadly Plague* 191
   Martin Luther

7. *The Merciful Hands of the Lord*. 211
   Ludwig Lavater

8. *The Work of Christ and the Christian's Duty* 231
   Jerome Zanchi

9. *A Godly Meditation on Death* 247
   Zacharias Ursinus

10. *On the Flight of a Minister in Persecution or Plague* 271
    George Abbot

11. *A Letter to My Mother* 295
    John Rawlet

Appendix A: *On Mortality* 313
   Cyprian of Carthage

Appendix B: *Prayer and Thanksgiving*.......................... 329
   Book of Common Prayer (1662)

Bibliography 331

Index of Subjects and Names 347

Index of Scripture References.................................. 357

Foreword

The father of modern medicine, Sir William Osler, wrote that "Humanity has but three great enemies: fever, famine, and war; of these by far the greatest, by far the most terrible, is fever."[1] I write this Foreword in the first week of January 2021, after 11 months of the SARS-CoV-2 pandemic. As a physician-scientist who founded and runs the Mayo Clinic's Vaccine Research Group, I have studied RNA respiratory viruses for the last 35 years. For the last 11 months it has been nearly the entire focus of my time—usually 12–16 hours per day, 6 days a week—as we have worked in the laboratory to understand immune response to this virus and attempted to build a novel COVID-19 vaccine platform. I have completed over 1,200 national and international interviews on the pandemic and given more talks than I can now count.

To be educated is to be prepared. Such a statement presupposes context and places value on the past. While the 2020 SARS-CoV-2 pandemic was a shock, it should not have been a surprise. Thus far, I have survived 4 pandemics: the 1957 Asian flu, the 1968 Hong Kong flu, the 2009 H1N1 flu, and (so far!) the 2020 SARS-CoV-2 pandemic. My previous roles as President of both the Armed Forces Epidemiological Board and the Defense Health Board, and as a member of the National Vaccine Advisory Committee, the Advisory Committee on Immunization Practices of the CDC, and the FDA's Vaccines and Related Biologic Products Advisory Committee, as well as my participation in many national and international tabletop exercises on infectious disease threats and pandemics, meant that nothing about what has happened in 2020 was particularly novel (other than the pathogen involved), nor unexpected to me or others in the world of infectious disease epidemiology. And yet the majority of the world, and the church, was unprepared. It need not have been.

To date, the SARS-CoV-2 virus has infected 100 million people worldwide, hospitalized tens of millions, and taken nearly 2 million lives. It has cost the United States over $16 trillion and disrupted virtually every aspect of life as we know it. And yet these effects pale in comparison to what

---

1. William Osler, "The Study of the Fevers of the South" *Journal of the American Medical Association* 26, no. 21 (May 1896): 999—1004.

generations past faced. In this book, *Faith in the Time of Plague*, Stephen M. Coleman and Todd M. Rester present much-needed new and revised translations along with republications of key treatises, letters, and writings from those Reformed theologians who came before us, who lived and ministered during times of plague. Like us, they wrestled with making sense of the events surrounding and slowly overtaking them. It is in this vein that I have gotten to know these men and their scholarly work. In November 2020 I completed a 60-page paper for a course at Westminster on the intersections of Reformation history, Reformed faith, and plague during the 16th–17th centuries in England. Once I'd taught myself to read Late Middle English, I spent weeks locating, reading, and synthesizing extant primary sources from this same time period. What a delight it is now to discover through this book rich literature from that era that has never been translated into English!

Faith in the Time of Plague provides us access to some of these key sources, and we collectively owe a debt of gratitude to Drs. Coleman and Rester for doing so. In particular, the translations of Voetius, Hoornbeeck, and Zanchi's writings will be relished by those who have found them previously inaccessible. Close study of these works reveals that the tremendous medical, social, ethical, political, and religious changes that occurred across the 16th and 17th centuries led to theological changes in thinking that can guide us through the very same issues in our churches and communities hundreds of years later.

Some brief context is important. In studying these works it's important to note that the word "plague" derives from the Latin word *plaga*, meaning "blow" or "stripe"—a reference to the idea of God's "strike" or "blow" against humans due to their sin. It's also important to recognize that the bubonic plagues ("black death"), which spread in successive waves throughout the Reformation time period, occurred hundreds of years before the germ theory of disease had been discovered and accepted. Prevalent belief among physicians and clergy of the day was the Galenic notion of plague as caused by poisonous vapors, or "noxious airs," as they called it. While many physicians, apothecaries, and public officials bravely stayed and fought these plagues, often losing their lives, it was the clergy, perhaps best exemplified in Martin Luther's letter to Reformed leader and pastor Johann Hess, that formed the core of public health responses to the pandemic. Such measures included separating the healthy from the ill, hygienic measures like fumigation, quarantine, and the limiting of large gatherings of people (yes, including church services), the development and funding of sick hospitals, and other provisions. In one case, at the urging of a young Reformed pastor, the entire village of Eyam, England sealed itself off from all others in a magnanimous attempt to prevent further spread of the plague. This stands in sharp contrast with the current challenge of public health efforts to convince people to maintain social distancing and observe proper mask use.

Plagues are just one of many points at which Christianity has provided the foundation and often the motivation for scientific solutions. Indeed, as others have pointed out, the doctrines of Scripture provide the very possibility of science. Paul Slack noted that from 1486 through the 1600s, the majority of books and publications in England dealing with the plague were, in fact, written by divines.[2] Yet the primary motivation of these 16th and 17th century Reformed and reformational theologians was not medical or even public health per se; rather, it was to ask and to answer great questions that transcended immediate concerns: What is the meaning of plagues? Are we "stricken" by God? Punished for our sins? Why do the righteous die alongside the wicked? In addition, important questions were asked of the clergy by the clergy: Shall pastors flee the plague? What were the limits and the requirements of love of neighbor and of Christian charity? Were their special requirements for the shepherds of God's flock during times of plague?

Each generation must answer these age-old questions, guided and informed by Scripture and the wisdom of the church fathers. This is the value of this outstanding book: access to writings by Reformed theologians living, pastoring, writing, and shepherding in the midst of devastating plagues to give us guidance today. Their writings illustrate a singularly important presupposition—that neither theology nor science can proceed without an epistemology and without an understanding that this world is contingent. This is perhaps even more important in our time when effective and evidence-based mitigation measures have been put at odds with political and syncretic religious ideologies. In the context of the church, appropriate distancing, wearing a mask, and proper hygiene should not be political statements; rather they are expressions of Christian charity and love for neighbor. We can do no better than to peer intently through the lens of history to learn how the towering figures of the Reformers reasoned and behaved as they were guided by transcendent truth. Through them we

---

2. Paul Slack, *The Impact of Plague in Tudor and Stuart England* (New York: Oxford University Press, 1985).

see a movement from the moralism so prevalent in our day to a Christocentric, salvific remedy borne of a right reading of Scripture.

It is for this reason, acutely pertinent to our "right now," that this book matters—and matters greatly. I wish it could be required reading for every pastor, every theologian, every church member, every public health official, and every physician. It turns out that theology, along with medicine and science, is legitimately interested in answers about the transcendent questions surrounding issues like plagues and pandemics! In fact, as others have pointed out, no scientist, no physician, and no public health official is absent an underlying philosophical or religious motivation for their understanding and recommendations regarding plagues and pandemics.[3] As the writings in this book illustrate, all streams of thought do not share moral or theological equivalence. For the modern mind it is likely to be shocking, as I admit it was often for me as I read this book, to see the profound depth of reasoning and the acuity of argument derived from Scripture and synthesized into patterns of thought and action. Doing so leads the reader from despair over current events into a profound doxology for our Creator and for his promise to his elect:

> And we know that for those who love God all things work together for good, for those who are called according to his purpose. For those whom he foreknew he also predestined to be conformed to the image of his Son, in order that he might be the firstborn among many brothers. And those whom he predestined he also called, and those whom he called he also justified, and those whom he justified he also glorified. (Romans 8:28–30, ESV)

The plagues of the 16th and 17th centuries and our own modern plagues and pandemics are all part of the unfolding eschatological drama that we see in Scripture. Plagues have purposes beyond our full comprehension. They neither surprise God, nor are they bereft of value to his elect. Todd Rester well understands the depth of this truth when he writes:

> Plague and disease deeply shaped the ministries of pastors and the congregational life of the early modern churches. A faithful pastor in

---

3. Charles Thaxton and Nancy Pearcey, *The Soul of Science–Christian Faith and Natural Philosophy*, (Wheaton, IL: Crossway Books, 1994).

this context needed a solid theology of God's providence, the dignity of every human being, especially of the sick and the infirm, a deep love of neighbor, a strong commitment to the duties of pastoral vocation, and a robust Christian prudence to navigate the physical and spiritual needs of his family, congregation, and community.[4]

We would do well to understand that indeed there is nothing new under the sun, and to marvel afresh that Scripture and the writings of those who went before us (including those in this book) rightly understood—even without the scientific knowledge we take for granted today—how to respond in God-honoring ways to the plagues of their day, for the benefit of all. May we be equally as intentional and God-honoring, guided by Scriptural doctrines, as they were then, in responding to the crises that confront us today.

Soli Deo Gloria
Gregory A. Poland, MD, FIDSA, MACP, FRCP (London)

---

4. Todd M. Rester, "Reforming Christians in a Time of Plague," *Westminster Magazine* 1, no. 1 (October 2020): 15.

Introduction

The advanced medical world that most of us have enjoyed in the West was greatly shaken by the dramatic and deadly spread of COVID-19. We have experienced the sobering inability to fight an invisible enemy. We have watched as statistics of death skyrocketed and overwhelmed hospitals, and as cities sheltered in place. The physical suffering of so many due to COVID-19 has seen many others endure the loss of daily activities, struggle with the loss of work and income, and strive to persevere through the frustrations and sorrows of lost family members and cancelled church gatherings and celebrations. When assembling has been possible, we've longed for former freedoms to fellowship now hampered by social distancing and ubiquitous masks.

This suffering, though rooted in real peril, is neither the first of its sort, nor the most deadly or horror-filled. Consider Petrarch's report of the Plague's carnage in 1348:

> Everywhere is woe, terror, everywhere. … I am not mourning some slight distress but that dreadful year 1348, which not merely robbed us of our friends, but robbed the whole world of its peoples.… And if that were not enough, now this following year reaps the remainder, and cuts down with its deadly scythe whatever survived that storm. Will posterity credit that there was a time when … almost the whole earth was depopulated?… Can it be that God has no care for the mortal lot?[1]

Indeed, historical records evidence regular visitations of haunting pandemics. Major plagues have played a role in the Judeo-Christian story from antiquity through the ancient and medieval worlds to the Reformation and to our day. The Bible records numerous plagues that impacted the life of the ancient covenant people (Lev. 13; Num. 25:1–9; 1 Sam. 24:10–17; 1 Cor. 10:6–13).[2]

Ancient accounts have preserved the sufferings of the Plague of Athens

---

1. Carter Lindberg, ed., *The European Reformations Sourcebook* (Malden, MA: Blackwell, 2000), 3–4.
2. See Peter A. Lillback, "Pastoral Principles Pertaining to Pestilence and Providence," *Unio Cum Christo* 6.1 (April 2020): 255–269.

(429–426 BC), the Antonine Plague (165–180 AD), the Plague of Cyprian (250–266), the Plague of Justinian (541–542), and the Roman Plague (590). The Medieval and Reformation eras agonized through the Black Death (1348–1349), the Sweating sickness (1485–1551), the London plagues of 1563–1564 and 1592–1593, and that city's Great Plague (1665–1666). These visitations of the grim reaper spared neither poor nor rich, believer nor unbeliever, sweeping away popes, emperors, and paupers.

America has faced pandemics too, such as the Yellow Fever Epidemic during Washington's presidency (1795) and the Spanish Flu (1918), a worldwide medical war fought as the First World War raged.

Recent years have witnessed pandemics and plagues such as AIDS (1981–present), SARS (2002–2004), Bird flu (2003–2005), Swine flu (2009–2010), MERS (2012–present), and the Zika virus (2015–2016). The world breathed a sigh of relief when it seemed the gruesome suffering of a 2018 Ebola outbreak was contained—only to be greeted a year later by COVID-19, which has since conquered the globe.

Paradoxically, times of plague not only bring forth great suffering and death; they have also produced knowledge and wisdom as omnipresent devastation provokes humanity to seek understanding, and to find new ways to live and to care for those who suffer. This is evident in Christian responses to plagues and pandemics. Scholars point to courageous and compassionate care for the dying as one reason for the rapid growth of the early church. "On Mortality"[3] by Cyprian of Carthage, written during the plague that bears his name (250–266), offers a powerful testimony to Christian witness and ministry during that time.

Further examples of beneficial results from deadly seasons of plague can be observed throughout the history of the church. Ministries of compassion and medical care have emerged, emulating the spirit of Jesus's Good Samaritan. Compelling examples of this are the orders of nuns who ministered heroically throughout the history of the Catholic Church. Deaconesses from Protestant Germany became the impetus for the modern nursing movement. The Medieval era saw the rise of the monastic order of the Hospitalers who originally cared for pilgrims en route to the Holy Land. Pastoral care for the sick not only developed scriptural counseling practices in preparation for death and enduring suffering, but gave rise to modern hospitals, which continue to bear the names of biblical figures,

---

3. See page 316 in this volume.

ecclesiastical movements, and denominations. Just as the wrath of man can ultimately praise the Lord, (Ps. 76:10) so the wrath of pandemics can bring forth good and glorify God (Rom. 8:28–30).

One such beneficial result is especially pertinent for our purposes: the extraordinary theological reflections of spiritual leaders who ministered in those perilous times. This anthology of spiritual treasure you hold in your hands is assembled from the repository of the Protestant Reformation. Presented here are writings by Martin Luther from Wittenberg, Huldrych Zwingli from Zurich, Theodore Beza from Geneva, Zacharias Ursinus from Heidelberg, Jerome Zanchi from Strasburg, Ludwig Lavater from Zurich, Gisbertus Voetius and Johannes Hoornbeeck from the Netherlands, André Rivet from France, and selections from England by John Rawlet, George Abbot, and the Book of Common Prayer. Diverse literary genres are represented, including theological treatises, meditations, biblical commentary, personal letters, hymnody, and liturgical prayer.

These, however, are but a sampling of the rich legacy of Reformed theologians who engaged the poignant theme of plague. A number of other valuable works by Reformed authors who sought to interpret God's purposes in times of plague are worthy of perusal as well, including:

- John Calvin, *On the Visitation of the Sick* (found in Vol. 2 of *John Calvin: Tracts and Letters*, published by Banner of Truth in 2009)
- Edmund Grindal, "Occasional Services for the Plague" (1563)
- John Hooper, "A Homily to be Read in the Time of Pestilence, Containing the True Cause of the Same; and Likewise a Most Present Remedy for as Many as be Already, or Hereafter Shall be Infected with Disease" (1553)
- Ludwig Lavater, (Zwingli's and Heinrich Bullinger's successor in Zurich, Bullinger's son-in-law), *Three Christian Sermons. . . of Famine and Dearth of Victuals* (1596)
- Thomas Vincent, *God's Terrible Voice in the City* (a Puritan's response to the Great Plague and Great Fire of London, 1665–1666)
- Thomas White, "A Sermon Preached at Paul's Cross on Sunday the Third of November 1577, in the Time of the Plague" (London, 1588)

In this work and those listed above, readers will find that deep and living faith emanates from these leaders of the church who ministered in a time of plague. Their trust in the sovereign purposes of our holy and good God are summed up well by the theological affirmations expressed so beautifully by Zacharias Ursinus's *Heidelberg Catechism*, Questions 1 and 27:

Question 1. *What is thy only comfort in life and in death?* That I, with body and soul, both in life and in death, am not my own, but belong to my faithful Saviour Jesus Christ, who with his precious blood has fully satisfied for all my sins, and redeemed me from all the power of the devil; and so preserves me, that without the will of my Father in heaven not a hair can fall from my head; yea, that all things must work together for my salvation. Wherefore, by his Holy Spirit, he also assures me of eternal life, and makes me heartily willing and ready henceforth to live unto him.

Question 27. *What dost thou understand by the Providence of God?* The Almighty and everywhere present power of God, whereby, as it were by his hand, he still upholds heaven and earth, with all creatures, and so governs them that herbs and grass, rain and drought, fruitful and barren years, meat and drink, health and sickness, riches and poverty, yea, all things, come to us not by chance but by his fatherly hand.

Yes, the Reformation fathers of faith affirmed that "health and sickness" were part of human life, not by chance, but by their Heavenly Father's hand. Hence their ultimate comfort was not to be found in this short life in a broken and fallen world, but in the sure eternal salvation won by the effectual work of Christ and guaranteed by the gracious saving work of the Trinity.

Finally, I am truly grateful that this new publication by Westminster Seminary Press, entitled *Faith in the Time of Plague*, is the fruitful collaboration of two Westminster Seminary professors and scholars: Todd M. Rester and Stephen M. Coleman. Todd, a church historian, and Stephen, an Old Testament scholar, have ably translated and edited many of these selections. Moreover, we all are deeply grateful for the Foreword provided by renowned Mayo Clinic vaccinologist, Gregory A. Poland. Greg is not only a leading expert in the medical treatment of plagues and pandemics, but has studied at Westminster, and serves as a member of the Westminster Seminary Board of Trustees.

It's my hope that the Lord will use *Faith in the Time of Plague* to lead us more fully to understand and to embrace the ever-relevant scriptural themes these historic leaders present, such as courageous ministry, loving compassion, wise medical practice, and practical living amid danger, the purposes of divine providence, and their earnest call for humble repentance and living faith. May these powerful pieces by our Reformation fathers challenge our faith so that we faithfully evaluate our day's rendition of the classic plague-time trilogy, "Cito, Longe, Tarde," that is, "flee quickly, go far, and return slowly." May we flee to Christ, stand far from fear, and give our hearts and lives promptly and sincerely to the High King of Heaven as we serve him, trusting his all-sufficient grace and loving providential care.

Soli Deo Gloria
Peter A. Lillback,
President,
Westminster Theological Seminary, Philadelphia
January 2021

Preface[1]

Blessed be God, even the Father of our Lord Jesus Christ, the Father of mercies, and the God of all comfort, which comforteth us in all our tribulation, that we may be able to comfort them which are in any affliction by the comfort wherewith we ourselves are comforted of God. For as the sufferings of Christ abound in us, so our consolation aboundeth in Christ. (2 Cor. 1:3–5, 1599 Geneva Bible)

At the beginning of 2020, not many of us were terribly interested in discussing plagues. Outside of the conclaves and conference rooms of historians, epidemiologists, and public health officials, who would have casually broached early modern mortality rates, disease transmission, plague diffusion, disease vectors, and medieval and early modern public health policy? After all, plague pandemics lay in the dark, distant corners of our corporate memory, somewhere in the gloomy umbral shade of the fourteenth century, far from the bright urgency of modern demands. Plague, and what life felt like in the midst of one, had to be imagined. But within a few short months it would be our sense of normal life that had to be imagined. As masks, social distancing, self-quarantining, and "flattening the curve" became part of our immediately foreseeable future, we no longer needed to use our imagination alone.

In times like these—times of change, uncertainty, and loss of control in a season of disease, death, and dying—it seems right to reflect on pastoral and biblical wisdom for Christian living and Christian ministry through the plague writings of pastors and theologians from a former age. Plague literature was, and is again, society's multifaceted literary response to plague, including everything from public policy and medical treatises to poetry and plays. Given the literary responses to the plague from various disciplines and layers of society, it is no surprise that a significant number of theologians and pastors participated in the genre. Frequently composed in the global academic language of the period, Latin, to publicize the works internationally, these writings offered biblical exposition,

---

1. Adapted from "Reforming Christians in a Time of Plague" by Todd M. Rester in *Westminster Magazine* 1, no. 1. The publisher is grateful for permission to publish this revised version.

doctrinal applications, and practical exhortations in particular crises. The plague writings of the Reformers collected and translated in this volume give us a clear view of how they believed Christians ought to respond to a pandemic and of what theological resources they reflected on. Of especially practical value, these works—prayers, hymns, theological treatises, and Protestant "art of dying well" tracts (*ars moriendi*)—are tested examples of doctrines, practices, and scriptural insights that remain relevant in ministering to congregants in perilous times; and their times were most certainly perilous.

Plague in the Early Modern Period

In addition to the more than 330 wars, armed conflicts, and rebellions between 1500 and 1700, plague was a common event in Reformation and post-Reformation Europe. Always a frightening occurrence in early modern Europe, due to its virulence and contagiousness, the plague (or the range of diseases included under the term) had a mortality rate on average of about 25% in this period. Viewed grimly, this mortality rate represents some improvement over the fourteenth century outbreaks, which had a mortality rate of 70–90%. During the seventeenth century, the percentage of population lost to plague was still staggering, whether in Italy (30–43%), the Low Countries, Rhineland, Alsace, and Switzerland (15–25% on average), England and Wales (8–10%), Spain (18–19%) or France (11–14%).[2] If you lived between 1560 and 1670 in southwest Germany, eastern France, or Switzerland, for example, you may have experienced any number of at least ten instances of plague that affected over 30 communities in each outbreak.[3] In one particularly virulent outbreak over 150 communities were affected.

Plague not only affected large cities or densely populated localities, but spread throughout rural regions along trade routes, in the wake of marching armies, and along the escape routes of refugees. The frequency of the plague was about every decade or so, sometimes lasting months, even years in both urban and rural communities. In the town of St. Gallen, Switzerland—a town of about 5,000 people (sizable for this period)—there were

---

2. Guido Alfani, "Plague in seventeenth-century Europe and the decline of Italy: an epidemiological hypothesis," *European Review of Economic History* 17, no. 4 (November 2013), 411.

3. Edward A. Eckert, "Boundary Formation and Diffusion of Plague: Swiss Epidemics from 1562–1669," *Annales de Démographie Historique*, (1978), 53–55.

outbreaks in 1610–1611, 1629, and 1635 that claimed at least a fifth of the population each time.[4]

Plague varied in severity; in some years there was a relatively low mortality rate, in others it was devastating. In Spain alone, for example, the outbreak of 1596–1599 accounted for approximately half a million deaths.[5] In London, during the outbreaks of 1592–1593, 1603, 1625, 1636, and 1665–1666 the death rate due to plague ranged from 4% of the population in mild instances up to 21% in severe ones.[6]

For a simple comparison, the estimated mortality rate of COVID-19 in the summer of 2020 (according to international, regional, and national reporting agencies such as the UN World Health Organization,[7] the USA Center for Disease Control,[8] and the EU European Center for Disease Prevention and Control)[9] ranged globally from less than 1% in a few countries to 12% in others, with most countries hovering somewhere between 4–8%. Out of approximately 25 million cases reported globally at that time, approximately 850,000 had resulted in death, for a global average mortality rate between 3–4%.

Our modern society chafes under the inconvenience of intermittent shutdowns of public marketplaces and social life. Yet, if you lived for any stretch of 75 years between 1500 and 1720—a big *if*, by the way—you would probably spend one-fifth to one-third of your life under plague-related civil ordinances and restrictions, implemented in half-year and years-long stretches. Perhaps not surprisingly, these restrictions were met with varying degrees of success and were accompanied by discord, civil unrest, and economic disaster as farms and markets faltered.

On the other hand, due to either a simple lack of medical professionals or their reluctance to expose themselves, the scholarship is clear that the burden of care for plague victims largely fell to religious orders and pastors

---

4. Ibid., 55, see especially table 2 "Comparison of plague losses of two continental cities and a larger maritime city," cf. 78–80, "Appendix: Swiss Communities Reporting Plague Outbreaks."
5. Ibid.
6. Ibid., table 2.
7. "Weekly Operational Update on Covid 19 for the week August 28, 2020," World Health Organization, accessed August 28, 2020, https://www.who.int/docs/default-source/coronaviruse/situation-reports/wou-28-august-approved.pdf?sfvrsn=d9e49c20_2
8. "CovidView for August 1, 2020," Center for Disease Control, accessed August 28, 2020, https://www.cdc.gov/coronavirus/2019-ncov/covid-data/covidview/past-reports/08072020.html
9. "Coronavirus disease 2019 (COVID-19) in the EU/EEA and the UK – eleventh update: resurgence of cases, August 10, 2020" European Center for Disease Control, accessed August 28, 2020, https://www.ecdc.europa.eu/sites/default/files/documents/covid-19-rapid-risk-assessment-20200810.pdf

in this time period. In 1641 in London, for example, Parliament entertained a novel European proposal to appoint a corps of doctors specifically to handle the plague in London.[10] But as a matter of frugality, only two doctors and two apothecaries were to attend plague victims in a city with an estimated 400,000 people. The proposal stalled and died in continual parliamentary debate. By comparison, London was comprised of at least 113 parishes within the city walls at the time, which coordinated pastoral and congregational outreach efforts with modest success. Further examples of pastoral care from the Reformers on this count are not difficult to come by. In 1519, the Swiss reformer of Zurich, Huldrych Zwingli (1484–1531), was away from Zurich when the plague broke out, but he rushed back like a fireman to a fire to serve his flock, even as mortality rates in that city reached 25%. It was not long afterwards that he contracted and almost died of the plague. Zwingli's "Plague Hymn" (*Pestlied*)[11] is a vivid written personal response to that experience.

We learn from a lament of John Calvin (1509–1564) in a 1551 letter to his colleague Guillaume Farel (1489–1565) that Theodore Beza (1519–1605) had contracted the plague while ministering in Lausanne.[12] Later, in 1588, Beza's first wife of forty-four years would die of the plague.[13] Franciscus Junius (1545–1602), a Bible translator, pastor, theology professor, and editor of the Belgic Confession, would die from plague during an outbreak in Leiden in 1602.

Plague and disease deeply shaped the ministries of pastors and the congregational life of the early modern churches. A faithful pastor in this context needed a solid theology of God's providence and the dignity of every human being, especially of the sick and the infirm; a deep love of neighbor; a strong commitment to the duties of pastoral vocation; and a robust Christian prudence to navigate the physical and spiritual needs of his family, congregation, and community.

As we can all attest, pandemics tend to reveal the seams and tensions within a society. It was no different in the sixteenth century. In one city, we have municipal and ecclesiastical records complaining that the undertakers

---

10. F.N.L. Poynterand and W. R. LeFenu. "A Seventeenth-Century London Plague Document in the Wellcome Historical Medical Library: Dr. Louis Du Moulin's Proposals to Parliament for a corps of salaried plague doctors," *Bulletin of the History of Medicine* 34, no. 4 (July–August 1960), 365–372.
11. See page 187 of this volume.
12. Shawn D. Wright, *Theodore Beza: The Man and the Myth*. (Ross-shire: Christian Focus Publications, 2015), 149; cf. S. Manetsch, *Calvin's Company of Pastors: Pastoral Care and the Emergence of the Reformed Church, 1536–1609* (Oxford: Oxford University Press, 2013), 284–289.
13. Wright, *Theodore Beza: the Man and the Myth*, 149.

and the cleaners were price gouging. Medical practitioners were overwhelmed, and hospitals were short staffed. People fled their homes and jobs for a season to the countryside and protested their civic obligations. Ministers, weighing their pastoral obligations to preach and care for their congregations, frequently declined municipal requests to supply chaplains to minister to the afflicted in the city's plague-house and hospital. Even doctors were not agreed on how infectious the plague was or how it was transmitted, increasing uncertainty about the actual risk of the plague. Why did it strike some and not others? How exactly does one remedy miasma (that is, "bad air," or better translated, "polluted air")? Additionally, it was exceedingly difficult to track cases of plague. Medical doctors and practitioners did not agree on which deaths were plague-related or due to some other cause. Strangers and travelers were suspect. Even the water supply was unreliable and just as likely to spread the plague as assist in its remedy. Those tasked with cleaning and disinfecting houses and public buildings did not always handle medical waste well, and infected bedding and straw was frequently dumped, out of convenience rather than regulation, on the banks of the local river—a source of the city's water supply.[14]

What pleading by the magistrates could not accomplish, sometimes force did. Plague spreaders, who spread the disease either in gross disregard of the magistrate's plague ordinances or who intentionally contaminated others, were prosecuted (115 cases), fined, imprisoned, sometimes tortured (flogging and amputations of the hand), and even executed (44 executions).[15] Invoking God's sovereignty, some Christians disregarded all concern for secondary causes of the plague. Others, paralyzed by fear of secondary causes, refused to fulfill duties to their home, church, and society. Many wavered between the extremes of indifference and anxiety. Basic life was constantly strained if not totally disrupted, and if the normal bonds of human and Christian fellowship were not yet snapped, they demanded constant maintenance.

This was the case in Geneva, Switzerland. That renowned city of Calvin's and Beza's pastoral ministry was struck by the plague at least five times between 1542 and 1572. Beza's own brother succumbed after fleeing the plague elsewhere, only to meet his death by it in Geneva in 1570. In September of 1571, the academy that trained ministers was almost shuttered

---

14. W. G. Naphy, *Plagues, Poisons, and Potions: Plague-spreading Conspiracies in the Western Alps c. 1530-1640* (New York: Manchester University Press, 2002), 108–21.
15. Ibid., 227–238. Cf. tables 10 and 11.

by civil authorities.[16] But Beza's persuasion managed to keep it open, if only because he was its sole professor, with only 4 students enrolled. While endeavoring to hold regular church services in 1572, the people often absented themselves. The magistrates and ministers of Geneva encouraged and pleaded with the people to seek the Lord in corporate repentance and prayer with mixed success. Plagues, like the one that struck Geneva, tested and shaped the character and identity of Christians in hundreds of similar outbreaks. But it was trials of this sort that concretized and personalized Reformed doctrines and approaches to pastoral ministry among congregants.

Plague and Theology

Theological questions among the Reformed in this period tended toward three primary categories: First, what is God's relationship to the infliction of a temporal evil? Is God the cause of evil? At the root of this question is a moral challenge to the character and goodness of God. Can God be good and still inflict evils as they are considered in themselves? In one sense, this is not too far afield from questions regarding predestination and reprobation. But in another sense, it is a much more poignant and practical application of God's goodness to real and present suffering. Second, if temporal evils can result in spiritual goods that have value in this life and the next, should the plague be avoided? And, related to this, if the plague is God's judgment of the wicked or chastisement of the good, is it permissible to seek to avoid it? Third, can a Christian physically leave their city and community in time of a plague outbreak? What of the duties of magistrates, ministers, and citizens? After all, how can someone love their neighbor and shun them at the same time?

Some in Beza's time in Geneva had argued that the plague was not infectious or grave, as not everyone was affected equally and to the same extent. Furthermore, some argued theologically that if the result of the plague is "to punish our sins, to test our faith, to drive us to repentance, and to drag hypocrites into the light. Who therefore can deny but that they flee a good who flee a plague, through which God causes these good things?"[17] Others even argued that avoiding the plague caused people to forsake Christian

---

16. Shawn D. Wright, *Our Sovereign Refuge: The Pastoral Theology of Theodore Beza* (Eugene: Wipf & Stock, 2007), 144; cf. Wright, *Theodore Beza: The man and the myth*, 148–149.
17. See page 23 in this volume.

duties to their neighbor; namely, whatever you would want people to do for you, so you should do for them. To the first point, Beza, in his *De peste quaestiones duae explicatae*[18] from 1579, cites Calvin to support his affirmation of mediating causes as a means of surviving plague.

On one side of the issue, some claimed that love of neighbor would preclude avoiding plague in any circumstance, since that would leave the most vulnerable forsaken, rupturing all human, natural, civil, and Christian ties. Beza noted that the commandment "You shall not murder" means that one's own life, or the lives of any who belong or depend on them, are not to be rashly put in danger of deadly infection, and one must take all wise precaution.

Regarding the duties of love of neighbor, Beza asserted that within the duty of love, there are degrees of obligation. "Everyone must have some understanding of his station and calling. For some serve in public offices, whether civil or sacred, but the rest are private persons."[19] Those in positions of authority and service then have a greater duty to perform their offices on behalf of others. Magistrates, especially Christian ones, have a duty, according to Beza, to remove sources of the plague as much as possible and to care for those that are sick.

Rivet, too, echoed this point, leaning on another Reformed exegete, Jerome Zanchi, for his interpretation of Philippians 2:30, in which he argued that the work of Christ was not to be abandoned out of one's own interest during pestilence. In the case where duty called pastors to minister to the sick, but none responded willingly, Rivet suggested a gathering of pastors where, after calling upon God in prayer, lots would be cast for who would minister word and sacrament to the healthy, and who to the sick. Of course, this would only work in places like Geneva, where there was an ample number of pastors. A different tactic might be needed in a region with fewer pastors. Rivet still suggested to his Dutch friend that this Genevan custom should be considered for the Dutch in time of plague. This would protect the large majority of pastors and their families and limit the spread of infection, he argued. Furthermore, he pointed out that Zanchi's instruction should not be taken simply for the individual pastor but must be taken in coordination with other pastors in the region. "In fact, because ministers are debtors to the healthy as well as to the sick, and to their own

---

18. See *A learned treatise of the plague*, page 6 in this volume.
19. See page 27 in this volume.

families, and they are assigned to the commonwealth and the church, those who may be infected do not comprise either the entirety or the greatest part of the commonwealth or the church. Why then, to the detriment of others, should ministers devote themselves entirely to the one part that is suffering?"[20] The duty and burden of the pastorate is shared in times of health, so also in times of plague. This is so that the body of Christ, though divided by plague, would be united spiritually.

Beza noted that even private citizens have a duty to be good citizens in the promotion of the public good, which includes supporting the magistrates in their efforts for the common good and supporting the efforts themselves. Then there are the bonds of families: Husbands are not free to abandon their wives, nor wives their husbands; nor parents their children, nor children their aged parents; so the citizen is not free to abandon a plague victim devoid of any and all support. Beza even included the relations of masters of households and their servants in this paradigm. It is times of trial and challenge that not only elicit from the Christian the maintenance of all their ties and duties, but demand intentionality, even while exercising all good and godly measure. "But I do not see how any serving in a public civil office may flee their charge in a time of plague. And for faithful pastors to forsake even one sheep through their withdrawal at a time when that sheep needs heavenly comfort most of all is too shameful, indeed too wicked, to even consider."[21] Whatever measure one takes in time of plague, it must be done out of diligent love of God and neighbor, in consideration of one's duty and one's dependents, with a clear conscience.

Plague victims and those who care for the sick have a duty of love of neighbor as well, Beza observed. "The sick must take heed that they do not abuse the love of their relatives and friends at a time when they desire to have themselves provided for. And those who continue to do their duties must not cast themselves heedlessly into the risk of infection. For this would happen from recklessness, rather than right and Christian judgement. . ."[22] Beza even gives a glimpse of his own experience of the plague when he recounts that, out of love for them, he forbade his friends to visit him—friends who were eager to show love and kindness—because he refused to be the cause of their death.

20. See page 45 in this volume.
21. See page 28 in this volume.
22. See page 28 in this volume.

For pastors and ministers, Beza offered this counsel in a time when there was great debate about the plague, its causes, its treatment, its infectiousness, and all manner of other questions: "But this especially must be agreed upon, that as our sins are the chief and true cause of the plague, so this is the only proper remedy against the same: that if the ministers would not dispute about infectiousness (which belongs to physicians) but, by their life and doctrine stir up the people to earnest repentance, love, and charity one towards another, then the sheep themselves would hear clearly and heed the voice of their pastors."[23]

Conclusion

On the heels of a devastating time of plague between 1567 to 1572, Geneva held out open hands of hospitality to religious refugees in the weeks following Sunday, August 24, 1572—when the Catholic League, aided by royal consent and the mobs of Paris, butchered about 2,000 French Protestants in the city during the St. Bartholomew's Day Massacre irrespective of age, sex, or station.[24] The religio-political violence spread to roughly fifteen other major cities and towns in France, bringing the number of the slain up to about 10,000. French Huguenot refugees streamed into Geneva and the surrounding area. So generous were private citizens that it was a full month before the city councilors needed to assist with the public purse.

Where did the city of Geneva and its people learn such hospitality? Was it precisely through the time of plague after the ties of family, church, and state were tested almost to the breaking point? How else can one comfort, except with the comfort with which they have been comforted (2 Cor. 1:3–5)?

Will Christians today respond in a similar way through this global pandemic and beyond? Will this time of testing prepare us for more intentional and faithful service, or will we slow in the things of God? Will we ponder and perform our duties or neglect and ignore them? Will we reflect on God's sovereignty and arrive at a greater sense of God's faithfulness and care? Will Christ's cause advance, by God's grace, in us and through us?

---

23. See page 29 in this volume.
24. Robert Kingdon, *Myths about the St. Bartholomew's Day Massacres, 1572–1576*, (Cambridge: Harvard University Press, 2013); Arlette Jouanna, *The Saint Bartholomew's Day Massacre: The Mysteries of a crime of State* (New York: Manchester University Press, 2013).

A Note on the Text

The body of extant plague writings is vast and much of it remains unavailable in English. The selections in this book were determined to a great extent by the treasures that came to light in translating the 1655 pamphlet *Variorum tractatus theologici de peste*, which makes up Part I of the book. This collection of tracts is an unparalleled Post-Reformation treatment of the plague, from pastoral and scholarly points of view. Part II consists of those Reformation and Post-Reformation works that Beza, Rivet, Voetius, and Hoornbeeck engaged with frequently (Zanchi, Abbot, and Ursinus). Alongside those pieces are additional contemporary works that we felt would be especially useful for pastors, scholars, and interested readers to have available in book form (Zwingli, Luther, Lavater, and Rawlet), and which give the reader a more complete picture of the Reformed tradition's branch of plague writings. Each of these eleven authors addresses the unique questions posited by the plague in distinct ways, yet each does so by definitively Reformed methods—grounded in Scripture, historically informed, and always with the issue of faith in Christ at the forefront.

Although predating the scope of the book significantly, Cyprian of Carthage's *On Mortality* is included in the appendix, both for its quality and because of that work's deep importance for the chapters that precede it. Also included are the relevant prayers from the *Book of Common Prayer* (1662), offered here as excellent samples of a faithful liturgical response in a time of plague.

It is our hope and prayer that the works presented once again in this volume will serve the kingdom of God by sharing with pastors, scholars, and laypersons the unique opportunities and responsibilities of Christ's church in times of crisis and peril.

Stephen M. Coleman & Todd M. Rester

Acknowledgments

It is our privilege to thank each of those who contributed to the research, production, and publication of this volume. We wish especially to express our gratitude to Jeff Hart and Framework for their support of the book, Rebecca Bylsma for proofreading the manuscript, Jessica Hiatt and Angie Messinger for their excellent design work, and Barry Waugh for his labors in indexing the book. A special thanks goes to Zachary Herbster whose timely assistance and work on the bibliography saved us countless hours and contributed greatly to the usefulness of this work. We're also grateful to Allen Guelzo for his encouraging early interest in and engagement with this material. Finally, Fortress Press has been very generous in allowing us to reprint Martin Luther's letter, "Whether One May Flee from a Deadly Plague."

It has been a pleasure to work with Westminster Seminary Press and we wish to thank the Director of Publishing, Josiah Pettit, and Operations Manager, Kyle Whitgrove, for their efforts in bringing this volume to completion. And of course, we owe a special thanks to the board of WSP—Peter Lillback, David Garner, Jim Sweet, Chun Lai, and Jerry Timmis—for believing in this project from the beginning and supporting it throughout. Our greatest debt, however, goes to Josh Currie who patiently and persistently kept this project on track. Thank you, Josh, for your inexhaustible patience and for your countless insights and contributions; this book is the better for them all.

We are delighted to dedicate this volume to our parents, Mike and Barbara Coleman and Les and Shirley Rester. Thank you for exemplifying that deep faith in Christ and that unwavering hope in the world to come that strengthens Christians at all times, and especially in times of suffering.

Part I
++++

Variorum tractatus theologici de peste

1

A Learned Treatise on the Plague

Introduction

When he succeeded John Calvin as head of the Genevan church in 1564, Theodore Beza (b. 1519) was already established as a leader within the broader reformation movement in Europe. He had, by this time, published numerous theological treatises, including his widely translated and circulated *Confession de la foi chrétienne* ("Confession of the Christian Faith"); served as a professor of Greek, first at Academy of Lausanne and then at the Academy of Geneva; played a prominent role at the Colloquy of Poissy; and completed a Latin translation of the New Testament and a French Psalter (begun by C. Marot). Though he was immensely accomplished as a scholar, author, and theologian, Beza, like Calvin before him, was first and foremost a pastor; and, also like Calvin before him, he pastored the Genevan church through incredibly tumultuous times—not the least of which were numerous seasons of plague which ravaged the city.[1]

Responding to widespread confusion about the cause of plagues as well as the proper Christian response, Beza composed his *Learned Treatise on the Plague* in 1579 (published in 1580).[2] In it he addresses two questions clearly stated in the title and which may be summarized as follows: 1) Is the plague infectious? and 2) May Christians flee from it? The answer to the

---

1. Major outbreaks of the plague in Geneva occurred in 1542–1544, 1564, 1568–1571, 1578, 1585, 1596.
2. "Beza's *Questions Regarding the Plague* was written in part to address local concerns and in part to refute a treatise written by a reformed pastor in Aarberg named Christophe Lüthard, which had argued that plagues are deadly, not because they are contagious, but because they are an expression of God's punishment against sinners. From this, Lüthard had concluded that it was inadmissible for Christians to take precautions or flee from the plague." Scott Manetsch, *Calvin's Company of Pastors: Pastoral Care and the Emerging Reformed Church, 1536-1609* (Oxford: Oxford University Press, 2012), 288.

first question may seem obvious to modern readers and therefore reflective of an earlier age of medical understanding, so that Beza's discussion of the matter would be of little interest to us today. However, Beza demonstrates that underlying the scientific question of the nature and spread of diseases is the theological question of causality. What is the relation of primary causes to secondary causes? Did God cause the plague or did my neighbor? If God wills that I should contract the plague, and his will is certain, what good does fleeing do? And how should this relation between primary causes and secondary causes inform how Christians think about God and respond to the hard providences that he, at times, is pleased to bring into their lives?

Beza unequivocally affirms the divine origin of the plague, and the fact that it is in some way an expression of God's wrath against sin for which all mankind is guilty. It does not follow, however, that because God is the primary cause that secondary causes are non-existent or should be ignored, whether they are the secondary causes by which the plague is spread or the secondary causes by which the plague may be avoided. In fact, it is with reference to these secondary causes that Christians must discern their responsibilities toward God and their fellow man. In the words of Beza, "But leaving those things secret which God has willed to keep secret from us, we must use those things which, with God himself going before us, nature tells us God has ordained to prolong our life so long as it shall please him. And if we do not do so, we will rightly be deemed to tempt and most grievously offend God."

For Beza, the simple answer to his second question of whether flight in times of plague is licit is an unequivocal "it depends." It depends upon one's station and circumstances. It depends upon one's office and relations. It depends upon so many factors that it is impossible to offer a one-size-fits-all answer. Since Scripture does not speak explicitly on the matter, Beza is content to commend "general precepts that are agreeable to the Word of God," exhorting believers to a careful consideration of what the law of love and one's duty toward God and man requires. Once this is discerned, Christians may move forward with freedom. There is freedom to stay and care for those in need, knowing that not a hair will fall from their head apart from the will of their loving Father in heaven; and there is freedom to go and preserve their life for the good of their family, their church, and their neighbor in the future. Beza's reflections challenge Christians both in his day and in our day to avoid easy answers to complex questions. What is licit for one may not be licit for others. What is wise and good for one may not be wise and good for others. Christians must refrain from placing themselves in judgment of their neighbors on matters about which the Bible is silent.

Though Beza's treatise is theological in content and polemical in tone, it is ultimately pastoral in purpose. The many profound and, at points, mysterious doctrines of the faith addressed here are not theoretical, abstract, and speculative exercises for Beza, but rather they are deeply personal realities of immense practical and doxological value in the daily life of every believer. Beza's pastoral heart is evident throughout the treatise, but it is perhaps most clearly seen in the prayers of the reformer which have been preserved and in which he weaves together these glorious themes of divine sovereignty, mystery, grace, calling, predestination, justification, adoption, sanctification, and glorification in beautiful expressions of faith and worship.

> But your children, O heavenly Father, instructed by your doctrine through the light of your Spirit, will in their hearts humbly reverence your decrees, which are always just, even in the first condemnation of all mankind, and will be content to magnify your goodness, for the grace that it has pleased you to bestow upon them in Jesus Christ, adopting them by him of your free mercy into your family. For they have learned in your school that the inaccessible brightness of your judgments dazzle the best sighted minds and spirits, yes wastes and consumes them when they presume to approach to enquire the secret causes. This do I know, neither will I know any more, that all things do work for the best of your elect, because that having known them before all ages, you have also predestined them to be made conformable to the image of your Son, called and justified them to be glorified.[3]

Beza, Theodore, *De peste ubi quaestiones explicatae una sitne contagiosa, altera an et quatenus sit Christianis per secessionem vitanda* (Geneva:

---

3. T. Beza, "Upon eternal death" in *Household Prayers*, as quoted in Shawn D. Wright, *Our Sovereign Refuge: The Pastoral Theology of Theodore Beza* (Carlisle: Paternoster, 2004), 134.

Eustathius Vignon, 1580); idem, "De peste . . ." in *Variorum tractus theologici de peste* (Leiden: Johannes Elsevir, 1655), 1–60. Cf. idem, *A shorte learned and pithie treatize of the Plague*, trans. John Stockwood, (London: Thomas Dawson, 1580).

A Learned Treatise on the Plague
In Which Two Questions are Solved: Whether or not the Plague is Infectious? And Whether, and how Far Christians may Shun it by Withdrawing?[4]

Theodore Beza

I confess that I have not been so acquainted with this question, "whether the plague should be considered among infectious diseases?" Until within these past few years, I believe it was never doubted that this sickness should be judged among all other diseases as especially contagious. As witness to this fact, I refer any uncontentious person to the judgment of writers from all countries who have addressed these topics. But now in our times people have begun to debate this question on the premise that many people so greatly fear this disease, and death which commonly follows it, that they forsake all duties—not only Christian ones, but even those of humanity—and they have greatly increased the very wrath of God, which is the chief cause of this sickness. Because of them, there is almost no place that this calamity has not touched; the bonds of human society being once ruptured, now the whole human race is being destroyed. And when asked to defend such ungodly behavior, these people frequently bring nothing else for their excuse than their fear of infection. As a result, those who think they have greater constancy than these others believe they cannot remedy the evil behavior more certainly than to teach that this sickness is falsely supposed to be infectious.

But because this unbelievable opinion can no more be proved by good reason than if someone should maintain with Anaxagoras that snow is black, or should labor to prove from the hypothesis of Copernicus that the

---

4. Initially, we thought to reprint the 1580 Stockwood translation into English. But upon comparison with the Latin, there were significant additions, omissions, and corrections needed throughout; what we offer here is a thoroughly corrected (if not new) translation that differs from Stockwood but was composed in constant comparison with that translation and the Latin. The level of revision the Stockwood translation required meant that it would be unprofitable for readers, whether popular or scholarly, to critically document all the differences.

earth really does move and the sun stand still as the center of the world,[5] I think that this dread, which brings with it a forgetfulness of all duty, ought to be and also must be abolished. Yet nor will I believe this disease is not infectious until someone shall teach me, either from the Word of God or by evident and good reasons to the contrary. For in the order of nature there are certain and most sure proofs of this, as long as the order of necessary causes agree among themselves.

For even were it established that the plague is the most infectious of all other diseases, indeed, even if death in the majority of cases inevitably results from it, I deny that therefore each person must abandon the station where God has placed them. I said I deny it because abandoning one's station is not to be preferred to the very life we owe to God and our country, and which human beings owe to each other, either for some public or private respect. And I would greatly prefer that the disputants would put their efforts of persuasion toward keeping people from fleeing due to their fear of the plague than striving to prove their odd opinion that the plague is not contagious. Indeed, I would rather have the consequent (as they say in the schools) in that same enthymeme denied, than the antecedent. For in this way not only by probable arguments, but also by necessary ones, they might actually accomplish what they want; namely, it is an exceedingly great sin when people, out of any fear of danger, sin against God or their neighbor. For what Christian has dared to call that into controversy? Or, if he should dare to do so, would he not be rebuked by the witness of his own conscience, even if everyone else were silent? For I do not think that there are any who hold with a good conscience that the plague must be fled in every instance, that is, without exception. Nevertheless, I still see that this point is disputed against by some, as if it were maintained by others. Yet, if anyone does hold that opinion (of flight in all circumstances of plague), I no more favor their error than that of those who, of the exact opposite opinion, think one must never flee the plague. But surely it is the part of a wise man to follow the golden mean, so that he does not flee when he should remain, nor make a heedless

---

5. Beza is hinting here that the most valid empirical challenge from astronomy to the Copernican theory of 1543 (for at this time it was merely a theory) was the need to demonstrate stellar parallax. Stellar parallax, the aberration of starlight due to the earth's change in position relative to the sun, was first demonstrated in 1728 by the astronomer James Bradley (1693–1762), providing direct evidence for the velocity of light and that the earth revolved around the sun. Cf. Nicolas Copernicus, *De revolutionibus orbium coelestium libri VI* (Petreius, 1543).

stand[6] when he should withdraw (for the term "fleeing" in this argument seems to me to be very improper), by which he offends against the very same charity which seemed to counsel him to stay. Moreover, before I come to the substance of the issue, I thought it fitting to preface these points for this purpose: that at the very start everyone would understand what I endeavor to defend and what to disprove. Then, since there are very many who think that this discourse on whether one ought to flee the plague depends upon the first question of whether or not the plague is infectious, let us examine the reasons and arguments with which they so confidently deny that the plague is infectious. That is a point that until now, by the way, everyone believed was not controversial; but they are infected with its denial.

These disputants want this question adjudicated with a consideration of what the plague is: its origin, its cause, by what means it is inflicted on us, its nature, and its purpose. I accept this condition as it is most appropriate and fair. But how shall we know these things? "By no means from any medical accounts *(physicae rationes)*" they say, "but only from the Word of God."[7] Then by all means let everything debated among physicians be obliterated, and instead of the books of Hippocrates, Galen, and other medical doctors, let physicians only read the Bible. In fact, let there be no difference between them and theologians, between the medicine of the body and that of the soul. "No, God forbid!" they will say, "for we do not condemn any medical account other than such as are contrary to the Word of God." Well said! So then, inasmuch as contagion originates from physical causes, and hence proceeds from them, let us inquire whether there is anything taught in the determinations of medical doctors regarding these physical causes that is repugnant to the Word of the Lord.

First Argument

They assert that the Hebrews call plague דֶּבֶר from דָּבַר, which also means to destroy with a sentence imposed by God. And the Greeks render

---

6. The word choice here *(consisto)* conveys more than simply remaining, but rather the idea of a soldier taking up a post. In military terms it means to hold one's ground and establish a position rather than to flee in the face of the enemy. E.g. Caesar, *Gallic Wars* 1.13

7. The Latin word *physica* is translated in the earlier English translation as variously *Physick*, *physical*, and *natural*. It does have a somewhat broader range than simply physical or natural and does encompass the idea of what we would deem medical as well. For the purposes of this reading, *physica* frequently carries the weight of the words physical and medical simultaneously.

it θάνατον, that is, death. I respond: Even so, so what? What relevance is that for this issue? For it does not follow from this point that because the plague is inflicted by God it does not proceed from intervening natural causes, unless on that account we want to remove all the natural causes of disease. After all, no one dies any kind of death unless ultimately God has decreed it.

Second Argument

"Indeed," they say, "but it is foolish to call the sentence of God, whereby he allots to every person not only their death but also the kind of death and its second causes, infectious." I respond: And who, I ask you, was ever so silly as to call the very sentence of God infectious? But what we assert is far different, namely, that contagion itself must be counted among second causes. For who can deny that many diseases are contracted by contact and touch? Who can deny some of these diseases are deadly, but others less dangerous, unless they want to contend that the sun does not shine at noonday? Certainly sin, with which we are all born infected, and from which all this mortality originated, is derived from a kind of spiritual infection not apart from the decree of God and has spread to all of Adam's posterity. Therefore, there is absolutely no force to this argument.

Third Argument

But after this, they also ask, "If contagion is counted among second causes appointed by God, how could we flee what has been ordained by God?" Doubtless they ask so that they may conclude from this that "even if it is granted that the plague is infectious, it is useless to seek a remedy against it by flight." I respond: But this too is a lead-headed reason. For if this conclusion is true, will it not be permissible to affirm the same of all second causes of death? If so, don't eat, don't drink, don't seek any remedy against any diseases. Send soldiers to the frontline unarmed, since the death ordained by God cannot be avoided. On the contrary, the state of the case is this: Certainly neither the death, its time, nor any kind of death appointed by God can be avoided. But we do not eat, use remedies against diseases, or arm ourselves against our enemies as if we thought to withstand God. Instead, leaving those things secret which God has willed to keep secret from us, we must use those things which, with God himself going before us, nature tells us God has ordained to prolong our life so long as it shall please him. And if we do not do so, we will rightly be deemed to tempt and most grievously offend God. It is so far off the mark to assert that, by using the means he established to avoid death, we should sin against him, even though sometimes we may use them to no effect; that is to say, this occurs when he reveals our departure to us, that we are about to die, when we thought our life would still be prolonged. Asa is rebuked in this way, not because he sent for physicians, but because he put his hope of life in the physicians.[8] So when experience has taught us that contagion creeps about among things near rather than far away, no one is to blame who, while not neglecting any part of their Christian duty, withdraws himself and his family. Indeed, the person to be greatly rebuked is the one who heedlessly casts himself and his family into the danger of infection. This is especially the case when, as the Apostle witnesses, someone who does not have such great care over his family as he ought to with a healthy godliness and charity is worse than an unbeliever.[9]

Fourth Argument

But let us see whether this next point is of any more solid stuff. "It is by those names that are attributed to the plague in the holy Scripture," they say, "that the quality and manner of it is sufficiently and thoroughly expressed. Therefore, because the plague is called 'the hand of God' (2 Sam. 24), 'the sword of God' (1 Chr. 21), and is also signified by the term 'arrows' (Pss. 38 and 91),[10] it does not proceed by contagion, for neither hand, nor sword, nor arrow wounds by infection." I respond: Although I might rightly call into doubt whether each of these proofs are brought forward appropriately, I too do not deny this conclusion. For elsewhere in another passage, such as Psalm 17:[14], David calls his enemies, who assaulted him by natural means, "the hand of God." And when it is said that the hand of God made us, this does not exclude physical generation. And it is clear that "arrows" in the Scriptures are all kinds of evils that God inflicts upon

---

8. 2 Chron. 16:12: "In the thirty-ninth year of his reign Asa was diseased in his feet, and his disease became severe. Yet even in his disease he did not seek the LORD, but sought help from physicians." (ESV)

9. 1 Tim. 5:8: "But if anyone does not provide for his relatives, and especially for members of his household, he has denied the faith and is worse than an unbeliever." (ESV)

10. Original cited: Ps. 31

humanity, using either the ordinary laws of nature only or the service of angels.

Second, I ask, how do they define the quality and manner of the disease? They will say, "By the very nature of each of those names." But I assert that by those metaphorical terms of hand, sword, and arrow, no more is signified about what manner or quality this disease is in itself, than what hail or scabies is when God is said to have struck Egypt with an outstretched hand. And finally, what is the cause and nature of every disease listed in the appendices to the law among the curses to be inflicted by God? What then? Surely it belongs to physicians and medical doctors to investigate the nature of diseases, insofar as they depend upon the laws of nature—which we see them do with such good success and certainty—so that they can predict both the diseases and their likely outcomes. But concerning supernatural and divine causes of sickness and other miseries: those a theologian explains, teaching that we must ascend far above nature and all physical things when one deals with avoiding and removing them. For the true and principal cause of these diseases is our sins, by which God has been provoked. And he raises and stirs up against us all these inferior causes to inflict just punishments upon humanity. Therefore, I assert that it is absurd to confuse these things that are so far distinct with their very different, yet not contrary, ends; but which are things only distinguished as ὑπαλλήλοις, that is, as subordinates or subalternates.

Third, since by this argument they contend that the plague is not infectious, on account of its often being called the hand, and sword, and arrow of God, I ask: is leprosy also the hand of God or not? Is it therefore infectious or not? And since it is infectious, were not the leprous therefore commanded to withdraw from the rest that were clean?[11] I ask this also, if there is no evil in a city except what the Lord has done, should those afflicted today with leprosy still be considered infectious?[12] And I would gladly ask of those who find fault with our withdrawal during a time of plague whether they think that those who are infected with leprosy are to

---

11. E.g., Lev. 13-14
12. Cf. Amos 3:6; *Elephantiacus*, or *morbus magnus*, was one of several Latin synonyms for *lepra*, leprosy, in the early modern period; this is not the disease caused by the Filaria worm and is known as Elephantiasis in modern medicine. Cf. Galen of Pergamum, *De Simplicium Medicamentorum temperamentis ac facultatibus*, 11.1.1 in *Galeni Opera Omnia* (Leipzig: C. G. Kühn, 1821-33), 12:314-16; cf. Luke Demaitre, *Leprosy in premodern medicine: a malady of the whole body* (Baltimore: Johns Hopkins University Press, 2007), 86-87. For early modern Latin synonyms for leprosy, see Simon Pelgrom, *Sylva synonymorum* (Amsterdam: Henricus Laurentius, 1635), 199-200.

be tolerated in the general company of human society? If they think that they are to be tolerated, why do they not cry out also against those who exclude the leprous? If they do not think they are to be tolerated, and think they must be avoided for fear of contagion, why, without exception, do they rebuke those that shun the contagion of the plague as the most harmful of all human beings? But perhaps they will deny that leprosy is the hand of God. Then let us speak of scabies, no matter whether it be a French or Spanish one—oh, why not even a German one? It is a punishment divinely inflicted for whoring, which in this age is considered a sport. I do not think anyone would dare deny that scabies is truly the hand, sword, or arrow of God that strikes whoremongers. But is it not therefore infectious? And does not a whore also infect many with this disease, who then again pollute another, so that this exceedingly filthy sickness is contracted, not only by sleeping together, but also by breathing and touching? And so it is even sucked out by infants from their nurse's breasts, and then nurses contract this disease by nursing an infant, which is either conceived by an unclean father or born of an unclean mother. Arguments like these, therefore, are the sort that need no refutation. It is certainly absurd to think it more preferable to assert that as many individual persons as there are, that many plagues are immediately (as they say) inflicted upon each person, than to say that this is the kind of disease where one person infects another. For whether God slays everyone with one stroke or whether, as happened to the Midianites, he struck them down by everyone wounding each other, and whomever he appointed to die, died, what difference does it make?[13] Again, there is no distinction in the matter we are addressing, whether someone is laid out by the bolt of God himself, or by another's infection.

Fifth Argument

Let us now come to what they allege regarding second causes, which they deny to be a certain position of the stars or a corruption of the atmosphere. I respond first that, as far as I know, medical doctors do not think any plague or contagion arises from those causes. I respond second: but let us even grant this, and furthermore imagine that they did list the actual natural causes of the plague. Now grant me this: why do they all at once

---

13. Beza is referring to Gideon's defeat of the Midianites recorded in Judges 7:22–23 in which "the Lord set every man's sword against his fellow and against all the army."

exclude natural causes, and with such certainty that they want people who hold that the plague is received by these second causes according to God's will to be considered poorly trained in the Holy Scriptures? "Because," they say, "the Holy Scriptures testify that the plague is inflicted by angels," such as in Psalm 88, 1 Chronicles 21, Ezekiel 9, and also in the account of Sennacherib, and in Revelation, where it mentions the worst kind of sore.[14] "For," they say, "that which God inflicts by angels does not belong to natural causes." I grant that, insofar as it concerns the angels themselves, who I concede are not reckoned among natural instruments. But what prevents God from commanding that the natural causes be stirred up by the angels themselves? For surely it is not debatable that both good and wicked angels do stir up the human will in some way, whatever kind of motion it is, such as when Satan is said to have entered into the heart of Judas[15] (unless perhaps we say it is permissible that good angels have somewhat less power than bad ones). And this is also clear in the account of Ahab, from the efficacy and power of the spirits of error.[16] And what sort of person would dare to deny that the will of man is to be reckoned among the principles, even the chief ones, of human actions? But if the human will is not excluded from the ministry of angels, why will we think that other natural causes must necessarily be excluded? Moses stretching forth his rod raised up lice and countless kinds of flies, suddenly brought out dreadful hail, and struck the Egyptians with the most grievous sores. And certainly the ministry of Moses was just as extraordinary as the ministry of angels. But then did not the lice and flies arise from putridity, did not the hail arise from vapors freezing through sudden compression,[17] and did not the sores also arise from the putridity of the humors?[18] When Satan received a concession from God, to suddenly stir up the wind and hurl fire from heaven and burn down Job's houses together with all his children, does it then follow that this occurred without any intervening natural causes?[19] Or would we not rather say that those princes of the air (as the Apostle, not without cause, calls them) suddenly made certain natural impressions upon the air? The devil sends the godly to prison in Revelation 2:10, but it is through tyrants

---

14. Isa. 37:36–38; 2 Kings 19:35–37; Rev. 16:2
15. Lk. 22:3
16. 1 Kings 22:19–23
17. *Ex vaporibus per* ἀντιπερίστασιν *repente concretis.* Cf. On the ἀντιπερίστασις and περίστασις of turbulent winds as the cause of hail, see Aristotle, *Meteorology*, 364^{b}14–30.
18. Beza is referring to the third, fourth, and seventh plagues in Exod. 8:16–32; 9:13–35.
19. Job 1:13–19

and persecutors of the Church. In the same book (Rev. 6:8), the pale horse, on whom Death the rider sits, receives power to kill by the sword, famine, pestilence, and the sending of wild beasts. Here, if we will understand that rider to be an angel, why will we not also say that he used natural material to cause the plague and famine equally as a sword and wild beasts, which themselves are also natural instruments? Then later (Rev. 9:1), the angels are commanded to stand in the four corners of the earth, and to compel the winds not to harm the land and sea with their blowing. From this it follows that when God commands, they send the winds out in a similar manner. From these it is evident without a doubt that there proceed a great many changes upon the air, and chiefly infection. Finally, whether natural causes are moved little by little by the force implanted in them, or otherwise are suddenly brought to their effects extraordinarily by God's command, they are natural; and to that extent their effects are also rightly judged natural, which no reasonable person can deny.

I respond third: If no natural causes may intervene in the plague, those whom the plague has touched cannot be comforted at all, much less healed by natural remedies. But experience and sense prove this to be most false. I respond fourth: I profess that I am one of those who so far detests the superstitious astrology of diviners,[20] the horoscopes of genethliacs, and all other kinds of impious predictions, that I could wish the ancient edicts of princes concerning those things were renewed and strictly observed. Nevertheless I think it is an error not to grasp something from the different concourses of the stars, the natural constitutions of the air, and the effects in our bodies that depend upon them. To behave as if the stars were only placed in their spheres to be gazed at or to distinguish time[21] is not a mark of judiciousness, but rather of perverse stubbornness. Farmers are daily aware of this. Storms shout out the same, and it is self-evident that temperate and intemperate [weather], and even contagion itself in some measure, may be foretold by skillful astrologers.[22]

---

20. Gk. μαντικήν

21. E.g. Craig Martin, "The Ends of Weather: Teleology in Renaissance Meteorology," *Journal of Philosophy* 48, no. 3 (2010): 259–82. Martin helpfully notes how Aristotelian conceptions of meteorology were frequently viewed as portents of the judgment of God and eschatology in the medieval and early modern periods. Beza's comments here seem to be in harmony with such views.

22. In sixteenth-century Europe, astrology included the relationships between meteorology, astrology, astronomy, and medicine, which were blurred. Here Beza is observing that while there are obvious superstitious elements found among astrologers, his category of natural physical causes covers a broad range of phenomenon.

I respond fifth: But now should we grant that those plagues, examples of which are drawn from Holy Scripture, were sent by angels and therefore occurred without contagion? Yet is it any less absurd to conjecture that no plague is sent except by angels, than to contend that no hail, showers, or lightning occur in the usual course of nature, since in many passages of Scripture we read that by the ministry of angels it has hailed, the most violent winds have blown, and that it has horribly thundered?

Their exception: "But," they say, "those examples of plague by angels are set forth to us as an example so that we may learn from them to judge rightly regarding mediating causes and the origin of the plague."

I respond to the exception: But who will deny that whatever has been written, has been written for that reason, so that we should be instructed? And everything mentioned in the Holy Scriptures regarding the ministry of angels—not only in the plague, but also in famine and other calamities—occurs first to destroy the wicked, and then to chastise and exercise the good. And they bring us the greatest profit so that we may learn both to fear and love God, who is not bound to the laws of nature, as the Stoic philosophers thought. And he has certain instruments of his judgements more fearful even than those which are perceived by our senses. But what you want—namely, that we are taught that angels do not employ any natural causes in executing the commands of God—does not result in the least.

I respond sixth: What about the fact that Scripture provides us examples of plague being sent without any mention of angels? Those against whom I dispute do in fact concede that Hezekiah was sick with the plague, but it did not say that he was stricken by angels. Through Moses and other prophets, the Lord frequently threatens the plague to sinners, and there is no doubt that these threats were not empty; yet there is never mention that he always sends them by angels. In some Psalms, the psalmist seems to hint that he was seized with the plague, nevertheless we never read he was smitten with any sore or wound that was given by angels. Therefore, all these points, unless I am very much deceived, accomplish nothing at all to remove contagious air as the secondary cause of this sickness.

Sixth Argument

But also upon what reason is the argument they set down founded? They assert that the plague is inflicted upon men by a singular providence of God. I respond: And what do they assert here that may not be affirmed of everything that happens in the world? For, as our Lord says, not even one sparrow falls to the earth apart from the providence of God, and the hairs of our head are numbered.[23] That singular providence, if it is extended to singular things, certainly is in itself such a universal genus that it is also singular in singular things.

Seventh Argument

They say next that, as often as the plague roams in the world, all those whom God decreed to preserve alive are excepted from this infection; and for the rest all other places are infectious, even if they are the farthest away from those who struggle with the plague. They also add further and say, "Why then do we fear contagion? Is it not foolish to fear what is not infectious to me?" I respond first: But for my part I cannot discern how these things are not entirely incoherent.[24] For how can all places be infectious to everyone if there is no contagion, unless perhaps they concede that there is? Second, I respond: But it cannot by any means be truly inferred from the certainty of God's providence that the plague is not infectious. And so, this argument runs beyond the proposed question. I respond third: Next, will we think that the amount of those who will die is more certain when God sends the plague than when he hurls other bolts? Now if they do not sin against the providence of God—who leaves things unknown to us with regards to his good will and pleasure, as is fitting—when they use medicinal remedies to both prevent and treat disease, why would we not also do the same thing when the plague is roaming nearby? Therefore, just as God appointed that some will not die of the plague, so he has also appointed remedies by which, as far as they can, people may avoid the plague. But in all kinds of diseases it is one and the same providence of God by which he has ordained what will occur with an immutable decree, even if the natures of the diseases do not differ so much among themselves. Now among the chief precautions in medicine against infection, a timely withdrawal is counted worthwhile, to which even the very nature and meaning of the word "contagion" attests; yet not all who flee will be safe, nor will all who remain die. Undoubtedly, when God sent a famine upon Egypt and the surrounding regions, he had determined who should die in that scarcity.

---

23. Matt. 10:29–30
24. Gk. ἀσύστατα

Yet for all this Joseph does not cease to provide the Egyptians with his utmost diligence and wisest counsel.²⁵ These same things the churches also did in the time of Claudius the Emperor, when they learned by Agabus the prophet that a famine would soon come.²⁶ The Lord also knew who should die in that cruelest war of the Assyrians in the days of Hezekiah, and yet both Hezekiah and the prophet Isaiah himself secured themselves within the walls of the city.²⁷ What more should I say? Paul assuredly knew that neither he nor any of those with him would perish in the shipwreck, yet he still said to the sailors who were preparing to flee from the ship, "You cannot be saved unless these men remain."²⁸ Christ also, though he well knew that his hour was not yet come, withdrew himself more than once when the Jews sought to kill him.²⁹

Eighth Argument

Finally, what they assume to be the most certain—namely, "That contingency is repugnant to the sure and steadfast decree of God"—even if it does not pertain to the topic much, yet who will grant it to them? We call contingent causes those which of their own nature can occur on either side. If anyone should remove them from the nature of things, I know not whether he would have any man of right judgment to agree with him. They say, from Augustine, that "the will of God is the necessity of things."³⁰ I respond: I grant this insofar as it pertains to the end and effects of the causes themselves. But as Augustine says very well, it does not follow that although all things which God has decreed will occur necessarily must occur, still that they would occur from necessary causes; as the Stoics did falsely conclude, and the same may be proved by certain and most evident examples.³¹ For do we not believe that Christ did in fact have human bones, and therefore

---

25. Gen. 41:46–57
26. Acts 11:27–30
27. Isa. 36–37
28. Acts 27:21–32
29. E.g. Luke 4:28–30; John 6:15; 7:30
30. Cf. Augustine, 6.15.24, "hoc enim non erat in conditione creaturae, sed in placito Creatoris, cujus voluntas rerum necessitas est." in *De Genesi ad litteram* in PL 34–1:350, idem, *Saint Augustine on Genesis: Two Books on Genesis against the Manichees and On the Literal Interpretation of Genesis: An Unfinished Book*, 2 vols. (Washington D.C.: CUA Press, 1990–1991).
31. Beza here is engaging debate regarding Augustine, *De Genesi Ad litteram* 6.14.24–6.17.28; cf. Cicero, *De Divinatione*. 1.38.82 in LCL 154:314–15 and Augustine, *De Genesi ad litteram* 6.17.28 in PL 34–1:350–51. Also see Augustine, *City of God* 5.9–10 in NPNF1 2:90–93. Cf. Cicero, *De Divinatione* 2.7 and idem, *De Fato*, 10.14.

such by their own nature might have been broken at any time? And yet in fact they could not be broken, for it was otherwise decreed by God.[32] Therefore contingently, which pertains to their own nature they were not broken, whereas notwithstanding they were such as might have been broken, and yet by God's decree they remained of necessity unbroken. Again, that Christ from the very time that he assumed our human nature was endowed with a mortal body, all Christians confess. Therefore according to his own nature he might have been slain by Herod along with the other infants; but by God's decree he could not. Therefore, that he was not then slain occurred contingently, if you consider the nature of his body, when it could have occurred otherwise. But, from God's decree, he could no more be slain by Herod than the will of God could be changed. Christ, when he was carried off to be crucified, was then undoubtedly of such health that he needed not at that time to have died. He died therefore contingently, if you consider the cause of his natural death; and yet he died of necessity, if you look to the unchangeable ordination of his Father, because his hour was come. And at the same time he died willingly because he laid down his life for us. So far therefore neither contingency nor a human will is repugnant to the most certain decree of God.

Ninth Argument

There remains one argument taken from experience, which in appearance seems the strongest, yet is of no force to destroy contagion. "If the plague," they say, "occurs from natural causes—from some certain constellation or from corrupt air—then certainly should not all be infected who dwell under the same constellation or breathe in the same corrupt air? But this is found to be false." I respond: Even reason itself proves the falsehood of this

---

32. Cf. Calvin, *Institutes*, 1.16.9; our modernized citation from the Norton translation and the Latin, idem, *The institution of the Christian Religion*, trans. Thomas Norton, (London: Reinolde Wolfe and Richard Harison, 1561), fol. 61r: "I grant there does not always appear the same reason, but undoubtedly we ought to believe that whatever changes of things are seen in the world, come by the secret stirring of the hand of God. But that which God purposes is of such necessity to come to pass, that yet it is not of necessity precisely nor by the nature of the thing itself. Just as there is the familiar example of the bones of Christ, for inasmuch as he had put on a body like ours, in no way will anyone deny that his bones were naturally able to be broken, yet it was impossible that they should be broken (John 19:33, 36): by this we see that not without cause were invented in the schools the distinctions of necessity in respect (*necessitas secundum quid*) and necessity absolute (*necessitas absoluta*), of consequent and consequence, whereas God had made the bones of his Son subject to frangibility, which he had exempted from being able to be broken, and so brought to necessity by reason of his own purpose, that that result could not happen, which naturally might have."

argument, for who is so ignorant that he does not know that one and the same cause does not always operate alike, much less equally? Indeed, the effects are different, according to the variety of the objects that are acted upon.³³ The same sun certainly hardens the mud and wilts the grain. One and the same north wind does not equally annoy men with cold. Everyone therefore sees how weak this reasoning is. But even let us grant that in some place every man will receive the corrupt air, yet many things may happen so that the same effect would not occur in all of them. For example, one man takes a preventative medicine, another does not. One immediately uses a good medicine, another very late, or never. Lastly, that which is the principal point must be considered: that Almighty God governs and moderates natural causes and their effects as it pleases him, so that it happens that contagion does not affect everyone who is exposed to it, as it is written in Psalm 91:6. Nor yet is it deadly to everyone that is infected; just like a poison that is drunk is not, as it is written in Mark 16:18. Therefore this argument also is no more valid to prove there is no infection in the plague just because many which keep company with those that are sick of the plague are not taken, or those that are absent are infected. As if the poison of a viper were not deadly, because Paul was bitten by one and felt no harm at all (Acts 28:5). Thus far concerning contagion.

AND WHETHER IT IS LICIT TO WITHDRAW IN PLAGUE

Now we must discuss withdrawal, for so I would rather call it than flight, although I do think it belongs to a wise person to flee peril with reason. There are some who, without exception, find fault with withdrawing from the plague and therefore consider it a nefarious wickedness, although they think that those who remain ought not to be reckless. There are, on the other side, those who hold that every man, as soon as the plague comes, ought to look out for himself [and withdraw], having no regard, or very little regard, for the fellowship and duties that Christian charity commands. Now, I for my part disagree with both of these, and especially with the latter, that they have the most lawful causes. But before I clearly declare my own judgement on this matter, I ask that first we would hear their disputes with each other. So therefore, they who think it not lawful to flee first of all

---

33. Lat. *Secundum objectorum patientium varietatem*: lit. "according to the variety of the patient objects" that is, of the objects being acted upon.

dispute philosophically against those that hold it not lawful to remain at all. The former allege, from Plato's *Gorgias*, that: (1) it is folly to fear death; (2) no one can be a temperate person who flees death, because it proceeds from an excessive delight in life; (3) no one is a just man that in the time of plague provides for himself by flight; and (4) he does not render to God or man his due.[34] To these arguments they add others, drawn from the Holy Scriptures, such as: (5) they do not think high enough of the providence of God, by whose unchangeable decree the course of human life is limited; (6) they distrust God, and do not believe his promise, "I will be your God, and the God of your seed;" (7) they are devoid of all charity, indeed, even more, of στοργῇ φυσικῇ, that is, all natural pity and affection;[35] (8) they tempt God according to the example of the Israelites (Exod.17:3, Ps. 78:18), prescribing to God the manner, time, place, and means by which he could save them; (9) they do not love God from their hearts because, loving earthly goods, they neglect heavenly ones; (10) they fear death too much, since they set themselves against the will of God, which is always good; (11) they think themselves stronger than God and that they can escape his hand; (12) they openly break the law of Christ, and nature, by which they are commanded to do to others as they would have done to themselves; (13) they do and teach what no Christian has done, but what was often customary by the heathen. And the latter, who under pretense of saving their lives argue flight without exception, have nothing to answer the former.[36]

And so if these allegations against those that do flee the plague are true such that they deviate the least bit from the laws of godliness and charity, I agree with their adversaries; and if they were found to not have the least spark of humanity, I count those worthy of all blame who flee from wherever they are to wherever they think fit to run. But if these arguments have been twisted against those whose withdrawal is motivated by just causes, who maintain the mean whereby they do not omit any part of their duty towards either God or their neighbors (which we claim most frequently occurs), then we affirm that all these arguments, however valid they may appear, nevertheless do not have any force if the circumstances are diligently examined. In fact, to their first biblical argument ([argument] 5) we

---

34. Plato, *Gorgias*, 522.d–523
35. Cf. Rom. 1:31 and ἄστοργος in Aeschines, *Speeches*, 2.146.
36. In the original Latin, this entire list of both sets of reasons philosophical and biblical is unnumbered. For the reader's convenience, we have numbered this schema parenthetically. This list will be referenced in the subsequent few points.

respond that even though the decree of God is immutable and his eternal providence has set immovable boundaries on our lives, nevertheless this does not subtract anything in the least from the ordinary and lawful means to guard our lives. No, not even if someone has received an oracle from God prolonging their life, as we have previously demonstrated from the clear example of Paul (Acts 27:14, 31). And much less is it the case that it is not lawful for us to use these means when it is yet hid from us what God from everlasting has decreed concerning the prolonging and ending of our life. Moreover, why should anyone be charged with distrusting the promises of God if they follow the methods prescribed by God to avoid evils in such a way that they wholly depend upon God, unless perhaps we can find this commandment expressly written somewhere in the Holy Scriptures: "While the plague is raging, you shall not flee." Counted among these methods are also preventative ones;[37] and among preventative remedies, withdrawing in an appropriate time, which even the very term "contagion" makes clear.

But this also is plain: Not only does one not offend against Christian charity and not tempt God who withdraws to avoid the plague in such a way that in the interim he does not omit any act of piety towards God or of charity towards his neighbor; but on the contrary, if he did not withdraw, he should be thought to provoke the wrath of God against himself and be worse than an unbeliever, since he is someone who needlessly puts himself in danger of deadly contagion, without any due care for himself or his family.

Their fifth and sixth biblical claims (arguments 9 and 10) are no truer. "They do not love God," they claim, "and, longing for earthly things, they neglect heavenly ones." I demand to know on what grounds? Because those who love God desire nothing more than to be with him, which happens to us through death? Or that they, on the contrary, fear nothing more than death? Not at all! The one who would consider only this ultimate goal set for himself, with the result that for the sake of his own benefit he may gain possession of the thing loved by any means, is rightly understood to love himself more than his friends. And so the same person who desires to be set free and be with Christ is also the one who even desires to be separated from Christ, like one accursed, for the benefit of his brethren (Rom. 9:3).[38]

---

37. Gk. προφυλακτικὰ
38. Original cited Acts 9:3

Also, he does not deliver up his life to enemies who lay in wait for him, but appeals to Caesar (Acts 25:11), and gives thanks for the restoration of his health (2 Cor. 1:11). What would they make of David, just as much a worshiper of God, who did not so much flee from Saul and Absalom as flee from death?[39] What of David and Hezekiah who each expressly prayed against death?[40] And so, one must not immediately think that anyone who flees death does not love God, just as on the contrary not everyone who longs for death must be accounted as one who loves God. But the only one who counts as loving God is the one that, while obeying the will of God with right reason and a good conscience, prepares himself for whether he is about to suffer or avoid death.

We also need to state the same point regarding the fear of death; namely, that if this fear rests upon a good reason and keeps within proper bounds, not only must it not be condemned, but in fact it must be approved of as a guardian of life implanted in us by God. Accordingly, the fear of death that is condemned from the writings of philosophers is only the one opposed to courage and the one that distracts us from what we owe to each other. But from the Holy Scriptures, the fear of death that is censurable is the one that fights against faith and love. Now it is one thing to destroy natural affections (which no one could do even if one wanted to do it) and another to keep them within their proper bounds, which even the philosophers rightly teach must be done. But just how this could be done rightly, only the Word of God shows through the Holy Spirit. Now regarding what they cite from Tertullian: in part they overshoot his target when he speaks of fleeing only in persecution, and in part they number among his blemishes what in fact has the highest agreement of the Church, so that their argument is like a runner whose course carries him away from the finish line. Certainly, no godly person—or at least anyone of average intelligence—ever condemned Jacob for his withdrawal, David for fleeing from Saul's rage or Absalom's condemnation, Elijah for running away from the path of Jezebel's fury, or the multiple escapes of Athanasius.[41] And on this point we do not take refuge either in the suffering of Christ or that passage in Matthew 10:23, "if they persecute you in one city, flee to another"; passages that, I confess, are not brought forward in an appropriate way. For what applies to Christ's fears rests upon a particular consideration and ought not to be brought

---

39. 1 Sam. 19, 21; 2 Sam. 15
40. Isa. 38:9–20
41. Gen. 27 (Jacob), 2 Sam. 15 (David), 1 Kings 19 (Elijah)

forward as an example because it concerns the mystery of our salvation, which only Christ could and did take upon himself. And specifically, in his bearing those fears, Christ saw and in fact experienced the terrible wrath of the Father, bearing the punishment due for our sins. By contrast, when we die, we are not alarmed by those terrors because we have a Father appeased and, through faith, can contemplate life in the very midst of death. But that saying of Christ is not in the least actually a command about flight, but on the contrary admonishes faithful pastors that if they are driven from one place, not being terrified by any threats, they should hurry to another, which we see the apostles do diligently afterwards.

But let us hear something else weightier perhaps. "There can be nothing sent from God," they say, "but that which is good. Indeed, there is nothing good, but that it comes from God. But the plague is sent from God, and therefore it is good; if not of its own nature, yet in view of the best end, namely, to punish our sins, to test our faith, to drive us to repentance, and to drag hypocrites into the light. Who therefore can deny but that they flee a good who flee a plague, through which God causes these good things?" And likewise, "Anything God sends upon all—that is, upon any one in the Church or Commonwealth—such as for example, the plague, he wills it to be endured by everyone. How can someone flee, if the plague must be endured? Therefore, those who flee the plague set themselves against the will of God. Indeed, they flee in vain, because it is vain to resist the will of God."

Could more absurd things than these have been said? Now, setting aside their fallacious usage[42] of the terms good and evil, to what end, I ask you, did they need to bring the nature of things into this disputation? The prophet says there is no evil (that is, no calamity) in the city, which the Lord has not caused.[43] Why then will we call famine, pestilence, war, and such things, good? "Because," say they, "they result in the good of the godly." I grant this, because the Lord does bring light out of darkness. But the godly are also brought out of their own sins. Surely sins, therefore, are not good? And does the one who resists sin resist God? To be brief, who does not see that to pray to God against things that by their own nature are harmful to us, and likewise to use just and lawful remedies to avoid them, if it could be done so that we commit their outcome to God, is a far different thing than what they rage on about—that we should hope to withstand God, or in

---

42. *Paralogismus*: cf. Gk. παραλογισμός: false reasoning, captious argumentation
43. Amos 3:6

some way escape his judgements? Abraham himself, Isaac, and Jacob did flee from famine, which was itself also sent from God, yet they cannot be said to have fled a good thing, or to have sinned in doing so. But as for that point which they make so much of, namely, "That those who flee the plague break that immoveable precept that humanity itself teaches: 'Whatever you would that others should do to you, do the same to them,'" it is fittingly turned back upon them that those who neglect to flee contagion, or any other danger, then neglect the duties of a Christian. So in no case does it accomplish anything against those who avoid the plague by withdrawing, unless they may be judged to have neglected to perform those duties they owe both to their country and to their neighbor. And I am truly amazed that those who, without exception, condemn withdrawing as being repugnant to charity do not consider that charity requires no less than that we provide for the healthy as we provide more help for those who are gripped with illness.

Finally, they say that as many as flee the plague do that which no Christian ever did, since there is no example of this in the holy histories. I answer that this is an exceedingly fallacious kind of argument, when it is evident enough that in the Holy Scriptures it is not in the least recorded what everyone did. And in many instances, the general rules of doctrine are sufficient material to establish those things about which we have no commandment or any particular example. Doubtless it is not recorded how often the people of Israel were visited with the plague, nor still how every person conducted himself in one. But they say they have altogether contrary counsel in the Holy Scriptures, for David calls us back to the tabernacle of the Most High (Ps. 91), as though someone who lawfully uses withdrawing did not flee to God. "But still," they say, "David did not flee that virulent plague mentioned in 2 Samuel 24, nor did he remove his household to any other place." I grant this. But how many particular circumstances forbid us to make of that a general conclusion? In fact, he personally was the cause of that plague, and rightly was so anxious that he bears witness that he was ready to redeem the public calamity even with his own destruction.[44] Next, when this plague did not continue beyond three days at the most, what room was left for him to deliberate? Where should he have fled when the plague raged throughout his entire domain, and yet there is not anything said, or at least very little, that it touched the capital city itself? Again, they

---

44. 2 Sam. 24:17; 1 Chron. 21:17

say Isaiah did not flee from Hezekiah when he was sick of the plague, as if we held that shepherds, in good conscience, might willingly and of their own accord abandon their sheep. Indeed, and what if I should take exception and mention that Isaiah did not come to Hezekiah but by the special command of God?[45] For so the history bears witness. "But," they say, "Jeremiah also and Baruch, as well as other godly men, did not flee from the city when it was besieged by the Chaldeans, although a great part of the people also died of plague as well as of famine." Neither do we say that we may rightly shun the plague by withdrawing if in doing so we abandon our obligation to God, our country, and all of our neighbors. But I cannot but be astounded that those who allege this example of Jeremiah have forgotten that he was captured at the gate of the city when he attempted to get out (Jer. 37:12).

Lastly, they offer an exquisite example of the church of Alexandria from the seventh book of Eusebius, *Ecclesiastical History*, chapter 20,[46] as if we approved of the withdrawal of everyone in all places and every circumstance, or as if we do not teach that such constancy and charity ought both to be praised and also followed, provided that it does not establish a general rule. For Eusebius does not say that each and every one did this, but only that very many of the Christians did.

And so, to conclude these things at last, there has not been anything alleged yet whereby the plague has been proved either not to be infectious or that withdrawal to avoid infection is to be condemned without exception. In fact, reason and experience both teach that withdrawal is one of the chief natural precautions during contagious diseases. For doubtless the very word *contagion* proclaims this: those things that are nearer to it are more in danger of it. And it is daily evident that by removing in a timely fashion to healthier places, many have been preserved. If anyone wants to take exception, maintaining that he would have been saved even if they had remained at home because God had so decreed it, what, I implore you, will he then say? Is it inappropriate to take other precautions and remedies for all other perils? Therefore, we ought to scorn as needless not only medicine, but also all prudence and wisdom, which is used to avoid dangers

---

45. Isa. 38
46. Beza probably cites chapter 20 of Eusebius's *Ecclesiastical History* (book 7), which describes Dionysius' festal letters, as the beginning of the account of which the pestilence in Alexandria is a part. The specifics of the pestilence and the Christian's response to it is found in chapter 22, especially paragraphs 7–10. Eusebius, *Ecclesiastical History*, 7.20–22 in *NPNF2* 306–307.

of all kinds. Nor should there be any difference between recklessness and discretion, between bravery and audacity. But the matter is far otherwise, because just as God by his everlasting and unchangeable decree has appointed the course of our life, so he has also ordained mediate causes, which we should use for the preservation of life.

It now remains for me to demonstrate to you when it is appropriate to withdraw. For just as in other indifferent matters, so also a person may employ withdrawing both well and poorly. And I am so far from persuading the same thing to every person without exception that, on the contrary, I confess that they offend much less who, when they might otherwise with a good conscience withdraw themselves, yet remain and risk and endanger their lives rather than that they might appear to have forsaken their neighbor or family. I confess, I say, that these offend much less than those who, being carried away with too much distrust or with an immeasurable fear of death, forget and neglect all the duties of humanity and have only this dictum before their eyes: "Flee quickly, far, and return slowly."[47] Surely these people are the most worthy to be thrust out of all human society, the bonds of which they break all to pieces. Now what must be preserved on this point, I think may be determined in the following way.

First of all, I think everyone must view the plague like the arrival of a messenger of divine wrath; because each person will stand before the judgement seat of God, everyone should condemn himself so that God may acquit him. And at the same time, it is decreed that each person will be summoned forward to plead their own case, and that this rod of judgment cannot be avoided by change of place but by change of morals.[48] And if one must die, it is decreed for the good of those who die, inasmuch as they are blessed who die in the Lord.

Another point is that no one should either withdraw or remain who has a doubting conscience about it. But rather, when he has learned out of the Word of God what his duty is, he ought to commend himself to God and persevere with constancy in it.

And even if in such a great variety of circumstances rules for every single thing cannot be established, yet it is not difficult to give certain general precepts that are agreeable to the Word of God, by which, like a kind of norm, individual cases may afterwards (as they say) be tested. Therefore,

---

47. Lat. *Cito, Longe, Tarde*
48. Lat. *neque locorum sed morum mutatione*

let those who intend to remain know that it is the commandment of God that "You shall not murder," and therefore that neither their own, nor the lives of any belonging to or depending on them, are to be thoughtlessly put in danger of deadly infection. On the other side, let those who intend to withdraw know that no one has such a great reason, either for oneself or for their family, that one may forget what one owes their country, their fellow citizens, and lastly to others to whom they are bound by the common bond of humanity and society or by any other kind of necessity. For love does not seek its own. And so, I confess that I cannot see any reason at all why someone should be prohibited from leaving (which should nevertheless be said without any sort of blame) who, either by reason of age or declining health, cannot help others. For if these were to remain, they could only seem to stay put that they may die with great loss to the commonwealth. For just as the cruelty of those who would thrust people out of their cities can never be blamed enough, especially if they are of the poorer lot, so it seems to me that these are to be greatly commended: both the godliness of parents who provide for the life of their children, without loss or damage to anyone else; and also the providence of magistrates especially must be praised who take care that the weak are well provisioned (without loss to the commonwealth), like a cultivated seedbed of citizens.

And here we meet that universal bond by which a person is especially bound to another and that cannot be dissolved without breaking humanity itself. There is also another bond binding every citizen to his country and city. But both of these bonds, I affirm, are to some extent natural and universal in order that everyone must have some understanding of his station and calling. For some serve in public offices, whether civil or sacred, but the rest are private persons. But there are manifold bonds between private persons that nature itself subdues, but that Christian godliness knits; and, unless they are distinguished so that each person may understand their duty in all things, it would inevitably happen that disorder would creep into all matters under the appearance of order. Therefore, let everyone help someone; every citizen a fellow citizen; everyone that needs their help, according to their ability. And let no one think of withdrawing whereby someone may be poorly cared for; still less that anyone would be swerved one bit—by contempt for anyone, or a disproportionate fear of death—from their duty to humanity. But in instances when one may take care, both for himself and his family, by withdrawing without neglecting his duty or public offense, I do not see any reason why someone could not do this, nor do I see why no one is obligated to do it. Still, so that no one flattering themselves would sin against their neighbor, it shall be the duty of a Christian magistrate to take safeguards: that anything that either breeds or nourishes the plague be removed so far as it can be, and that there is consideration for those visited with this sickness so that no one is driven to be anxious for anyone. But I do not see how any serving in a public civil office may flee their charge in a time of plague. And for faithful pastors to forsake even one sheep through their withdrawal at a time when that sheep needs heavenly comfort most of all is too shameful, indeed too wicked, to even consider. Moreover, the bonds of private persons are diverse and manifold. Among these, the one that God testifies is necessary to give the chief place to is the natural commingling of blood, namely, the bond of marriage, so that certainly in my judgement a husband cannot in good conscience leave his wife, or a wife her husband, especially if one of them is visited with the plague. And how much parents owe their children, and children their parents, or relatives their relations, the very laws of nature declare; laws that Christian charity is so far from dissolving that, on the contrary, it draws them closer together. Indeed, for servants to forsake their masters—or for masters, who have made use of their servants' service when they were healthy, to neglect their servants when sick (which too often happens)—is cruelty. Yet the obligations of all these bonds are not equivalent, and therefore that which is less immediate must give place to the one that is more so, since many duties cannot be discharged at once.

Then, just as there is room for someone even among those who are present to forsake their duty unless those who remain do their duty, so the sick must take heed that they do not abuse the love of their relatives and friends at a time when they desire to have themselves provided for. And those who continue to do their duties must not cast themselves heedlessly into the risk of infection. For this would happen from recklessness, rather than right and Christian judgement, to many who, although they used to shun those that were sick of other diseases, now visit those with the plague so that they may seem to despise death. This contempt of God's judgments I tolerate less than I do the excessive weakness of the fearful. But how others are affected and disposed in craving the presence of their friends I do not know. When I myself was visited with the plague twenty eight years ago[49] in Lausanne, several of my friends wanted to come to me—and the one that stands out beyond the rest is Pierre Viret, of blessed

---

49. Circa 1551

memory, who was prepared to come to me; and also John Calvin himself brought me every kind of kindness by a messenger sent with letters—but I did not permit anyone to come to me, lest, by the great loss of such great men, I would have been thought to have provided for myself through loss to the Christian commonwealth. Nor did it grieve me to refuse their coming, although perhaps the same could not be said of me if I were in their place. But if, in calamities of this sort, the magistrate does provide as much as can be done in time —both that by such lawful means as are not repugnant to Christian charity the infection may be prevented, and also that those sick with plague lack nothing—he shall doubtless do very well both for the sick and the healthy. He shall also remove many questions, which are customarily raised in this argument. But this especially must be agreed upon, that as our sins are the chief and true cause of the plague, so this is the only proper remedy against the same: that if the ministers would not dispute about infectiousness (which belongs to physicians) but, by their life and doctrine stir up the people to earnest repentance, love, and charity one towards another, then the sheep themselves would hear clearly and heed the voice of their pastors.

FINIS.

2

A Letter to a Friend

Introduction

Born in 1572 to Huguenot parents, André Rivet studied theology at Berne and La Rochelle, after which he served first as chaplain and then as pastor to the Duke of La Trémoille.[1] In 1617, Rivet was elected president of the Synod of Vitré. Three years later he was appointed professor of theology at Leiden, where he distinguished himself not only as an exegete, theologian, and polemicist, but also as a pastoral theologian. In 1646, Rivet would leave Leiden to assume his last post as rector in the new Orange College of Breda, where he remained until his death in 1651. Rivet's eminence as a theologian is well summarized by Archibald Alexander, the first professor of Princeton Seminary, who wrote:

> The learned need not be informed, that in that age when theology was more thoroughly studied than in any other since the apostles' days, Andrew Rivet had no superior, whether you contemplate him as an exegetical or polemical theologian. His acquaintance with the Christian fathers was most exact and extensive; and he knew how to estimate their labours, and what deference was due to their authority, of which he gave full evidence in the work entitled *Critici Sacri*, which is now the best guide on this subject which the young theologian can follow. Rivet's theology was as sound as it was extensive.[2]

---

1. Eugène and Emile Haag, *La France Protestante*, 10 vols. in 8 (Paris: Joël Cherbuliez, 1846–1859), 8:444; "Destined from his infancy to the holy ministry by his parents, who were animated by an ardent piety united with a great zeal for the Reformed religion . . ." editors' translation; cf. *Allgemeine Deutsche Biographie*, 56 vols. (Leipzig: Duncker & Humblot, 1875–1912), 28:707–708; G. P. van Itterzon, "Rivet (Rivetus), André (Andreas)" in *Biografisch lexicon voor de geschiedenis van het Nederlands protestantisme*, 6 vols. (Kampen: Kok, 1978–2006) 2:375–78.

2. Archibald Alexander, *Thoughts on Religious Experience* (Edinburgh: Banner of Truth, 1967), 197; cf. André Rivet, *Critici Sacri Libri IV*, 4th ed. (Geneva: Pierre Chouët, 1660).

There was not always agreement among the Reformed on what the plague was biologically or what the proper civic policy was, but there were those like Rivet who strived toward theological consensus and social unity. Rivet's pastoral sensibilities are evident in his irenic seventy-page *Letter to a Friend* (1636) in which he considers God's sovereignty and goodness in the face of secondary causes like the plague, as well as practical considerations for pastors.

And in this regard, Rivet urges not only words, but deeds. Plague, according to Rivet, is an opportunity for widescale deep repentance—publicly and privately, individually and corporately, for offending God through disobedience to both tables of the law, for sins against God and against neighbors. Rivet observed that the "sons of the physicians teach—with not one excepted that I know of—that the plague is contagious and spreads like some kind of poison, which infects the air that we breathe." Furthermore, argues Rivet, since from the beginning of the world every animal has been granted the right to protect itself, its body, and its life, so "one must not think that God has granted less to human beings, who can predict what will harm them, so that they can take precaution by all lawful means." In sum, Rivet maintains that, "Even as our faith rests upon God—while we pray with supplications and vows to avert evils that his hand has inflicted and beg his mercy that the assault of the destroying angel is either hindered or thoroughly checked—meanwhile all of the secondary causes and aids provided by God that can be lawfully used must not be neglected."

What might be the most rewarding for the Christian is Rivet's unblinking treatment of mortality. By God's grace, Rivet was himself well prepared for death, and he showed those who visited with him in his final days what it looks like to "go toward it and through it" with faith in the risen Christ. Shortly after preaching a sermon on Christmas day, 1650, Rivet fell ill. Realizing that he was not likely to recover from the illness, he offered the following prayer to God:

> Great God, thou art my Father, thou hast given me both life and a new life; thou hast taught me from my youth, and I have declared thy wonderful works; forsake me not now in my old age. Hitherto, through thy peculiar favor, thou hast preserved me sound in my body and my faculties, and the functions of my mind have not been impaired, so that a little before I was oppressed by this disease, I found

myself as apt and ready for the exercise of my vocation as in my flourishing youth. O Lord God! If it be thy will that I should longer attend upon thy service, thou canst assuage my disease in one moment; but if thou has decreed otherwise, thy will be done. This one thing I beg with most inward affections that thou wilt make me conformable to thy goodwill—let not thy good Spirit depart from me, that in this conflict thy strength may make me a conqueror. Accomplish this, O Lord, for thine own sake, and since thou hast employed me in thy work, grant that I may die an honourable death, and such as may be an example unto others: that I may stand fast in that sound doctrine which I have taught, and may make a good confession thereof before witnesses, that thereby thy church may be both instructed and edified. Let me apply to myself by a lively faith all the promises of the Gospel, and let them put forth their efficacy in me, unto my joy and eternal consolation, that nothing in the world, neither affliction nor distress, may separate me from thee, or cause me to doubt of thy love and favour. Thou knowest my weakness and infirmities: permit not the grievousness of my pain to cast me into impatience or murmuring. Either make my pains tolerable, or furnish me with fortitude and constancy sufficient to bear them: that I may not offend with my tongue, keep thou the door of my lips![3]

God answered Rivet's prayer, as he was able to spend the next two weeks of his life in constant prayer and in visitation with many who came to see him. On the day of his death, January 7, 1651, Rivet prayed the following:

The sense of divine favour increaseth in me every moment. My pains are tolerable, and my joys inestimable. I am no more vexed with earthly cares. I remember when any new book came out, how earnestly I have longed after it—but now all that is but dust. Thou art my all, O Lord; my good is to approach unto thee. O what a library have I in God, in whom are all the treasures of wisdom and knowledge! Thou are the teacher of spirits—I have learned more divinity in these ten days that thou hast come to visit me, than I did in fifty years before.[4]

3. Ibid., 197–98.
4. Ibid., 207.

His final words were those of the apostle Paul, "I have fought a good fight. . ." Though others had to finish what he was not able to say, Rivet mustered enough strength to utter his Amen before passing into glory.[5]

André Rivet, *Andreae Riveti ... Operum Theologicorum*, 2 vols. (Rotterdam: Arnoldus Leers, 1652), 2:405–12; idem et al., *Variorum tractatus theologici de peste*, (Leiden: Johannes Elsevirius, 1655), 63–138.

A Letter to a Friend
André Rivet
Translated by Todd M. Rester

O most excellent man,

After you departed from us, I pondered a great deal and for a long while upon that question, which is motivated and precipitated by this most calamitous time; on that scourge, which all confess is being inflicted by God, either immediately or through secondary causes that infect the air and spread that pestilential disease, which has killed so many people in so many places and runs riot everywhere throughout these provinces. A few godly and certainly God-fearing men question whether one ought to take precaution for that evil, either by keeping separate or staying away from visiting those who either have been infected or have visited infected places. Other equally godly and prudent men assert that this can be done, and even must be done, yet with many appropriate requirements and qualifications applied. I am not one who thinks that I can construct a case for or against either side such that I would lead all parties to one viewpoint. Yet with you I will say what I feel and, after presenting others' views, I will present what seems to me just and fair, and on what my mind has settled at this point. But I should require this one thing from you and all good people, so that we would all agree on this matter: these deadly epidemics, and this pestiferous plague that has caused and does cause such carnage daily and has miserably depopulated so many of the most flourishing cities, has been inflicted by God who has been incensed by our sins; and there is not

---

5. Ibid., 207.

a more ready and prompt remedy than—throughout all members of the commonwealth, public and private—that we witness in word but also in deed that our former corruption of life and morals displeases us; and we will seal the same testimony with a true emendation, with our morals ordered to the will and Word of God, and first giving proof to God and then under God to all people; with the magistrate focusing upon violators of both tables [of the Law], restraining lurking wickedness, and checking all injustice and insolence with the bolts of laws and punishments; with subject peoples keeping themselves in their duty, humbling themselves under the hand of God, and considering that, for their good, God either inflicts or is about to inflict chastisements and trials, the use and benefit of which we gather from the Word of God and our own experience, even in these times of mortality and pestilence. These are the sorts of benefits harvested from that exquisite work by Cyprian the Martyr, *On the Mortality*,[6] [composed] on a similar occasion for the use of the ancient church and placed before our eyes. I would desire that little book frequently set in the hand, day and night, of those who in this current situation are excessively anxious and worried. It is also incumbent upon godly and faithful servants of God especially in this to build up failing godliness on this occasion and—as it were, kindled by the fire of this affliction—to inflame godliness more and more with the breath of their exhortations, which reach all the way to heaven and dissipate the corruption of the infected air. I do not doubt that in this desire I would have the agreement and accord of all good people with me.

But with this remedy presupposed first and foremost, we can consider whether others ought to be applied whereby plague can be avoided, either when one takes precaution against the evil, or even avoids or reduces it, and whether we strive to do so publicly or privately. In almost all other dangers and diseases such an approach is generally not even up for debate, and it is thought advantageous from its present usefulness and past experience, as well as to be necessary in some measure. But it seems, in this case, this approach is cast into doubt by quite a few people. It is even openly condemned by certain people, who do not think it is permissible for Christian and faithful men to avoid infected places, to abstain from familiar association with those who have been infected with the plague,

---

6. Plague in ancient and medieval times was frequently called simply "the Mortality," not the Black Death, a title originating among historians circa 1755. Cyprian of Carthage, "Treatise VII–On the Mortality" in *ANF* 5:469–475, reprinted here in Appendix A.

or to provide for some sort of retirement and flight for a change of air for themselves and their families.

We do not deny that this approach is not free to everyone, and not all the time. Such is dependent on the circumstances of places and persons, for whom flight and retirement would not only be inappropriate but would be the crime of deserting one's station with respect to God and men. Instead, we will attempt to show that, with circumstances changed and all things duly considered, one who does not take the necessary precautions for himself, even by a change of places and air, can even run headlong into the censures of having tested God and of foolishness. The plague is contagious and communicates itself like some kind of poison, infecting the air that we breathe. All the sons of the physicians teach this, with no exception that I know of. In addition to the reasons which they apply, which are neither few nor weak, they have experience to support them. Although that experience may be mistaken sometimes, and the physicians' ability to defend against that poison is less than sufficient, nevertheless in many instances experience teaches that those who rashly cast themselves into danger fall into it and suffer the penalties of their own foolishness. If from the beginning it has been granted by nature to every kind of animal to guard themselves, their body, and their life, one must not think that God has granted less to human beings, who can predict what will harm them, so that they can take precaution by all lawful means We do not think it lawful, however, if anyone established in a public calling, whether in the commonwealth or church, should cast off all care for those who suffer and for those living in danger to their body and soul and leave them destitute of all necessary assistance. For this must always be presupposed: the public authority must take heed that those who groan under the hand of God do not lack the necessary support, however infected they are. We only say that this of all things must be their concern, especially for those who rule. This is not demanded of everyone. Indeed, this duty belongs to a magistrate and pastor, according to their office, so that those who are not established in an office or not necessary for it should take care that they do not meddle in their affairs. And on this reasoning [the pastors and magistrates] must assist the sick, which is not an imposition on the healthy, because both ought to be consulted.

To be certain, the most learned theologians among us consulted on this matter agree in the main on this opinion. Among whom Calvin, in epistle 362, expressed himself briefly but, as in his customary way, energetically.

Among several questions posed to him was this third one: "Is it right to change locations for the sake of fleeing the plague?" He responds, "This question seems to arise from the stupidity of those who have never been endowed with even a bit of humanity. Therefore," he says,

> will it then be impermissible to chose healthy air? Therefore, in private dwellings will it also be impermissible to prefer an opportunity for health? Therefore, will it be impermissible to watch out for noxious excrement? Therefore, one ought not fear any contagion? Thus, they hand us paradoxes, the result of which is to strip us of all sense. Meanwhile our counsel is not to indulge the cowardice of those who abandon their vocation at the first hint of danger. Just as if a husband had abandoned his wife, or a wife her husband, or children their parents, or in turn parents their children, so it is if a pastor consulted himself and abandoned his church, or if a magistrate quits his office. Finally, no less than fire or sword, the contagion of plague can be avoided provided that no office is neglected.[7]

You mentioned to me that there was once a treatise published by the venerable Beza, which I have not happened to see, yet I did read what was cited from it by certain people, namely Paul Tarnow in *On the Sacred Ministry in Three Books*,[8] and it is listed in the *Epitome of Conrad Gesner's Library* among Beza's extant works.[9] But because you have hope of a new edition, I do not doubt that it will become known to all what was the general and perpetual opinion of the Genevan Church; that as much as she could, in asserting the providence of God and his arrangement of the final ends of human beings, she was beyond even any hint of the slightest suspicion, and

---

7. Cf. Ep. 362 in John Calvin, *Epistolae et Responsa*, 3rd ed. (Hanover: Guilielmus Antonius, 1597), 706; cf. Ep. 3212 in *Calvini Opera* 18:104–5.
8. See bk. 3, ch. 2, "Is it licit for a pastor during a prowling plague, to withdraw from the sheep committed to his trust?" ("An liceat pastori, grassante peste, secedere ab ovibus sua fidei commissis") in the Lutheran theologian Paul Tarnow (1562-1633), *De sacrosancto ministerio, libri tres in quibus de ministerii evangelici in ecclesiis Lutheranis veritate et efficacia . . . et praeter theoreticas quaaestiones complures, pleraeq; omnes practicae . . .* (Rostock: Johannes Hallervordius, 1624), 1299–1309.
9. Beza's 1580 work does not appear in Conrad Gesner (1516–1565), *Epitome Bibliothecae Conradi Gesneri* (Zurich: Christopher Froschouer, 1555). Most likely, Rivet is referencing the updated version of 1583, Conrad Gesner et al., *Bibliotheca Instituta et collecta a Conrado Gesnero, deinde in epitomen redacta . . . tertio recognita . . . per Iosiam Simlerum . . . postremo . . . per Iohannem Iacobum Frisium* (Zurich: Christopher Froschouer, 1583), 780. This reference work advertises itself as "nearly the most exhaustive catalogue of all books written from the beginning of the world until this day, extant and non-extant, published and spread everywhere in libraries."

to very many it would seem she even transcended it; yet regarding those final ends she always thought in such a way that she judged that no means should be condemned whereby either evils could be guarded against or goods could be procured. I know that when the plague was prowling about there, a hospital was established for it; not only were medical doctors and practitioners elected to it who would be present with the sick as much in that public place as in private dwellings, but even a domicile separate from others was outfitted for them. Among the pastors, some were chosen by lot, after an invocation of the name of God, who must be present with those who had fallen ill, with the remaining pastors being exempted who would then administer the Word of God and sacraments to the healthy as well as to those who were suffering from non-contagious illnesses so that in this way they would be mindful of both. And while a pastor comforted one, the others would not be endangered as more and more the evil grew worse. And in this way they also looked after human society, so that all things were done appropriately and in order. Concerning private persons, there is another rationale; provided they do not abandon the members of their household, they can withdraw from others and, being mindful of themselves, retire from all engagement with those infected with the plague, and they can also shun those places in which it ravaged.

This was the opinion of that most learned man Jerome Zanchi, which he expounded in his commentary on Philippians 2:30, in which he discusses Epaphroditus as a minister of those "who on account of the work of Christ drew all the way near to death, without consideration of their own life."[10] With these words he later shows that, for everyone individually called by Christ, this work shall never be abandoned. Thus one correctly infers that not even due to pestilence will the work of Christ be deserted, and one must not consider fleeing. But, however much these words may be true in general and should be understood simply, one judges that they must be understood in different ways according to the circumstances. And since he expounds on the topic further on the occasion of relating what had once been debated between him and a certain pastor from Chur, Switzerland, I will condense his disputation on it so as to omit nothing of those matters treated on both sides, to convey the weight of the matter. At that time the pastor was contending, not least, that "no one and in no way ought to avoid

---

10. Jerome Zanchi, In *D. Pauli apostoli Epistolas ad Philippenses, Colossenses, Thessalonicenses et duo priora capita primae epistolae D. Iohannis, Commentarii*, 2nd ed. (Neustadt: Wilhelm Harnisius, 1601), 222–227. See page 234 in this volume.

comforting those afflicted with a pestilence, much less ought one to leave places infected with such a plague." Zanchi says that, to the contrary, both must be done, provided that they were done for a legitimate reason; that is, so that what duty God has enjoined upon us we would not disgracefully neglect, to both the injury and defrauding of the Church and of our neighbor. On the contrary, these arguments were proffered which concerned on one hand all believers and, on the other, only pastors, upon whose solution depends the resolution of the whole question.

First, from this point that pastor attempted to prove that the pestilence was not a contagious disease but only a scourge inflicted by God immediately, which he was proving from the example of the plague whereby God drew attention to David's sin after the census of the people (2 Sam. 24). Second, from the providence of God, which cannot be resisted; he has enumerated whom he wills to be snatched away by the plague, and whom he wills to be spared, and that cannot be avoided by any carefulness of men. Third, from charity, which does not seek its own, but what is Christ's and one's neighbor's.

To these things, which are common to all, Zanchi responded to the first point that it is false that the disease is not contagious; experience, in addition to various reasons, vanquishes this point. His opponent was even compelled to acknowledge this. It does not follow that if the plague is a scourge of God, it is not contagious. For leprosy among the people of Israel was also a scourge of God, yet it infected others with its contagion. The same thing must be said of elephantiasis, scabies, and similar evils, which, if it is licit throughout the law of God to avoid them, then it will be no less licit to shun a pestilence for the same reason. I add that it is not always true that a plague is inflicted immediately by God without the influence of secondary causes. The contrary is plainly evident in many passages, where either the superior causes or even inferior ones that corrupt the air in an extraordinary manner are the first beginnings of this evil, which grows little by little with the corruption increasing.

To the second point Zanchi responded that the providence of God does not destroy second causes but establishes them, because through them his decrees are executed. Hence the decree whereby he decreed to destroy these or those people and to save others does not impede human effort to save themselves, not only by using remedies which are at hand or prescribed by doctors, but also other remedies among which is this one: that those not obligated by their vocation to a specific residence (*ad residentiam* as they say) may avoid infected places. Why in plague ought not that be done which is done in famine, war, persecution, and similar circumstances? For what sort of person will deny that God moderates all things so that not even a hair of one's head would fall to the earth apart from his providence? Yet no one ever appointed a trial date[11] for those who fled a famine, just as they who had regard for themselves and their own departed from Palestine to Egypt. No one ascribes vice to those who are not suited to soldiering if they should flee from war and travel to other places where they can enjoy peace. Since these also would be among the means established by God, especially with us this decree of God must not be inquired into; since these things are unknown, it so belongs to us to lean upon the providence of God, to which our life is subject, so that we would omit none of those things which are conducive for the preservation of life and wellness. Indeed, even if we were certain that God had decided to save us from the plague, yet [our duty] would not cease or rather [allow us to] be negligent in our care, lest we cast ourselves into danger. Indeed, Paul had known what God had decreed concerning himself and his sailing companions (Acts 27). Yet he did not want the sailors to snatch themselves away, with the others abandoned. Indeed, he said to the centurion, "If those men would separate themselves, likewise you all will perish" (Acts 27:31). Although in fact he knew they would not perish, yet he was not ignorant of the fact that the means whereby the ship could be saved consisted in the effort of the sailors. From which it is inferred that lawful means do not obstruct divine providence but are subordinate to them. One must think likewise about the plague, that it does not resist divine providence, which includes those who labor publicly, so that intemperate air is improved with flames kindled with either sulfur dust or other means; or those who employ preventive measures privately; or even those who, as much as they can conscientiously, move away from infected places.

To the third point, charity does not require that everyone should attend to all the unwell. They could be helped by those who are elected for that task. Also, it is contrary to charity if, in order to care for one, someone harms many; [for example,] if someone infects their own family, or if someone unnecessarily leads others into danger. The rule of charity is that one has regard for many, and one must be so guided that we do not injure charity under pretext of it. Jerome Zanchi argued the matter in this sense.

---

11. *Diem dixit*: lit. "he appointed a day," that is, for trial to address accusations; e.g. Cicero, *Pro Milone*, 14.36.

Georg Sohn (c. 1552–1589), also a professor at Heidelberg, in his *Theses on the causes and cure of plague*, in tome one [of his *Opera*],[12] embraced the same opinion: "To those who can leave without inconvenience to the Commonwealth or the Church and with love of neighbor intact, the remedy of flight is granted, and in these cases that saying of the doctors has place, 'Fly quickly, go far away, and come back slowly!'"[13]

The English theologian, William Perkins, a godly man and highly experienced in cases of conscience, while explaining the sixth commandment of the Decalogue in the affirmative part— wherein the conservation of our life and that of others is stated—answers this question: "Is it permissible for a person to flee in time of plague?" He responds, "Those impeded by their calling may not leave; it is forbidden for them to flee. These sorts are magistrates and pastors inasmuch as they are caretakers of souls. But those who are free and unobligated, and not bound to any calling, are permitted to flee."[14] He asserts these chief reasons: (1) anyone is free to seek their own security and safety, provided that they do so without damage and detriment to others; (2) it is permissible for a person to flee war, famine, floods, fire, and other similar crises of life; why not also the plague?; (3) with the number and assembly of the common people diminished, so also the danger is diminished.

But to the objections he responds in this way: (1) "Flight is a sign of distrust." He responds: "Distrust is a sin, which is not located and committed in the thing itself, but in the person." (2) "This is offensive." He responds, "The offense is taken, not given." (3) "Fleeing is deserting one's neighbor, which is repugnant to charity in the highest degree." He responds, "Not in the least, provided that their kindred are present, as well as magistrates and ministers of the word." (4) "All people are obligated to visit the sick, and that from the divine ordination and establishment." He responds that "among the Jews, the lepers had been excluded, and so also now those were excepted who were affected in some way with a disease most nearly corresponding to leprosy, and if there is some danger of contagion." Thus William Perkins.

---

12. See the Reformed professor of theology and Hebrew at Marburg (1574–1584) and professor of Old Testament at Heidelberg (1584–1589), Georg Sohn, *Operum Georgii Sohnii Sacrae Theologiae Doctoris... continens scripta auctoris methodica*, 2nd ed. (Nassau-Siegen: Christopher Corvinus, 1598), 1:150–153.

13. *Cito, longe, tarde, cede, recede, veni*: commonly attributed to Galen and Hippocrates on the plague.

14. William Perkins, *The Workes of that famous and worthy minister of Christ in the universitie of Cambridge Mr. William Perkins*, 3 vols. (London: John Legatt, 1626), 1:58.

George Abbot (1562–1633), who was later the archbishop of Canterbury, eruditely handled the same question in the school of theology at Oxford University in question five titled *On Flight in Persecution and Plague*,[15] where he most learnedly refuted those who, under the pretext that contagion is a divine visitation and because each person is assigned their time of living, infer that it is not permitted to any person to remove themselves. He proves that this is futile because with equal reason someone could cast themselves into the sea or headlong off a cliff, because he would not die unless his hour would have come. Yet our Savior refers to this sort of thing as testing the Lord (Matt. 4:7). Just as God Almighty has ordained the ends, so also the means, and we must in every way diligently seek them out. What pertains to the visitation of God shall certainly be the rod of God, and if he may have stricken us with it, we should endure it patiently; yet it is not necessary that we should foolishly present ourselves to it, lest we should seem to have seized his hand with violence upon ourselves. Also sword, famine, the teeth of harmful beasts, and others of the same sort God lists among his harshest scourges.[16] But the examples of godly men teach us to avoid these things if we could, such as when David fled from Saul's spear and the patriarchs withdrew to Egypt due to a famine.[17]

He adds that everyone ought to flee occasions of one's own demise. There is a special command about avoiding bloodshed; and if that applies to others, then certainly it applies to us as well. If it is not permissible in any way to inflict death upon someone else, then certainly it applies to ourselves also, in which case both of these are wrong: either embarking on a path which leads to death, or approaching the means to it. And just as in other cases, so also in the case of the plague, which certainly is a murderer (Ps. 91:6), and one that so quickly is carrying off many thousands of people.

God, who provided for his own people against the contagion of leprosy and willed that the leprous should live separately lest they infect others, is not displeased if we should withdraw for a time in order to shun a contagion so dangerous and harmful to life. The custom of the Turks must not be approved, who indiscriminately blunder into a place infected with the plague. It is fitting for Christians to restrain themselves, and importunate

---

15. "V. De fuga in persequutione & peste" in George Abbot, *Explicatio sex illustrium quaestionum* (Frankfurt: Jonah Rosa, 1616). See page 274 in this volume.

16. See e.g. Deut. 28:15–68

17. 1 Sam. 19:1–10; Gen. 12:10–16; Gen. 42

people must not quarrel with their brethren who withdraw themselves, their children, and their family due to the necessities of the times. To those God granted the fittingness of the matter, let them use it in good faith. But those absenting themselves while their brethren yet languish miserably should not be absent but should assist, direct, and comfort them with counsel, assistance, and whatever means they can. This is the sympathy of Christians. Thus far Abbot.

While writing in his commentary on 1 Chronicles 21:15, Ludwig Lavater (1527–1586), who is rather inflexible on this question, still acknowledges that "nothing prohibits us using preventative measures,[18] such as when we burn various odors whereby the air is improved and the poison is driven away; such as when we observe a good diet." He adds, "Most people think nothing is more useful than flight, such as when they take themselves away from pestilential places to healthy ones as quickly as possible. But one must see what a consideration of our duty demands."[19] That is certainly a necessary caution and must be observed by all who are wise, but from these remarks it is apparent that he does not condemn flight absolutely.

Once regarding the same question, Urbanus Rhegius (1489–1541) wrote a grave and weighty letter to Antonius von Berckhusen, the mayor of Hanover, which is found in the second part of his *Opera*, folio 91. Moreover, he resolves the matter in this way:[20]

In the commonwealth, whoever is not engaged in some office, whether economic or political, so that nothing would lapse due to his absence, and if his absence results in no detriment or inconvenience, and if he vehemently fears for himself and his life, can in good conscience flee, lest he test God. And yet he must fly in such a way that he hands over and commits his will and his entire self to the good and holy will of our heavenly Father, who even in the midst and in the depths of the sea can save his own, just as he saved Jonah; but although he can save in that way, yet, like Jonah, one must not therefore foolishly cast oneself into the sea contrary to the Word

---

18. Lat., Gk. *remediis*, προφυλακτικοῖς

19. Ludwig Lavater (1527–1586), a Reformed theologian who taught at Zurich, handles the plague in the context of his treatment of David's sin in 1 Chron. 21:13–17. His locus on the plague, *De Peste*, occurs after his comments on 1 Chron. 21:14. See idem, *In libros Paralipomenon sive chronicorum, Lvdovici Lavateri Tigurini Commentarius*, 2nd ed. (Heidelberg: Andreas Cambierius, 1600), 74r–74v. See page 214 in this volume.

20. See the letter dated August 1, 1540, in Urbanus Rhegius, *In omnis generis afflictionibus, in persecutionum procellis, in pestis*, aliisque morbis (Frankfurt: Petrus Brubachius, 1545), fols. 45v–55v; idem, *Opera Vrbani Regii Latine Edita* (Nürnberg: vom Berg und Neuber, 1562), 2:91r–93v.

and Will of God. For this would be to test God, who can find and deliver us in all circumstances—and slay us—whenever he wills.

Therefore, whoever is not fastened and bound by the bond of his calling, ministry, or any function, if he would have nothing that he should perform due to public mandate, then it is licit for him to avoid the plague in whatever way that he can and may change his residence and fly. Yet, he must always do this in the fear of God. Many holy men of renown in the Old Testament, such as Abraham, Isaac, Jacob, Elijah, Paul, and others, fled the danger of death. Indeed, it is stupidity and foolishness to cast oneself without cause into danger of death. Thus Rhegius.

All these theologians were orthodox, without ever being spattered with any spot of suspicion that they ever detracted anything whatsoever from divine providence or predestination. Yet with one consent they teach that faithful people can withdraw from infected places and take heed in flight for themselves and their families, with such reasons and in such ways which they do not see as repugnant to Christian charity.

The more difficult question regards magistrates and ministers of the church, especially when one considers their flight and withdrawal. For, since it belongs to these to look out for everyone, both the healthy and the sick, they could not rightly do this if they should change their location. Nearly all agree they are obliged to stay in residence, nor can they withdraw without scandalous effect. So also these theologians I have adduced supposed. Georg Sohn, in a few but expressive words, speaks thus, "The three little adverbs of the doctors, *cito, longe, tarde*—that is, 'Leave quickly, fly far, and return slowly'—and the remedy of flight do not apply at all to those whom reason commands to remain, either due to a public office, whether ecclesiastical or political, or due to Christian charity. For our calling or love of neighbor must never be violated (John 10:11, Matt. 25:42). And so if those fly, they heap injury upon injury."[21]

So also Rhegius, in the work cited above: "The one who enters into some public function, whether ecclesiastical or political, must administer the office of his function, and he cannot flee with a good conscience."[22] To these, he only concedes this after spiritual remedies have been applied "in the fear of the Lord for all bodily remedies and all means," by which the

---

21. See Georg Sohn (1552–1589), "XV. De Causis et Curatione Pestis", §37–38, in *Opera*, 2nd ed., 3 vols. (Herborn: Christoph Corvinus, 1598), 1:153. This disputation is part of a set of nineteen disputations delivered at Marburg between 1574–1584.

22. Rhegius, *Opera*, 2:92r.

plague can either be expelled or defended against, and by which we may fortify ourselves against the plague so that we may not become infected, provided that these means are not contrary to faith and charity.

Yet, it must be noted in this case, even if they should remain in a common place, such as in the city, and should exercise their offices in the commonwealth and the church, all are not obligated to go to the suffering, and to associate in person with them. In fact, because ministers are debtors to the healthy as well as to the sick, and to their own families, and they are assigned to the commonwealth and the church, those who may be infected do not comprise either the entirety or the greatest part of the commonwealth or the church. Why then, to the detriment of others, should ministers devote themselves entirely to the one part that is suffering? And perhaps they will not debate so much regarding the magistrate, if it is sufficient to care [for the sick] through others, so that they may administer the things necessary for the sick in a suitable and timely manner through those who must and who are ordained to that task. But pastors must execute their task αὐτοπροσώπως, that is, personally, because such are the functions of their ministry, which could not be performed through another, nor would those functions be sufficiently provided for in their absence. And so, when there is only one pastor, it seems necessary that he should care for his congregation; he should invite those suffering to repentance and instruct them rightly regarding a blessed and good death.[23] For then, standing steadfast in his calling, "a thousand may fall at your side, and ten thousand at your right hand, but it will not come near you" (Ps. 91:7). Because even if God should see fit to do otherwise, that pastor will be blessed who, in contempt of death, would have died in his duty.

And this is certainly worthy of the greatest consideration. But notwithstanding, even in this necessity, we must attend to two points. First, where there is a plurality of pastors, it can be carried out by the method that we have mentioned was the custom at Geneva: that one or other from the group is delegated, who might be chosen by lot, and they would attend to the infected. Yet the rule of prudence must be applied in their approach; that is, they should not draw so near when they could be heard at a distance from the sick person, so that they do not draw close if precautionary measures are not adhered to, unless perhaps necessity urges it. And they should not infect their own family. As long as they are engaged in that work, the

---

23. Lat., Gk. *de beata εὐθανασίᾳ*

magistrate should procure a public residence for them with the necessary staff for that purpose. Then the rest of the pastors could easily exercise the remaining duties in the public assembly of the church, and in consolation of those afflicted, such as those suffering with other diseases that are less dangerous, who otherwise would shun the presence of their pastors if they knew their pastors indiscriminately frequented infected buildings. So also some of the most learned theologians think, even those who seem more rigid on this matter, such as the Jena theologian, Johann Gerhard (1582–1637). In his *Theological Commonplaces*, Gerhard says, "Still it must not seem blameworthy if a church is equipped with several ministers of the Word, and it is agreed among them to commit the office of visiting the sick to one of them. Or it could also be extraordinarily useful to the church that one or several of them could perform these tasks and then scatter to safe places."[24] How beneficial the view of Paul Tarnow is, the recent professor in Rostok, and how he proves it is found in his work *On the ministry*, book 3, chapter 2.[25] So also Zanchi in the work cited, asks, "Why does the church not appoint one or two, or even several [pastors] to do this task according to the necessity of the times, who would undertake the care of all the sick? Then you would free those who are more necessary to the church from this task of visiting [the sick]."[26]

The basis for this opinion is this: the wellbeing of every member must be provided for, but especially that of the whole body, and especially so that the entire church is not deprived of the ministry of its pastors. For which reason it also follows that where there is only one pastor common to the entire church, it must be seen if the sick could be succored in another way that does not render the pastor useless or suspect to the rest of the congregation. For in these regions, even outside of the danger of contagion, it has been established that pastors should be relieved of some part of the burden, with comforters supplied from another rank. This is a more difficult matter when the Lord's Supper is administered to the bed-ridden,[27] for then it seems to be work that requires a pastor. Although several people think that

---

24. Sic "*Locorum Comm. Tom. 6. Pag.* 496", see Johann Gerhard, "De Ecclesiastico Ministerio" §290, *Theologici Loci*, 9 vols. (Frankfurt & Hamburg: Zacharias Hertelius, 1657), 6:170.

25. Paul Tarnow, *De sacrosancto ministerio, libri tres in quibus de ministerii evangelici in ecclesiis Lutheranis veritate et efficacia . . . et praeter theoreticas quaestiones complures, pleraeq; omnes practicae . . .* (Rostock: Johannes Hallervordius, 1624), 1299–1309.

26 Cf. Zanchi, *Commentarii*, 223–227. Rivet's statement is not an exact quote from Zanchi but seem.s to be a summary of his position.

27. *Clinici* from Gk. κλινικοί.

it can be done through an intermediary,[28] just as was once done when the wafer of the Eucharist was moistened for the Serapion, which was brought from the minister to the invalid by a boy, as Eusebius of Caesarea tells us in his *Ecclesiastical History*.[29] But an example does not make a law, especially when it is a single one and it is repugnant to the institution of our most holy Lord. Therefore, in his *Cases of Conscience*, bk. 4 ch. 9, [case 6], Friederich Balduin (1575–1627) thinks it is more desirable that when a pastor should visit a sick person, he should take precaution that the sick person is brought out of their hovel into a sunny place so that the pastor speaks to him there, and he would hear him out of range of the diseased wind.[30] He should prepare the holy supper and perform the things remaining which pertain to this act in such a way that he would be in less danger of infection. Finally, he adds that the holy supper is not so necessary that in the midst of danger of the plague, due to one or another sick person, the entire assembly elsewhere should be brought into the danger of infection. We know that the Supper was established to this end, that it was to be administered in the assembly of the church. And we exhort each believer, provided that they are well and the opportunity presents itself, that they should frequent communion. We scarcely have anyone in this struggle who demands it, because they know that it is not so necessary nor also fitting. And so they confirm their communion with Christ by other means privately; by the remembrance of a past perception of the Sacrament, and by the present word, whereby their faith is strengthened. And certainly it is not in vain that they think their leading men should be excepted from a task of this sort; men who, as long as they live, are exceedingly beneficial to the Church so that by their death they leave her desolate and deprived of the most useful instruments. Especially if they would be such who also teach in their schools, for by this reasoning, as I understood it, Dr. Beza of Geneva was excepted—despite his reluctance for being excepted—from those who attend upon the sick. And it is not unjust that Dr. Zanchi took issue with the incident when Dr. Heinrich Bullinger of Zurich returned infected with the pestilence from a visit to a certain woman suffering from it, and he infected his entire family such that then his wife and two daughters died, when he

28. Lat. *per interpositam personam*
29. Eusebius of Caesarea (265–339), *Eccl. Hist.*, bk. 6, ch. 44 in *NPNF2* 1:290
30. See "What must be done in rural areas in time of plague when a pastor has no colleague? How must the holy supper be given to the infected, so that perhaps the whole church would not be infected with a fear of the pastor?" in the Lutheran pastor and theologian, Friedrich Balduin, *Tractatus luculentus posthumus . . . casibus nimirum conscientiae* (Frankfurt: Caspar Wachtler, 1654), 654–55.

could have provided for the sick woman's wellbeing and comfort another way than by access to such a great man. "Should he not also," Zanchi says, "have loved his family and the Church, and reckoned concerning both?"[31] Therefore he concluded that the public good must be set before a private one, and the greater good before the lesser one. Emperors must not be exposed to dangers in the front line; there is no debate on this in an army. I could add here Zacharias Ursinus (1534–1583), a former Heidelberg theologian, *Theological Exercises*, part 2, page 514.[32]

This was also the common opinion of the Gallican Reformed Churches, as is evident from the national synod held in Vitré, in the province of Brittany in May 1583, wherein, in the name of the Churches in the Low Countries, three delegates were received: pastors Michael Forest, minister of the French Church at Mechlen; Dr. Jean Boulins, minister of the church at Ghent; and Jean Charan, minister of the Gallo-Belgian church at Bruges. Moreover, in the *Matieres Generales*, article 25: "on the question proposed by the deputies of Poitier, if it is expedient that ministers should visit those infected with the plague, the company leaves this to the prudence of the consistories concerned. They judge that this is not to be done at all, unless in the gravest and most urgent cases, so that one would not expose the whole church to a great peril for the sake of an individual person, unless the minister could comfort the sick without danger and the sick from a distance could hear the pastor comfort from afar, without risk of being infected. This is why we advise the minister who sees the approaching danger, in the ordinary course of preaching, to exhort his congregation to patience and to comfort them, and this by a text of Holy Scripture that would be appropriate and suitable to such an end."[33] From this, three points are gathered. The opinion of those churches is: (1) the disease is contagious; (2) each person must prudently take heed to themselves, and they must not foolishly frequent infected places; (3) when there are few pastors that are common for an entire church, things must be arranged in such a way as to provide for the comfort of the sick, so that the greatest part of the church is not harmed, as long as the pastor is not rendered useless due to the convenience of a few. Nevertheless, in all these points, the rule of Christian charity and prudence must be applied.

31. Zanchi, *In D. Pauli Apostoli Epistolas ad Philippenses, Colossenses, Thessalonicenses... Commentarii*, 2nd ed. (Neustadt: Wilhelm Harnisch, 1601), 223. See page 234 in this volume.
32. Zacharias Ursinus, *Zachariae Vrsini, Vratislaviensis Scholasticarum in materiis theologicis exercitationum*, 2 vols. (Neustadt: Matthaeus Harnisch, 1589–90), 2:514–516.
33. Cf. Jean Aymon et al. (eds.), *Actes Ecclesiastiques et civils de tous les Synodes Nationaux des Eglises Reformées de France*, 2 vols. (Charles Delo, 1710), 1:161.

I do not see that the papist theologians that wrote on cases of conscience think differently, which is also evident from their practice where their theology especially thrives, such as in Italy, Spain, and several other places. For they take especial heed that those who have even just the slightest suspicion of infection do not visit others and are not received at all in infected cities. For which reason the questions of the Summists, on the oath of those who come from contagious locales, concern whether they could deny it when their oath was given, if they knew that they could not create any danger for those receiving them, and whether they could lie with an equivocation. In fact, all respond that "they can so swear, if those coming from a place of plague rightly believe that neither themselves nor any of their property was infected with the plague. Otherwise, by no means is it permissible to swear when there is a danger of contagion."[34] The custom, even if it ought especially to be disapproved of, still shows among them that flight from the contagion is not so much recommended as commanded by their laws. Indeed, even the Canon Law decrees "if it should happen that a pest should befall a place of study, then the scholars (*scholastici*) and professors can withdraw to a certain nearby city or town, and then resume the privileges which were granted for a school (*studium generale*) in the place chosen," as Pierre Grégoire has it in his *On the Republic*, bk. 18 ch. 6, no. 10.[35] I hear that Gabriel Biel and Ludovicus Baer wrote a treatise on flight from the plague, with Molanus indicating such in his *Bibliotheca materiarum*, but I have not seen them, nor does a manifest matter require multiple witnesses.[36]

---

34. Latin, *Sic Toletus lib. 4. Summae cap. 21, Lessius de justitia et jure, cap. 42. Dub. 9, n. 47, Sanchez Moral. Tom. 2. Lib. 3. Cap. 6. Num. 35* : Francisco de Toledo, S.J. (Toletus, 1515–1582), "An liceat iurare et quomodo" in *Summa casuum conscientiae, sive instrucio sacerdotum in libros VIII distinctos* (Cologne: Rhenana Societas Jesu, 1610), bk. 4 ch. 10 §6, p522; Leonardus Lessius, S.J., "Dubitatio IX: Utrum si alio sensum quam alter intelligit iures, obligeris, et quale peccatum hoc sit" in *De Justitia et jure* (Paris: Rolinus Theodoricus, 1610) cap. 42 dub. 9 num. 47, pp621–22; Thomas Sanchez, *Opus Morale in Praecepta Decalogi*, 2 vols. (Antwerp: Martinus Nutius et Fratres, 1644–1622), 1.3.6 no. 35, 1:24. All of these Jesuit cases of conscience explore the limits of when it is sinful to knowingly lie and break an oath, if the oath taker in good conscience is not seeking to subvert the intention of why the oath is given. Specifically, if a city seeks to bar entry to anyone who has come from a locale infected with plague, is it permissible to swear an oath contrary to the truth but not the intent of the oath, if the oathtaker is not (yet) infected with the plague, and thus gain entry to a city? These Jesuits said yes.

35. Pierre Grégoire of Toulouse (c. 1540–1597, jurist), *De Republica libri sex et viginti* (Frankfurt : Nicholas Hoffman, 1610), 730.

36. This volume is an index of books arranged in a topical catalogue of Roman Catholic exegetes, doctors, and scholastics: Jan Vermeulen (Molanus), *Bibliotheca Materiarum* (Cologne: Joannes Kinchius, 1618), 124; Gabriel Biel, *Contra pestilentiam, sermo medicinalis, quaestio de fuga pestis* (Hagenau: Heinrich Gran, 1510).

Yet the opinion of Ludwig Baer (1479–1554), if anyone would care to know, may be found in the nineteenth digression of three books of digressions in the *Commentary on 1 Timothy* by Claude d'Espence (1511–1571), a doctor at the Sorbonne, in which d'Espence summarizes that little work from Musculus and adds other things as well as a worthy consideration of church history.[37] The summary is this: in time of plague or in another dangerous time, due to the danger that must be shunned, those who are free can flee. Those who are entrusted with public office must not, nor can they in good conscience. Nevertheless, not only are they free to use remedies and preventative measures, but they are also all obligated to do so. The ones who remain should not condemn those who depart as weaker ones. The one who flees should not argue that others are like tempters of God, but they should leave it to the judgment of God, so that each is led by the Spirit. Whatever it may be, let one take heed to the sick and those in the throes of the disease, so that they would not lack any necessary assistance. Let each person provide for their own households, or for others established under their care. One may see the rest in d'Espence in the place cited and weigh it accordingly.

This is especially evident when the transfer of the Council of Trent to Bononia was granted under this pretext by the Roman pontiff, "because prelates wanting to depart from fear of disease could not be justly detained." Thus, "for the security of the Council it is beneficial and suitable to move it to the city of Bononia for a time, as it is a better equipped place." These are the words of that decree, session 8, on the eleventh day of March, 1547.[38] Indeed, this was in reference to a plague; one they were either safeguarding against or seriously acknowledging was prowling about there.

Therefore, regarding this business, from the opinion of these men whose judgments I have referenced, I think that there is just cause why I will not depart, which seems to me to keep faith with God and conjoins charity with prudence. I do not doubt that this pestilence is being inflicted by God for just reasons, which is also threatened upon the stubborn (Lev.

---

37. Bk. 3, ch. 19: "On flight in time and danger of plague" (*de fuga in tempore ac periculo pestis*), Claude d'Espence (Claudius Espencaeus), *Opera Omnia quae superstes* (Paris: 1619), 253–55. For "Whether in time of plague … it is licit to flee or not? And if when … is it not?" see Ludwig Baer (also Bär, Ber, Ludovicus Berus), *Ludovicus Berus . . . ad Quaestionem ei propositam, utrum uidelicet tempore pestis, uel ex alia causa, ad uitandam mortem, seu mortis periculum, fugere interdum liceat, nec ne? Et si quando liceat, an tunc praestet, non fugere?* (Basel: Joanes Oporinus, 1551).

38. *The canons and decrees of the sacred and oecumenical Council of Trent*, ed. and trans. J. Waterworth (London: Doman, 1848), 67–8, commentary on Session 8, pp. cxvi–cxx.

26:25, Deut. 28:21, Num. 14:11–12, Jer. 24:10, Ezk. 6:12). I know that "plague has gone before God, and pestilence preceded his feet, coming as at noon and from the holy mountain to Paran" (Hab. 3:3–5). Those nations were not ignorant of the fact that they had been stricken with the most savage pestilences by a god who had been angered; for which reason it also happened that they strove to placate their gods in various ways. So the Romans, when the plague was rampant, established theatrical games for this purpose, which Orosius mentions in bk. 3, ch. 4, *Against the Pagans*.[39] And elsewhere the books of the Sibyls were read thoroughly so that they might inquire what ought to be done; likewise in book 4, ch. 5.[40] It is fairly evident to us what must be done, if only we had the heart to undertake it. The pages of the Sibyls do not teach us, but the books of the prophets do, with God himself contesting that there is only one remedy: true repentance. "If," he says in 1 Kings 8 and 2 Chronicles 6, "I shall have inflicted plague on my people, and, humbling themselves, my people upon whom my name is placed will have prayed and sought my face, turning back from their evil ways; in turn, I, hearing from heaven, will pardon their sin and heal their land." One must especially lean upon this exercise, without which these accomplish nothing: flight, precautions, purging of buildings, treatment with sulfur smoke or powder, or with kindled fires, or any other remedy derived from natural causes. They are in vain when first and foremost God has not been placated, when they think they can enter into a covenant with death. "We have cut" they say, "a covenant with death and we have enacted a precaution with the grave. The overwhelming scourge will pass by, but it will not come near us, because we have arranged our lie and we have hidden ourselves with lies" (Isa. 28:15). But these things are useless; God will flush them out of their hiding place. "He will inflict his plague upon their cities, and their blood will be in their streets" (Ezek. 28:23).

No less must those be despised who abuse the name of confidence in God and contrive to show their contempt of death, who are not moved by so many funerals; in the middle of which, they indulge in the character of their school, the kind who in "that time, the Lord God of hosts calls them to weeping and mourning, to baldness and the wearing of sackcloth, and they turn themselves to joy and gladness, killing oxen and slaughtering sheep, eating meat and drinking wine. 'Let us eat and drink, for tomorrow

---

39. Paulus Orosius, *Adversus paganos historiarum libri septem* (Mainz: Petrus Cholinus, 1615), 138–9.
40. Orosius, *Adversus paganos*, 228–30.

we die'" (Isa. 22:12–13). I certainly shudder at this senselessness.[41] It is even said in certain places, when the plague was ravaging even more, that there was heard nearly every single day those who clamor for more wine, drinking, and dancing in the homes of recent widows, in the alleys and avenues of the cities. These came frequently from a funeral, not only for simple gatherings for a drink and repast, but also for wedding banquets of those assembling, men and women whose spouses recently had been placed in funeral urns. What barbarity! What stupidity! This is scarcely even done by brute beasts! This reminds me of Augustine in book 1 on *The Morals of the Catholic Church*, chapter 34: "I have known many who most luxuriantly drink over the dead; and over those buried, they bury themselves in feasts made for corpses and call their gluttony and drunkenness 'religion.'"[42] It certainly always displeased me, and many others, this custom of drinking together after a funeral concluded, whose origin cannot derive from anywhere else than the funeral feasts of pagans. But if it must be indulged in sometimes, would it not be best at a time when few are dying and those but coming to their natural fate? Why must either the same thing or even a quite licentious thing be done when we are called to weeping, mourning, and ashes? Why therefore the amazement if against such things the Lord of hosts would have revealed himself? Let me not live restless, "if that iniquity of yours will be expiated until you should die."[43] Thus, when among the Corinthians, they condemned the church of God and scorned it—while one was starving another was drunk, and they profaned the table of the Lord. "Therefore among them there were many sick and weak, and many fell asleep, because they did not judge themselves so that they would not be punished by the Lord" (1 Cor. 11:30–31). If we should not tremble at these judgments of God, then what at the last should we hope for ourselves, except that God will pronounce the same thing that he did about the Israelites in Isaiah 1:5? "Why would you be utterly struck down? Will you increase your apostasy?... The whole head is infected with the same sickness, and the whole body is limp." Because these people are given to

---

41. Gk. ἀναισθησίαν
42. Augustine, *On the Morals of the Catholic Church*, bk. 1, ch. 34, sec. 75 in *NPNF1* 4:62.
43. In this brief section, Rivet is adapting Isaiah's prophecy against Jerusalem and applying it to the situation of his own day: "In that day the Lord GOD of hosts called for weeping and mourning, for baldness and wearing sackcloth; and behold, joy and gladness, killing oxen and slaughtering sheep, eating flesh and drinking wine. 'Let us eat and drink, for tomorrow we die.' The LORD of hosts has revealed himself in my ears: 'Surely this iniquity will not be atoned for you until you die,' says the Lord GOD of hosts" (Isa. 22:12–14, ESV).

drinking parties and orgies, cupidity and greed have joined themselves; they eye the property of the dead and scurry about, either in order to plunder it or to somehow claim some title to it, so that in their open disregard for any danger they hardly even consider the burial of the infected corpses. And yet not a few of such people are loudest among those who would take prudent caution; indeed, with their "if it pleases God" they would even preach their own faith and charity! Therefore, do you think these are signs of faith in God, to revel while he strikes with affliction? Should you not rather be those who tremble at God's judgments and beg his help?

Even as our faith rests upon God—while we pray with supplications and vows to avert evils that his hand has inflicted and beg his mercy that the assault of the destroying angel is either hindered or thoroughly checked—meanwhile all of the secondary causes and aids provided by God that can be lawfully used must not be neglected. Now certainly it is evident to everyone that even pestilence has its own natural causes, as often in its origin as in its steady progress. What hindrance is there—indeed, what opposition is there—to our endeavor to, as much as we can, retard the plague's force with God's blessing? Who does not know that sometimes plague arises from filthy homes and clogged sewers? Sometimes the cause is in the sun—if its heat burns with excessive ardor then it draws diseased vapors from the earth whereby bodies are distressed, and due to the unaccustomed change of air they become faint, consumed with pestilential diseases. Certainly Diodorus Siculus, in his *The Library of History* (bk. 12), teaches that [the cause is] from stagnant water heated by the warmth of the sun, and breathing air thick with foul odor with which the air is infected. The by-products are also exceedingly humidified and virulent as an unboiled fluid, which is especially harmful—infecting grazing [animals] and the summer air, if it is not cooled during the Etesian winds (the time of the north-westerly trade winds).[44] Marsilio Ficino adds in his *Antidote of Epidemics,* chapter 2, "When it is more universally present, the vapor of the plague in the air is created from certain malign constellations, especially when Mars is with Saturn in the conjunction with signs visible to humans, from the eclipse of celestial lights."[45] But this also characterizes what we have said in particular plagues, that the cause is in the winds and malign

---

44. Diodorus Siculus, *Library of History,* bk. 12, ch. 58 in *LCL* 384:44–47
45. Marsilio Ficini, *Epidemiarum Antidotus* in *De vita libri tres* (Paris : Eliaias le Preux, 1616), 338 ; idem, *Marsilio Ficino, Three Books on Life: A Critical Edition and Translation,* C. V. Kaske ed. and trans. (Arizona Center for Medieval and Renaissance Studies, 2019).

vapors of bogs and sewers, and equally from the motions of the earth. But it is always regnant in thick, marshy, foggy, and fetid air. Not a few of which causes concur in these regions [of the Netherlands], and especially in those places and towns in which the plague commonly ravages.

So what is to be done now? If the magistrate who has care of the commonwealth and its subjects should command that the sewers are purged so that stagnant waters flow and are renovated, that exceedingly humid air is tempered with frequent fires, and that infected buildings are not inhabited by new residents until fumigated after a thorough washing, will not more healthful air return? Ought the magistrate then be charged with impiety, as if he were resisting the extended hand of God and desired to fight against God?[46] But, in fact, would he not be rebelling against God if—when the safety of the people committed to him has been delayed until those things which are first and foremost above all the priorities to God[47] were procured—he did not move every stone and try all legitimate pathways by which the force of the disease may be in some way dispatched? And so we have contended that it pertains to the magistrate's duty not only to establish and command those things that have been spoken about, but also to confine those who, devoid of all charity towards their neighbor, intermingle themselves with others with impunity immediately after they have left infected places without any indicating sign whereby either the buildings or persons that have not yet been sanitized could be distinguished, and then they sit among the healthy in churches and other public places, and those who in open shops set forth their wares for sale on that very day, or perhaps only a short while after, cadavers have been removed from their shops. Certainly in these places there is such great carelessness that no one ought to be amazed that the plague *does* spread. Instead we ought to wonder how it could happen that it would ever stop.

A DIGRESSION ON BURIALS IN CHURCHES

At this point, however, permit me to digress a little (yet not far) off topic, and I will tell you what I think about the corpses of the dead that are buried and interred, even in a time of contagion, not only in the cities, but in fact inside the very churches themselves, where we meet for the worship of

---

46. Gk. θεομαχεῖν
47. Gk. πρὸς τὸν θεὸν

God. Of that practice in general, I publicly published my opinion several years ago.[48] But then I never would have thought I would see an example of it in our time. Not even papists inter corpses infected with the plague in their church, which I confess, not without horror, that I have seen done in these regions. Even while a holy sermon is being held the crypts are opened before the eyes of all and, with the caskets of the recently dead laid by and others looking on, [the new one] is cast into the earth. In fact, this custom seemed to me not too far from the customs of those who infect public fountains, because these people can hardly find a more effective way than if they would immerse such corpses in the water. Still, I mean no offense and no ill intent at all,[49] because I know what they are trying to do with these customs; namely, they are trying to show some kind of charity and display of respect towards the dead. But surely honor could be shown to the dead in a different way than one that is harmful and dangerous to the members of the church who are still living and breathing.

I have read not a few who wrote as firsthand witnesses[50] about the customs and rituals of different pagans and nations regarding the burial of the dead. I have also heard of others who had several homes throughout various places of the habitable world. I want to call them as witnesses whether have they ever seen or heard—either in the whole Orient, or that part of Europe which the sultan of the Turks occupies, or in the diverse kingdoms and territories of Asia, or in Africa, or even among those whom we consider to be barbarians—places designed for worship filled with the bodies of the dead? Or whether that is also present in the practice of Christians that have been scattered among the nations? When I recently addressed this burial custom in multiple points, I remember I was told how polished and clean they kept those places, and how far removed their custom is from this custom of burying the bodies of the dead in their cities; that such a practice was not even granted to their emperors themselves.

I do not think it is necessary to demonstrate this point with many [examples]. Among the heathen at one point burial was not even permitted within the walls of their cities. Among the people of God, the matter is beyond controversy: the burial of the dead happened outside the cites, and of those whose burial is mentioned in the Holy Scriptures all the dead were

---

48. Cf. Rivet, on Gen, 47, disp. 171, in *Opera Omnia*, 3 vols (Rotterdam: Arnoldus Leers, 1651–1660), 1:654–656.
49. *Absit invidia verbo . . . pessimo animo.* Cf. Livy, *The History of Rome*, 9.19.15
50. Gk. αὐτόπται

carried out of the cities (Gen. 25:9, Mark 5:2, 14, Luke 7:12, John 2:3, 31)—with perhaps only the kings excepted, who were buried in the city of David but in a place chosen outside of the society of the living, frequently in crypts and caves found in gardens. I will not insist on this, but according to their law, the Athenians once buried their dead outside the religious limits of their city.[51] They called the gates of their city ἠριαῖαι,[52] because the dead were brought there for burial because the tombs had been constructed at the gates of the city, on the borders of fields, or at roads. In the *Law of the Twelve Tables*, there was a warning, "You shall not bury or cremate a dead person in the city."[53] Emperor Hadrian prohibited the interment of the dead not only at Rome, but even in any city of the empire with the added reason, "so that the holy law of the free towns should not be polluted" (*De religiosis et sumtibus funerum*, bk. 47, tit. 12),[54] or, as the jurist Paulus states, "Let not holy sites of a city be polluted" (Paulus, *Opinions*, Bk. 1, title 21, §2).[55] For the law of the Roman priests did not permit "a public place to be obligated by the private religion of burials," as Cicero thought.[56] We have the testimony of Varro in book 5 in the Latin language: "There were monuments on tombs along the road, which admonished passersby both what these had done and that they [too] were mortals."[57] There are those who expressly treat of the rite, custom, and laws of the ancient funeral, whose books it is not fitting or needed to describe here. We must only direct our attention to this case, which is borne out by the law of the Romans: that

---

51. *Poemeria*: from *post moerium*, "beyond the wall." In ancient Rome, the *poemeria* were not coextensive with the city walls, but indicated an uninhabited, consecrated space on both sides of the city wall. Cf. Livy, *Ab Urbe Condita*, 1.44; idem, *History of Rome 1* in *LCL* 114:154–55.

52. Derived from ἠρίον, a burial mound with a crypt built into it.

53. Rivet's citation: *Ne quis hominem in urbe sepeliret, neve ureret*. cf. C. G. Brun et al, *Fontes juris romani antiqui*, 2 vols., 6th ed. (Freiburg: 1893), 1:35. As cited in Cicero, *De leg*. 2.23.58: *hominem mortuum in urbe ne sepelito neve urito*. Cicero supposes that the law is due to the fire hazard of the funeral pyres, not a point of religious observance. For mention of this point in a source Rivet utilized, see Giglio Gregorio Giraldi, *De Sepultura ac vario sepeliendi ritu libellus* (Basil: Michael Ising, 1589), 12.

54. Cf. *Codex Justinianus*, lib. 3, tit. 44, "De religiosis et sumtibus funerum," §12: Diocletianus et Maximianus. "Mortuorum reliquias, ne sanctum municipiorum jus polluatur, intra civitatem condi, jampridem vetitum est." For the debate on the priority of Roman imperial law prohibiting burials in cities or a local municipal law (the law of a free city) allowing burials in cities, see *Digesta* lib. 47, tit. 12, "De sepulcro violato, §3.

55. S. P. Scott (ed.), *The Civil Law, including the Twelve Tables, the Institutes of Gaius, the Rules of Ulpian, the Opinions of Paulus, the Enactments of Justinian, and the Constitutions of Leo*, 3 vols. (New York: AMS Press, 1973), 1:267.

56. Cicero, *De Legibus*, 2.23 in *LCL* 213:444–5.

57. *Monumenta in sepulchris secundum viam fuisse, quae praetereuntes admonerent, et se fecisse, et illos esse mortales.*

[sickness] has perpetual force to pollute cities by the bodies of the dead, certainly not with moral or ceremonial pollution as among the Jews, but certainly with a physical one that consists in this, that not only is the air surrounding open monuments and the vapors evaporating from the earth infected, but also the water of wells, which are used throughout these lands and which cannot but be endued with some quality of buried stench. Recently, I was reading in Lylio Gregorio Giraldi that there certainly was a most ancient custom of houses built within the city for the bodies of the dead, and also that the religion of the Lares and Penates had endured, who were worshiped by the heathen for the sake of this house.[58] But soon the custom arose, which was ancient and upheld by all—as Giraldi mentions in his book *On a different rite of burial*—so that foul and repulsive things [were excluded], which he proves with the same laws adduced which we recently mentioned.[59] Also he adds subsequent points that are especially relevant to our topic: "For these reasons corpses were buried outside the cities; I see especially among others to be mentioned that, of course, the city would be free from the putrid odor of corpses; not to mention that they would infect the air with pestilence, and so that those travelers passing by there would be inspired to praises and would be admonished to meet death with outstanding and memorable deeds. Nor, if it should so happen, approaching enemies would be out in the open among those graves, and accordingly they would also be repelled from the walls of the city with quicker awareness."[60]

Further on, he also inveighs at length against customs today: "Now our Christians (for the holy customs of our ancestors have utterly perished!) not only build crypts and shrines for the bodies of the dead inside the city, but even, if it please God, in the temples themselves, in which not only the ashes and remains of the wealthy are preserved and the religion of our ancestors is honored, but indeed, even the foulest corpses of the nefarious, of the most wicked and impious of persons, which I most bitterly grieve is done contrary to the laws and customs of the ancients."[61] Other than this point, this author is devoted to the holy rites of papists, among whom this custom grew from superstition and greed. Now what he says about the ancients must not be understood only as referring to the Roman heathen,

---

58. Giraldi, *De Sepultura*, 259.
59. Giraldi, *De Sepultura*, 3. Rivet only summarized the point Giraldi made from Seneca.
60. Giraldi, *De Sepultura*, 260.
61. Giraldi, *De Sepultura*, 260.

but also to Christians, among whom this custom was not in use in the early and purer ages, nor in subsequent ones. We have the witness of the *Constitutions* of the Christian Emperors wherein this was prohibited, as in ordinance 159 (*capitularium* CLIX) of Charlemagne and Louis, "So that no one henceforth should bury the dead in a church." And in ordinance 47 (*capitularium XLVII*), "so that regarding burying the dead in basilicas, that custom is preserved which was established from the ancient fathers."[62] And certainly Jean Etienne Durante (1534–1589), the president of the parliament of Toulouse, who wrote *The rites of the Catholic Church* (that is, what he calls *catholic*), in book 1, chapter 23, confesses that "this was the religion of the ancient fathers, that the bodies of the dead were not to be buried inside the Church."[63]

Regarding the canon extant up until now from Gratian's *Decretum* (pars IIa, causa 13, qu. 2, c.), set forth in the canon and written at the Council of Vaison, I looked for it in vain in the edition managed by Jacques Sirmond, *Ancient Councils of Gaul*.[64] But the one which is cited by Gratian is the same words contained in the Council of Nantes, which is thought to have been held around the year of Christ 900, although Sirmond estimates that it is more ancient. The words of the canon are: "It must be prohibited according to the customs of the ancients that in the church by no means are any to be buried, but in the atrium, or portico, or outside the church. But within the church, near the altar where the body of the Lord is prepared, by no means should anyone have license to bury."[65] The seventeenth canon of the Synod of Trebur (895) prohibits any laity from being buried in the church and commands that "By no means are they to project [above ground], but with paving stone placed above and no apparent trace of a tomb, the reverence for the Church is to be preserved. But where this is difficult to do on account of the multitude of bodies, the place for a cemetery and common

---

62. Reginonis abbatis ... Libri duo de ecclesiasticis disciplinis (Vienna: Joannes Thomas de Trattnern, 1765), 77.

63. See ch. 23 "De coemeteriis" §5 "Mortuorum corpora, an in Ecclesiis sint sepulturae mandanda" (on cemeteries, §5 "whether it is commanded that the bodies of the dead ought to be buried in churches") in Jean-Etienne Durante (*Joannes Stephanus Durantus*), *De ritibus ecclesiae catholicae libri tres* (Paris: Denis Moreau, 1644), 1:218.

64. In scholarship of canon law, this particular council is frequently cited as the Council of Vaison (either *Concilium Varenses*, *Concilium Vasenses*), or the Council of Nantes (*Concilium Nannetense*). Cf. Gratian, *Decretum*, Pars IIa, c. 13, qu. 2, cap. 15, in *Corpus iuris canonici* (Graz: Akademische Druck-u. Verlagsanstalt, 1959) 1:726; "Concilium Nannetense (658)" in Jacques Sirmond, *Concilia antiqua Galliae tres in tomos* (Paris: Sebastian Cramoisy, 1629), 1:495.

65. Gratian in *Corpus Iuris Canonici*, 1:705.

burial ground should be considered, when the altar has been moved away and established where it is suitable that a sacrifice to God may be religiously offered."[66] From this it is clear that they judged at that time that it did not bring honor to the Church to bury the dead in it, and that sacraments are not to be religiously administered in places filled with bodies. But it is the express decision of the Council of Braga, (*Concilium Braccarensis*), which is Braga in Spain,[67] whose canon is found in the *Decretum* of Burchard of Worms, bk. 3, ch. 157: "It is fitting that the bodies of the departed in no way are to be buried in the basilica." And they add that "until now the cities of Gallia retain this most constant privilege that in no way within the limits of the walls of the cities is the body of a dead person to be buried."[68] There is Canon 36 of the first Council of Braga under King Ramirez, in which that privilege is not restricted to the cities of Gallia but applied in general, although Burchard added the name Gallia without mentioning the addition. According to Baronius, this council was held in 563 AD.[69]

Durantius acknowledges it as "this godly custom of the ancients" and that it was "renewed and restored by Charlemagne." It had only been granted to emperors at that time that they might be buried within the vestibules of the churches or in the portico. It was not granted to any other people. "But today," says Durantius, "with this custom received outside the laws and customs of the ancients, Christians who are neither emperors nor priests, to whom that privilege was permitted afterwards, and even the laity generally are buried within a church, as well as many others."[70]

But it is apparent that this custom was invalidated through bad morals, ambition, superstition, and avarice. For when people saw that it was a privilege attributed to the great men that they might be buried in the vestibules of the churches, next, little by little, they were buried in the basilicas themselves, which had even been granted to bishops and other ecclesiastics. Those who had some authority also sought that privilege, so that it was granted to churches in which they aspired to be buried that they left something in a will, from which it happened afterwards that the gates were opened to all when money was offered. Although in the beginning

---

66. Giovanni Dominico Mansi, *Sacrorum Conciliorum Nova et Amplissima Collectio*, 53 vols. (Florence, Venice, 1758–1798), 18:141–2.
67. Braga has been part of the Kingdom of Portugal since 1179.
68. Ch. 4, Concilium Braccarensis is included in Burchard of Worms, *Decretorum Libri XX*, in Migne, *PL* 140:705. There were at least 9 councils in Braga from the sixth century onward.
69. Cesare Baronio, *Annales Ecclesiastici* (Antwerp: Plantin, 1588–1607), 7:519.
70. Jean Étienne Durantius, *De ritibus Ecclesiae Catholicae libri tres* (Lyon, 1606), 144, 1.23.7.

very many people complained to the councils and prohibited the sale of the burial rite, as was mentioned previously in the Synod of Trebur.[71] And in the Council of Nantes, "it is forbidden," they say, "for all Christians to sell land to the dead and to deny the burial owed."[72] Regarding which, Jerome previously said in a question on Genesis 32, "Let those who sell tombs, and are not compelled to, know that they should accept the price but also, should they extort it from the unwilling, their name is tarnished and some measure of their merit dies."[73] And Gregory I, book 7, Epist. 15 rebuked Januarius, the bishop of Sardinia, because he demanded 100 *solidi* from that renowned woman Nereida who wanted burial for her daughter. Moreover, he admonishes them "not to presume to be tempted anew in others," and he prohibited them "that nothing could be asked for or demanded."[74] But Gregory himself, who wanted to address the mode of avarice, imprudently relaxed the reins when in the *Dialogues*, bk. 4, ch. 50 he taught, "It is profitable for the dead, whom mortal sins do not weigh down, if they should be buried in the church, because their relatives come several times a day to the sacred places of their own, look at their graves, remember them, and pour out prayers for them to the Lord."[75] Now once this had been admitted and superstition grew in those days, there was no one who would not solicit for and who did not want this privilege; for which reason there arose fowling for wills, endowments, and bids in churches, according to one's rank and proximity to the greater or lesser altars. And once the gates were opened, greed[76] flooded in, and totally occupied the place so that again the house of God had become a den of thieves, where there was nothing that was not for sale, and it was not permitted for anyone to die and be buried for free.

Therefore, what is to be done when the superstitious themselves acknowledge that it is contrary to the customs of the ancients and to the honor of God and religious worship for churches to be opened to cadavers

---

71. See ch. 15 "de sepultura mortuorum", ch. 16 "ut sepulturam morientium nemo vendat", and ch. 17 "ut nullus laicus in Ecclesia sepeliatur" in *Acta et Decreta Concilii Triburiensis* (Schöffer, 1525); also Giovanni Dominico Mansi, *Sacrorum Conciliorum Nova et Amplissima Collectio*, 53 vols. (Florence, Venice, 1758–1798), 18:140–2.

72. See ch. 6, "Concilium Namnetenses" in Mansi, 18:168.

73. See Gen. 32:16 in Jerome, *Liber Hebraicarum Questionum in Genesim* in PL 23:973; idem, *Saint Jerome's Hebrew Questions on Genesis* trans. C. T. R. Hayward (Oxford: Clarendon Press, 1995), 57.

74. In modern English editions, this is bk. 9, ep. 3, *Registrum Epistolarum Gregorii* in NPNF2 13:1–2.

75. Gregory I, *Dialogorum libri quatuor* in PL 77:411–12; idem, *The Dialogues of Saint Gregory, surnamed the Great*, ed. E. G. Gardner (London: Philip Lee Warner, 1911), 245–6.

76. Gk. αἰσχροκερδία

and transformed into tombs for the dead; and for those who otherwise profess that they are against all the superstitions and abuses of the papists to retain this terrible custom, even one so well known to be so to those who have degenerated into it? And how dare they conjoin this public injury with common rights, available to all who can buy it, so that it is no longer even a privilege for the poor? Or does superstition still have place in the souls of certain people who think the sanctity of a place benefits the souls of those bodily husks laid there? It perhaps could be conceded by the papists, who even still are generally buried there. But even when they allege a pontifical right to pollute churches, which are filled with as many living heretics as dead ones, I cannot persuade myself that papists dwelling with us, with the religion of the place adduced, would expect such a burial. Therefore, what reasons move us to procure the same for ourselves? "Ambition drove and greed vexed."[77] Do I speak what is true? I do not see how this conclusion could be avoided if it is reduced to these two cases. The wealthy—or those who want to be such—do not want to have their grave in common with the poor. They think it results in more honor if they are laid to rest within the crypts of the church than if they await the resurrection in a common cemetery under the open sky. Thus my tears. I know I have glossed over the fact that part of that money goes to the poor and to other uses for the church. But both could be provided for by means other than that which is neither honest nor joined without danger. "My house will be called a house of prayer," says the Lord (Jer. 7:11, Mark 2:17). Therefore, it must not be constructed for the purpose of becoming a common grave. *The dead do not praise God, nor do any who descend to the place of silence!* (Ps. 115:18) Churches are not silent places! But these must resound in them: the Word of God, the songs of believers, and the sound of prayers. Why then are the dead within the churches, when they cannot hear the Word of God or pour out prayers, and when prayers on their behalf are not to be offered to God? And even if they could (hypothetically speaking), would the presence of the bones and remains be necessary for that?

Someone may perhaps say that the living desire that the dead may rest in the churches so that they may continue to witness to their faith, as well as

---

77. *Impulit ambitio, vexit avaritia*: This Latin phrase is first found in Theodore Beza's poem in a "broadside" (a publication spanning one full folio sheet) congratulating Queen Elizabeth upon the defeat of the Spanish Armada in 1588. The poem appeared on one broad sheet in Latin, with translations into English, Dutch, Spanish, Hebrew, Greek, Italian, and French. idem, *Ad Serenissimam Elizabetham Angliae Reginam Theodor. Beza* (London, 1588). The full Latin couplet is: "*Tanti huius rogitas, quae motus causa? Superbos Impulit Ambitio, vexit Avaritia.*"

their hope of a future resurrection, even after death, and to commemorate that they lived in that profession which was exercised in those places. But that cannot be asserted since they even open the door to those who would abhor our holy places. Next, if one would do it for that reason, why would it be granted for only certain persons, with others excluded who did not pay? Perhaps they would maintain that they have the tombs of their ancestors there. But this cannot be asserted either because many are buried outside of there, and also many of their ancestors rest elsewhere. Later, when the churches will belong to the common law, what reason can be given that there it is bought for one person or the possession of a tomb is claimed? Now what comes of the fact that very many ancients, moved by foolishness and superstition, still chose a tomb for themselves and for their own? It is precisely for this reason that much better customs must be established in the future, so that they ought to abstain from such burials lest some of the leaven of superstition would be suspected to be remaining among them.

Regarding the ambition I spoke about, the walls themselves confirm it. The instruments of idolatry have been cast out of the churches, the images that had been changed into idols have been carried off or scraped off, in order that the marks of our vanity might be substituted in their place. The result is that our church walls and columns are crowded with placards on every side by those with a desire to emulate them. Each one tries to surpass their neighbor, so that finally it results in the school for our humility and self-renunciation being changed into a monument for our pride. On these same walls, which are inscribed with the commandments of God and the profession of our faith, are affixed—if I should say it as delicately as possible—the profane pedigrees and crests of men. All these things bring with them such great expenses and burdens of unnecessary costs that many surviving families feel the inconveniences of that exorbitance dearly. I do not doubt that many godly pastors of the churches groan over these and similar things and wish they might be corrected; and they endure what they do not approve of, in imitation perhaps of Augustine in Epistle 119 to Januarius, ch. 19, who said that there were many things which he could not approve of, but due to the scandals that needed to be avoided with either very many saints or turbulent persons, he could not freely disapprove of them.[78] But

---

78. See instead Augustine, Ep.55, ch. 19 §35 in *PL* 33:221-2; idem, *Letters, Volume 1 (1–82)*, Fathers of the Church series, trans. W. Parsons (Washington D.C.: Catholic University of America, 1951, 2008), 290. There are two letters to Januarius, epistles 54 and 55 in modern numbering, that are sometimes entitled *Ad inquisitiones Januarii, Libri Duo*.

still, in the intervening time the matter continued so that there is a great amount of injury to the commonwealth and the church; they will judge in agreement with me that a remedy is necessary, which must be expected partly from the pastors and partly from a godly and prudent magistrate. By the pastors so that it would be established from the Word of God among the people, who then would not adhere to these customs as if they were necessary, and who then would be led away from all superstition and vanity. Then the people would know that it is especially in their interest that this inveterate custom would not creep in any longer. Because if this were to happen, once the pastors and people have come along to the same mind it will not be difficult by common pledges to move the average, godly magistrate to leave the churches free for living believers. And the earth would no longer be moved within [the churches], which is hardly sufficient to render so many bodies into dust anyway, and from which it even happens sometimes that bones still wet with blood and rotting gore are brought before our eyes. If these cemeteries should be in the neighborhood of the cities, they could be carefully attended so that, if perhaps it were not safe for citizens to go to them because of the military equipment of the enemies, they would have a place prepared in their own bounds.[79] Otherwise, they should choose spacious areas outside the cities for cemeteries, even if the magistrates would want them encompassed with walls and fosses. In them Christians of all ranks of society could be buried decently, especially during a time when pestilence is prowling about. For in this way there will be no risk, like there is in enclosed spaces, that the vapors would fill the whole place and infect those attending the funeral. There will be no weak fear to stumble upon, which nevertheless arises from this cause and can deter even a steadfast man. The timid do not come to the place of preaching, and that comment of Chrysostom applies here; in a sermon about faith and the law of nature, concerning those conducting a funeral outside the city, he stated that "Before one gains entrance to the whole city and the whole fort there are tombs, so that a combatant trying to enter the city—which has rule and flourishes in wealth and power as well as in other dignities—having seen first what has happened previously, sees what he is to consider afterwards. Before the gates there are tombs. In front of the fields there are tombs. Everywhere in front of one's eyes is the school of our

---

79. *Pomeria*: open ground bounded on either side of a city wall with stone borders in order to delimit range of fire from the walls.

humility."[80] Why, even in France, there is scarcely any city one may see that does not have its cemeteries outside the city.

In order that this would obtain in these provinces of the Netherlands, it must be wanted more than simply hoped for. Still, if it does not seem wise that the ancient custom, although introduced contrary to reason and good morals, should be thoroughly changed, at least then change should happen due to what necessity urges and what experience teaches—that it ought to have been established from the beginning that infected cadavers, without regard for peoples' preferences, should be carried out to a decent place outside the cities. Then there would be no need to seek out areas near the churches for where the multitude of heaped up bodies could be placed, but rather ground elsewhere. And certainly not to mention that there would then not be such horrendous sights, so abhorrent to all decency. This I place among those matters that pertain, at such a time as this, to the care of magistrates, who are debtors to the people that have submitted to them, so that the republic and the church would not endure any more damage. I also hope those who have neglected it thus far will be careful with respect to their own danger, and that they would take measure for these abuses, whose disordered source I do not doubt that I have uncovered.

From this digression, I now return to our custom and what I said at the beginning. Again I insist that there is nothing necessary in this disputation but the amputation of vices, with which I hope all agree, as with this: that the duties of charity must never be interrupted, not in any event. Only, each one must consider what more charity urges for the very many and diverse opportunities for charity that occur; and diligently each one must expend what their calling demands. And in doing so, let us steer clear of the two rocks against which Zanchi warns us: stupid boldness and exceedingly vicious fear. Otherwise, it would happen that, fearing nothing, we ourselves and others would likewise perish. Here also it would happen that, desiring to save our life, we would desert the work of Christ. Therefore, standing in the middle, let us trust in the Lord and be courageous, and nevertheless let us not neglect the means of preserving life and health. We will also moderate our concern for both in such a way that nothing will detract from what we owe to God and to our neighbor. In addition, since a meditation upon death is useful at any time, we will deem it especially necessary when so many funeral processions pass by outside our homes. "For,"

---

80. See Pseudo-Chrysostom, *De fide et lege naturae* in PG 48:1085.

as I will say in the words of Seneca, "death is nearby at our side, but since we never consider it unless it affects someone else, we daily have proofs of our own mortality."[81] Since we have such frequent and numerous deaths before our eyes, let us fix them upon our heart, and with all else set aside, let us meditate upon this, lest we dread the word "death" too much; but let us make it a very familiar thought to us, that if it should happen, we could even go towards it and through it to meet our Bridegroom, who, through death, abolished the power of death.

May God strengthen this mind in us, and in you as well, with all your family and friends; and may God keep you safe for the sake of the public good.

> Farewell,
> At The Hague, February 15, 1636.

---

81. Seneca the Younger, *Ep. 101* in *LCL* 77:160–61.

3

A Treatise on the Plague

Introduction

It is difficult to overstate the importance of Gisbertus Voetius for the history of the Reformed church in the Netherlands. It has been said of him that "Few men have in any age exercised greater influence over the church of their time and country."[1] For those unfamiliar with life and work of the Dutch reformer, Joel Beeke offers a helpful analogy: "Voetius was to the *Nadere Reformatie* (usually translated as the Dutch Second Reformation) what John Owen was to English Puritanism. Though largely unknown and ignored by English-speaking scholarship, Voetius is nearly as well known to students of Dutch Post-Reformation orthodoxy as Owen is to students of English Puritanism."[2] Voetius was a towering figure in his day, tireless in his labors to preserve and promote Reformed orthodoxy in the face of numerous errors and heresies afflicting the church, including Arminianism, Rationalism, Labadism, and Socinianism.

Gisbertus was born in 1589 at Heusden to devout parents deeply committed to the Reformation. From 1604–1611, he studied at Leiden where he witnessed the theological rift created by the controversial theology of Jakob Hermanszoon, who is known more commonly simply as Arminius. Strengthened in his own Calvinist convictions through the teachings of Franciscus Gomarus, Voetius was an outspoken critic of Arminianism, which no doubt contributed to his appointment to the Synod of Dort (1618–1619).

Voetius pastored first in Vlijmen (1611) and then in his hometown of Heusden (1617), and in 1634 was appointed professor of theology and

---

1. *Cyclopedia of Biblical, Theological, and Ecclesiastical Literature*, Vol. 10, ed. John M'Clintock and James Strong (New York: Harper and Brothers, 1891), 809.
2. "Gisbertus Voetius: Toward a Reformed Marriage of Knowledge and Piety," in *Protestant Scholasticism: Essays in Reassessment*, ed. Carl R. Trueman and R. S. Clark (Carlisle: Paternoster, 1999), 227.

Oriental languages at the newly formed Illustrious School of Utrecht (later Utrecht University) where he would remain for the rest of his life.

Voetius is a complex thinker, yet his program for teaching was as simple as it was unwavering. Beeke summarizes it well: "His ideals were clearly set forth in his inaugural address, *De pietate cum scientia conjugenda* (On Piety Joined with Knowledge). Piety and knowledge are not to be separated. They are to promote each other's welfare, for they are wedded together. The mind must assist the heart and life, and the heart and daily living ought to reinforce the mind."[3] This marriage of heart and mind, piety and knowledge, is clearly evident in Voetius's *A Treatise on the plague, or A spiritual antidote for the plague*. Here Voetius explores the issue of the plague theologically, first with respect to God as sovereign over the plague, and then with respect to man and his duties in the plague (both to God and neighbor). Voetius differentiates between efficient causes: A primary cause, that is God; secondary causes, like fevers, flies, and bad air; and meritorious causes, such as human sinfulness. So, while one might speak of the efficient causes of disease as natural, physical, and proximate, the meritorious causes are those that elicit God's wrath.

The spiritual antidote that Voetius recommends for the plague can be divided into private and public aspects. First, the private remedy is that signal measure of the grace of God in the heart of the believer that must be prepared in daily doses "with a renewed faith by believing it, by watching carefully with a firm hope, by desiring it with a kindled love, by demanding it with devoted prayers." Second, that spiritual remedy requires "fighting against the fear of death through Christian faith and fortitude." Indeed, "so that you may find a faith and heart fortified in Christ against death, exercise yourself in preparation for death and meditation upon the brevity and vanity of this life." Third, "there is the consideration of the fatherly divine providence on which, like a couch of heavenly security, we may recline our hearts." We can do so because there is no chance or fortune that befalls our health or life, since nothing happens that is not for our good. Fourth, there is the renewal and stirring up of our repentance through a careful scrutiny of our inmost parts, for the practice of repentance and the exercise of new obedience. "Only here we advise, on the occasion of a plague, to stir up all the public and private exercises of godliness, especially even for sympathy and charity towards our brethren and especially to a neighbor destitute of other help."

---

3. Ibid., 231.

The public remedy included the frequent celebration of fasts, the removal of scandal, the repression of sins—such as extravagance in banquets, clothing, buildings, funerals, and theater—and the pursuit of righteousness and justice where there had been violence and oppression. The spiritual antidote, according to Voetius, especially centered on the public preaching of the Word and the celebration of the sacraments. In these the hope for healing, not just physically and temporally, but spiritually and eternally, is made manifest in the heralding of the gospel of Jesus Christ and the sealing of that gospel on the hearts of believers who partake of the sacrament by faith.

In his *Treatise*, Voetius demonstrates an intellectual breadth and depth that is nothing short of breathtaking. His bibliographic work alone is impressive even by modern standards of research. His command of multiple languages and disciplines, likewise, outdistances all but our greatest polymaths. His ability to synthesize multiple strands of thought into a deeply coherent and logically compelling argument showcases the best of what the Reformed scholasticism of his day had to offer.

As Voetius closes his treatise on plague, his concluding line is both powerful and provocative: "Conquer the fear of death and you will conquer the fear of plague." At the end of the day, the fear of death is only conquered through faith in the one who conquered death itself. As Voetius puts it:

> The faith, apprehension, and taste of the goodness and grace of God in Christ, if we have in fact ever tasted how sweet the Lord is in forgiving our sins (Ps. 103-4), in imputing and gifting the merits of Christ (2 Cor. 5), in adopting us as his children, and that by sealing us with the seal of his Spirit (Rom. 8). Provided God is gracious to us with the special grace of the elect (Ps. 106), this grace is sufficient for us. In all these things we will be more than conquerors. There is nothing that will separate us from his love (Rom. 8).

Gisbertus Voetius, "Tractatus de Peste, seu pestis antidoto spirituali," in *Variorum Tractatus Theologici de Peste* (Leiden: Johannes Elsevirius, 1655), 139-249. Gisbertus Voetius, *Selectarum Disputationum*, 5 vols. (vols. 1-4, Utrecht: Johannes Waesberg, 1648-1667; vol. 5, Utrecht: Antonius

Smytegelt, 1669), 4:292–325. We have inserted the 1667 addenda throughout the text according to Voetius's notes in the 1669 *Selectarum Disputationum*, indicating these paragraphs to the reader.

A Treatise on the Plague, or a Spiritual Antidote for the Plague
Gisbertus Voetius
Translated by Todd M. Rester

The agreement and practice of all churches and preachers teaches that theologians must treat the plague theologically, wherever and whenever this evil happens to strike. To that end, treatments on this topic have been written by our Theodore Beza,[4] Ludwig Lavater,[5] Thomas Fabritius, Heinrich Möller—in a meditation on Psalm 91[6]—and Lucas Trelcat Jr.;[7] from among the papists by Jerome Praevidello,[8] Gianfrancesco Ripa,[9] and recently Filiberto Marchini in a large enough volume entitled *The Divine War*;[10] and I need not mention the letters of Calvin and Rivet, or Zanchi's commentary on Philippians 2, nor those points which the casuists and commentators everywhere note on the Decalogue and the Scripture passages of Psalm 91, Exodus 9, 1 Samuel 24, 1 Chronicles 21, and Ezekiel 5 and 14. Following

---

4. Theodore Beza (1509–1615), *De peste quaestiones duae explicatae, una sitne contagiosa, altera an et quatenus sit Christianis per secessionem vitanda* (Geneva: Eustache Vignon, 1579).

5. Ludwig Lavater (1527–1586), *Von der Pestilentz, zwo Predginen: die ein vom Ursprung der Pestilentz, wohar die sye, item warumb sy regiere unnd wie man sich darinnen halten sölle . . . beschriben durch Ludwigen Lavater, Dienern der kirchen zuo Zürych* (Zurich: Christoffel Forschower, 1564); idem, *De Pestilentia concio Lvdovici Lavateri, in qua ostenditur, vnde sit et quare immitatur: item, quo pacto se gerere debeant, qui illo morbo corripiuntur*, trans. Joannes Pontisella (Zurich: Froschen, 1586); idem, *Van de peste, een seer Christelijcke onderrichtinghe* (Deventer: Jan E. Cloppenburch, 1599).

6. Heinrich Möller (1530–1589), *Enarrationis Psalmorum Davidis . . . novissima editio* (Geneva: Pierre et Jacques Chouet, 1610), 905–14.

7. Lucas Trelcat Jr. (1573–1607), "Tableau, ou Discours Chrestien, sur la consideration de la briefvete de ceste vie" in various authors, *Remèdes contre le mal-reiglé mespris, l'oubliance, et la trop grande apprehension de la mort, cueillis au jardin de vie* (Geneva: Jacques Chouet, 1604), 1–87. Cf. idem, «Antidotum pestis, seu Tractatus Christanus de Causis et Remediis eiusdem» in *Opuscula theologica omnia* (Leiden: Johannes Orlers & Johannes Maire, 1614; Amsterdam: Henricus Laurentius, 1614), 503–[584]. Page numbers are lacking [581–584]; what is labeled p581 starts the *Oratio Funebris* for Johannes Kuchlinus.

8. Hieronymus Praevidellus, "De peste et eius privilegiis" in Gregory XIII (patron), *Tractatus universi iuris*, 22 vols. (Venice: Franciscus Zilettus, 1584–1586), 18:171v–87r.

9. Gianfrancesco Riva di San Nazzaro (d. 1535), *Tractatus de peste* (Leipzig: Jacob Apelius, 1598).

10. Filiberto Marchini (1586–1636), *Belli Divini, sive pestilentis temporis accurata et luculenta speculatio theologica, canonica, civilis, politica, historica, philosophica* (Florence: Sermartelliana, 1633).

in their footsteps, specifically because not a few studious persons urgently requested it, we have included [in this treatise] what we previously stated about this plague, and in the usual exposition of ordinary common topics (*loci communes*), where: (1) we will point out the causes of this evil and (2) its antidotes, (3) we will decide on the principal controversy of flight from the plague, and (4) we will respond to some problems and cases.

Chapter I: The Inflicting Cause

We have stated that the efficient cause is first an inflicting cause and then a meritorious cause. That efficient cause is either primary or secondary. According to Amos 3:6, God is the primary cause of all evils and sorrows and thus also its author. A majority of commentators enumerate three common and widespread (*epidemica*) scourges of God: famine, war, and plague (Lev. 26; Deut. 28; Jer. 14, 21, 24, 27, 29, 32, 34, 38; Ezek. 6). A fourth is added with wild beasts, namely in Ezekiel 5 and 14. Otherwise, you would not be incorrect to number seven general kinds of human calamities with the medical doctor Girolamo Cardano in *On the variety of things* (bk. 8, c. 45): earthquake, flood, gale, animals, plague, war, and famine.[11] Plague is attributed to God with its own particular rationale, as it is a *malum θεήλατον*, an evil sent by God, first in its origin and then in its occurrence and effect, and by other astounding consequences, about which see below. Certainly [this is true] in its origin because it is more immediately from God, and there is a lesser apparatus of means in nature, at least that could be grasped and diagnosed by us. Hence it is called "the hand of God" in Exodus 9:3. And that ministry of Moses and Aaron does not bear upon that plague, as the commentaries of Pereira, à Lapide, and Rivet note.[12] The pagans saw not a few diseases, especially the plague, as something subject to the divine. Hence Homer in Book 1 of *The Iliad* sings of the plague as inflicted by the arrows of the Greek archer Apollo.[13] Because it brings a present destruction upon many in its occurrence and effect and exercises divine vengeance

---

11. Girolamo Cardano, *De rerum varietate libri XVII*, 2nd ed. (Avignon: Matthieu Vincent, 1558), 447.
12. Benito Pereira, S. J. (Benedictus Pererius, 1536–1610), *Selectae Disputationes in Sacram Scripturam*, 3rd ed., 5 vols (Lyon: Horatius Cardon, 1607–1610), 1:270–73; Cornelius à Lapide (1567–1613), *Commentaria in Pentateuchum Mosis* (Antwerp: Jacobus Meursius, 1659), 403; André Rivet, *Commentarii in librum secundum Mosis* (Leiden: Franciscus Heberus, 1634), 215–16; idem, *Opera Theologica*, 1:857–58.
13. Homer, *Illiad* 1.9–10

against human beings—in Hebrew דֶּבֶר from the root דבר, which in the Piel means "he perished, he slew" (2 Chron. 22:10)—thus plague in Psalm 91:6 is joined with קטב, that is, a destruction or ruin; and it is called the destruction of plague in Hosea 13:14. In that respect it is both the hand of God and flying arrows (Ps. 91:5 with Deut. 32:24), and in Chaldean[14] מותא, "death" (Ezek. 5:17),[15] in Exodus 9:3, 15 מותנא (Ps. 106:30–31, 2 Sam. 24:21), and in Syriac מותנא, "deaths" (Matt. 24:7). And so in the Greek of Revelation 6:8 a fourth of the earth is slain "with sword" (ἐν ῥομφαίᾳ), "with famine" (καὶ ἐν λιμῶι), "and with death" (καὶ ἐν θανάτωι), that is, in a plague. The French call a prowling plague idiomatically *la mortalité*. Besides this, by the rabbis it is called אנדר לומוסיא, and a defective form דר לומוסיא (which is from the Greek, ἀνδρός λοιμός, a plague-infected person), as can be seen in Rashi on Genesis 6:13 and in *Bereshit Rabba* §32.[16]

The second cause is either supernatural or natural. The former is a good angel (2 Sam. 24:16 with 1 Chron. 21:15–16; 2 Chron. 32:21). Many commentators (e.g., Nicholas of Lyra,[17] Alfonso Tostado,[18] Marchini, etc.) contend, on the basis of a comparison with Ps. 77:49, that the angel who struck the firstborn of Egypt was an evil one. Yet I do not force their reasons [on anyone], which we gather through an analogy from Job 1:7–8. For if Satan could inflict sores on Job, and if therefore through himself or through magicians he mixes other poisons and breathes them on human beings, why could he not stir up a plague and infect its contagion on others? On magic provocations of the plague, see below.

Here at least it must be noted that malign maladies are inflicted upon people by the devil with the just permission of God (Luke 13:11; 12:16), which we have treated in our disputations on demons and magic. I need

---

14. An old name for Aramaic
15. Orig. 5:16
16. *R. Sel. Jarchi*: Rashi is the common acronym for the medieval French Rabbi Shlomo Yizchaki (1040–1105). The name Jarchi (ירחי, "moon") most likely derives from the town of Lunel in Provence, France, from which he or his ancestors were supposed to have lived. Perhaps the most accessible text and translation of Rashi's commentary on Genesis is *Pentateuch with Targum Onkelos, Haphtaroth and Rashi's Commentary*, vol. 1; trans. M. Rosenbaum and A. M. Silbermann (New York: Hebrew Publish Co., 1973).
17. Cf. Ps. 77:49 in Nicholas of Lyra (c.1270–1349), *Biblia Sacra cum Glossis, interlineari et ordinaria, Nicolai Lyrani Postilla et Moralitatibus*, 7 vols. (Lyon, 1545); 3:200v.
18. See qu. 48 "An Angelus percuties Aegyptios fuerit bonus, vel malus?" on Exodus 12 in Alfonso Tostado (c. 1400–1455), *Opera Omnia*, 27 vols. (Venice: Balleoniana, 1728), 2:144–46. This theologian is variously named Al(f)onso Fernández de Madrigal, Tostado, or as Abulensis since he was the bishop of city called *Abulensis* in Latin, that is Ávila, Spain; "Tostado" is likely a derogatory reference to the sun-tanned complexion of a farmer, which occupation his father held.

not mention lunatics, those possessed, and so forth, which were treated in their own disputation. The natural and definite cause [of plague] is anxiously sought for, yet there has not been anything demonstrated so far other than its undefined occult quality, and that it is like a kind of venom, because it is so great and of such a kind that all the study of medical doctors[19] is scarcely able to describe it; doctors who, after all their investigations, after their countless experiments, having separated them from diseases of intemperateness into diseases of the entire substance or of occult qualities, confess they are compelled to categorize this as holy fire. The testimonies of all are examples to us: Jean-Antoine Sarazin in his *Commentary on the Plague*, ch. 2;[20] Follinus in *Amuleto* bk. 1, chs. 3–6;[21] Sennert, *Institutes*, bk. 2, pt. 2, ch. 12, and *On Fevers*, bk. 4, ch. 1;[22] Gulielmus Marcquis, *Ten Problematic Questions on Plague*, problem 1;[23] Julien Le Paulmier, *On Contagious Diseases*, "On pestilential fevers," ch. 5–6.[24] So it is not in an inept way that the papist theologian Filiberto Marchini will give the reason why he affixed the title for his speculation regarding the plague as *Divine War*, its etiology[25] appearing at the beginning in the prolegomena sections: "That it thrives among common people is a foolish and depraved opinion, as if when some city or province is affected by pestilence those seeking its origin on earth rather than in heaven either attribute it to natural causes or to another human cause of a special occurrence."[26] Yet we do not say that inferior causes have no place here, but rather that these causes and their mode of operation are very frequently hidden from us, so that—led with much more admiration, reverence, and fear of the judgments of God—we say what Pharaoh's magicians said of the gnats: "Behold, the finger of God" (Exod. 8:19). From which one is

---

19. Gk. ἰατρῶν παῖδες

20. Jean-Antoine Sarazin (Johannes Antonius Saracenus, 1547–1598), *De Peste Commentarius* (Lyon: Louis Cloquemin, 1572), 10–31.

21. Hermannus Follinus, *Amuletum Antonianum seu Luis Pesterae Fugae* (Antwerp: Hieronymus Verdussius, 1618), 9–34.

22. See Daniel Sennert, *Institutiones Medicinae*, 2.2.12 and *De Febribus*, 4.1 in *Opera*, 3 vols. (Lyon: Jean Anotoine Huguetan, Jr. & Marc Antoine Ravaud, 1650), 1:364–69, 2:138. Let the reader note that the 1656 *Opera* consolidates volumes 1 and 2 into one tome, utilizing continuous pagination. The edition cited here utilizes separate volumes with separate pagination.

23. Gulielmus Marcquis, *Decas Pestifuga seu Decem Questiones Problematicae de Peste* (Antwerp: Caesar Ioachim Trognaesius, 1627), 1–37.

24. Julien Le Paulmier de Grentemesnil (Palmarius, 1520–1588), *De Morbis Contagiosis Libri Semptem* (Paris: Dionysius Du-Val, 1578), 300–308.

25. Gk. αἰτιολογίαν

26. Marchini, *Belli divini*, fol. §§r.

prone to gather an adjunct [characteristic] peculiar to this disease, that it possesses many characteristics in itself that must be marveled at, which have not only sapped the ingenuity of physicians but have by far overcome it; regarding which Sennert, at the end of book 4, chapter 1, ingeniously remarks, "yet such is the nature of pestilential poison, and any differences in any pestilential constitutions, which no one has explained satisfactorily up to this point."[27] These are such things, as J. C. Scaliger says in his *Exercises* 218, §8, as are concealed in temperate souls, and sport with those curious ones.[28] But the secret miracles of nature we should delineate typically[29] for the admiration of the works of God and his glory. Moreover, the secret miracles of nature are found in its origin, in its poisonous or malign and secret quality, in its contagious spread,[30] in its concomitants, and in its effects and antidotes.

(1) In its origin because the motion of the earth would sometimes yield an opportunity for it when the air is dry and hot, or sometimes when humid and cold; sometimes in famine, and sometimes by the constitution of waters when they are poisoned, whether by the stink of animals, vegetables, or fossils when trapped in the air (Gulielmus Marcquis, prob. 1), or when there is no other such occasion evident.[31]

(2) In poison, which is so manifold that relatively every person in its presence may be exposed, no matter what type of nature, whether mineral, vegetable, or animal to some extent. And daily new species of plague arise, which Gulielmus Marcquis (prob. 1) clearly proved after he had observed all others. Besides monkshood (*Aconitum napellus*), and arsenic (about which see Follinus, bk. 1, ch. 6), he points to henbane (*Hyoscyamus niger*), aspidium, scorpion venom, black Hellebore, Euphorbia, cicuticum,[32] mandrakes, cantharidin, and so forth.[33]

(3) In contagion, which is so astonishing in its procreation, its generation, its vector, whether air or stench, its force and method of dissemination, and so forth; regarding which see Sennert, bk 4. ch. 2, in which

---

27. Sennert, *De Febribus* in *Opera*, 2:138.
28. Julius Caesar Scaliger (1484–1558), *Exotericarum exercitationum Liber XV, de subtililate*, 633–34 in 1557 edition. Note well that there are four editions with different paginations: 1557, 1582 (667–69), 1612 (667–69), 1620 (278–79).
29. Gk. ὡς ἐν τύπῳ
30. *contagio*
31. Marcquis, *Decas Pestifuga*, 1–37.
32. Having consulted historians of pharmacology and medical researchers, the poison Voetius references is unknown.
33. Ibid., 1–37; Follinus, *Amuletum Antonianum*, 28–34.

he vividly describes a rampant plague in the time of Evagrius, bk. 3, ch. 28.[34] For us here especially one grows more amazed at the diversity of application to objects distinguished in their number. There are some that infect cattle but not humans and vice versa. In Exodus 9 there is again what infects these people but not others; what affects some peoples frequently, others exceedingly rarely, and still others never, as Scaliger in his *Exercises*, number 32 gives testimony regarding black people. It is because in one place there are more wealthy people than poor, and vice versa; again, more women than men, and vice versa (see Marchini, part 10, prob. 2); more younger people than aged. And then there are those who never come near those infected with plague, or rarely do, and those who are continuously present with them.[35] There are those who flee more than those who remain in the midst of the fire, as they say, and then there are those who live in a house with the infected and others who dwell elsewhere; and to this point, there are some more robust and healthy than those of afflicted or questionable health. Finally, it easily infects certain people with only a glance or through a fomite, but others scarcely become infected even though they handle it, a memorable example of which is in Evagrius, *Ecclesiastical History*, bk. 3, c. 28. Experience teaches many things, Guillaume Marcquis noted in some part from writings about the plague (prob. 1).[36]

1667 Addendum to Chapter I: Where secret miracles of the plague are mentioned in "(3) in contagion," add: Because when the plague prowled about most savagely in Heidelberg and the Palatinate, within a few months fifty pastors of the churches were carried off, the city of Heidelberg was despoiled of citizens, and the Academy lost students—part of whom were carried off, part of whom were scattered—so that not even one in the college of wisdom (because it only had one) neither suffered nor was put to the test, as Pareus witnesses in book 2, exercise 50 of his Exercises.[37]

(4) In its effects, because it pervades so many parts of the world (e.g. in the year 1382 and 1450), and because it inflicts such great carnage in

---

34. Sennert, *De Febribus* 4.2 in Opera 2:139–42; 3.28; Evagrius Scholasticus, *Historia Ecclesiastica* in PG 86-2:2653–54; idem, *The Ecclesiastical History of Evagrius Scholasticus* (Liverpool: Liverpool University Press, 2000), 162–63.

35. Scaliger, *Exotericarum* (1557), 131–32; Marchini, *Philosophica de Pestilentia Problemata* (Florence: Sermartelliana, 1633), 13–14.

36. Marcquis, *Decas Pestifuga*, 13, 18, 21, 33.

37. David Pareus, *Exercitationum Philosophicarum et Theologicarum Libri IV* (Heidelberg: Lancelotus, 1610), 262–63.

so brief a time, so that it is spoken of elegantly and conscientiously by Sarazin, in the previously cited treatise, chapter 1, as "like the character of a divine avenger."[38] Once it so savaged Athens that there was hardly anyone who was not touched by death, the disease, or mourning (about which see Thucydides, bk. 2, and Lucretius bk. 6).[39] Such pervaded nearly the whole world in the year 1030. Another plague under Vespasian in Rome destroyed ten thousand people per day, as Eusebius witnesses in his *Chronicle*. Likewise there is the plague in Constantinople by Nicephorus, bk. 15, ch. 10; Procopius bk. 2, *De Bello Persico*, and another under Leo [III] the Isaurius.[40] In 1345, for five whole years it ravaged the whole world and carried off half of the population. Under Benedict VIII, to which Plantin testified, many more died than survived. Furthermore, very many other examples may be sought from the historians and writers about the plague, or if anyone would study a sketch, from the chroniclers and *eclogarii* who annotate histories, such as among others Seth Kalwitz in his *Chronology* and Zwinger in his *Theatre of Human Life*.[41] One must marvel especially at the effects of this disease because it does seize and snatch away people who hardly ever feel [un]healthy so suddenly and unexpectedly. Scaliger, in the passage cited, states that the urine and pulse of some people infected by the plague does not differ from the healthy. Relevant here is Domenico Terilli, who, in his treatise on *The Causes of an Unexpected Death*, chapter 5, when the plague was ravaging throughout the year 1576, gave a horrendous account of very many who had given themselves to sleep and quiet at night, but by morning were immersed in the deepest slumber and did not ever wake up again afterwards.[42] Cardano refers in book 8 of his *On the variety of things*, ch. 45, to those who previously had been well but were dead between six to eight hours later from the plague of 1524 in Milan.[43] Protasius Rovellus mentions that he saw fresh bread that had been exposed to night air not only become moldy but swarm with worms; and next there was a

---

38. Sarazin, *De Peste Commentarius* (1572), 2.
39. Thucydides, *Peloponnesian War*, 2.47.3–2.54.5 in LCL 108:340–57; Lucretius, *De Rerum Natura*, 6.1138–1286 in LCL 181:578–591.
40. Nicephorus Callistus Xanthopoulos (c. 1265–c. 1335), *Eccleisasticae Historiae*, bk. 15, ch. 10 in PG 147:33–36; Procopius, *On the Persian War*, bk. 2.
41. Seth Kalwitz (Calvisius, 1556–1615), *Opus Chronologicum ubi tempus astronomicum per motus et eclipses*, 4th ed. (Frankfurt: Anthonius Hummius, 1650); Theodor Zwinger, *Theatrum humanae vitae* (Basil: Eusebius, 1586).
42. Domenico Terilli, *De causis mortis repentinae distinctiss. Tractatio* (Venice: Damian Zenarius, 1615), 13–15.
43. Cardano, *De Rerum Varietate*, 340–343.

great amount of putrid air.[44] Agricola, in book 2 of *On the Plague*, writes that eighty people in an assembly called together for prayer died in one moment, without any previous notable alteration.[45] Likewise Sennert, in chapter 2, page 639, references stories and incidents from various authors.[46]

(5) In the concomitants and connections of this evil, this disease causes a horror and amazement because so many different kinds of diseases and symptoms are customarily joined with the plague, such as: blindness (Nicephorus, bk. 15, ch. 16), delirium, fever, insomnia, profound sleep, thrush and ulcers of the mouth, angina, pleurisy, vomit, buboes, carbuncles, and diarrhea (Sennert enumerates these in bk. 4, ch. 1, and from Lucretius: *On the Nature of Things* bk. 6; Seneca in *Oedipus*, Act 1).[47] In this regard, compare the history of Evagrius in the passage cited, Procopius, *On the Persian War*, bk. 2, and Thucydides, *On the Peloponnesian War*, bk. 2.[48] You should be familiar with the astounding accounts of the plague from those three historians. In his treatise, *On Martyrdom through the Plague*, pt. 4, ch. 3, pp. 543–544, the Jesuit Theophilé Raynaud tells of the most sorrowful and unspeakable effects of a frenetic delirium and cruel insanity that befell the region of Cavares[49] and Lyon in the year 1564 and 1629.[50]

---

44. This is an anecdote from "our friend Prothasius Rovellus" in Cardano, *De Rerum Varietate*, 342; cf. Cardano, 342 cited by Simon Oomius (1630–1706), *Des Heeren Verderflicke Pyl, ofte Twee Boeken van de Pest* (Amsterdam: Willem van Beaumont, 1665), 97.

45. Georg Bauer (Georgius Agricola, 1494–1555), *De Peste Libri Tres* (Giessen: Caspar Chemlin, 1611), 58.

46. Sennert, *De Febribus* 4.2 in *Opera* 2:139–42

47. Sennert, *De Febribus* 4.1 in *Opera* 2:139; Lucretius, *De Rerum Natura*, 6.1138–1286 in LCL 181:578–591; Seneca the Younger, *Oedipus*, Act 1, 1–201 in LCL 78:18–33.

48. Evagrius, *loc. cit.*; Procopius, *On the Persian War*, 2.22–33 in LCL 48:451–473; Thucydides, *On the Peloponnesian War* in LCL 108:340–357.

49. An area that the Gallic *Cavari* tribe settled in the days of Emperor Augustus. In Voetius's day, this would have been a way to describe the region around Avignon, France.

50. Theophilé Raynaud S.J., *De Martyrio per pestem* (Lyon: Jacques Cardon, 1630), 543–544; Cf. idem, *Omnia Opera*, 20 vols. (Lyon: Boissat & Remues, 1665–1669), 18:515. In 1646, this book was censored *donec corrigatur*, "until it is corrected" by the papal Congregation of the Index, which censured and prohibited books. The issue was under what circumstances one became a martyr. In 1619, Jesuits at the University of Salamanca insisted that one could become a martyr for dying in defense of the doctrine of the immaculate conception of Mary, which at the time was not considered an article of faith. It had been asserted by Roman Catholic doctors as early as 1541 that it was heretical to maintain that one became a martyr defending to the point of death the doctrine of the immaculate conception of Mary. Likewise, Raynaud came under fire for asserting that one became a martyr without reference to articles of faith but through suffering plague well. See Henry Charles Lea, *Histoire de l'Inquisition au moyen age*, trans. S. Reinach 3 vols. (Paris, Société Nouvelle de Librairie et d'Édition, 1902), 3:737. This French translation is more accurate and greatly corrected. The note on Raynaud is an addition in the French edition. Cf. Henry Charles Lea, *History of the Inquisition in the Middle Ages*, 3 vols. (1888), 3:610. On Raynaud's trials with the papal Index, see S. Tutino, *Uncertainty in Post-Reformation Catholicism: A History of Probabilism* (Oxford: Oxford University Press, 2018), 237.

Jean-Antoine Sarazin also mentions $παραπληγία$[51] or mentagra,[52] and madness in chapter 1.

(6) In the antidotes, because there is such great variety and such great uncertainty in specifics regarding this or that specific plague or poison in this or that city—indeed, in this or that family or person—that a great number frequently would perish before the nature of the poison is known. Hence it happens that there is a remedy at hand for this one but destruction at hand for another. And then there are different therapeutic opinions of medical doctors and empiricists regarding phlebotomy and other things, as one can see among the authors cited above. So that by the stubbornness of the evil, or its uncertainty, the victims very frequently are driven to hopelessness, which happened in the plague at Athens in Thucydides, book 2. Even today, after such frequent experience, there are not lacking those who are overcome; because against all other poisons their own remedies are readily at hand, but against the plague nothing has been found yet. Sennert speaks in this way in the book cited (pt. 4, ch. 3): "Although the most prudent doctors confess that a true and specific remedy of the pestilential poison remains hidden from humanity."[53] And Julien Le Paulmier in his book *On the Pestilential Fever*, chapter 17, lamented this "because by the ancients there have been found a remedy for the Spanish disease, the poison of a rabid dog, and a scorpion, and certainly this remedy was so safe that anyone who had need might use it freely and recover." He mentions that as of yet none for the plague has been found with these words, "It must be apparent," he says, "lest we would deny the recognition of the inscrutable counsel of God, and so that we would regard this incurable disease as a scourge against humanity."[54] And even the most outstanding physician, Diomedes Amicus, in his book *On Plague*, chapter 30, teaches that in the pestilential plagues the remedies advance nothing for relief.[55] Nevertheless, I do not adduce these points in order to lead people away from remedies, but I would teach them rather to marvel at and have regard for the smiting hand of God.

51. Cf. Jean Antoine Sarazin, *De Peste Commentarius*, 8, where Sarazin cites Pliny with reference to the disease Lichens ($λείχην$) of Emperor Tiberias Claudius, see Pliny, *Natural History*, bk. 26, chs. 2-3 in *LCL* 393:264-67.
52. In ancient Rome, Mentagra was an eruptive disease of the chin and face that could mar appearance and was thought to spread through kissing.
53. Sennert, *Institutiones Medicinae*, 4.2 in *Opera*, 2:152.
54. Julien Le Paulmier, *De Morbis Contagiosis* (Frankfurt: Claude Marnius & Johann Aubry, 1601), Bk. 7, Chap. 17, 447-450.
55. Diomedes Amicus, *Tractatus tres exactissimi... De morbis omnibus communibus generatim... De peste singillatim... De variolis* (Venice: Haeredes F. de Franciscis, 1599), ch. XXX, 68-71.

Chapter II: The Meritorious Cause

The sins of human beings are the meritorious cause of plague. Among those crying out and widespread, the eminent ones that ravage everywhere are extravagance, pride, self-exaltation, and especially that magnate of them all, the violation of justice (2 Sam. 24), and the many oppressions and slaughter of good people (Exod. 9, 12; 2 Chron. 32). In his book *On the Delays of Divine Vengeance*, Plutarch tells of when Delphi was struck by the gods with famine, plague, and horrible diseases due to their slaying of Aesop.[56] From Ezekiel 5:14, Jeremiah 29, and Exodus 9 and 12 we gather that contempt and abuse of the divine Word is the cause of plague. Likewise you have regarding the Lord's Supper in 1 Corinthians 11:30. Gregory of Nyssa in his *Life of Gregory the Wonderworker* makes the cause of plague the worship of demons, magic, theatres, and spectacles, which are the appendages of "demonolatry."[57] In their genus, the final causes, which we conjoin with the effects, are the punishment of and avenging towards resolute sinners—a chastisement aiming towards their conversion—and the proof and stirring up of the converted (Amos 4 with Ezek. 14). In their species, I will express them in the words of Cyprian in his *On the Mortality*:

> By the dread of the mortality and of the time the lukewarm are inflamed, the slack are nerved up, the slothful are stimulated, the deserters are compelled to return, the heathens are constrained to believe, the ancient congregation of the faithful is called to rest, and the new and abundant army is gathered to the battle with a braver vigor to fight without fear of death when the battle shall come, because it comes to the warfare in the time of the mortality. And further, beloved brethren, what is it, what a great thing is it, how pertinent, how necessary, that pestilence and plague which seem horrible and deadly search out the righteousness of each one and examine the minds of the human race, to see whether they who are in health tend the sick; whether relations affectionately love their kindred; whether masters pity their languishing servants; whether physicians do not forsake

---

56. Plutarch, *Moralia. On the Delays of Divine Vengeance* in *LCL* 405:232-33.
57. Gregory of Nyssa, *De Vita B. Gregorii Thaumaturgi* in *PG* 46:955-58; Gregory Thaumaturgus et al., *St. Gregory Thaumaturgus Life and Works*, trans. M. Slusser (Washington D.C.: Catholic University of America Press, 1998), 85-87.

the beseeching patients; whether the fierce suppress their violence; whether the rapacious can quench the ever insatiable ardor of their raging avarice even by the fear of death; whether the haughty bend their neck; whether the wicked soften their boldness; whether, when their dear ones perish, the rich even then bestow anything and give, when they are to die without heirs. Even although this mortality conferred nothing else, it has done this benefit to Christians and to God's servants, that we begin gladly to desire martyrdom as we learn not to fear death. These are trainings for us, not deaths: they give the mind the glory of fortitude; by contempt of death they prepare for the crown.[58]

Thus far Cyprian.

(1) First consequence: In the definition of the Jesuit theologian Cornelius à Lapide, which I think he fetches from Ficino in his commentary on Exodus 9,[59] plague is a certain venomous vapor condensed in the air, hostile to the vital spirit, which can infect every humor; but especially blood, then choleric, third phlegm, and fourth melancholy. This is neither theological enough (as from our theses 1 and 2 and whatever is evident enough) nor is it logical and medical, as above all others Follinus and Sennert will teach you, who carefully inquire into the definition of plague.

(2) Filiberto Marchini, the Florentine regular and theologian, in his *Divine War*, prolegomena, §§4 (published in 1633 in his Italy that is so near to France) declares the end and outcome of the plague with this fable in place of an example: "But with what more should I follow up? Out of this pestilential calamity that has savaged among the inhabitants of Lyons these past four years, and has raged throughout nearly all of France, has it not resulted in for the most part the destruction of Calvinism, the expulsion of heresies, and the restoration of the ancient catholic religion as Jean Grillot, writing a testimony of the Lyonnaise plague, testifies?"[60] Do tell of the circumstances, O good historian, so that you might discharge your trust: who, what, where, by what means, why, how, and when?

---

58. Cited from Cyprian, "Treatise 7—On the Mortality", *ANF* 5:473. See page 316 in this volume.

59. Cornelius à Lapide, *Commentaria in Pentateuchum Mosis* (Antwerp: Jacobus Meursius, 1659), 403. Cf. Marsilio Ficino, *Il Consiglio di Marsilio Ficino Florentino contro la pestilentia con altre cose aggiunte appropriata alla medesima malattia* (1522).

60. Marchini, *Belli Divini*, fol. §4v. cf. Jean Grillot S.J., *Lyon Affligé de Contagion ou recit de ce qui s'est passe de plus memorable en cette Ville, depuis le mois d'Aoust de l'an 1628 jusques au mois d'Octobre de l'an 1629* (Lyon: François de La Bottiere, 1649), fols. Aiii r–Aiii v.

Chapter III: Spiritual Remedies

There are preventative measures and remedies of the same kind, which are for all diseases, indeed and for afflictions in this life; an abundance of which writers produce on the cross, or patience, or on the comfort of believers. Now we point out only certain specific and proper ones that have been applied for this present matter, first privately then publicly. Therefore, the private preventatives:

(1) That badge of God's grace on the heart (Heb. 13:9)—a dose that must be prepared daily by a faith renewed for believing it, by a firm hope expecting it, by an ignited love desiring it, and by devoted prayers entreating it. Moreover, the preparatory and preamble of it would be reading and meditation upon Psalm 91 and 103, or Romans 8, or Hebrews 12 and similar passages. To which if anyone would then add the reading of that golden sermon of Cyprian, *On Mortality*, or Möller's meditation on Psalm 91,[61] it certainly would not be a waste of effort.

(2) There is fighting against the fear of death through faith and Christian fortitude. For when that is utterly overcome there is nothing that causes us to fear the plague so. For here is a stimulus of the plague, that this contagion, this poison, this fear of all fears[62] would contain in itself most certain death. There are also other contagious diseases, making one no less miserable, much more frequent than plague, like dysentery, kidney stones, a continuous fever,[63] and so forth, but people do not turn pale at the mention of these nor do they flee. What is the specific difference? The fear of death. In order that you may find your faith and heart strengthened in Christ against death, however, you must exercise yourself in preparation for death and meditation upon the brevity and vanity of this life. We have treated of this topic in the lectures *On the Ascetic Christian*, where we have also pointed out other authors.

(3) There is contemplation of the divine fatherly providence on which, like a couch of heavenly security, our souls recline. For upon that providence depend health and sickness, life and death, and the mode and moment of sickness and death. It presides over all second causes, and it powerfully extends from beginning to end. Nothing befalls our health or life as an accident or fortune; nothing comes to pass that is not for our good

---

61. Heinrich Möller (1530–1589), *Enarratio Psalmorum Davidis ex praelectionibus Henrici Molleri*, 8th printing (Geneva: Samuel Chouët, 1660), coll. 823–34.
62. Gk. φοβερῶν πάντων φοβερώτατον
63. *Synochus putrida*: one theory at the time held that this sort of fever was due to an excess of blood that had "calefactioned," become hot.

(Matt. 10:30–31; Rom. 8:28). We will not expend ourselves in an explanation of this remedy. See the authors cited on the providence of God in our dissertation on *The End of Life*, and the arguments which we brought to bear there.[64]

(4) There is the renewal and exercise of our repentance, so that we would carefully scrutinize our inmost parts (Zeph. 2:1–2; Lam. 3:39–43) rather than the hand of God and this fire consuming our households. Indeed our repentance penetrates and pervades our veins, arteries, and innermost heart, so that we will be preserved from every infection and contagion (2 Cor. 7:12 with James 1:27; Jude 23) so that the contagion of plague would not touch us. Anything further regarding the practice of repentance and the exercise of new obedience must be treated expressly elsewhere. We teach here only this: the occasion of the plague is for the purpose of stirring ourselves up in all the exercises of public and private piety, and especially for sympathy and love towards brethren, and especially toward any isolated neighbor.

Public preventative measures are partly ecclesiastical and partly political: First, frequent celebration of fasts (Joel 2:12). Second, the removal of scandals and repression of sins (e.g. luxuriousness in feasts, clothing, buildings, ornate observance and pomp in funerals, dances and comedies, oppression and violence), the raising up of all and anything that has collapsed in morals, discipline, and both rule and jurisdiction (Isa. 58:3–10; 1 Cor. 2:30–32). And third, the needed care and comfort of those suffering from the plague. Let us not have so much concern for ourselves and the healthy with rigid observance of certain laws that we would be cruel to the souls and bodies of those persons or houses that have been infected with plague (Isa. 58:7–12; Ps. 41:1, 23; Jas. 2:13–14). However, this is what happens: having been excepted from the necessary duty of godliness or friendship, healthy people, who were present either with someone laboring with the plague or present in infected buildings on a given occasion, are excluded from the sermons and exercises of piety and from every assembly of people in the marketplace, in the byways, in common life and in its preservation. This is why healthy people, together with the sick of that family, are everywhere and most strictly enclosed in houses that have been closed up, and this enclosure frequently lasts for at least a full three months, six

---

64. Voetius, *Dissertatio Epistolica, De Termino Vitae ad... Johannem Beverovicium*, 2nd ed. (Utrecht: Esdras Wilhelmus, 1641).

months, or longer, with the specific result that, without any conversation, without any refreshment of a walk through fresh and less infected air, without any visits to less infected buildings, courtyards, or other places, and without any exchange of air in their houses, people are sickened by the contagious, putrid, fetid, and deadly air in their melancholy solitude and sickness. And finally, it happens that healthy people, or those who brought it from another area (where perhaps some are suffering from the plague), with a great inconvenience to themselves and their affairs, are shut out of our cities and provinces for a long time. Are these the works of piety and Christian mercy to the sick, the dying, and to travelers? They would say that there is an exception in the case of plague. But I will respond with that remark of Bernard of Clairvaux's on Romans 13:1, where he proves that everyone, even clergy, are subject to the magistrate: "The one who studies to exclude," he says, "studies to deceive."[65] Where Scripture does not make an exception, we must not.

Chapter IV: Proper Antidotes

Now it remains for us to indicate in three points the remedies against the plague, which has already assaulted ourselves or our domestics. Moreover, these remedies are partly common and partly specific. The former are what are applicable in all the calamities of this life, namely in lethal or dangerous diseases. (1) The first of these is a purgation and resignation of our own will, and a denial of ourselves so that we may be entirely at rest in God's fatherly will (1 Sam. 2; 2 Sam. 16; Ps. 39; Job 1). The practical authors must be consulted, who comment on patience and comfort, on self-denial, or on Matthew 17, Mark 8, Luke 14, on the third petition of the Lord's Prayer,

---

65. *Qui studet excipere, studet decipere*: Voetius attributes this statement to Bernard of Clairvaux and utilizes the quote elsewhere in his work, cf. Voetius, *Politicae Ecclesiasticae*, 2:275. Nowhere does Voetius indicate the precise reference in Bernard of Clairvaux (1090–1153). E.g. For one passage where Bernard utilizes Romans 13:1-2 in a work on papal authority to Pope Eugenius to argue that the pope is not the only power, see Bernard of Clairvaux, *De Consideratione*, bk. 3, ch. 4, §17 in *Sancti Bernardi Opera*, 9 vols. (Turnhout: Brepols, 1957-1998), 3:444–445; idem, *PL* 182:768; "You are mistaken if you think your apostolic power, which is supreme, is the only power instituted by God. If you think this is the case, you differ from him who says, 'There is no power except from God.' Likewise, what follows, 'The one who resists power, resists the ordinance of God.' Even though this is principally yours, it is not solely yours. The same one says, 'Let every soul be subject to higher powers' (Rom. 13:1-2). He does not say 'to *a* higher power' as if in one person, but 'to higher powers' as if in many. Therefore, yours is not the only power from God; there are intermediary and lesser ones. Just as also those whom God has joined together must not be separated, so those whom God has made subordinate must not be made equal."

and on similar passages already cited. (2) An admiration and celebration of our God's mercy, who draws back to himself lost or wandering sheep who are pleased with their own impetuousness; he places them on his shoulders and restores them to the path of life, although it is a narrow path. "Greater is what we deserve, but less is what we suffer."[66] Our sins merit punishments, but behold, the sparing hand of God! Behold, the heart of mercy, the cords of his love, the saving remedy, that good ill of chastisement, that sweetest bitterness, that loving wrath, the most profound depth of mercy, the path to heaven, and heaven itself on earth! (3) The faith, apprehension, and taste of the goodness and grace of God in Christ, if we have in fact ever tasted how sweet the Lord is in forgiving our sins (Ps. 103–104), in imputing and gifting the merits of Christ (2 Cor. 5), in adopting us as his children—and that by sealing us with the seal of his Spirit (Rom. 8). Provided God is gracious to us with the special grace of the elect (Ps. 106), this grace is sufficient for us. In all these things we will be more than conquerors. There is nothing that will separate us from his love (Rom. 8). (4) Hope, desire, and contemplation of a better life, if in fact we finished our race. If God would lead us back from the gates of hell, how much greater should our gratitude be, and how much more heavenly our manner of life on earth, with which Jerome elegantly characterizes Blaesilla in his nineteenth letter to Marcella.[67] All these things must be drawn from the common places on eternal life, on a blessed death or on the art of dying, and on the practice of Christian hope. These and other common means must be applied by the entire people and to the church, a summary of which is that a public fast against common calamities is distinctly pointed out to us by God himself (Joel 2:12, 15). On the method of celebrating a fast, see what I have said elsewhere.[68]

The specific remedies of the plague, which are opposed to our haughtiness, terror, and the misery of this evil, we will only point out must be enlarged upon by the spiritual trainer:

(1) *Many things cause the present death.* I respond: you have already been taught that death is not death for you, but a passageway to a better life.

(2) *It snuffs people out so suddenly and unforeseen.* I respond: There is

---

66. *Majus est quod meremur, minus est quod patimur*: Often attributed to Augustine of Hippo, e.g. Prudentius, *Brevarium Psalterii* in *PL* 115:1456.

67. Cf. "Letter XXXVIII to Marcella" in *NPNF2* 6:47–49.

68. Voetius, pt. 1, bk. 2, tract. 4, chs. 1–2 in *Politicae Ecclesiasticae* (Amsterdam: Joanne à Waesberg, 1663–1669), 1:970–999.

no sudden death for those who have Christ as their life (Col. 3; Phil. 1:23). The lamps of the righteous are not extinguished by extinguishing, even if they should walk through the valley of death, because Christ enlightened them and will shine upon them in perpetual brightness, even illuminating that darkness (Eph. 5; 2 Cor. 3; Ps. 23; John 8:12). To that end, those maturely accustomed to the yoke of Christ, indeed who even daily hear his call to salvation, will never preoccupy themselves with darkness or a sudden death (John 11:25–26). Finally, it is reckoned to your profit that this torment is briefer, this contest is shorter than the vexations of a long-lasting disease; the victory easier, and the passage from this life easier, in that death that is fitting to lead to immortality and glory. For this desire truly belongs to the godly (Phil. 1:23; Rom. 7:24; 2 Cor. 5:4–8).

(3) *It is an outrageous disease.* I respond: But it is not outrageous for God to call forth his own from this place through this disease. It is attested that this is the experience of all ages. There are noted examples from so many servants of God, among whom are Johannes Oecolampadius, Jacobus Kimedoncius, Franciscus Junius, and so forth. According to these examples—for those who love God—it is never an outrageous visitation or strange hand so much as the hand of their heavenly Father. When God sometimes appears to his own like he is masked, but that mask draws them to faith, and through all the shadowy and covered things he draws them into his very sanctuary, one should consider the heart of their Father.

1667 Addendum to Chapter IV: Where there is mentioned by name those extinguished by the plague, Oecolampadius, Franciscus Junius, add: Wolfgang Fabritius Capito, Martin Borrhaus (from Melchior Adam, *On the Lives of German Theologians*), Jacobus Kimedoncius, a Heidelberg theologian [circa] November 26, 1596 (from book 2, exercise 7 of Pareus's *Exercises*),[69] Theodore Bibliander, and the renowned Conrad Gesner (from *The Life of Gesner* by Josiah Simler in the year 1566 in quarto where it mentions Bibliander on page 18), Thomas Erpenius (from the funeral prayer of Gerard Johann Vossius); and Theodore Beza was stricken with the plague, but yet was not extinguished.[70] You have something about Oecolampadius in the *Lives* of Melchior Adam, and in the oration of Polanus on the life

---

69. David Pareus, *Exercitationvm Philosophicarvm & Theologicarum Libri IV* (Heidelberg, Johannes Lancellotus, 1610), 98-101; Melchior Adam, *Vitae Germanorum Theologorum* (Frankfurt: Jonah Rosa, 1653), 399-402.

70. Josiah Simler, *Vita Clarissimi Philosophi et Medici Excellentissimi Conradi Gesneri Tigurini* (Zurich: Froschouerus, 1566), 18.

and death of Oecolampadius delivered in the year 1593, and which appears with his commentaries on Malachi in the year 1597, published in octavo.[71] On Franciscus Junius, Sr., Franciscus Gomarus is mentioned in his funeral oration, from which there is a brief narrative excerpted regarding his disease and death, in the 1613 edition (i.e. second edition) of his works published in Geneva in folio.[72] If anyone should read these lives closely (which one would not do without profit), one will see how godly and outstanding men confirmed our opinion about flight from plagues with their own practice; and myself, my colleagues, and successors taught by our example in our pastoral ministry at Heusden, Netherlands from the year 1625 and following (when the plague ravaged there for some time) and supplied to the sheep and citizens suffering from it some measure of help and comfort in life and death with all our might. Notwithstanding that, my colleague, by the grace of God, survived until the year 1626 [after] he was afflicted by God with that disease for several months before his children died; and my wife, who in the same year was most gravely tormented, passed through the same fire, a little before one of my children suffered with it.

(4) *This is a terrible disease beyond others—first in oneself, and then also especially because all our friends and relations frequently desert the one suffering.* I respond: First, the same thing also befell Christ (Ps. 22:12; Matt. 26:40), and you have begun to be made like your head; advance on in this course. Second, however many desert you, yet God will not desert you (Isa. 42:15; Ps. 27:9–10; Isa. 54:6–7). He is your shepherd (Ps. 23:1, 4). He restores you on the couch of infirmity (Ps. 41:3–4). He has his left hand underneath you and with his right he embraces you (Song of Sol. 2:6). He is at hand in your necessity so that he may rescue you (Ps. 91:15). Where he is, there is strength, comfort, food, drink, medicine, doctor, friend, relation, shepherd, lord, father, inheritance, life, victory, light, jubilee, triumph, and finally God and all things. Third, whatever may be terrible in this disease, it is less now that God is not terrible towards you (Jer. 17:17), now that Christ lifts up the loving light of his countenance upon you, now that he regards you, who had the terror of death, hell, and the plague (Hos. 13:14; 1 Cor. 15:55–56).

71. Adam, *Vitae*, 45–59; For his biography, see Johannes Oecolapadius, *Ioannis Oecolampadii . . . Commentarorum in Prophetas*, 2 vols. in 1 (Geneva: Jean Crispin & Nicolaus Barbier, 1558), vol. 2, fol. *ii recto–*vi verso. For Amandus Polanus von Polansdorf's oration, see "De sancta vita et beato obitu Oecolampadii" in A. Polanus von Polansdorf, *Analysis Libelli Prophetae Malachae . . . adiunctae sunt orationes quatuor . . .* (Basil: Conrad Waldkirch, 1597), 210–42.

72. Franciscus Junius, *Omnia Opera Theologica*, 2nd ed. (Geneva: Samuel Crispin, 1613), 1:22–23.

(5) Finally, so that I may deal fully with the mass and antitheses that remain: the hand of God is that which not only presses down but also uplifts, it not only wounds but also heals. It is God's staff, not of fury but of correction, not of a torturer but of a father (Heb. 12:7-8). The striking angel is also the messenger of death, but to you the angel of deliverance and the forerunner of salvation (1 Cor. 15:54, 57; 2 Tim. 4:7-8; 2 Cor. 5:1-2). It is a whirlwind and tempest from the face of God, but in that storm is your God, likened to a whirlwind and gale (1 Kings. 19:13, 21; Job 38:1). They are the arrows of the Almighty, but let fly from a gentle and sweet hand, in which way Gregory of Nazianzus calls his afflictions "bitter arrows from a sweet hand."[73] It is a poison, but to the poison and corruption of sin; not a destructive one, but an alexipharmic poison, an antidote which the greatest doctor of souls has prepared from a poison that delivers from poison and preserves against poisons. So a poison is driven out with a poison, a disease is destroyed by a disease, a plague by a plague, rot with rot, and stench with stench. Let the variegated[74] wisdom of our God be a blessing. It is a fire, but one that consumes our enemies, purifies friends, and illumines our households. In this fire, to us God is the burning bush (Exod. 3), appearing for our deliverance. It is a burning fire, you will say, that devours and drains away our vital spirits. But nevertheless, it burns with and leaps forth flames of the fire of his very love for us, which, while it burns our flesh and melts our hearts (Ps. 37:26), lights the lamp for that perfect day with a heavenly heat, and consumes these frigid and earthly members; it smelts off the dross of God's children so that they are set like the most purified gold in their Lord's treasury. Briefly, the very last thing that this fire threatens to sweep away is nothing other than yourself, as in Elijah's fiery chariot, carrying you away to heaven to rejoice and reign forever with Christ. This is the chief of the chief points: this plague—so ineffable, so abominable, so horrendous, so disastrous, and so harmful to sinners and men of this age (as they are called in Psalm 17:14), which is nothing other than a pestilential plague—is but a forerunner of the infernal one of burning. To the children of God it is at the same time like the plague of sins, which, through the grace of God and through the plague of Christ's death (Hos. 13; 1 Cor. 15), is also the antidote

---

73. Gk. ἐκ γλυκεῆς παλάμης πικροὺς ὀϊστούς: cf. Gregory of Nazianzus, *Carmina* 2.1.19 ln 30, "Cχετλιαχτικον ὑπὲρ τῶν αὑτου παθῶν" in *PG* 37:1273; idem, *Selected Poems of Gregory of Nazianzus: I.2.17; II.1.10, 19, 32: A Critical Edition with Introduction and Commentary* (Göttingen: Vandenhoeck & Ruprecht, 2009), 109–112, 189.
74. Gk. πολυποίκιλος

to that poison; it is health, life, a passageway to life, to such an extent that they even rush forward to embrace death, and they do not fear whatever time it would seem fit to God to call them and lead them home.

Chapter V: Forbidden Antidotes

Now must be detected and overthrown those disastrous and harmful antidotes which are customarily applied by the heathen, papists, and others. Moreover, they are either magical, idolatrous, superstitious, or exceedingly carnal.

There are various magical ones. In the year 1522, on Pope Adrian VI's watch,[75] in Rome there was a shocking instance of demonolatry publicly exercised by a certain Greek named Demetrius Spartan, who calmed the plague that had arisen at the time with an auspicious propitiation, that is, a *prospera litatio* (thus a worshiper of Jupiter speaks) of a sacrificial bull at the amphitheater.[76] Half of the bull's horn was slit in such a way that it went unnoticed, and the magician had rendered the bull so tame, that when the magician wanted he would lead it with a lengthy magic song in its right ear and by a slender thread attached to the whole horn. See the history (which we previously cited in *The Desperate Cause of the Papacy*, book 1, §4) in bishop Paulo Giovo's *Histories of his Time*, vol. 2, bk. 21,[77] where even that heathen papist bishop harshly censures the Flemish Adrian VI because, new to the Roman palace and inexperienced in Italian affairs, he did not want to constrain that plague with severe laws in the Italian style, and neither did he impose anything that would have restrained that pagan demonolatry.

---

75. Lat. *sub oculis Hadriani VI*: given the debate surrounding this claim, it is better to take this phrase broadly, but Voetius does seem to have believed Pope Adrian VI was in attendance as it occurred "under the eyes of Adrian VI."

76. Voetius is almost directly citing the Roman Catholic source, Paulo Giovo (1483–1552), bishop of Nocera, Italy, who served as a physician during this time in Rome, see P. Giovo, *Historiarum sui temporis*, 2 vols. (Florence: Lorenzo Torrentini, 1550–52), 2:11. Another source Voetius may have consulted here, which is cited above, is Georg Bauer, *De peste libri tres* (1611), 57–58. The details of this account are highly debated in the period. It is true there was a Greek magician, Demetrius Spartan, present in Rome, who claimed he could abate the plague with a sacrifice of his blessed ox to Jupiter. Roman Catholic accounts claim the pope's vicar interdicted the magician's attempted sacrifice; others claim the sacrifice did occur but at midnight. None of the Roman Catholic accounts indicate Adrian VI was actually present, but according to Giovo, because of the hope of the credulous multitude, "no one dared shun the superstition." The fiasco occurred only days before Adrian VI was installed. For a more critical account, see Ludwig von Pastor, *The history of the popes: from the close of the middle ages*, trans. R. F. Kerr, 40 vols. (London: Paul, Trench, Trübner & Co., 1910), 9:66.

77. P. Giovo, *Historiarum*, 2:11, cited by Voetius, *Desperata Causa Papatus* (Amsterdam: Joannes Jansson, 1635), 32.

This is of the same stuff as the invocation of Aesculapius under the form of the Epidaurian serpent (about which Livy speaks in book two; Valerian Maximus in book 1, chapter 8; and Plutarch on Coriolanus) when an enormous pestilence arose at Rome.[78] For there is no doubt that the devil and magic were present in this business. Nor must magic be passed by, whereby it is asserted that the cadavers of sorcerers (who, even dead and buried, were reputed to induce plague) must have their heads chopped off; an example of which, in his *Four Books on Fevers*, Sennert cited from chapter 11 of Hercules of Saxony's (1551–1607) book *On Lice*.[79] The most learned philosopher and physician is as patently[80] amazed as I surely am; "the cause of this matter," he says, "is not easily opened; it belongs to the mind avid for truth to be diligently undetermined on it."[81] Also, all amulets are of a magical character, one of which we will address below.

Idolatrous and superstitious remedies include the feasts of the gods,[82] stage plays which were used by the consuls Titus Sulpitius and Petreius Licinius in 291 B.C. (462 A.U.C.) and brought to Rome for this purpose, that the traveling gods would have sacred buildings or temples devoted to some divine spirit, sacred practices, and so forth, as Livy attests (bk. 1.5, bks. 7.10–11, 27).[83] The Athenians raged with similar and worse idol-mania, saying that the altar to the Unknown God and the oracle of Sparta, when consulted, responded that a virgin must be sacrificed annually. See Plutarch, parallel 35,

---

78. See instead Livy, *History of Rome*, bk. 1010.47.6–7 in *LCL* 191:540–543, where Livy references the Epidaurian serpent, compare to Valerius Maximus, *Memorable Doings and Saying* (*Facta et Dicta Memorabilia*), 1.8.2 in *LCL* 492:104–105; Plutarch, *Lives. Caius Marcus* Coriolanus, XII–XIII in *LCL* 80:144–149.

79. Sennert, *De Febribus* in *Opera* 2:144; cf. Hercules of Saxony (Herculis Saxonia or Ercole Sassonia, 1551–1607), chapter 11, "Whether sorcery could be the cause of lice?" (An maleficia possint esse caussa plicae), *De Plica quam Poloni Gwozdziec, Roxolani Koltunum vocant* (Laurentius Pasquatus, 1600), 42–53, especially 51–52. While inquiring whether the *maleficia daemonum*, the sorcery of demons, could be a cause of lice and plague, Hercules relates a rather gruesome and graphic tale from 1572 of a sorceress in the region of the city Leopolis in the kingdom of Poland (now Lviv, Ukraine) who had been buried in the local cathedral. As the story goes, the plague started soon thereafter. In order to dispel the plague the corpse of the sorceress was exhumed and decapitated.

80. Lat. *patienter mirari*: a correction from *patienter* to *patenter* is in order, as Sennert was not "patiently amazed."

81. Sennert, *De Febribus*, 389. cf. idem, *Opera*, 1st ed., 4 vols. (Lyon: 1656), 1:797.

82. *Lectisternia*, e.g. Livy, *History of Rome*, 1.13.6; 5.13.6; 7.2, 27; 8.25; 21.62; 22.1.

83. Voetius seems to be translating a portion from Ludwig Lavater here, who cites Livy utilizing the names Titus Sulpitius and Petreius Licinius, cf. Ludwig Lavater, *Van de peste, een seer Christelijcke onderrichtinghe* (Deventer: Jan E. Cloppenburch, 1599), 71–72. In Livy, *History of Rome*, 7.2 the consuls mentioned who introduced *lectisternia* in times of plague were Gaius Sulpicius Peticus and Gaius Licinius Stolo, whereas Livius Andronicus is mentioned as the Greek playwright who introduced regular lyric and dance.

where he refers to the same thing regarding the city of Falerii, and the Souda does as well on the term περίψημα, a scapegoat.[84] And these are the Gentiles. The Jews ascribe exotic and astounding names, which contain the nomenclature of the angels who brought the plague, to their rooms, baths, and homes; among these, there is the name *diridon*, which was then carried through the entire alphabet (such as *adiridon, bediridon,* and so forth), and when written in large letters, they claim it is the most effective remedy (See Buxtorf, *Synagoga Judaica*, ch. 33).[85] Then refer to the superstitious Talmudic observance which they prescribe in Bava Kama, fol. 60, "Let no person in time of plague walk in the middle of the road because the angel of death, to whom power is given, publicly kindles it in the middle of roadways."[86]

In the papacy, besides sorrow for sins and reconciliation with God (which we also acknowledge, when taken rightly) these things are prescribed (See Marchini in his prolegomena fol. §§§§ recto): supplications, which they call either processions, auricular confessions, the dominical body (that is, the idol of the Mass), or public and private veneration (regarding Masses for the purpose of shunning the mortality or in time of pestilence, see *Missale Reformatum* in the appendix, fol. 69; regarding masses for the plague of animals, see the ancient *Missale*, Paris, 1506 fol. 213;[87] these latter ones, the Jesuit Baille expressly defends in his *Catechism* part 1, qu. 20);[88] the invocation of the saints; imploring the Blessed Virgin

---

84. (Pseudo-)Plutarch, *Parallela Minora*, §35 in *LCL* 305:306–309; I. Bekker, ed., *Suidae Lexicon, Græce & Latine* (Berlin, 1854) 850.

85. Johannes Buxtorf, *Synagoga Judaica, das ist Jüden Schul, darinnen der gantz Jüdische Glaub und Blaubens ubung* (Basel: Sebastian Henricpetrus, 1603), 598–599. Cf. idem, *Synagoga Judaica, auscpiciis authoris jam olim Latinitate donata* (Basel: Ludwig König, 1641), 422–424.

86. See Bava Kamma 60b, 8 in *The Schottenstein Edition Talmud Bavli* (New York: Artscroll 1990–2012): "The sages taught: if there is a plague in the city, a person should not walk in the middle of the road, due to the fact that the Angel of Death walks in the middle of the road, as, since in Heaven they have given him permission to kill within the city, he goes openly in the middle of the road. By contrast, if there is peace and quiet in the city, do not walk on the sides of the road, as since the Angel of Death does not have permission to kill within the city, he hides himself and walks on the side of the road."

87. E.g. *Missale ad consuetudinem ecclesie Romane* (Paris: Thielman Kerver, 1506), fol. 213 recto. Cf. Jacques de Paméle, *Liturgica Latinorum Iacobi Pamelii . . . duobus tomis digesta* (Cologne: Gervinus Calenius, 1557), 2:446–447. The *"missale reformatum"* Voetius has in view could be the 1506 Kerver printing as it does utilize *revisum* in the subtitle.

88. See instead, treatise 2, q20 or pt. 3, q22 in the Latin or German translations. Guillaume Baile S.J. (Guilelmus Bayllius, 1557–1620), *Catechisme et Abbregé des controverses de nostre temps, touchant la Religion*, 2nd ed. (Lyon: Pierre Rigaud, 1625), 143–148, 336–337; idem, *Catechismus seu Epitome complectens tractatus IV capita*, trans. Henri Lamormain (Lyon: Matthaeus Formica, 1626), 120–123, 282–283; idem, *Controversiarum Catechismus, das is kurtzer bericht auff 124 Strittige Religionspuncten* (Munich: Cornelius Leyserius, 1642), 126–130, 289–290; Voetius's citation is incorrect as well as vague; he is most likely referencing either the Latin or German translation, rather than the

Mary, and the resort to her temples and images, especially the recitation of that hymn to Mary that was sent down from heaven for this purpose and given to the monastics of Santa Clara of Coimbra, Portugal, if what Francisco Gonzaga said was true in his chronicle, part 8, p. 310.[89] And to this point Marchini, whose superstitious nonsense the Jesuit Guillaume de Pretere has by far surpassed in his *Remedies Against the Plague* (published in the vernacular Dutch edition of Antwerp in 1636)[90] where, after the indicative causes and signs of the plague, he places eleven patron saints, doctors, and marshals in the first battleline of spiritual antidotes against the plague (which, as a technical term commonly employed in this material, he explains from Jan Gerartsen):[91] First, Sebastian, whom they customarily invoke and worship in this case in Portugal. We add from Lorin's *Commentary* on Wisdom 18:19 that this saint is everywhere considered to be the one who expels the plague. When his image was carried about (which Paul the Deacon describes in bk. 6, ch. 5, *The History of the Langobards*), the horrible plague at Rome that occurred in the year 680 AD ceased.[92] The monument of this event, he says, is still extant in the entryway of a minor basilica, San Pietro in Vincoli, where the mosaic of Sebastian is still worshiped. See this history explained more in Baronius in the notes of his

---

French original, as the division of the work into parts and questions occurs only in the translations. In the translations, treatise 1, q. 20 addresses a question of *sola Scriptura*, which is not at issue here. However, treatise 2, q. 20 addresses the sign of the cross and its usage with sick animals and demon possessed people (Fr., "corps des animaux irraisonnables travaillez de maladie, es corps assiegez par les diables," p. 145–146). Treatise 3, q. 22 rebukes the Reformed for not bringing the Mass to the sick.

89. Voetius drew this citation from the marginalia of Marchini, *Belli Divini*, fol. §§§§ recto, which reads "Francis. Gonz. pa. 8. Chron. pag. mihi 310". The correct citation for the series is Francisco Gonzaga, *De Origine Seraphicae Religionis Franciscanae*, 3 vols. (Venice, 1603), 3:941–942. Note well, volume 3 has a slightly different title, idem, *Tertia huius operis pars omnes provincias omnesq. tum fratrum tum quotue sororum Ultramontanae familiae conventus complectens* (Venice, 1603).

90. For Voetius's reference to de Pretere's *Remedios contra Pestem*, see Guillaume de Pretere, S.J. (1578–1626), *Gheesteliicke Remedien teghen de Haestige Sieckte, ter oorsaecek vande devotie die binnen Antwerpen betoont wordt besonderlijck in het aen roepen van de H. Moeder Godts ende andere Heyligen patroonen ot Marschalcken teghen de haetighe sieckte* (Antwerp: Jan Gnobbaert, 1624). The 1635 edition does not seem to be extant in modern research libraries. Also noteworthy is De Pretere's *Catechismus* (Antwerp, 1623), which was kept continuously in print in Belgium until 1800 by the Society of Jesus.

91. Lat. *Goropius Becanus*: See Jan Gerartsen of Gorp, (Johannes Goropius Becanus, 1519–1573).

92. Jean de Lorin S.J. (1559–1634), *Commentarius in Sapientiam* (Lyon: Horace Cardon, 1607), 665; Voetius cites Lorin's reference here to Paul the Deacon, which is incorrect (i.e. *Lib. 6. Cap. 2. De Gestis Longobardo*), instead see Paul the Deacon (ca. 720–ca. 799), *History of the Langobards*, bk. 6, chs. 5–6, trans. W. D. Foulke (Philadelphia: Dept. of History, University of Pennsylvania, 1907), 254–257; cf. plague of 566 AD in Liguria, bk. 2, ch. 4, 86–87; idem, *Historia Langobardorum*, in *Monumenta Germaniae Historica Saec. VI–IX*, ed. G. Waitz (Hannover: Bibliopolis Hahniana, 1878), 213–215, cf. 74.

Martyrology, January 20, and in Marchini, part. 10, prob. 8;[93] but Marchini admits there are no traces extant in the deeds of Sebastian to explain why he was then chosen as an expeller of plague. No cause can be imagined, therefore, except that hieroglyphic or kabbalistic stab of an arrow, as the plague among the Greeks is called the arrow of Apollo and in Scripture the arrow of God. Second, Hadrian in Flanders. Third, Christopher in Spain and Belgium, from which this couplet arises, "Those who St. Christopher's semblance spy / surely, on this day no bad death shall die."[94] Fourth, Anthony throughout the whole of Belgium. Fifth, St. Rocco in Italy, to whom heaven sent down this remark, "To those who suffer plague and flee to St. Rocco's patronage, I make known they will escape that contagion." Sixth, Benno of Hildesheim in Bavaria, whom he says six monks in Antwerp now commend and display to be worshiped. Of course his relics are preserved in a Jesuit church there. Seventh, Makarius, the Armenian Patriarch of Antioch by those in Ghent. He mentions briefly and panegyrically that the seventh of these, when shown in time of plague, resulted in life and miracles. One of these, in the year 1616, was said to be in the mountains of Hannover, when the body of St. Makarius was sent by Cameracus, which Cornelius á Lapide mentions in his dedicatory epistle to the commentary on the Pentateuch.[95] Eighth, Remigius in France. Ninth, Oswald in England. Tenth, Laurence in Burgundy. Eleventh, Fregidandus in Brabant. But as with all attendants, as the queen and supreme doctor at the head of them all, he sets the Blessed Virgin Mary first—several examples of deliverance through her were mentioned by the mediation of her likeness, and why she is worshiped at Guadalupe, Spain like another Diana of the Ephesians is discussed by Nuñez in his *Hispania*, ch. 61.[96] He also prescribes this mode of worshiping the saints: through the formula of prayer to Mary used in the monasteries of Bernard; then through a heavenly antiphon sent down from heaven, which we indicated above is found in Marchini; then through formulas of prayer to any of the first seven attendants; and last through five

---

93. Cesare Baronio, *Martyrologium Romanum* (Cologne: Ioannes Gymnicus, 1603), 58; Marchini, *Philosophica de Pestilentia Problemata* (Florence: Sermartelliana, 1633), 17. The edition of Marchini's *Belli Divini* used here includes the *Philosophica de Pestilentia Problemata* as an appendix with a separate pagination.
94. *Christophori sancti speciem quicunque tuetur / Ista nempe die non morte mala morietur.*
95. Cornelius á Lapide, *Commentarius in Pentateuchum Mosis* (Antwerp: Joannes et Jacobus Meursius, 1648), fols. *2r–*7v.
96. Luis Nuñez (Ludovicus Nonnius, 1553–1645), *Hispania* (Antwerp: Hieronymus Verdussen, 1607), 189–193.

psalms of Mary from the Psalter of Bonaventure (which he then puts forth in the vernacular language), affirming from the published work of Karl Stengel—that great Benedictine spiritual alexeterian[97] of Dillingen—that in Rome in 1470 through the recitation of these psalms to Mary in the convent of Augustinians the plague was clearly lifted from the people.[98] He intersperses one or another prayer to God and to the name of Jesus, and commends also these spiritual preventatives: the names of Jesus, Mary, and Anna, whether said with the mouth, or written on their homes, or said in one's heart; or the Lamb of God; the names or images of these marshals of the pest, inscribed in one's house or room; carrying around capsules with relics; the sign of the cross; blessed candles; fasts with penance; and pilgrimages (p. 143, 169). And certainly at the climax of this little book, which contains 185 pages, we add this exclamation commonly employed by the Sorbonne theologian D'Espence, "Now shame on Rome."[99]

There is no refutation we would supply here because only to display these things is to refute them; the others we treat individually elsewhere: the lamb of God, the cross, and so forth. Meanwhile, reader, given the time, you could consult our disputations on blessings, exorcisms, the *Agnus Dei*, the cross, pilgrimages, rosaries, superstition, and magic.[100] They well enough worship these "saints" of ours, among whom are the chimerical Christopher, and Rocco, who is not worshiped at Rome having never been canonized; although, despite the pope's snarling in vain, he is worshiped at Venice as a saint. We discuss this elsewhere, when we speak about chimerical saints.[101] There is another little book in the vernacular Dutch, published in Antwerp in 1645, entitled *The Lives of St. Rocco, St. Joseph, and St.*

---

97. Lat., *Alexeterio*: derived from Gk. ἀλεξητήριος, one who defends or averts, historically among ancient Greeks, a title of Zeus. Voetius is mocking Stengel because the bulk of Stengel's work has to do with hagiography, the images of the saints, and the cult of the saints and martyrs. The currently extant corpus of Stengel's Latin works numbers 89 volumes.

98. Karl Stengel O.S.B. (1581–1663), *Commentarius Rerum Augustanarum ab urbe condita ad nostra usque tempora* (Ingolstadt: Gregory Haelin, 1647).

99. *Habeat nunc Roma pudorem*: Charles D'Espence (1511–1571) was a French theologian who was involved in the Council of Trent and also was known for his arguments against the views of Theodore Beza on predestination, C. D'Espence, *Traité contre L'Erreur Vieil et Renouvelé des Prédestinés* (Lyons, 1548). He was also the rector of the Sorbonne. Cf. Juvenal, *Satire* 2.38.

100. Cf. Voetius, "Section IV de Titulo Alexipharmaci et Magia Papatus," *Desperata Cavsa Papatvs . . . Præmissa etiam velitatione de Magia, aliisque Abominationibvs Papatvs* (Amsterdam: Joannes Janssonius), 24–39; Voetius here argues against Jansen, treating of various Roman Catholic prayers of exorcism and various other magical formulae.

101. Voetius presided over four disputations and included an appendix on chimerical saints in Voetius, *Disputationum Theologicarum*, 3:472–539.

Hubert, patron saints against the plague.[102] For the superstitious and idolatrous burning of candles, which they carried in their hands during five days and everyone was listening to Masses in order to shun this mortality, see the constitution of Clement VI, which missal was previously published in Paris in 1506, p. 222. Also add the feast of the purification of Mary, or in Greek called the *Sypapante*, that was instituted in the year 544 AD.

1667 Addendum to Chapter V: Near the end, where it is about Mary, who is counted by the papists among the patron saints of the plague, add: From Ferry de Locre, bk. 2, chs. 11 and 13, regarding Mary Augusta (referenced by Nicolas Vignier, part 2, *Theater of the Anti-Christ*, p. 1001),[103] when Antwerp was afflicted in 1603 they made a vow to Mary of Zichem or Aspricollenses (whose miracles and worship occurred in such grandiose ceremonious ways by Justus Lipsius, that I may use a Sedulian phrase, as George Thomson learnedly expressed) and it sent to her the gift of two silver candlesticks with this inscription: "Receive, holy parent, from an Antwerp vow, a gift / which it gives, and the harsh pestilence or plague does not grow." And at Brussels in the same year, for a similar cause, they sent as a gift a silver crown with this inscription, "To the queen of heaven, the most holy mother of God, the blessed virgin Mary, a suppliant Brussels offered it afflicted with a disease in the year 1603."

And we will pass by the exorcisms that Borromeus, the archbishop of Milan, opposed to the plague in 1630, and which Marchini refers to and praises in his appendix of philosophical problems, p. 47.[104] This train of evidence closes out the papistico-magical stamp of their writers or the seal of their engravers, because although publicly approved and even employed by clerics in Italy in 1630, Marchini at least rightly refutes magic (Marchini, ibidem, prob. 33).[105] On the invocation of the seven angels who serve before God (cf. my disputation on the heavenly hierarchy)[106] and swearing by their names, whether and in what way this should be customarily done,

---

102. Anonymous, *Het Leven van den H. Rochus, S. Ioseps, ende den H. Hubertus patroonen teghen de peste* (Antwerp, 1645).

103. Ferry de Locre, (Ferreolus Locrius, 1571-1614), *Maria Augusta Virgo Deipara in septem libros tributa* (Aras: R. Maudhuy, 1608), 110-16, 118-21; Nicolas Vignier, *Theatre de L'Antechrist, auquel est respondu au Cardinal Bellarmin, au Sieur de Remond, a Pererius, Ribera, Viegas, Sanderus et autres qui par leurs escrits condamnent la doctrine des Eglises Reformes sur ce subjet* (Geneva: Philippe Albert, 1613), 1001. Vignier refers to Locrius as Friol de Locres.

104. Marchini, *Philosophica de Pestilentia Problemata*, 47.

105. Ibid., 44–45.

106. Voetius, "disp. 46: De hierarchia Coelesti et Angelis Tutelaribus" in *Selectarum Disputationum Theologicarum* (Utrecht: Johannes à Waesberg), 1:882–905.

elsewhere we will perhaps recount our inquiry on carnal remedies to which people customarily flee when distressed by a carnal effect of fear without any prudence, godliness, or love; to which we referred first as an excessively fearful and sinful reason for shunning the plague, which was written down publicly elsewhere, which we uncovered above, and Lavater handles, as do other theologians and doctors; and then there is the exceedingly base and disorderly flight of the plague-fleers, of which not only theologians disapprove, but also outstanding doctors, and which we are now about to discuss.

Chapter VI: The principal question, how the plague must be avoided

Therefore, the principal controversy is whether and how the plague, that is, the one that has infected cities, houses, and people with plague, ought to be fled. Here: 1) we will detect and remove the false charges and subterfuge with which the state of the controversy is customarily involved; 2) we will establish the genuine state of the controversy; 3) we will confirm our view with reasons; 4) we will draw out the principal consequence, and then other ones from there; 5) we will respond to objections.

To the first point, the state of the controversy is not, nor is it disputed by our adversaries whether the plague is bad, whether it is a dangerous disease, whether it brings the most present destruction to the majority, whether the danger ought to be fled; but whether by leaving without necessity one is tempting God, whether in the nature of things something may be contagious, and whether there may be contagious diseases, and whether the plague is one of them. Certainly, since regarding these things many of those fleeing the plague are inflating [its severity] so that they may cover the shamefulness of their cause and lull their conscience to sleep. Who does not see that they instantly prevaricate and engage in sophistry through their ignorance of logical method? This, however, is the genuine state of the controversy: whether the remedy of flight according to the creed of physicians—"Flee quickly, go far, and return slowly" (which Lavater, and his Latin translator Johannes Pontisella, call a meager Christian one)—ought to be applied by all, since of course there is no help more available or certain.[107] In agreement with theologians and Christian doctors, as in

---

107. See Pontisella's dedicatory letter in Ludwig Lavater, *De Pestilentia Concio*, trans. J. Pontisella (Zurich: Froschower, 1586), fol. 3r.

my opinion, we deny that certain doctors affirm this dictum so absolutely without respect to God, Christian conscience, and moral virtues. We also add that all believers are obligated to discharge their duty in spiritual and physical matters, first to their own households, and next to their brethren, friends, relatives, and any other neighbor, as their vocation, ability, and circumstances allow.

Let us now prove the prior part of our assertion in this way. First, since none of these kinds of human actions can be absolutely prescribed by a medical doctor as a medical doctor, the circumstances of the actions must be weighed and then it must be concluded whether or not these actions are permissible. Now since actions are subject to right reason and the divine law, there are no actions in the individual that are purely natural and adiaphora, hence it happens that human beings cannot here follow the leading of nature, as livestock do, avoiding evils and pursuing goods. Now surely one must not seek what is morally good or evil, or belongs to virtue or vice, from medical doctors inasmuch as they are medical doctors; for they simply and merely point out the connection and consequences of natural causes together with their effects. But one must seek these elsewhere. For example, a doctor may indicate that there is somewhere some secret and rare antidote—perhaps some food or drink—which leads to this or that effect. But this fact in itself does not give license to anyone to procure it irrespective of its owner's consent.[108] Considering certain diseases, one might say sex (Ambrose, *Ep.* 66, Lodovico Settala's *Problemata*, sec. 4, q. 17) or even a large draught of an inebriating potion can take away some of its ill; yet on that fact alone a Christian does not conclude that illicit sex or drunkenness in that case are not sins.[109] Second, such flight is not without some unbelief and distrust against God's promises (Isa. 65; Matt. 10; especially Ps. 91), which were all accomplished for believers. Third, not only does this advance a heartless and dishonest flight, however much they persuade themselves of fleeing like Jonah; yet, although they shun a contagion through contact and through a fomite, as much as it depends upon natural causes, by that very action they still do not avoid the same contagion and infection insofar as it depends upon the smiting angel, whether good or bad, and insofar as it depends upon that peculiar one and by the inexplicable choice and application to people, because we have acknowledged God

---

108. *sive volente sive nolente domino* : lit. "with the owner willing or not."
109. Ludovico Settala (1552–1633), *In Aristotelis Problemata Commentaria*, 3 vols. (Lyon: Claude Landry, 1632), 1:272–274.

above, in thesis one, in the things to be marveled at in the plague. Even Sennert himself in the passage cited conceded that the plague is sometimes inflicted immediately by God without the ordinary concursus of secondary causes. A crowd of other doctors state that it is even contagious across distances—I would like someone to explain to me what good flight would do in either case. Fourth, from equivalents, because in every other danger—in dangerous diseases, indeed even in contagious ones—piety, love, and custom teach people not to desert their neighbor so, and not to counsel flight only for themselves. Moreover, these are those types of dangerous diseases: hydrophobia, elephantiasis, leprosy, tuberculosis,[110] dysentery, English sweating sickness,[111] measles,[112] smallpox,[113] rotten fever[114] (which elsewhere in Belgium is called either camp disease or Mansveldian disease,[115] from the army of Count Mansveld in the year 1625), Spanish Plague,[116] conjunctivitis,[117] scabies, peptic ulcers,[118] and so forth. Fifth, because of such crude prophylactic measures for the plague, there are neither rules nor examples in the Old or New Testament that persuade us even by the least consequence. It is certainly amazing that Moses, Aaron, Joshua, David, and other leading men in the Church and State, when there was a plague prowling among them, did not turn back in this way, so that at least they taught us by their own example, namely, not to tempt God. Sixthly, we add an argument *ad hominem*, because those fugitives themselves, who first flee everything and shout about the things that must be fled—even with mercilessness towards their very own flesh, their children, relatives, friends, and companions of the same faith, and so forth—now here they are: when the plague has invaded them and their dwellings, or the hand of God has dragged them back from flight, they speak otherwise and not only do not disapprove of love in visiting, comforting, bringing help, and so forth but also extol it to heaven. Seventh, finally, there comes the consensus

---

110. Gk. $\phi\theta\iota\sigma\iota\varsigma$: lit. "consumption"

111. Lat. *Sudor Anglicus*: English sweating sickness was a disease of unknown etiology and epidemiology active between approximately 1485–1551 but was highly contagious and rapidly deadly. G. Thwaites et al., "The English Sweating Sickness, 1485–1551" in *The New England Journal of Medicine* (1997), 336:580–582.

112. Lat. *morbillus*

113. Lat. *variolus*

114. Lat. *Synochus Putrida*

115. Lat. *Morbum castrensem, Mansveldicum*

116. Lat. *lues Hispanica*

117. Gk. $\dot{o}\phi\theta\alpha\lambda\mu\iota\alpha$

118. Lat. *mala ulcera*

not only of the theologians cited below, but also of Christian medical doctors, who are acquainted with giving counsel to Christians. A preeminent example is Gulielmo Grataroli of Bergamo, France—who was converted to our religion and is jealous for it, on account of which he settled his residence in Basil when he left Italy behind—who in his book on the plague, page 884, says: "Those adverbs—*cito, longe, tarde*—are the most useful. Because those who cannot do it either are not willing to be affected by Christian charity, or they are especially concerned to dwell in a ventilated place."[119] And Jean-Antoine Sarazin in ch. 6, p. 156, "But this caution must be applied, lest a total fortress in flight should be established, as if safety in its entirety were to depend upon it. For how is it that mortals hope to evade the finger of a wrathful God by their own subterfuge; and can they escape his sight? But indeed who would even dare to think this, unless he is thoroughly unacquainted with divine immensity?"[120] And with several other points regarding God's immensity he connects the passage Psalm 139:8–9, from which he concludes that "One must not take comfort from the corner of a cave, but from peace with the eternal God. . . the only ward of evil[121] who was, is, and will always be. But it should seem neither poorly considered nor useless if people of a weaker nature, and who are nearly weighed [in the balance] by fear. . ." And note this well:

> . . . and with thanksgiving, that refuge and fortress, will be taken away [i.e. die] when God grants. . . But in taking heed to this danger, again, they must apply this caution, lest while they consult for themselves they allow those present with them and whom they must hold dear to be deserted, as if forgetful of their calling which is certain by reason of their public office, whether Magistrates, Pastors of the Church, physicians and surgeons who earn public funds, and as many others as are bound by their office to bring help to the sick. But by reason of one's relationships it seems just to remain for spouses, relatives, and neighbors.[122]

---

119. *Libr. De peste p. 88.4*: Voetius cited this edition: Gulielmo Grataroli, "Pestis Descriptio, causae, signa omnigena, et praeservatio" in *Opus non minus Luculentum quam iucundum lectu* (Cologne: Petrus Horst, 1571), 884; the first edition of this tract is: idem, *Pestis Descriptio, Causae, Signa Omnigena et Praeservatio* (Paris: Federicus Morellus, 1561), 17.
120. Sarazin, *De Peste Commentarius* (1572), 156.
121. Gk. ἀλεξίκακος
122. Ibid., 156–157.

Problem 1: Whether those traveling or sojourning for a time somewhere, who by no part of their calling or any other necessity are at all bound to one place more than another: is it permissible for them to depart? Response: I affirm, yet only without an astonished distrust and chaotic flight; indeed without any scandal, and only if extreme necessity (with other deficiencies) does not compel them to take up the office of the Samaritan (Luke 10, Isa. 58:7).

Problem 2: Whether it is licit for infants, children, and a similarly weak crowd, who are not employed for anything, but are a burden, to leave somewhere for a time? Response: I affirm that also in other diseases, dangers, and impending or calamitous circumstances.

Problem 3: Whether heads of households,[123] who have fixed residences somewhere, who sustain their family by the honest labor of their hands, and who enjoy their privileges and comforts as much political as ecclesiastical: is it licit for them to desert their city with their family for a time? Response: I at least am not willing to be the source for that. Although I would consult certain ones of the theologians who do not generally approve of this, I do not argue against this strongly, nor do I oblige anything.

The latter part of our assertion regarding offering help to the sick, I prove in this way: First, from the duties of love that we owe to brothers and neighbors: "you shall love your neighbor as yourself" (Matt. 22; 7:12; Heb. 13:1, 13, 16), even to our own loss and risk (1 Cor. 13:5, 7; 1 John 3:16–17). However, among those duties, help must be rendered to the sick and dying. Second, from the peculiar bond between spouses, siblings, relatives, friends, and so forth whereby they are mutually bound to duties to each other in these and other cases (1 Tim. 5:4, 8; Rom. 1:31; Eph. 5–6). Third, from the special command regarding rendering works of mercy to those in calamities and sickness (Ps. 41:1–3; Matt. 25:36, 43). Moreover, there is not any exception here or elsewhere regarding contagious and dangerous diseases. Where there is greater danger, there fraternal love binds us closer; there it also extends itself in a more illustrious way (1 John 3:16). With this command must be joined the example of Jesus Christ, which the apostle brings to bear there. Fourth, from the great prize and promise made by God to mercies of this sort (Ps. 41:1–4; Matt. 5:7, 25, 36, 43; Jas. 2:13). Among those promises is also the protection of God against the terror of the night, and the arrows flying at midday (Ps. 91). Fifth, Christian

---

123. Lat. *patresfamilias*

bravery also persuades the Christian soldier to offer himself bravely, when the occasion is presented, to dangers of this sort, to despise death, and to rest in God's providence, and that from a sincere love of God and neighbor (Acts 20:24; 21:13–14; Phil. 2:3). Regarding the contempt of death and faith in God's providence, these have been treated previously. Sixth, it approaches the consensus and practice of the godly. There is much from many sources: Cyprian, *On Mortality*; there is the illustrious example of the Christian Church about which Eusebius writes in bk. 9, ch. 7 and bk. 7, ch. 17; Nicephorus in bk. 6, ch. 20, where we see the Epistle of Dionysius, the bishop of Alexandria, and the paraphrased interpretation of the same by Rufinus;[124] and especially the erudite sermon of Lavater, published in turn in German, Latin, and Dutch, which also inserted his comments on Ezekiel 14, and his comments on 1 Chronicles 21.[125] The meditation of Ps. 91 in Trelcat the Younger's *Antidote*, page 535.[126] William Ames, *Cases of Conscience*, bk. 5, ch. 7, q. 5 has many things about loving one's neighbor, which can be most apt for this business.[127] Sohn's *On the Causes and Cure of Plague*, tome 1; Perkins on the 6th commandment of the Decalogue; Calvin in his letters page 454, from the edition in folio; Beza in the *Diatribe* on the plague that has been published. Ursinus in his *Theological Exercises*, part 2.[128]

---

124. Eusebius, *Ecclesiastical History* in NPNF2 1:360–361; Nicephorus, *Ecclesiasticae Historiae* in PG 145:1167–1170; Rufinus of Aquileia, *The History of the Church*, trans. P. R. Amidon, (Washington D.C.: Catholic University of America Press, 2016).

125. Cf. n2 supra and the sermon referenced as inserted, in Ludwig Lavater, "Homilia XVIII De Pestilentia" in *Propheta Ezechiel . . . homilis seu commentariis expositus* (Geneva: Jean Crespin, 1571), fols. 26v–33r; for two sermons on plague in German paired with Cyprian's *De Mortalitate*, see Ludwig Lavater, *Von der Pestilenz zwo predginen die ein vom ursprung der Pestilenz wohar die sye item warumb sy regiere unnd wie man sich darinen halsten sölle* (Zurich: Christoffel Froschower, 1564); in Latin, idem, *De Pestilentia Concio . . . ex Germanica Lingua in Latinam*, trans. J. Pontisella (Zurich: Officina Froshower, 1586). See also a sermon on Ezekiel 14 which briefly mentions courage in time of plague and in other trials, idem, 138–139. There is a brief excursus entitled *De Peste* (On Plague) after his comments on 1 Chron. 21:14–15 in Ludwig Lavater, *In Libros Paralipomenon sive Chronicorum Commentarius* (Zurich: Christophorus Froschouerus), fol. 78r–79r. However, there are additional questions on the plague posed and answered in his comments on 1 Chr. 9–15, fols. 76v–80r. For Lavater's comments on 1 Chr. 21:9–17, see page 214 in this book

126. Lucas Trelcatius, Jr., *Opuscula Theologica Omnia*, 512, 537–540.

127. See bk. 5, ch. 7, §§11–15, William Ames, *De Conscientia, et ejus Jure, vel Casibus, libri quinque* (Amsterdam: Joannes Janssonius, 1631), 277–278; idem, *Conscience with the Power and Cases Thereof* ([London], 1639), 130–131; idem, *Vyf Boecken vande Conscientie en haar Regt of Gevallen*, trans. C. V. Wallendal (Amsterdam: Jan Pieterse Kuypen, 1660), 507–508; idem, *Von dem Recht dess Gewissens und desselben begebenden Fallen in V Büchern verfasset* (Nuremberg: Wolfgang dess Jüng & Johan Andreas Endter, 1654), 571–573.

128. Georg Sohn (c. 1552–1589), "XV. De Causis et Curatione Pestis", *Theses de Plerisque Locis Theologicis* (Siegen: Christophor Corvinus, 1598), 150–153 in *Opera*, 2nd ed. (Nassau-Siegen:

1667 Addendum to Chapter VI: Near the end where Ursinus's *Exercises* is cited, add Pareus's *Exercises*, bk. 2 exercise 49; Alsted in his *Cases of Conscience*, ch. 43; especially Szegedi, in his *Common Places*, "on Death," table 2, where he rigidly disputes against flight.[129]

In the summary of the matter, they agree with us, although they grant flight to free men. Let not anyone allege that those doctors did so from unfaithfulness and lack of humanity[130] (whereby one withdraws himself even from the closest bonds of blood and affinity). The papist casuists and practical theologians feel the same way and exhort to Christian bravery so that they may boast of their own merits on this score and of their daily trophies as excessively brave. You may gather these from the book of Filiberto Marchini, *On the Plague*, and the Jesuit Raynaud on *Martyrdom through Plague*, and in a vernacular book of the Jesuit de Pretere. It must be added, and at this point analogically applied, that whatever the moralists and practical theologians comment on mercy, fortitude, and love of neighbor, Christian doctors do not dissent, as we have indicated previously, whose counsels persuade flight, shunning those infected with the plague with this limitation: "as much as Christian mercy or sympathy permits," which parenthesis was piously and prudently placed at the beginning of the *Antidote* in the year 1636 by the most renowned Utrecht medical doctor.

Chapter VII: A secondary question, a Response to Zanchi & Joseph Hall

From the principal question decided, we deduce this corollary: if certainly no believers can absolutely withdraw themselves from suffering brethren,

---

Christopher Corvinus, 1598), vol. 1, pt. 6. NB: The pagination in this volume resets multiple times. *Theses de Plerisque Locis Theologicis* comprises one pagination that includes parts 5 and 6 in *Opera* vol. 1; William Perkins, *The Workes of that famous and worthy minister of Christ in the universitie of Cambridge Mr. William Perkins*, 3 vols. (London: John Legatt, 1626), 1:58; Ep. 247 in John Calvin, *Epistolae et Responsa*, 3rd ed. (Hanover: Guilielmus Antonius, 1597), 454–455; cf. Ep. 4187 in CO 20:456–457; Theodore Beza, *A Treatise on the Plague*, see page 6 in this volume; Zacharias Ursinus, *Scholasticae in materiis theologicis Exercitationes*, 2 vols. (Neustadt: Matthew Harnisch, 1590), 2:513–514..

129. David Pareus, *Exercitationes*, 255–261. Johann Heinrich Alsted (1588-1638), *Summa Casuum Conscientiae Nova Methodo Elaborata* (Frankfurt: Paulus Jacobus, 1628), 179–182. Let the reader take note that this is not the same work as Alsted's *Theologia Casuum exhibens Anatomen Conscientiae et Scholam tentationum* (Hanover: Conrad Eifridus, 1630). István Szegedi Kis (Stephanus Zegedinus, 1505-1572), *Theologiae Sincerae Loci Communes de Deo et Homine* (Basil: Officina Pernea, 1585), 252-254.

130. Gk. ἀστοργία

then likewise pastors of churches are not free from this support and work of love. The corollary must be held against the dangerous disputation of Zanchi on Philippians 2, which seems to smack excessively of the Italo-medical custom; and also against Joseph Hall in his *Epistles*, decade 4, epistle 9, who discusses the conscience of ministers too much according to the custom or law received in England at that time.[131] The reasons are: First, because the reasons brought forward previously for the duty of all believers towards those struggling with the plague constrain pastors more strongly, at least in what pertains to spiritual care. The second is taken from their office and titles; they are pastors, spiritual fathers, guardians and overseers, dispensers, and so forth who must feed with word, example, and assistance (as Gregory the Great rightly states in his *Pastoral Rule*), not only publicly but also privately and in homes (Acts 20:20), and at least in season and out of season (2 Tim. 4:2), especially in the case of necessity. Third, because the Church must not dwell in their hearts in a meager way and they must, by Paul's example, want to live and die for the sheep (2 Cor. 7:3), and by Christ's example, lay down their own life for the life of the sheep (John 10:11–12, 15; 1 John 3:16). Fourth, because not only out of love for the rest of Christians but also out of justice they cannot be immune or plainly withdraw themselves, and that on account of public funds also. Fifth, because there are also other contagious and dangerous diseases as noted above in chapter six, but no one will say that ministers must not, or at least cannot, abstain totally from visiting those sick, nor take to flight in those 160 cases, therefore much less in the case of plague. Sixth, because all ecclesiastical decisions—with whom the authors who write about church polity and the duty of pastors must be compared, namely, the Helvetic confession article 17, and the decisions of the Dutch Church—impose on them the comfort of the sick. Moreover, there are no decisions among us, nor even synodical decisions, which in the case of this disease interdict their duty. But on the contrary, the 1574 Synod of Dordrecht for a particular question teaches the contrary practice for nearly all pastors.[132]

---

131. Girolamo Zanchi, *In D. Pauli Apostoli Epistolas ad Philippenses, Colossenses, Thessalonicenses Commentarii* (Neustadt: Matthaeus Harnisius, 1595), 156–163 see page 234 in this volume; Joseph Hall (1574–1656), Dec. 4, Ep. 9, "To Mr. E. A.: Ep. IX, A Discourse of fleeing or staying in the time of pestilence, whether lawfull for minister or people" in *Epistles containing Two Decades*, 3 vols. (London: E. Edgar, 1608–1611), 2:197–203

132. See *punten* 33–36, *Acta* (1574) in F. L. Rutgers (ed.), *Acta van de Nederlandsche Synoden der Zestiende Eeuw* (Utrecht: Kemink & Zoon, 1889), Series 2, 3:202–203, where there are directions regarding the visitation of the sick, the role of ministers in the visitation of *Pesthuysen*, and the burial of the dead with a limitation on the number of attendants at the graveside.

And so especially does the practice of the Church of Geneva, where they commit the duty by lot to some of the ministers, which Beza references in his treatise on the plague; and it is most plainly evident that Calvin and the rest of the Genevan theologians felt that this is included in the pastoral office. The words of Francesco Porto of Crete intimate their perpetual practice. In his *Response to the Letter of Pierre Charpentier* (Charpentier was a certain professor of law at that time there, and then later an apostate and traitor), Porto stated, "I know that you, when not even one from the college left his office on account of the plague, set the worst example—it pleased you to run away, leaving your post deserted."[133] Scultetus, in his *Sermons* on Isaiah, chapter 38, page 496, not only concludes the matter most clearly regarding ministers but also regarding others in the case of necessity.[134] In nearly the same way Georg Sohn determines the matter in his *Theses*, page 195.[135] George Abbot agrees with them in his *Questions* or lecture 5, page 195, Oxford edition, 1598, except on what is more binding due to necessity in, I think, the English custom.[136] The Lutheran theologians do not differ here from us, such as Johannes Gerhard, *Theological Common Places*, tome 6; Tarnow, *On the Minister*, book 3; Balduinus in *Cases of Conscience*, book 4, chapter 9, case 6; and expressly Wigand in his treatise *On Persecution*, page 270, and from the most recent work of Melchior Sylvester Eckhard in *On the Conscientious Pastor*, class 2, section 5, question 3.[137] An example of them all is the manly counsel of Luther, tome 3, Jena edition, as well as in Philip Hahn, *Counsels* or

---

133. Francesco Porto of Crete (1511–1581), chair of Greek at the Academy of Geneva from 1562–1581. Pierre Charpentier was a jurist at Toulouse, Geneva, Strassburg, and Paris. Cf. Francesco Porto, *Ad Petri Carpentarii Causidici virulentam epistolam, responsio Francisci Porti Cretensis, pro Causariorum quos vocat, innocentia* (Geneva, 1573), 5.

134. Scultetus, *Idea Concionum in Jesaiam prophetam ad populum Haidelbergensem habitarum* (Geneva: Pierre Aubert, 1618), 496.

135. Sohn, *Theses* (1598), 150–153 in *Opera*, vol. 1, pt. 6

136. George Abbot, *Quaestiones sex totidem praelectionibus in schola theologica Oxoniae* (Oxford: Joseph Barnes, 1598), 195; cf. idem, *Explicatio sex illustrium Quaestionum* (Frankfurt: Rosa, 1616), 149–151, see page 274 in this volume.

137. Johann Gerhard (1582–1637), *Locorum Theologicorum*, 9 vols. (Frankfurt/Hamburg: Zachariah Hertelius, 1657), 6:170–171; Paul Tarnow (1562–1663), bk. 3, ch. 2, *De Sacrosancto Ministerio, libri tres* (Rostock: Hallevordius, 1624), 1299–1309; Friedrich Balduin (1575–1627), *Tractatus Luculentus, Posthumus, Toti Reipublicae Christianae Utilissimus de Materia rarissime antehac enucleata, Casibus nimirum Conscientiae* (Wittenberg: Helwigius, 1628), 1098–1100; Johann Wigand (1523–1587), *De Persecutione Piorum* (Frankfurt: Werdestein, 1553), 127; Melchior Sylvester Eckhard (1600–1650), *Pastor conscientiousus, hoc est: Variae quaestiones, de casibus & rebus dubiis, ministri personam propius tangentibus* (Ulm: Balthasar Kuhnen, 1651), 217–219.

Theological Judgments and Requirements of a Minister, published in German in the year 1650, treatise 7, page 45.[138]

The papists impose this with all those caretakers of souls. After all that Marchini amasses in part 1, chapters 2–3, with part 3, chapters 1–2 he treats this case with the reasons adduced from the pastoral office (John 10; Ezekiel 24), from the law of love and righteousness (Thomas IIaIIae, q. 26, art. 5, and q, 185, art. 5; *Quodlibetal* 12, q. 18 art. 3), and countless authorities from the canonists, casuists, and so forth.[139] To these he adds examples of Carolus Borromaeus, bishop of Milan in the year 1576, and of other regulars, whose orders and names he mentions in part 10.[140] Moreover, he inserts the famous letter 180 of Augustine to Honoratus on the flight of pastors in the time of the calamity of war.[141] Busaeus in *Garden of Christian Virtues*, in the chapter on Fortitude, praises, besides the example of Borromeus, the example of Bernardinus Senensis, and of the new order established in Rome for ministry to the sick.[142] The Jesuit Raynaud in his treatise on *Martyrdom through Plague*, part 3, chapter 3, commends the Alexandrian presbyters and deacons, of whom he mentions *Roman Martyrology* for February.[143] Afterwards he references Cyprian, Gregory the Great, Benedict, Aspertus, Bernardinus, his own Jesuits in the year 1558, and so forth.[144] Jan Vermeulen grants this in his *Theologia practica*, and Marchinus himself, with many other casuists, grants that the bishop or parochial can sometimes care for his sheep mediately through a substitute.[145] But this does nothing for our ministers, where there are no lazy and beneficed bishops with the power to substitute, nor do they have place for dispensations of non-residence. Gabriel Biel in his sermons

---

138. See Philip Hahn (Philippus Haenen, 1558–1616), *Consilia sive Iudicia Theologica et Requisita Ministerii totius Ecclesiae, New verbessert und vollständig Kirchen Buch*, 3 vols. (Braunschweig: Andreas Duncker, 1647) 3:45; cf. idem, *Consilia* (Braunswchweig, A. Duncker, 1647), 3:47. Hahn cites Martin Luther, *Ob man fur dem sterben flieben muge* (Wittenberg: 1527), fol. Aiii recto; cf. Luther, *Luther's Works* (1999) 43:122, see page 194 in this volume.

139. Marchini, *Belli Divini*, 3–14, 58–64; The summary Voetius provided here of John 10 and Ezekiel 24 and the citations of Thomas are in pt. 1, ch. 2, Marchini, *Belli Divini*, 7

140. Marchini, *Belli Divini*, 241–267.

141. Marchini, *Belli Divini*, 10–14.

142. Joannes Busaeus S.J., *Viridarium Christianarum Virtutum ex Sacrosanctae Scripturae* (Mainz: Joannes Albinus, 1610), 285–301.

143. Théophile Raynaud, *De Martyrio per Pestem* (Lyon: Iacobus Cardon, 1630), 411–14. cf. Baronio, *Martyrologium Romanum* (1603), 148.

144. See Raynaud's detailed exposition of these figures in chapter 4, ibid., 423–463.

145. Jan Vermeulen (Molanus, 1533–1585), *Theologiae Practicae Compendium* (Cologne: Birckman, 1590).

on time, in the three medicinal sermons against pestilence, subjoins the question about flight in plague, where he certainly proffers eruditely, and seems to determine enough in this part, except that in the custom of the papal casuists he totters back and forth between a blessed exception and restriction.[146]

1667 Addendum to Chapter VII: Where the papist authors are cited that prohibit flight for those who care for souls, add to these Becanus, part 2, *Theologia Scholastica*, tome 1, tract 3, ch. 6, q. 4.[147]

A consequence: (1) That it is licit, and exceedingly praiseworthy even, with certain danger of death to take care of friends suffering with the plague, Marchini rightly proves from reasons and authorities of Cyprian, *On Mortality*; Augustine, *On Friendship*, ch. 10; Jerome on Micah 7; Lactantius, *Divine Institutes*, bk. 5, ch. 18; Ambrose, bk. 3 on duty, ch. 12. (2) Nevertheless, likewise it seems exceedingly incongruous, as he concludes, that those afflicted with the plague, or those especially suspected of it, must be punished as homicidal and traitors to the country if they should not warn the healthy and live openly with them (part. 2, ch. 6). (3) If indeed pastors of the churches cannot withdraw themselves from visitations of the sick, much less is flight licit for them, or importunate desertion of the ministry.[148]

Chapter VIII: Twelve Objections Answered

From this pious opinion some in the papacy, both in the past and today, retreat, not so much out of judgment as from the emotion of fear, and from there turn to a vicious practice, from which two perverse principles produce at last their opinion. Tostado on Genesis 14, column 7, to a great degree appears to favor this opinion, whose decision afterwards, Marchini limits in part 2, ch. 6.[149] Nicolaus de Clemanges, a celebrated theologian in his own time, urged flight without any limitation, see epistle 27, where

---

146. Gabriel Biel, *Sermones Dominicales... hyemales estivales de tempore... Sermones Medicinales [con]tra Pestem Epidimie*, 2nd ed. (Hannau: Henricus Gran, 1510), fols. 150v–152v, esp. 152v. Note well that there are multiple editions and printings of the *Sermones Dominicales* that do not always include the "medicinal sermons."
147. Martinus Becanus S.J. (1563-1624), *Theologiae Scholasticae Pars Secunda... tomus prior* (Mainz: Joannes Albinus, 1619), 267-70.
148. Marchini, *Belli Divini*, 53–55.
149. Alonso Tostado, at marginalia "An et quomodo pestis fugienda est" in *Commentaria in Genesim: Mendis nunc sanè quam plurimis diligenter expurgate* (Venice: Sessa, 1596), 479-85; idem, *Opera Omnia*, 1:530; cf. Marchini, *Belli Divini*, 53–55

from our [country] Johannes Lydius, the editor of Clemange, in the margin sensibly wrote this censure, "not a theological counsel in the least."[150] Marchini in chapter 12 marvels that certain most learned men, and not a few, withdrew by their own counsel and persuasion from godly works, and asks why, unless they were threatened with terrible infernal punishments.[151] Among the Reformed there are not lacking among the wealthier and rather powerful persons especially, but also the simpler rustics, who certainly did not fulfill this duty in that way; but of those who rave in such a way that people ought to turn back from those heroic works when the infernal punishment was proposed, I know of none. But let us hear the reasons of both of these persons and of any others.

Objection 1: No one must cast himself into that danger, therefore [it is licit to flee the plague]. I respond: First, it is conceded that [one should not do so] without necessity and not rashly. Second, absolutely, so that no one would cast themselves [into it], but they would not say [the same for] those who call the medical doctors, surgeons, servants and maidservants, pastors, priests, and comforters for help. Because if they offer that service contrary to the salvation of the soul and the commandment of God, these cannot in good conscience ask this from them. Third, if this argument were to have place, then no one would vow themselves to the army, no citizen would take up arms for hearth and home, no one would fight a fire, and no one would help shipwrecked sailors, and finally no martyr would be burned alive. God forbid! God forbid! That golden opinion of Thomas Bilney, a martyr in England in Marian times, must be applied to this pestilential fire, "O I feel by experience," he says, "and have known it long by philosophy that fire by God's ordinance is naturally hot, but yet I am persuaded by God's holy word, and by the experience of some spoken of in the same, that in the flame they felt no heat, and in the fire they felt no consumption. I constantly believe, however that the stubble of this my body shall be walked by it, yet my soul and spirit shall be purged thereby, a pain for the time, whereon notwithstanding follows joy unspeakable."[152]

Objection 2: Order must be preserved in love so that I would prefer

---

150. Lat. *Consilium minime theologicum*: See Nicolaus de Clemanges, Ep. 27 "On a certain general pestilence and its causes according to the doctors as much as to the divine Scriptures", *Opera Omnia* (Leiden: Johannes Balduinus, 1613), 99.

151. Marchini, *Belli Divini*, pt. 1, ch. 12, 37

152. Voetius's Latin citation corrected from the English of John Foxe, *The Ecclesiastical Historie, containing the Acts and Monument of Martyrs*, 3 vols. (London: 1641), 2:277. Cf. idem, *Fox's Book of Martyrs: The Acts and Monuments of the Church*, 3 vols. (London: George Virtue, 1851), 2:309.

my bodily safety to the life of my neighbor. For I am not obligated to love him more than myself. Response with Marchini: First, the order of love demands that no one rashly, and without the urgent and just necessity of a friend, expose one's life. Second, a friend is not to be loved more than ourselves, but an honest man is to be loved more for his virtue. Just as when someone exposes his life to danger for the sake of saving his country or keeping his faith.

Objection 3: A person is not the lord of his life; therefore he must flee all those struggling with the plague. I respond: God is the Lord of life; one freely spends it for God from a just and urgent cause on account of an upright and praiseworthy goal. But otherwise they also are martyrs, either citizens who guard the walls against a hostile invasion or those who run to being burned, and so forth.

Objection 4: If in persecution it is licit to flee from city to city, therefore also in time of plague. I respond: It is not always licit nor for everyone, but that case is decided elsewhere. Next, not every kind of flight and at every time is objectionable to us. At least, theologians generally determine that ministers of the Word must not flee in persecution and must not desert the sheep. See, among others, George Abbot, who eruditely and clearly handles this in his *Six Questions* or lectures, question 5.[153]

Objection 5: A house, which is being devastated with fire, we leave behind; what then of a house infected with plague? I respond: we concede that also in other diseases. If in fact the house were not spacious and did not afford enough room (I have learned how such is offered in Italy by the prefects of health from Marchini in the place cited) certainly this convenience must not be condemned.

Objection 6: Those who visit others infected with the plague in some way commit suicide,[154] for it is just as if they leaped into the fire. I respond: First, those who with an obligatory goal and way bravely offer themselves to some danger for the honor of God and the wellbeing of our neighbor do not belong to this subject, no more so than the martyrs, citizens and soldiers defending the fatherland, doctors, surgeons, and others who care for the soul or body of the sick. Second, there is a different method for fire and contagion of plague. Fire always burns promiscuously those whom it touches, without any choice of persons or suspension of its action; but the

---

153. George Abbot, *Explicatio Sex illustrium Quaestionum* (Frankfurt: Jonas Rosa, 1616), 129–151. See page 274 in this volume.

154. Lat., Gk. *rei, αὐτοφωνίας*

plague does not act in the same way, as experience teaches. In what suicide properly consists, we teach in the disputation on the same topic.[155]

Objection 7: Leprosy absolutely had to be fled in the Old Testament, therefore also in the New Testament. I respond: The one feverish with this argument deserves no response in theological schools. The one who touched a cadaver, one who has had their period, and so forth contracted ceremonial uncleanness. But what is this to the contagion of the plague?

Objection 8: I am immediately absolved from every duty of those succoring the sick, provided that I would not fail in prayers before God, and I would not be lacking both in counsels and in gifts through others to them. Response: If children should say this to their parents, husbands to their wives, and brothers to their brothers, and vice versa, it seems to me I hear that ancient *corban* of the Pharisees (Matt. 15:5).

Objection 9: The one who fears can flee with good conscience and withdraw from all those even necessary duties of love, even towards parents, wife, children and so forth. I respond: First, the vehemence of the affections in a person does not absolve from sin, as not only theologians teach, but even Aristotle and his moral philosophers. Second, this at least is inferred from this: one must flee an inordinate fear and repent. By no means is that one bound to repent and emend himself any other way who does not confess, instead of fear, the truth of faith, or does not join himself to the public assembly of the orthodox. For instance, a [further objecting] case is set forth that if anyone is so seized with fear that he would offer no duty to the sick—indeed he will burden the sick man, and in presenting himself to the sick man will bring to himself either destruction or danger of it—ought he not rather abstain and thus in his conscience be at rest? Response: With this hypothesis posed, that anyone prudent in counsel would abstain for a time, lest of course he would add sin upon sin; nevertheless in doing so neither is the damage taken away nor his sin—no more than when someone swollen with a burning wrath or contention towards their neighbor abstains for a time from meeting for dinner with them, or a son abstains as long as he is drunk from visiting with help and assistance his father who is on his deathbed. Therefore, how much more also must this defect be vigorously corrected.

Objection 10: God's plagues and ills that have been inflicted must be fled. Response: But for this reason, not all the afflicted must absolutely flee:

---

155. Voetius, *Selectarum Disputationum*, 4:244–92

when there are those who would lack our assistance. By no means must all paupers, the poorly clothed, the starving, and the sick be shunned.

Objection 11: One can spare the pastors of the Church, because so much depends upon their safety or the damage done to the Church, and this can be easily cared for through others. I respond: First, we are not disputing here whether and by what means the public good of the Church, the necessity of the sick, and the maintenance of the healthy could easily be provided for (especially when the shunning of contagion is quite vigorously circumscribed in certain laws). Nor also are we disputing whether the comforting of the impoverished sick is regarded as so great that it must be rendered immediately by the pastor or the entire ministry of the Word, because otherwise the ministry would suffer. But we are only handling this topic now, that we should teach that this duty of comforting must not be separated from the pastor's ordinary function, as if pastors are not bound to it *jure divino*, that is, by a divine right. Indeed, as if they would sin in their pastoral office if they would visit such sick people. Second, in all the churches, especially in smaller hamlets and villages, I do not see how one could spare the ministers unless we then want all those dying to be devoid of comfort. Third, nevertheless one must not treat of this with such thrift that we cause the hands of those who are well-intentioned to go slack, or that we break others who are endowed with only a mediocre courage, or finally so that we would not detract the least bit from those outstanding men who everywhere in the Netherlands have not deserted their office and do not want to spare themselves or their labor in this way (of whom not a few have died as vigilant watchmen and leaders standing in their station). Fourth, this duty must not be cared for through others in such a way that these become vicars or substitutes (whom the Reformed Church does not acknowledge), but only assistants who lighten part of the load, and finally so that the integral parts of the ministry are not alienated from ministers and fractured, and then transferred to others. Fifth, finally, whatever those assistants do, in more serious cases of conscience—especially if the wretchedly sick were to desire their counsel and comfort—in these instances pastors must not be plainly excluded from the performance of their office.

Objection 12: I have heard sometimes also this exception, that it is not obligatory nor is it even possible that one person can visit all those suffering; thus it is sufficient for someone to assist their household servants and their own family. I respond: Certainly, love begins at first with them, but God does not command that it precisely terminate there. In the giving of alms, the ability of one person does not extend to giving the same amount[156] to each and every person in comforting and assisting the suffering and infirm. But then by a bad inference one is led to the negative claim that in no way are we bound to visit anyone in such a case.

Chapter IX: Eight Questions and Cases

Let us respond now to some cases and questions. The first is whether comets could be rightly said to foretell the plague? Response: Not definitely, but indefinitely, for they do foretell some scourge and judgment of God, but that is either plague, war, famine, and so forth. Yet one must take heed that before an event, we would apply this prediction to certain people or certain cities. From the unusual occurrence of frogs, rats, and reptiles, plague is not otherwise presaged than through certain medical, rural, and nautical forebodings, as Vallés observes in *Sacred Philosophy*, ch. 30.[157] On the many kinds of portents, see the annotations of Cardano in his *On the Variety of Things*, bk. 15, ch. 78, and especially Marchini, prob. 20, and Girolamo Fracastoro, *On Contagion*, bk. 1, ch. 13.[158] But on how certain or uncertain these presages may be, we have spoken about in our disputation *On displays and prophetic signs*.[159]

Second: Must plague be attributed to evil angels as instruments of divine wrath? Response: I affirm from the arguments adduced in thesis one, and experience teaches this. Now if you believe Paul the Deacon in his *History*, book 3, chs. 5–6, regarding that plague in 680 A.D. under Pope Agatho (r. 678–681) that thoroughly ravaged Rome and Pavia, not a few demons were seen holding fiery swords and spears in their hands, who sometimes struck the doors of some houses with double-edged swords and spears and, as many as were so struck, on the next day in the same family there were those who died.[160] Gregory of Nyssa on the life of

---

156. Lat. *mutuo gratuito*
157. See ch. 30 on divination in Francisco Vallés (1524–1592), *Sacra Philosophia*, 6th ed. (Lyon: Jean-Antoine Huguetan & Marc-Antoine Ravaud, 1652), 147–171. Francisco Valles was a humanist and physician in Spain.
158. Cardano, *De Varietate Rerum* (1558), 713–718; Marchini, *Problema* (1633), 26–29; See bk. 1, ch. 13 "De Signis contagiosum" in Girolamo Fracastoro (Hieronymus Fracastorius, 1476–1553), *De Sympathia et Antipathia Rerum liber unus . . . De Contagione et Contagiosis Morbis et Curatione, libri III* (Venice, 1546), fols. 37v–38v.
159. Voetius, "De Signis Prima, de Naturae miraculis ostentis et prodigiis" in idem, *Selectarum Disputationum*, 2:902–922.
160. Instead see Paul the Deacon, *History of the Langobards*, 254–257.

Gregory the Wonderworker reports, "If a certain specter came to some dwellings, in which the calamity"—that is, the plague—"was threatening, certain destruction followed."[161] Procopius in book 2, *On the Persian War*, affirms that the plague ravaging in the year 544 AD under Justinian "had arisen from the appearance of demons in human visage, for as many as they met, these thought themselves stricken by some man, and the disease suddenly broke out upon them."[162] Pope Gregory the Great (although he is frequently credulous in his narrations) in book 4, chapter 36 of his *Dialogue* says that people upon whose heads were seen to appear flaming arrows, and who sensed no sickness, were laid low by those flying down.[163]

Third: Is the plague natural or supernatural? Response: both.

Fourth: Are they therefore miraculous? Response: no.

Fifth: Is the pestilence a milder plague than famine or the oppression of enemies? And why? Response: 1) I affirm from 2 Samuel 24. And I am amazed that Marchini denies this in his prologue, §1, as well as does Tostado on 2 Samuel 24, who thinks David did not choose the least but the greatest evil because it would be common to him and his subordinates.[164] 2) The reason is because a fury, a devastation, carrying away, and perturbation of the senses and affections are not so dominated in the plague, nor do we forget God and the internal and external divine worship, nor do we fall into so many sins, but on the contrary devotion and acts of piety especially thrive at that time. See for example the comments of Peter Martyr Vermigli on 2 Samuel 24, Lavater on 1 Chronicles 21, and David Pareus in his *Theological Exercises*, bk. 2, exercise 22.[165]

---

161. Gregory of Nyssa, *Life of Gregory the Wonderworker*.

162. Procopius, *On the Persian War*, 2.22-33 in LCL 48:451-73

163. Gregory I, *Dialogues*, trans. O. J. Zimmerman O.S.B., *The Fathers of the Church* series, vol. 39 (New York, 1959), 239; "This Stephen, as you recall, died three years ago of the horrible plague which devastated Rome. During that time arrows could be seen hurled down from the sky, carrying death to many individuals. A soldier at Rome was struck down in this way. He did not remain dead very long, however, for shortly after dying, he came back to life and told what happened to him."

164. Cf. Marchini, *Belli Divini*, fol. §§2v; Tostado, *Opera*, 13:281-82. Note well, Tostado's commentary on the four books of the kings enumerates 2 Samuel as 2 Kings; 2 Kings it lists as 4 Kings.

165. See Peter Martyr Vermigli (Petrus Martyrus Vermilius, 1499-1562) on 2 Sam. 24:10-17, *In Samuelis Prophetae Libros Duos . . . Commentarii* (Zurich: Christophorus Froschouerus, 1564), fols. 320r-322v; idem, (Zurich: Johannes Wolphius, 1595), fols. 316v-319r; Ludwig Lavater on 1 Chron. 21, *In Libros Paralipomenon*, fol. 78r-79r and see page 214 in this volume; David Pareus, "Exercitatio XLV: De electione pestis prae bello et fame 2 Sam. 24 et 1 Chron. 21" and "Exercitatio XLVI: Paraphrasis exegetica historiae de pestis cohibitione et aversione 1 Par. 21 et 2 Sam. 24" in *Exercitationvm Philosophicarvm & Theologicarum Libri IV* (Heidelberg, Johannes Lancellotus, 1610), 246-250.

Sixth: Do those who die from the plague while serving others out of love become, properly speaking, martyrs? Response: They move this question, and among those who affirm it is Marchini in part 1, chapter 7; and the Jesuit Raynaud, in his rather thick treatise, *On martyrdom by plague*, disputes in its favor.[166] We say that it is a mere game of equivocation on the term "martyr" and follow those who deny it, in agreement with: Biel, conclusion 9, in his treatise "On flight during plague," which is extant among his sermons after Lord's Day 24, Pentecost;[167] D'Espence, bk. 3, digression in ch. 19; Gabriel Vázquez, part 3, disputation 153, ch. 3.[168]

Seventh: Could a doctor flee? And is he obligated to visit those infected with the plague, if someone should desire his labor? Response: These move this question: Bañez in IIa–IIae q. 33, art. 3, dub. 4; Suarez, *On Laws*, bk. 3, ch. 30, note 4; D'Espence on 1 Timothy, digression, bk. 3, ch. 19;[169] Bonacina, Salas, Sanchez, de 'Buoni,[170] and Benzon, who are cited by Marchini in part 1, ch. 8,[171] where he distinguishes between a medical doctor brought for one purpose and one brought into every circumstance. So then Marchini says one can be compelled, but that it in no way can be done unless there is imminent necessity and that with an

---

166. Marchini, *Belli Divini*, 20–24, esp. 23 where he references Raynaud part 3 and 4 in their totality; Raynaud, *De Martyrio per Pestem*, 384–633.

167. Gabriel Biel, *Sermones Dominicales* (1510), fols. 150v–152v, esp. 152v; cf. page 105 n146 in this book.

168. See D'Espence, *Digressiones in 1 ad Timoth. Pauli Epistolam*, bk. 3, ch. 19; "De fuga in tempore ac periculo pestis" in *Opera Omnia* (Paris: Claude Morelle, 1619), 253; Gabriel Vázquez, on IIIa q. 68 art. 3, disp. 153, ch. 3 *Commentarium ac Disputationum in Tertiam Partem Sancti Thomae*, 3 vols. (ca. 1549–1604), 2:382–385.

169. See Domingo Bánez O.P. (1528–1604), *Scholastica Commentaria in Secundam Secundae S. Thomae* (Douai: Petrus Borremans, 1615), IIa–IIae q. 33 art. 3 dub. 4, concl. 1–4, 3:478–480; See Francisco Suarez S.J. (1548–1617), *Tractatus de Legibus ac Deo Legislatore in decem libros distributus* (Lyon: Horace Cardon, 1619), bk. 3, ch. 30, no. 4, p. 193; D'Espence, *Opera*, 253.

170. Martino Bonacina (1585–1631), *Summae Moralis Theologiae sive Tractatuum de Casibus Conscientiae* in *Opera Omnia Moralia*, 3 vols., 2nd ed. (Lyon: Gabriel Boissat & Laurence Anisson, 1639), disp. 4, q. 1, punct. 16, prop. 2, §§9–14, 2:227–228; idem, *Tractatus Tres de Legibus, de Peccatis, et de Praeceptis Decalogi* (Brescia: Joannes Baptista Bozzola, 1622), 591–592; Juan de Salas S.J. (1553–1612), *Tractatus de legibus in Primam Secundae S. Thomae* (Lyon: Jean de Gabian, 1611), q. 96, tract. 14, disp. 10, sect. 9, §47, 242; Tomás Sánchez S.J. (1550–1610), *Opus Morale in Praecepta Decalogi* (Antwerp: Joannes Meursius, 1614), bk. 3, ch. 16, §§10–15; Omobono de 'Buoni C.R.S.P (b. 1569), *Commentarii Resolutorii de Examine Ecclesiastico et Disquisitionibus Moralis ac Practicae Theologiae Christianae Philosophiae et Casuum Conscientiae*, 3 vols. (Bologna: Nicolò Tebaldini, 1623–1627), tract. 15, ch. 8, q. 25, 3:346–347.

171. Marchini, *Belli Divini*, 25; cf. Bonacina, *Summae*, disp. 2, q. 8, punct. 2, §6 and §11 in *Opera Omnia Moralia*, 2:137–138; Salas, q. 96, tract. 14, disp. 12, sect. 1 in *Tractatus*, 271–274; Sánchez, *Summa* bk. 1 ch. 18 no. 4; Suarez, *De Legibus*, loc. cit.; Rutilio Benzoni (Rutilius Benzonus, ca. 1542–1613), *Speculum Episcoporum et Curatorum in quo de Fuga in Peste, Fame, et Bello per tres libros* (Venice: Minima Societas, 1595), bk. 1, disp. 1, q. 1, vers. 2, fols. 2v–3r.

increased payment. But it seems to me a hard and quite imperious reason that he adds: "because for the sake of obviating a common loss, a legislator can legislate obligation, even with evident danger to their life."[172] But by far the harshest, if not the most atrocious reason which he states is: "Pharmacists (*pharmacopoei*) and surgeons, if they should attempt to flee after a commandment of a legislator, can be punished with death as an example to others."[173] Whatever the case may be, because this care belongs to the doctors (as Gulielmus Marcquis profusely argues in prob. 2), they must rather be stirred up by reasons that should result in them being led to their duty by the persuasion of love in the example of Levinius Lemnius: "Never let them conduct themselves without undaunted courage, having cast themselves upon confidence in God, and with a zeal to comfort the common people and their citizens" (*The Secret Miracles of Nature*, bk. 4, ch. 17).[174]

Eighth: Whether contagion is only through a fomite, such that certain persons even want to scrupulously avoid them to the point of burying coins from infected places in the earth or casting them into the sea, as well as stones, metals, and other objects so that, by the divine will, for some brief period of time they ought to be soaked in a harsh vinegar, as this practice is held in Florence and Palermo, according to Marchini (part 10, ch. 11, p. 257).[175] And whether, from the prescription of Ficino in his *Advice against the Plague*, ch. 23, "everyone ought to flee conversation with people so that there would always be a space of at least three feet of open air between your friend, and from an infected person at least nine feet,[176] and you must take heed that he never breathes his breath upon you, and between you and him there is always sun, fire, and odors."[177] Response: 1) The most outstanding

172. Marchini, pt. 1, ch. 8 "An Medici possint cogi ad residendum," §7 in *Belli Divini*, 25.
173. Marchini, *Belli Divini*, 25 §§7–8, "For this is the most just law with respect to the common good, because the natural law itself teaches that common good must be preferred to the private one ... §8 Extend this same point and it must be said that surgeons and pharmacists, [who] must not flee in time of plague ... because their work is so necessary in this time ... that if they should attempt flight after the command of the legislator, they also can be punished with death as an example to others."
174. Levinus Lemnius, *Occulta naturae miracula Libri IIII* (Bibliopolis [Amsterdam]: [Officina Paltheniana], [1598]), 581–585.
175. Marchini, *Belli Divini*, 257.
176. Three feet: Lat. *bicubitus*, Ital. *due braccia*; nine feet: Lat. *sex cubiti*, Ital. *sei braccia*
177. *Remed. Epidemic. ch. 25*: Instead cf. ch. 23 in Ficino, *Il consiglio* (1522), fol. 47r–48r, "... che tu fugga le conversazioni maxime a digiuno et quando conversi stia discosto dal compagnio due braccia almeno et alluogho aperto, et quando e disosperto stia etiam piu dilungi almeno sei braccia et allo scoperto, et fa chel vento non venga dallui inverso te. Intra te et lui fia sole, fuo, odori o vento chesoffi inverso lui."

doctors do not think [the danger] is that much. Mercuriale, *On the Plague*, ch. 12, says that it seems to him that "simpletons refuse to handle money for fear of contagion."[178] Likewise, even Jean-Antoine Sarazin, ch. 6, p. 26, where he also adds this, "For this reason he approaches to marvel at the exceedingly careful caution of our people, since many families live together in buildings. If either a sick person laboring with the plague or a corpse extinguished by plague has been carried down by spiral staircases, even made from solid stone, they think entering or leaving by the same means is full of danger."[179] 2) And if through a remote consequence and suspicion the scrupulous think that something of contagion can cling somewhere, I would suggest to them what Bernard in sermon thirty-one on Song of Songs says to such persons scrupulous of a doctor's diet, those observant of food, and neglectors of customs: "Remember," he says, "I beg you, you are a monk,"—I substitute Christian—"not a doctor; you are not about to be judged for your health, but your profession. I beg you, certainly spare first your peace [of mind], next spare those serving by their labor; spare your community[180] from sorrow; spare conscience; I do not say your conscience, but another's."[181] But that saying is τὸ λίαν ἀκριβὲν ψεῦδες, ["the exceedingly precise falsehood"], because in theoretical sciences, in the civil practice of men, in medical diet, that must be observed everywhere; with only the law of God excepted and matters of conscience, in which that verse in Ephesians 5:15 obtains, ἀκριβῶς περιπατεῖτε, ["Look carefully how you walk"]. Flight from the contagion must be moderated by your calling and love of neighbor. 3) By no means, if you so fear all those things—if under every stone you find a scorpion, if you shudder at the shaking of every leaf—may the commander now desert his army, the soldier his post, parents their family, magistrates and judges their court, and ministers their church; and, as in what happens elsewhere, they would commit it to a substitute or a reader. Now then, this will be from the natural law of contagion: spare oneself (that is, the more precious souls) and expose the less precious ones to this danger. Soon it will be your departure from this world—at least

---

178. Girolamo Mercuriale (Hieronymus Mercurialis, 1530–1606), ch. 12 "How contagion acts in a healthy body" (Cap. XII Quomodo contagium agat in corpus sanum), *De Peste in universum, preasertim vero de Veneta et Patauina* (Venice: Paulus Meietus, 1577), 31–39, esp. 35.
179. Sarazin, *De Peste Commentarius* (1572), 26.
180. Lat. *domus*: here, the monastic community.
181. See Bernard of Clairvaux, *Sermones in Cantica Canticorum*, Sermon 30, §12 in PL 182:939; idem, *St. Bernard's Sermons on the Canticle of Canticles*, 2 vols. (Dublin: Browne & Nolan, 1920), 1:363.

from your world. For the air there (as the physicians teach and Sarazin in the passage cited) is either corrupt according to its substance, or it is putrid and contains in itself the seeds of the pestiferous contagion. If anyone should take exception that he does not extend this scrupulous flight too far, I reply, you bind yourself by the same consequence and by the same conscience (even with overturning your calling and piety), and this man or that woman acts sparingly towards your own life as they take counsel for their own health; or both should apply that moderation which we ourselves require, so that the nature and method of physicians would not become the norm of your conscience, your specific calling, of piety towards parents, or love[182] towards children, but vice versa. Nearly the same thing must be judged regarding the duration of contagion in a fomite, such as a garment of linen, wool, or silk; which if you think about the analogy of poison that can lay dormant for a dozen years or in fact even fifty years (as observes Mercuriale, ch. 14, *On the Plague*, and Marchini, prob. 28) at least I do not see when garments of this sort could at last be handled without reservation. Compare that with our problem 14.[183] Therefore all these things must be burned with fire. And, finally, who will put an end to reservations and anxious observations? Again, therefore I instruct with that saying: Do nothing excessively.[184]

Chapter X: Ninth, is it necessary to put distance between ourselves and the contagion?

Ninth: Is it necessary to put distance between oneself and the contagion? Response: 1) Sennert in bk. 4, ch. 2, p. 688, proves his distinction between contagions through a fomite, which he calls a mediate one, and so wants it subdivided into that which has only air intervening and that which is propagated through garments and other objects.[185] In general, this certainly can be said. But they think from the observance of some bird that the plague

---

182. Gk. στόργης
183. Mercuriale, *De Pestilentia*, 39–45; e.g. Marchini, *Belli Divini*, 160; Noting that problem 28 is generally stated in the preface (What length of time are fomites usually considered contagious in clothing, garments, etc?), it is not paginated to the text, see e.g. pt. 7, ch. 3 dealing with whether items that have come in contact with plague should be burned. Marchini states in §3, "How much more so, because goods infected with the plague are of no value or estimation; they bring death with only one contact or even being in their proximity."
184. Lat. *Ne quid nimis.*
185. Sennert, *De Febribus*, 4.2 in *Opera* 2:139–142

has been brought into this region, or a contagion into that city, at a distance from another region and city; and that this necessarily occurred through the air, and was not inflicted immediately by the hand of God or the ministry of angels (which Sennert and other physicians do not deny; among whom there is Le Paulmier, *On Contagious Diseases*, "On the plague" bk. 1, ch. 6, who asserts that the plague is never inflicted without physical causes) upon this city or that region equally, and upon a city or region on which it was inflicted first in the whole world.[186] How then should we think about other diseases, droughts, floods, and fires? 2) If indeed it is such a spiritual dissemination and penetration of contagion at distance (as Sennert says in the passage cited and Follinus does in chapter 8) so that even from the sharing of air, winds, and so forth with the remotest regions infected with plague, and from only the glimpse of infected buildings or people (e.g. Nicephorus, *Ecclesiastical History*, bk. 17, ch. 18, and Guido tract. 2, doct. 2, ch. 5, which Giuntini in his book *On the plague*, ch. 1 calls *peste basilistica*, the *basilistic plague*) someone contracts the plague; therefore they should tell, it seems to me, what they think of that disorderly flight of *cito, longe, tarde*, of the three foot distancing, of that stubborn and often cruel flight from infected plazas, homes, and people—or how I could manage to flee so that I would escape the air in which the whole wide world is suffused?[187] Especially if it should be so corrupt, as Cardano speaks of it in his *On the Variety of Things*, bk. 8, ch. 45, cited above. Or what at least will be the limits of flight so that I would be certain that the air in which I rest does not in some way have that astral, spiritual contagion in it? Giovanni Filippo Ingrassia on the plague in Palermo (in Marchini's problem 29) says a distance of fifty paces constitutes a space that is not suspect.[188] But what then will be done so that the most remote air from the sick is not brought with a blowing breeze to the well, if indeed then one must especially take heed of wind from that region where the plague is prowling about so that it would not flow to us, as

---

186. Le Paulmier, *De Morbis Contagiosis* (1578), 300–308.

187. Follinus, *Amuletum* (1618), 38–44; Nicephorus, *Ecclesiasticae Historiae* in PG 147:265–268; Francesco Giuntini (Franciscus Junctinus, 1523–1590), it is not known which work this is.

188. Marchini, *Philosophica Problemata*, 37; cf. Giovanni Filippo Ingrassia (Philippus Ingrassias, 1510–1580), *Informatione del Pestifero et Contagioso Morbo ilquale affligge et have afflitto questa citta di Palermo, et molte altre citta, e terre di questo Regno di Sicilia nell' anno 1575 et 1576* (Giovan Mattheo Mayda, 1576), pt. 1, ch. 7, p. 53; cf. idem, *Informatione del pestifero et contagioso morbo*, ed. L. Ingaliso (FrancoAngeli, 2005).

Fracastoro warns us in book 1, chapter 13 of *On contagion*?[189] Fabio Paolini affirms in his commentary on Thucydides (book 1 with the authors cited there) that once it was brought from Ethiopia to Athens by the wind, and from Babylon to Italy.[190] Likewise Herculanus confirms that the plague was brought from Slovenia to Venice in 1456 A.D. in his *Commentary on the Fourth Book of the Canon of Avicenna*.[191] Therefore we would have to abstain entirely from public life, even when we flee from an infected city; and therefore *cito, longe, tarde* is insufficient, for then one must always fear and beware that the plague we left behind from one city or from some remote corner of the earth does not blow upon us. Indeed, it would not even suffice to hide indoors, if in fact the wind could easily propel some infected air, or some astronomically-influenced and most subtle exhalations,[192] inside one's home. Even more, the very astral atoms as vehicles of contagion on their own might even penetrate to the innermost parts of buildings. I do not say this so that we would torment ourselves in an excessively anxious way, if not a superstitious way, with judging and monitoring those crafty little things in order to avoid any or even the most remote contagion, even to the point of neglect of love and duty towards God and neighbor. And in this way we would make ourselves doubly and even trebly miserable.

Tenth: Why are the majority who devote their effort to the physical and spiritual comfort of the sick more immune from plague than some others? Response: With the reasons of others rejected, Sennert in ch. 2, brings forward probable reasons taken from second causes.[193] But it is most certain that it is derived from the special protection of God according to Psalm 91.

Eleventh: In what way is plague stirred up by magicians? Response: The methods of devilish operations are various and entirely hidden from us. Often they immediately affect bodies; equally as often they also employ

---

189. Girolamo Fracastoro, *De Sympathia... De Contagione* (1546), fols. 37v–38v.

190. Fabio Paolini (Fabius Paulinus, 1535–1605), *Praelectiones Marciae sive Commentaria in Thucydidis Historiam seu narrationem de Peste Atheniensium* (Venice: Juntae, 1603), 146–155.

191. See tract. 4, ch. 3 "Signa pestilentiae aeris" in Giovanni Arcolani (Joannes Herculanus, 1390–1484), *De Febribus... In Avicennae Quarti Canonis Fen Primam Dilucida atque Optima Expositio* (Venice: Iunta, 1552), fols. 151r–152r. Cf. Avicenna (Ibn Sina, 980–1037), *The Canon of Medicine (Qanun fi al-tibb: The Law of Natural Healing): Volume 4: Systemic Diseases, Orthopedics and Cosmetics*, trans. H. Doostdar, ed. L. Bakhtiar, 5 vols. (Great Books of the Islamic World, Inc., 2014). For the Arabic text, see E. al-Qashsh and A. Zay'ūr, eds., *Al-Qānūn fī l-tibb*, 4 vols. (Beirut: 1413 A.H./1993 A.D.)

192. Gk., Lat. ἀποῤῥίας, *et subtilissimos halitus*

193. Sennert, *De Febribus* 4.3 in *Opera*, 2:150

their proxies, namely magicians, through the application of natural causes in order to produce poison and infection. For several examples, see Cardano in his *On Subtlety*, bks. 2 and 18, *On Poisons*, ch. 17, and *On the Variety of Things*, bk. 15, ch. 80;[194] Gulielmus Marcquis, prob. 1, pp. 4–6; Aretius, the problem on enchantment, Marchini, preface, fol. §§ verso; Pierre Grégoire of Toulouse, *Syntagma*, bk. 34, ch. 11; Althusius, *Dicaeologica*, bk. 1, ch. 102, §§17–18.[195] It seems to me extremely disagreeable what is dreamt up by Grégoire. Marchini proves it in the place cited: "Magicians induce plague somewhere by stirring up the putrid matter of their own body by the force of their own imagination, through which they send out rays from their infected eyes and animal spirits, and they vitiate nearby air, whereby it is contracted by others. Then plague is procreated in human bodies."[196]

Twelfth: Could someone with a good conscience exchange their labor for people infected with the plague for a certain price? Response: I affirm, against Jean Briard, *Quodlibetica* 3, (whom Raynaud references in pt. 3, ch. 1, p. 392) who condemns of the highest stupidity and gravest sin those who waste their life for money.[197] We add this precaution: only if the supreme end would be the glory of God, the salvation of a soul, and the good of our neighbor. Now a fair wage for such dangerous work is not in itself evil.

Thirteenth: What must be done by the godly, especially by pastors of churches, where through rigid laws or tyrannical custom it is not licit to give mercy towards those most dear and necessary to us? Response: They

---

194. Girolamo Cardano, *De Subtilitate Libri XXI* (Lyon: Guilelmus Rouillius, 1559), 44–137, 633–678; idem, *The De Subtilitate of Girolamo Cardano Volume 1* (Arizona Center for Medieval and Renaissance Studies, 2013); idem, *De venenis libri tres* (Padua: Paolo Frambotti, 1653), 36–39; idem, *De Varietate*, 728–41.

195. See "Problema 1: Num Pestis sit venenum? Et num unum vel plura veneni genera pestem efficiant?" in Marcquis, *Decas Pestifuga*, 1–5; see "Locus CXLV Fascinatio," Benedictus Aretius (1505–1574), Reformed professor respectively of philosophy and theology at Bern, Switzerland (1548–1563, 1563–1574), in *S. S. Theologiae Problemata, hoc est Loci Communes Christianae Religionis Methodice Explicati* ([Lausanne]: Isayas le Preux, 1617), 815–819; see "Tituli Explicatio pestis cur divinum bellum" in Marchini, *Belli Divini*, fol. §§ verso; Pierre Grégoire of Toulouse (Petrus Gregorius Tholosanus, 1540–1597), French Roman Catholic jurist, see "Cap. 11 De Maleficiis et incantationibus homines, animalia aliasque res interimentibus, vel iisdem nocentibus" in *Syntagma Iuris Universi, atque Legum pene omnium gentium, et rerum publicarum praecipuarum in tres partes digestum in quo divini et humani juris totius naturali* (Frankfurt: Officina Paltheniana, 1599), 670–671; Johannes Althusius (1557–1638), *Dicaeologica libri tres, totum et universum jus, quo utimur methodice complectentes* (Frankfurt: Christophorus Corvinus, 1649), 386.

196. Marchini, *Belli Divini*, fol. §§ verso

197. Raynaud, pt. 3, ch. 1, *De Martyrio per Pestem*, 392–393; cf. Jean Briard (Briardus, d. 1520), *Quaestiones Quodlibeticae* (Theodorus Martinus, 1518), fols. 32r–32v.

will teach that both the magistrate and people are responsible for the necessary love towards the afflicted in such a case of necessity. Next, they will display their love toward those beloved to them in some measure, if not publicly, at least privately. Finally, if they could not hide and therefore it is forbidden to them all public conversation and ministry, they will keep their souls in patience. Meanwhile, they will not abandon their domestics, and especially their wife, parents, and children, even if one were to have to abstain from all ministry for a season. For then there will not be any sin in them, but in those who through their own excessive fear reject and impede their ministry.

Fourteenth: What must be stated regarding that plague that originated at Justinopolis[198] from contact with the sheets that, twenty years prior, had carried the sick and transported the dead to their grave, and it arose [in the time of] Trincavellius and Francansanus, as Sennert tells it in bk. 4, ch. 3, from which contagion, ten thousand people died? Response: "Let Apella the Jew believe. I won't."[199] Why not rather ascend to God than handle this with devised, and often insipid, reasons that attribute all things to nature and evident causes and learn to admire nothing as divine, nothing as unusual, in these judgments of God?

Fifteenth: Could a health official[200] extract those having the plague, or those suspected of having it, from their own home and city when they are unwilling to leave, and confine them to a public infirmary? Response: Marchini moves this question and responds to it in the affirmative in pt. 7, ch. 1, with the adduced example of the leprous (Lev. 13–14, Num. 5), besides civil and canonical law. He makes an exception for the nobles and religious persons, and he grumbles about monastics and priests, seeming to intend a distinction between them. We have one exception to his rule, namely we reject it as unsupported by any reason.[201]

Sixteenth: Ought the preaching of the Word and other assemblies for the exercise of godliness be impeded on account of plague? I deny it, but Marchini advances this exact opinion in pt. 4, ch. 7, but with reasons that are partly strange and partly false, without any suitable or clearly proven ones.

Seventeenth: Ought movable goods that are pestilential or at least

---

198. Modern day Koper, Slovenia.
199. See Sennert, *De Febribus* 4.3 in *Opera* 2:150; This is a quote, "Credat Judaeus Apella, non ego," from Horace, *Satires*, bk 1, satire 5, lines 100–101; approximate meaning, "Tell it to someone who cares."
200. *Praefecti sanitatis*
201. Marchini, *Belli Divini*, 127ff.

suspected of being such be burned with fire by the magistrate, and in fact without any compensation? Response: I deny it against Marchini, pt. 4, ch. 3.[202] His reasons are frivolous because those goods, he says, are of no value or account as proximity to them only brings death. We thoroughly discount that disputation.

Eighteenth: Is a statute, and certainly one on pain of death, Christian if it does not admit anyone to markets or permit any travelers, and then prohibits anyone's exit from the city? Response: I deny against this same Marchini, who in ch. 5 praises Pope Urban VIII as the one who, with this panacea, freed the entire Roman jurisdiction from plague when it was nearly entirely infected. What a most worthy miracle for an infallible and almighty papalist faith!

Nineteenth: For the purpose of keeping the plague at bay, is it licit to employ the work of Jewish physicians? Response: Marchini denies this but still with some exceptions. We absolutely deny it due to the reasons adduced elsewhere against the Jewish practice of medicine among Christians. The reader should only remember that Jews, on account of their dissemination of the poison and plague in France in the year 1320, were expelled from it entirely.[203]

There are also other considerable problems that Marchini treats; but because properly they concern philosophy and medical pathology, and the determination of certain ones is quite uncertain, and in addition these have been sweated out by others already in their explanations, we do not want to

---

202. Marchini, *Belli Divini*, 104ff.

203. Voetius here repeats a common "blood libel" claim. This prejudiced, unsubstantiated claim is grievous and obscures the full meaning of his prohibition against visiting Jewish physicians. While it doesn't reduce the gravity of or excuse the prejudice of the libel, this prohibition is probably best understood as a religious critique rather than in ethnic terms. Elsewhere, Voetius pointedly states that Judaism "opened the door to the magical arts with their pseudo-philosophy of the Talmud and Kabbalah." In other words, he considered Jewish medical practice of the time to be so shaped by religious philosophy that it bordered on, if not actually engaged in witchcraft, magic, superstition, mysticism, and false worship; things forbidden to Christians. For more on Voetius' engagement with Judaism, and in the context of evangelism and missions, see especially his disputations "De Judaismo" and "De generali conversione Judaeorum ad Rom. 11:25-27" in *Selectarum Disputationum* 2:79-83, 124-55; J. A. B. Jongeneel, "The Missiology of Gisbertus Voetius: The first comprehensive protestant theology of missions," *Calvin Theological Journal* vol. 26, no. 1 (1991):47-79; Gideon van der Watt, "Gisbertus Voetius (1589-1676): Some perspectives on his influence on developments in the South African Dutch Reformed Church's Missiology and Mission Practice" *In die Skriflig*, vol. 53, no. 3 (July 2019):1-9; Voetius, "Tractatus 1: De Plantatione Ecclesiarum" in *Politicae Ecclesiae* (Amsterdam: Waesberg, 1663-1676), 4:293-342; translated into Dutch, idem, *De Plantatione Ecclesiarum: Tractaat over de Planting en de Planters van Kerken*, trans. D. Pol (Groningen: Firma Bouwman & Venema, 1910); H. A. van Andel, *De zendingsleer van Gisbertus Voetius* ("Gisbertus Voetius's Doctrine of Missions") (Kampen: J. H. Kok, 1912), 16-18, 175-82.

be delayed with rehashing them.[204] But these are the chief ones: (1) Why is the disease of the plague so difficult to cure? (2) Why does it strike down some and not others? (3) Is the pestiferous poison naturally congenital in human bodies? (4) Why are those confined to monasteries and prisons, the elderly, and the middle-aged carried off less often? (5) Why are bodies extinguished by the plague so very mollified? (6) How and why can one person uninjured by the plague harm others with it? (7) Are fish immune to the plague? (8) Are there regions that are immune to plague? (9) Will feral carnivores come in contact with cadavers extinguished by the plague? (10) Would the plague take hold of the same person twice or frequently? (11) Why are the rather healthy laid low by the plague before others? (12) Should the buboes under the armpit or inguinal area be frequently compared? (13) Why are the blemishes of the plague visible on the back and chest, but not on the face? (14) Why are these blemishes visible *post-mortem*, when they were unseen before death? (15) Whether putrified air is the cause of pestilence? And how is that contagion communicated on the air? (16) Whether plague is induced by a foul smell, and to this point, by a glance of it, hearing of it, one's imagination, or fear of it? (17) In what part of the year does plague arise and cease, respectively? (18) How long does plague customarily linger and thrive in a province? (19) What sort of contagion is more pernicious? (20) What are the pathognomic, or characteristic, signs of the plague?

Consequence: If Egyptians and Turks do not flee under pretext of fate and their morbid and fatal deity, then they recklessly seek out the dangers of the plague and condemn all remedies, as certainly Prospero Alpini testifies in chapter 15 of his book, *On the Medicine of the Egyptians*,[205] and so does Busbecq in his *Turkish Letters*.[206] Certainly many of the godly and

---

204. *Nolumus iis recoquendis immorari*: lit. "We do not want to be delayed with re-smelting them."

205. Prospero Alpini (Prosperus Alpinus, 1553–1617), bk.1 ch. 15, *De Medicina Aegyptorum libri quatuor* (Venice: Franciscus de Franciscis Senensem, 1591), 27–28; cf. Sennert, *De Febribus* 4.1 in *Opera*, 2:133.

206. Lat. *Busbequius in legatione Turcica*: E.g. Ogier Ghiselin de Busbecq (Augerius Busbecquius, 1522–1592), *Legationis Turcicae Epistolae IV* (Monaco, 1620), 359–360; idem, *The Turkish Letters of Ogier Ghiselin de Busbecq*, ed. E. S. Forster (Baton Rouge: Louisiana State University Press, 2005), 189, "The Turks hold an opinion which makes them indifferent to, though not safe from, the plague. They are persuaded that the time and manner of each man's death is inscribed by God upon his forehead; if, therefore, he is destined to die, it is useless for him to try to avert fate; if he is not so destined, he is foolish to be afraid. And so they handle the garments and linen in which plague-stricken persons have died, even though they are still wet with the contagion of their sweat; nay, they even wipe their faces with them. 'If,' they say, 'it is God's will that I should die, then die I must; if not, it can do me no harm.' Thus contagion is spread far and wide, and sometimes whole families are exterminated."

zealous of our religion in the Netherlands, whom I do not want to openly mock or indirectly accuse of Turkishness, should be far from that opinion. If they are not those who flee the plague, are not so fearful and so unfeeling as to desert their own, then they still do not in the least have a resemblance to the Turk, nor do they recklessly tempt God. They do not reject means, nor do they condemn medicine; but they do not prefix or set nature before grace, medicine in front of their Christian faith, private desire ahead of God's glory, their own particular good ahead of the public good of virtue, but the exact opposite. So they have been taught by their pastors (whom this slander also touches far and wide). If some by zeal and desire to do good for their neighbor sometimes seem to do something imprudent, it is not so much that he must be sharply harassed—much less as a pretext then to seek a base, fearful flight. It is less evil here to sin by way of excess [boldness] than in the defect. Compare what we have said above, especially Lavater in his treatise *On Plague*, and his commentary on 1 Chronicles 21 whose opinion I agree with there entirely, with which also especially the [Reformed] writers of Switzerland, Germany, and the Netherlands agree.[207] Nor on the chief point do the French and others disagree with us. Although some among them seem to decide the matter too much according to the laws and customs of their own country elsewhere. It is no shame to conclude with a saying of Suleiman the Emperor of the Turks, who used to say that the "pestilences are the arrows of God, which do not stray from their mark. If he willed to strike someone with this bolt, no flight and no hiding will profit." And the determination of the Talmudists in *Sanhedrim*, folio 29, "Although the plague were to prowl about for seven years, nevertheless no one will die except the one whose years have been fulfilled." And Chagigah, folio 4, "Will someone depart when it is not their time?" What if these sayings are taken in a reasonable and Christian way, as we taught must be accepted as our fatal end in our disputation *On the End of Life*, so that no more would this slander of Turkishness impact us by some plague-fleers. These are base placards and defamatory pamphlets of the Neo-Pelagians, which thunder against nothing except Turkishness, Manichaeism, atheism, and so forth, and not the orthodox teaching of our churches.

Conquer the fear of death and you will conquer the fear of plague.

---

207. Ludwig Lavater, *De Pestilentia Concio Lvdovici Lavateri* (Zurich, 1586); idem, *In libros Paralipomenon, sive Chronicorum Commentarius* (Zurich: Christoph Froschuer), fols. 78r-82r. See page 214 in this volume.

4

A Theological Dissertation on the Plague

Introduction

Johannes Hoornbeeck (b. 1617) served faithfully from both pulpit and lectern from 1639 until his death in 1666.[1] Born and raised in Haarlem, the Netherlands, Hoornbeeck matriculated at Leiden University in 1633. Two years later, when an epidemic of plague broke out in Leiden, he transferred to Utrecht University, attending lectures there until the plague subsided in September of 1635. It was during this time at Utrecht that he first met Gisbertus Voetius, his mentor and later his colleague in the theology faculty. Hoornbeeck would interrupt his studies again in 1637, returning home after the death of his father. But he was able to complete his training at Leiden in 1638 and, in 1639, accepted a call as a pastor in a Dutch Reformed church near Cologne, Germany, where he served until 1643. Among his expatriate congregants in Cologne was the young Petrus van Mastricht (1630–1706), who would later matriculate at Utrecht University.

Although at one point forced to leave Germany due to religious strife with Roman Catholics, Hoornbeeck was promoted to the rank of doctor of theology in the final months of 1643. By May of 1644, he had received four separate calls: a pastoral call at Maastricht, another at Graft, a call to be a theology professor at Utrecht, and another at Harderwijk. He chose

---

1. For the most significant biographies of Hoornbeeck, see the "Vita clarissimi Hoornbeekii" in *De Conversione Indorum et Gentilium libri duo* (Amsterdam: Johannes Janssonius, 1669). Most other bibliographical dictionaries rely upon this *Vita*; e.g. A. J. van der Aa, "Hoornbeek (Johannes)" in *Biografisch Woordenboek der Nederlanden*, 21 vols. (Haarlem, 1852–1878), 8-02:1230–1234; De Bie and Loosjes, "Johannes Hoornbeek" in *Biographisch Woordenboek van Protestantsche Godgeleerden in Nederland*, 6 vols. (1907–1949), 4:277–286; "Hoornbeeck" in *Nieuw Nederlandsch Biografisch Woordenboek*, 10 vols. (1911–1937). There are at least three variant spellings of Hoornbeeck's name in the secondary literature and in the period. The most common ones are a mild variant of Hoornbeeck or Hoornbeek.

Utrecht and served as professor of theology there from 1644 to 1654, before moving to the University of Leiden, where he would remain until his death at the relatively young age of 49, leaving behind a formidable and wide-ranging corpus of publications.

Hoornbeeck's published works, which number well over one hundred, generally fall into three categories: theological, polemical, and pastoral or practical. Among his theological works, he was best known for his two-volume *Theologia Practica*, published in Utrecht (1663, 1666, 1689), and Frankfurt and Leipzig (1698). For a flavor of his polemical works, his most noted pieces are perhaps first his *Summary of Controversies with infidels, heretics, schismatics, that is, heathen, Jews, Muslims, Papists, Anabaptists, Enthusiasts and Libertines* (1658, 1676, 1697) and then another two-volume work titled *Socinianism Confounded* (1650–1662).[2] Were we to cease our consideration here, a modern might be tempted to discount Hoornbeeck as an ivory tower scholastic in the rarified academic air of a bygone era. However, the grounded nature of his pastoral ministry among the flock is evident in a sampling of the following titles: *A Theological Treatise on the Method of Preaching* (1646),[3] *The Denial of Self* (1653), *On Spiritual Progress* (1654), *Sincerity and Hypocrisy* (1654), *On Godliness* (1656), *The Sense of Divine Grace* (1658), *The Calling of Man the Sinner to Christ* (1661), *The Certainty of Salvation* (1664), *On Faith* (1661), *The Approach of the Soul to Christ* (1661), and *The Spiritual Warfare* (1664).[4] The list could go on, most of which remains untranslated. His deep concern for confessional orthodoxy fed, and was fed by, his pastoral care for souls. The result is a treasury of work from a titan in an age

---

2. Johannes Hoornbeeck, *Summa Controversiarum Religionis*, 2nd ed. (Utrecht: Johannes à Waesberg, 1658); idem, *Socianismi Confutati*, 2 vols. (Utrecht: Johannes à Waesberg, 1650).

3. Johannes Hoornbeeck, *Disputationis Theologicae De Ratione Concionandi* (1646); idem, *Miscellanea Sacra* (Utrecht: Gulielmus vande Water, 1689), 225–274; found as an appendix with a separate pagination, as Hoornbeeck, "Methodus Concionandi" in Andreas Essenius, *Compendium Theologiae Dogmaticum*, 2nd ed (Utrecht: Franciscus Halma, 1685), 1–69; idem, *Tractatus Elegantissimus de Ratione Concionandi* (Frankfurt, 1703); a recent translation into Dutch, idem, *De Eerste Homiletiek in Nederland: Ontstaan, Vertaling, Inhoud en Verwerking van de Homiletiek De Ratione Concionandi van Johannes Hoornbeeck*, trans. T. Brienen (Kamben: De Groot Goudriaan, 2009).

4. Johannes Hoornbeeck, *De Abnegatione sui* (Utrecht: Johannes à Waesberg, 1653); idem, *De progressu spirituali* (Leiden: Johannes & Danielis Elzevier, 1654); idem, *De Sinceritate et Hypocrisi* (Leiden: Johannes & Danielis Elzevier, 1654); idem, *De pietate* (Leiden: Johannes Elzevier, 1656); idem, *De sensu divinae gratiae* (Leiden: Johannes Elzevier, 1658); idem, *De vocatione hominis peccatoris ad Christum* (Leiden: Johannes Elzevier, 1661); idem, *De certitudine salutis* (Leiden: Johannes Elzevier, 1664); idem, *De fide* (Leiden: Johannes Elzevier, 1661); idem, *De accessione animae ad Christum* (Leiden: Johannes Elzevier, 1661); idem, *De pugna spirituali* (Leiden: Johannes Elzevier, 1664).

of titans of Dutch Reformed theology—a treasury that was drawn on by later theologians like Herman Bavinck, Abraham Kuyper, and Gerhardus Vos, to name a few.

While Hoornbeeck's ministry must be understood in the context of the Dutch Further Reformation or *de Nadere Reformatie* (literally "the closer reformation"), Hoornbeeck was not concerned with the spread of the Gospel in the Netherlands only. One scholar has aptly noted that "Hoornbeeck belonged among the Dutch theologians of missiology, but he was not the first."[5] Within the Dutch Further Reformation, a body of sixteenth and seventeenth century pastors formulated a corpus of theology characterized by emphases on godliness and piety for the individual, the church, society, and the state. But, as Oosterom has observed, adherents to this cause were not concerned exclusively with *het innerlijk leven* ("the inner life") as the *Nadere Reformatie* is sometimes characterized. Instead, many of the movement's leaders displayed an outward emphasis in their theory of missions (*de zendingsgedachte*).[6] This mission-minded group included theologians that reached back into the very early days of the Reformation among the Dutch and Belgians, such as Adrianus Saravia (1532–1613),[7] Justus Heurnius (1587–1651),[8] Willem Teellinck (1579–1629), Godefridus Udemans (1582–1649), Jodocus van Lodensteyn (1620–1677), to name a few, as well as Gisbertus Voetius,[9] the mentor and colleague of Johannes Hoornbeeck, who ought to be included in their ranks.

It was this Hoornbeeck who was not content with a scholastic theology that only aimed at disputation. "I have noticed that many people think it sufficient for a theologian to be able to hold debates with Roman Catholics, with Socinians, Anabaptists, Remonstrants, and that kind of people, safe from most people except those mentioned here and safe from the parts of their task with respect to those other people, which is to teach, convert, and

---

5. See B. Oosterom, "Johannes Hoornbeeck als Zendingstheolog" in *Theologia Reformata* 13, (1970): 81–101, here 85.

6. Oosterom, "Johannes," 81.

7. Saravia outlined and defended an Anglican approach to global missions, see ch. 17, "Mandatum omnibus gentibus praedicandi Evangelium, Apostolis in coelum receptis, etiam Ecclesiam obligat, ad quam rem apostolica authoritate opus est" of *Diversis gradibus Ministrorum Euangelii* in Adrianus Saravia, *Diuersi Tractatus Theologici* (London: Societas Stationariorum, 1611), 18–19; idem, *A Treatise on the Different Degrees of the Christian Priesthood* (Oxford: John Henry Parker, 1840), 161–166.

8. Justus Heurnius, *De Legatione Evangelica ad Indos Capessenda Admonitio* (Leiden: Officina Elzeviriana, 1618).

9. Inter alia, Gisbertus Voetius, "De missionibus ecclesiasticis" in *Politicae Ecclesiasticae* (1676) 3:322–348.

save, as much as we can, all the nations."[10] With these words, Hoornbeeck signals his broad and rigorous view of the mission of the church to extend beyond national confessional states, local universities and their debates, and the proximate concerns of nationalist mercantile colonialism.

Between 1635 and 1669 there were multiple outbreaks of plague in the Netherlands, as indicated by burial data.[11] With respect to the work which follows, it is a scholastic treatment of a set of pastoral questions contemporary to 1658—right in the middle of a simmering period of ongoing outbreaks in various cities and locales in the Netherlands. This work therefore combines all of the doctrinal, polemical, and pastoral concerns that one might find in the rest of Hoornbeeck's published works with a specific application to the present need. In *A Theological Treatise on the Plague* Hoornbeeck is deeply concerned with what state of heart and mind a Christian must maintain before, during, and after a plague, and with how someone ought to prepare their heart to serve during a plague and perhaps even to suffer during one. It is in this way that Hoornbeeck demonstrated and modeled, as did many of his colleagues in the *Nadere Reformatie*, that doctrine is for living to God—and that blessedly, even if that living includes preparation for death.

+ + + + +

Johannes Hoornbeek, *Dissertatio de peste theologica* in *Variorum Tractatus Theologici de Peste* (Leiden: Johannes Elsevirius, 1655), 250–380.

A Theological Dissertation on the Plague
Johannes Hoornbeeck
Translated by Todd M. Rester

The Sacred Page commends that singular prudence in the tribe and sons of Isaachar being exceedingly understanding of the times, , whereby they could wisely counsel Israel in what ought to be done at

---

10. See Hoornbeeck, Johannes, *Johannes Hoornbeeck (1617–1666) On the Conversion of the Indians and Heathens*, Ineke Loots (ed. and trans.) and Joke Spaans (ed.), (Brill: Leiden, 2019), 35. This is Loots's English translation. Cf. Hoornbeeck, *De Conversione*, fol. Mm r.

11. Daniel R. Curtis, "Was Plague an Exclusively Urban Phenomenon? Plague Mortality in the Seventeenth Century Low Countries" in *The Journal of Interdisciplinary History* 47, no. 2 (2016): 139–170.

any time on any occasion (1 Chron. 12:32). This the Savior calls "signs for knowing the times" (σημεῖα τῶν καιρῶν γινώσκειν) in the Gospel (Matt. 16:3). And the Sacred Page teaches in this way—that theologians, according to their condition and state of the times, handle anything anywhere that belongs to the wise and pass on, either verbally or in writing, those things that ought to be especially adapted as useful to the present situation of things. From this we think that theologians especially are to be animated and equipped for any occasion—whether some head of doctrine is stirred up, or reigning sin, or some public disaster brings devastation—as the circumstances change so that they are not disturbed by any injury. Because it is rightly useful and edifying to be of service to ourselves and our own as present need demands, or, as in David's phrase of Holy Scripture, to be useful with divine counsel in our own generation (Acts 13:36), we would ascertain what holy doctors and writers of every era have observed.

To pass by some other things, it was noted by Jerome in his *Chronicle* in the year of Christ 340 in the fourth entry of Emperor Constantine (i.e. 280th Olympiad, 4) that a severe earthquake shook nearly the whole Orient and overthrew and swept away many cities;[12] the same was noted by Ephrem the Syrian who had an oration, *On the Earthquake*, which is extant in the edition of Vossius, tome one.[13] Under Emperor Valentinian, by various signs and destructions when the Orient was afflicted in a miserable way, the earth and fields convulsed in a highly unusual way that not only devastated Constantinople but also Cappadocia and elsewhere in the year

---

12. See Jerome, *St. Jérôme Chronique: Continuation de la Chronique d'Eusèbe, années 326–378*, trans. Benoît Jeanjean and Bertrand Lançon (Rennes: Presses Universitaires de Rennes, 2004), 84: "Multae Orientis urbes terrae motu horribili consederunt." Cf. M. R. Sbeinati, R. Darawche, M. Mouty, "The historical earthquakes of Syria: an analysis of large and moderate earthquakes from 1365 B.C. to 1900 A.D." *Annals of Geophysics* 48, no. 3 (June 2005), 385: "In the year 341, Antioch was shaken by a violent earthquake for three days (Theophanes). An earthquake at Antioch lasted for three days in the year 341–342 (Cedrenus)... In 334, [there was] a strong earthquake in Syria and the near East. It was said there were 40,000 victims. Antioch was destroyed. In 340, an earthquake destroyed Beirut, killing a large number of people. In 341, a destructive earthquake in Antioch, followed by many shocks." Based on the Latin phrasing that Hoornbeeck employed, cf. Cesare Baronio, 367 AD §XXXII, *Annales Ecclesiastici*, 12 vols. (Venice: Laurentius Basilius et Antonius Tivanius, 1705–1712), 4:166, "S. Hieronymus in Chronico hoc ipso anno quarto horum Imperatorum affirmat."

13. Lat., *Ephraem Syrus, orationem illam habuit De terrae motu*: See idem, "Adversus eos, qui dicunt Terraemotus a terrae inflatione fieri" in *Operum Omnium Sancti Ephraem Syri*, ed. Gerardus Vossius, 3 vols. (Rome: Jacopo Torneri, 1589–1598), 1:90–92. Here Ephrem takes issue with those who attribute the earthquake more to natural second causes than to the divine first cause. See also idem, *Ephraemi Syri Opera Omnia quae exstant Graece, Syriace, Latine*, eds. Yusuf ibn Siman as-Simani et al. 6 vols. (Rome: Typographia Vaticana, Johannes Mariae Henrici Salvioni, 1737–1746), 1:342–343.

367. Gregory of Nazianzus, when his father was present but silent during the public mourning, had an elegant sermon, *On the plague of hail* (see *De Plaga Grandinis*, σιωπῶντα διὰ τὲν πληγὲν τῆς χαλάζης), certainly directed to the people, but also to his father.[14] And a whole century before those, when a tremendous plague (which more properly concerns our argument) prowled throughout nearly the whole world and Africa in 256 A.D., Cyprian wrote an outstanding and timeless sermon, *On the Mortality*. Pope Gregory, when a severe plague was rampant at Rome in 590 A.D. preached a sermon that is extant in book 11, ep. 2 of his *Register of Letters*,[15] and in Gregory of Tours, *History of the Franks*, bk. 10, ch. 1.[16] And so on; there are others elsewhere.

In our era, when the plague arose and made a horrendous assault, the argument that rather urgently needed to be handled by theologians was first questions and then cases of disturbed consciences, to which it was necessary to answer also with various writings published in the light of day. Among his letters, Franciscus Junius, the truly incomparable professor of theology in our academy,[17] and one who died from the plague on October 13, 1603, treated this question or case at some point (in the year 1596 if I am not mistaken): "What must a minister do in the time of plague?"[18] On the same argument compare the creeds and writings of the most outstanding men: Beza, Rivet, and Voetius—whose treatise on this matter above I have shown to the printer and is now the third to be printed. I would have added Wilhelm Zepper if it were not extant only in German, and his *Account of the Plague*, in which he set forth his exposition of Psalm 91, would make a good book itself.[19]

---

14. Gregory of Nazianzus, "Oratio XVI: in patrem tacentem propter plagam grandinis" in *PG* 35:933–964; idem, "Oration XVI: On his father's silence, because of the plague of hail" in *NPNF2* 7:248–254.

15. See Gregory I, "Registrum Epistularum" in *Opera*, 5 vols, 2nd ed. (Rome: Typographia Camerae Apostolicae, 1613), 4:778–779; idem, "bk. 11, ep. 2" in *The Letters of Gregory the Great*, trans. J. R. C. Martyn, 3 vols. (Pontifical Institute of Medieval Studies, 2004).

16. Gregory of Tours, *Gregorii episcopi Turonensis libri Historiarum X* in *Monumenta Germaniae Historica*, ed. B. Krusch and W. Levison, 2nd ed. (Hanover, 1951); idem, *The History of the Franks*, trans. L. Thorpe (London: Penguin UK, 1974), 403–407.

17. I.e. Leiden University

18. As of yet, it is undetermined to which letter of Franciscus Junius this refers, or if it is still extant.

19. Wilhelm Zepper (1550–1607), *Auszführlicher Bericht von Sterbensläuften: Darinn vermöge götlichen Worts angezeigt vnd erwisen wird, was von der plage der Pestilentz zu halten, auch wessen alle, vnd ein jeder, derer Stätte, Flecken, Häuser, Leiber oder angehörige mit dieser plage heimgesucht, oder auch durch den zeitlichen Tod hinweggenommen werden ... Sampt angehester Erklärung des XCI Psalmen, zu trost in Sterbensläuften gericht* (Herborn: Christoff Raben, 1607).

In considering the matter myself, I look at it from a twofold perspective: first of God inflicting the plague, then of man and his duties; in which someone must conduct himself in relation to withdrawing from that affliction or sustaining it, or someone must conduct himself in relation to others with the plague. I have carefully distinguished and considered the questions and cases concerning both heads, with the addition that individual cases could be handled briefly with our sort of judgment and response. Of course, it is a serious affliction that affects people gravely, and it infects violently and slays them quickly. These are its certain three adjuncts and common criteria.

OF GOD INFLICTING THE PLAGUE

God's parts are everywhere supreme. He, according to his nature and providence, is the supreme director and governor of all things that are made (Matt. 10:29–30), of all evils or afflictions in general (Isa. 45:7, Lam. 3:37–38, Amos 3:6), and finally of the kinds of diseases or afflictions (Lev. 26:25, Exod. 5:2–3, Deut. 27:21–22, 2 Sam. 24:13, 15, Ezek. 14:21, Amos 4:10). No other higher cause can be imagined nor other lesser causes ought to be considered without that one. But here questions can be posed:

Question 1: Does God inflict the plague mediately or immediately, with causes and through causes—inferior and natural ones, by altering, changing, and commixing them—or even without them? I respond: Sometimes in this way or sometimes another. He can do something this way or that. And now just as God can immediately inflict life and death, or mediately by the natural order and causation, so finally he can do in cases both of disease and plague. Josephus says that what happened in the time of David in so brief a space—from dawn until breakfast, 70,000 men; or in the army of the king Sennacherib, 180,000 were struck down in one night—did not happen through natural and ordinary causes, but by the hand of God or through an angel, which Holy Scripture witnesses to in 2 Samuel 24:15–16 and 2 Kings 19:35. But concerning the plague that the Assyrians underwent, this opinion is by no means improbable, which Josephus also follows, who calls it a λοιμικὴν νόσον, that it was a "pestilential sickness" in *Antiquities*, bk. 10.[20]

---

20. Hoornbeeck: *Antiq. Lib. X. cap. II*; see instead Josephus, *Jewish Antiquities*, bk. 10, ch. 1, §5 in *LCL* 326:168–9, γὰρ θεοῦ λοιμικὴν ἐνασκήψαντος αὐτοῦ τῷ στρατῷ νόσον, "For God had visited a pestilential sickness upon his army" (1937 Marcus translation) In 10.2.1, King Hezekiah is smitten, according to Josephus, with νόσῳ χαλεπῇ, "a severe illness," idem, *LCL* 326:170–71.

Question 2: Without a doubt this is a grave affliction, but must it be counted as the gravest of all? I respond: It certainly is among the most grave because it is among God's threats and judgments, and next this is also evident to people's common sense. But still it is not the gravest because God does not rank it in the first place among evils that he threatens, nor did the king[21] hesitate to choose that option before the other ones; and the one who has more of a sense of the divine [knows] he is accustomed to threaten it certainly more than other afflictions. For this one thing has that which draws people's hearts more promptly and quickly to God and divine meditations and concerns, unlike some other evil where we frequently delay on inferior and proximate causes and do not so immediately fly to God and cling fixed upon Him. There this more certainly and easily happens with people, and the nature of this disease is hidden from physicians themselves to such a degree that they are ignorant of how to describe its form with certainty. What is secret and divine is unique to this evil, more so than to any other disease or calamity.

Question 3: In such a common and epidemic mortality, how will we judge whether it is a punishment or a chastisement? Of course, everyone knows these are different and as the former is distinguished into its kind of fault and punishment—or, even better, into its kind of fault and affliction, or into its unsightliness and sorrow—so the latter kind of chastisement is properly spoken of differently than a punishment. Thus this case is brought forward because when the plague is considered proof of divine wrath, insofar as people conclude we are and live under the wrath of God and so then because they dread dying in this way, they think that they have a grave case. I respond: Whether you consider the pestilence either in itself materially to be a punishment just as other evils, diseases, and death, or subjectively in man to hold the place of a punishment among the wicked according to the diversity of the subject, still for the godly and those redeemed in Christ it cannot be anything else than a chastisement, but not strictly and formally a punishment: "For those who are in Christ Jesus there is no condemnation" (Rom. 8:1). Clement of Alexandria observes that distinction between τιμωρίαν, vengeance and punishment, and κόλασιν, chastisement, in *Stromata*, 7: "Just as boys are chastised by a schoolteacher or father, so we are chastised by providence. But God does not punish, οὐ τιμωρεῖται. ἔστι γὰρ ἡ τιμωρία κακοῦ ἀνταπόδοσις, κολάζει μετα τοι πρὸς τὸ χρήσιμον καὶ

---

21. Referring to king David in 2 Sam. 24:14

κοινῇ καὶ ἰδίᾳ τοῖς κολαζομενοις that is, "for punishment is the repayment of evil, but he chastises to the good of those being chastised both commonly and privately."[22] So often what is good in itself tends toward evil on account of the malice of the subject—whether benefits of any kind bodily, such as food or drink, or spiritually, such as the Word of God. Similarly, yet conversely, evils tend toward the good when they befall good people, as Rabbi Gamze was accustomed to say, גם זה לטובה, "even this is good" (cf. Rom. 8:37–39).

Question 4: Is the plague contagious or not? This has already been proved by so many arguments, examples, and experiences that a person who wants to question it is exceedingly ignorant, and to deny it is outrageously stubborn. And because that error frequently lays hold of someone as if against the support of divine providence and even in support of human recklessness, not even medical doctors but theologians debated about it, and demonstrate how it does not belong to God to use falsehood, as Job says: "Will you speak iniquity on God's behalf, or will you speak deceitfully for him?" (Job 13:7). As if either that affliction could not result in great destruction or the providence of God could not miraculously and certainly preserve people even in the midst of such fires, when the contagion slithering about snatches others away or, about which we are now speaking, the plague is endowed with the ability to infect? Or as if acting through lesser and even natural causes is repugnant to either divine predestination or providence? These things have been discussed and proved many times by others, and they are taught and known with few resisting them anywhere, so that I could seem to want to abuse your leisure if I were to delay on this point any longer.

Of Man and His Duties

I pass now to the second part, which encompasses a person's duties in this matter. These are to be referred to in five classes: First, whether it is licit or necessary to flee. Now, we cut this point short because others offer many things elsewhere that we may consult. As to what follows: in the second place, what heart and mind is appropriate to have towards those affected with an imminent plague, and how should they view it? Third, when a plague is now present and is actually inflicted, how to avoid it? Fourth,

---

22. Clement of Alexandria, *Stromata or Miscellanies*, bk. 7, ch. 16 in *ANF* 2:553.

what is our duty towards others who are suffering with the plague? And finally, what is our duty towards the departed? To these heads, I think all the points that are customarily asked and treated can be referred.

Regarding Flight from the Plague
The greatest difficulty adheres to the first case regarding flight from plague since, first of all, the notion and name of "flight" offers itself as the first thing to be discarded. Although it is an ambiguous term, a harsh one, and one commonly explained in a subsequent part, here I think it should be omitted. The reason is because it cannot be formed with one certain definition to which all would agree, and because where a definition does occur the term must be discarded lest one would sport with perpetual ambiguity and fallacy. At least it would offer an assertion and investigation of the truth to change the name of the thing defined, and to substitute and pursue another in its place. In fact, "fleeing" seems to connote a certain affection of heart and argues for timidity, the opposite of courage, which to a certain extent should be placed among the vices, and then one is not allowed to approve of it. But should you leave off that ignoble part of the heart, this is not properly speaking "fleeing." Therefore, I prefer you should say "leaving," "departing," or "avoiding," or if there is some other more meaningful and more innocuous term than "fleeing." Beza also saw and noted how much ambiguity this term has.

Now by no means do I deny that in the common usage of the term, "fleeing" means some sort of withdrawal among as many sacred writers as secular ones. But in the present circumstances, besides the use of the term, we should look at the substance chiefly, indeed only, for we think that it is by no means harmful that an ambiguous and harsh term must be changed to a better one. Especially if on this question we also have regard for the commonly received sense of fleeing, where not only common people take offense to the term "flight," but others generally do as well.

So far for the term, but this is not enough to be done with it yet. I certainly think that the entirety of the question here, whether it is licit to flee or depart, must not be discharged with an immediate answer of either an affirmation or denial of the question. Because we are handling it theologically and as a case of conscience, one must begin with a person's heart; and first of all it must be firmed up and formed against any intemperance of affections. Seeing that, eventually we would either declare in favor of the affirmative or the negative. A soul always sins when it is impatient or meticulous beyond measure. And at least in the case of plague one must take care above all as to whether something is neglected. Although perhaps it may be licit to withdraw, yet with respect to your soul you did not depart without sin. So both the answer to the question and the right formation of conscience depend upon this condition. Therefore, I would instruct a person's heart first in the sort of thing that ought to be done here, and then I will answer the question, lest someone already would form an answer in advance. Then if the answer does not address the entirety of this business, it certainly does the chief part of it. Because if you would answer immediately and simply with a part left out, that it is licit to depart in some cases, people think to themselves that this is the whole matter in any case, which it is by no means at all! If you would take heed first to the heart, an unambiguous conclusion results: anyone that departs does so from some other cause than the one by which people frequently and commonly sin and offend others. Hence one must begin in counsel and in its answer, or with a person who is asking sincerely.

Otherwise, with respect to the thing itself or the question, we first set forth certain distinctions, and then the conclusions from which the decision of the proposed question follows by itself. But those things which it touches are, since we are inspecting two things in this question, the *object* that must be fled or shunned and the *subject*, or the one who turns aside from the plague. We distinguish between these two by reason of: 1) the object considered as evil in itself, for the pestilence is not in the genus of goods, but of ills—then as an evil, the judgment of God. The former is with respect to us, the latter to God; the latter with respect to the efficient cause, the former with respect to the subject; the former with respect to our sense, the latter concerns the closer mind or spirit. 2) The shunning is either of a place infected by the plague, or even of a person. 3) In withdrawing or withdrawal, besides the bodily departure, we especially consider the affection, as has been said, of the soul, wherein it occurs just now. 4) Natural affection, or the character and sense of nature, first towards any evils and then towards plague; and spiritual affection, which surpasses, rules, and supplants, although it does not extinguish, nature and natural things—even if a spiritual person lives not according to his own nature and flesh, but according to the Spirit, who tames his natural affections, and conceals and extinguishes their light and ardor, as it were, just as the sun does to lesser stars.

Now I conclude in this way: 1) inasmuch as it is an evil, by no means must it be wished for or desired; 2) therefore, it must be prayed against; 3) finally it must also be shunned, of course only with just methods. No one that I know can resist these, even if they are founded on a nature of evil and its natural aversion to it. For just as in the rest of the evils—disease, famine, and war, with which plague is frequently joined—is it not entirely right to turn aside from them, and by any means or remedies to cure or prevent them? What the proper method of acting is and the conditions required in those cases must be observed no less here than there.

This case seems more doubtful: is it permissible to shun those things that are not simply ills *qua* ills and ones inimical to nature, but ills *qua* judgments of God? Surely it is by no means permissible for you to be indignant that God is judge either to visit the sins of men in the covenant, nor is it permissible for you to resist, and remain silent as if to elude those arrows by your avoidance and flight. So again, one must remember the chief parts of this decision at every point: but truly, in a mind rightly composed, no part of righteous patience or fortitude disparages that either these are imminent bolts of lightning and you should not audaciously object to them, or that you should take care to yourself that the inflicted bolts are extracted and you heal them. But in fact, prudence commands you not to avoid them by any means. For either God desires that you are plucked out of them as from the midst of the waters with Noah, or saved with Lot from a general fire of the country, or even healed from a lethal disease with Hezekiah. You must certainly explore the means that are at hand and that divine providence would suggest are to be laid hold of, whereby you would submit to him, and God would desire you either unmolested or delivered. Of course, the means ought to be just and lawful. On the contrary, if you should neglect them you would be rightly accused of imprudence, recklessness, and tempting God. For our religion teaches us that means and the use of them are not to be separated from the providence of God, nor do the secret decrees of God withstand or object to the revealed rule and law of our actions.

The Christian's Attitude Toward an Imminent Plague
In turning aside from the judgments of God and the plague, since nearly the whole question impinges on the heart, this must be explained at once. And if not in this topic, before we fully decide the proposed difficulty regarding flight or withdrawal, then when? Although we would answer that question afterwards, it also belongs to this topic to know what and what sort of mindset we approve of or reprove.

Therefore, question 1: I ask, what is a fitting mindset toward an imminent calamity and plague? When should we resist it and when are we constrained to meet it? For there are duties of godliness, some towards a future and pressing affliction, and others towards an affliction present and hanging over you. And then certainly it is necessary to foreknow some things and to care for others; of course, these things must be sought from the innermost discipline. That is so that we may know the condition of the afflictions of this life as necessary, common, and useful in every way. Εἰ δέον ἐστί, "if it is necessary," says Peter, that is, "for a moment" if necessary "you may have had to suffer various trials" (1 Peter 1:6). Many passages teach the common condition of people and believers (Job 7:1; 14:1; Heb. 12:6–8) and also the same use of afflictions (Heb. 12:10) ὁ δὲ ἐπὶ τὸ συμφέρον. "But God disciplines us for our good."

Moreover, it is necessary for us to take care of ourselves and our soul by the following: First, that we would be in a state of grace, and seek the kingdom of God before all else and his righteousness (Matt. 6:33). Second, that we are in the faith and in the life of faith, for the just man would live out of his faith (Rom. 1:17, Eph. 6:16). Third, that we are certain of those among us (2 Cor. 13:5). Finally, that we are instructed in the witness of the cross, which teaches us to bear that cross patiently and well, from which that passage of James 1:5 must be received, "if anyone would lack wisdom," which is right to understand as true for any kind of wisdom.

Question 2: To what heart do we commit ourselves in order to endure this present affliction now, and thus the plague? I respond: You would have said it all if you had said "a patient heart." But this is the kind of virtue that has broad latitude and various degrees, and its own ἔργον τέλειον, "perfect work" (Jas. 1:4), which can be learned by carefully going through particulars with application made to the present question: First, there is the point that the heart and hand of divine visitation are sensitive, and not ἀναίσθητος, unfeeling, harsh, stubborn, or unmindful of the one who is suffering, persecuted, or bent down. How greatly God most gravely detests contumacy (Isa. 1:5; 42:24–25; Jer. 5:3; Prov. 23:34–35; Exod. 8:15; 9:34; 2 Chron. 36:13); and how ἀναλγησίαν, insensibility, and ἀπαθεῖαν, apathy, are also detested by Taurus, a philosopher, albeit a Stoic one, in Aulus Gellius (bk. 12, ch. 5).[23] Second, we would draw from the plague and other ills a humble mind: "Humble yourselves, therefore, under the mighty hand of

---

23. Aulus Gellius, *Attic Nights*, bk. 12, ch. 5 in *LCL* 200:372–383

God"²⁴ (1 Pet. 5:6; cf. Jas. 4:10; 2 Chron. 7:14; Deut. 8:3; Dan. 4:37; 5:22; 1 Sam. 3:18). Third, [we would learn that patience possesses] calmness and self-sufficiency²⁵ or satisfaction, of which the apostle bears witness in Philippians 4:11–12 (cf. Job 1:21). And Marcus Aurelius says regarding himself in bk. 10, §14, "The well-instructed and humble heart says to Nature that gives and takes back all we have, 'Give what you will, and take back what you will.' And he does not say this puffed up with any pride, but obediently and with good will."²⁶ Fourth, it is necessary to receive even ills and afflictions with a grateful heart (Jas. 1:2; Heb. 10:34; Ps. 119:71; Rom. 5:2–3). "A Christian, even when condemned, gives thanks," says Tertullian in his *Apologetic*,²⁷ and also in his book *On Patience*: "In fact, it is right for us to rejoice and congratulate ourselves that we are worthy of divine chastisement. 'I' he says, 'chastise those whom I love.' O how blessed is that servant, on whose correction the Lord is intent, with whom he deems worthy to be angry, whom he does not deceive by concealing admonishment."²⁸ For which reason, when this sentence was pronounced by the judge, "It pleases the court to punish Thascius Cyprian with the sword," the voice of Cyprian answered, "Thanks be to God!" The holy anthem is "A worthy martyr is worthy to God." Chrysostom in his eighth homily on Colossians says, "This tongue does nothing holier than to give thanks to God in the midst of adversities. Certainly, it does no less than the tongue of the martyrs. Both are crowned alike."²⁹ And regarding himself, in his letter to Cyriacus:

> For even when I might flee from the city, I will not concern myself with this at all, but I was saying within myself, 'Even if the Empress³⁰ wants to exile me, let me go into exile, for 'the earth is the Lord's and the fullness thereof' (Ps. 24:1). And if she wants to cut me in two, let her cut me in two. So likewise Isaiah also suffered, I have him as an exam-

---

24. Gk. ταπεινώθητε ὑπὸ τὴν κραταινιὰν χεῖρα τοῦ θεοῦ
25. Gk. αὐταρκείαι
26. Marcus Aurelius, *Meditations* in *LCL* 58:274–275
27. Tertullian, *Apology*, in *ANF* 3:18
28. Tertullian, *On Patience*, in *ANF* 3:714
29. See on Col. 3:5–7, John Chrysostom, *Homilies on Colossians* in *NPNF1* 13:298; cf. idem, *Homiliae XII in Epistolam ad Colossenses* in *PG* 62:357–358.
30. On Chrysostom's banishment by Empress Eudoxia with Theophilus, the patriarch of Alexandria, in 403 at the Synod of 'the Oak' (*Synodus ad Quercum*; Quercum, "The Oak" was a suburb of Chalcedon), see Socrates Sozomen, *Ecclesiastical Histories* in *NPNF2* 2:148–149; for an account with the specification of the charges, see C. J. Hefele, *A History of the Councils of the Church*, 5 vols. (Edinburgh: T. & T. Clark, 1876), 2:430–439.

ple. If she wants to toss me into the sea, I am mindful of Jonah. If she wants to cast me into a furnace, likewise the three children suffered. If she wants me thrown to the wild beasts, then let her, I am mindful of Daniel who was cast into the lions' den. If she wants to stone me, then I have company with Stephen the first martyr. If she wants to take my head, let her take it, then I have company with John the Baptist. If she even wants to take away my property, then let her, naked I came from my mother's womb, naked I will also depart (Job. 1:21).[31]

Histories regarding Emperor Maurice[32] constantly reference that he cried out to his wife and his children, who were executed violently before him by the command of Phocas, with the same pious phrase, "You are just, O Lord, and your judgment righteous."[33] Among the Jews the family of the holy ones or of those sanctifying God as holy[34] is celebrated because even in every adversity and persecution they ceaselessly praise God with: כי ככל השמרית קדשו את השם[35]

To those words and the example of Chrysostom, I cannot but remember the blessed martyr Bradford in England in the times of Mary, who likewise responded approximately with: "If the queen should grant me my life, I would thank to her. If she should desire to send me into exile, I would thank her. If she would burn me, I would thank her. If she would imprison me forever, I would thank her."[36] And there are very many examples of this sort throughout all of history. Fifth, it is necessary to endure afflictions with a brave heart, and sustain them, which is fighting the good fight[37] (1 Tim. 6:12; 2 Tim. 4:7). Note Augustine's remark: "O Lord, burn here, cleave here, only spare in eternity."[38] Sixth, both in faith and confidence[39] recline upon

---

31. Chrysostom, *Ep. Cyriaco Episcopo Exsulanti* in *PG* 52:683–684.
32. Emperor Maurice (539–602) was emperor of the Eastern Roman Empire from 589 to 602. Maurice and his sons were executed in a coup d'état led by a general named Phocas.
33. See Theophanes the Confessor, *Chronographia*, AM 6094–6095; idem, *The Chronicle of Theophanes: An English Translation of Anni Mundi*, trans. H. Turtledove, 2 vols. (University of Pennsylvania Press, 1982).
34. Heb. קדושים.
35. Though השמרית is likely an error, the sense is something like, "Even when things were bad, they sanctified God (lit. the name)."
36. John Bradford, *The Writings of John Bradford*, 2 vols. (Cambridge: Cambridge University Press, 1848–1853), 1:500.
37. Gk. τὸν καλὸν ἀγῶνα ἀγωνίζειν
38. This prayer is frequently attributed to Augustine, e.g. Peter Lombard, *Commentarius in Psalmos*, Ps. 6:2 in *PL* 191:105.
39. *Fide et fiducia*

the divine promises, especially that one in 1 Corinthians 10:13, "God is faithful, who does not allow you to be tempted beyond what you can bear, but with the trial, will make also a way of escape, so that you may sustain it." Finally, before all things, the soul must be freed from the fear of death, which when evils seem to pile up terribly, then people struggle with such great dread and favor flight. Hebrews 2:14–15 is opposed to this, because Christ destroyed "the one who has the power of death"[40] and redeemed all those who through the fear of death "were subject to lifelong slavery,"[41] and many other passages point to this end. Therefore, it is right for such a heart to be equipped and armed for all kinds of afflictions, and first to endure and then sustain the plague. For which reason it will not trouble us much, this question of flight of plague, either in raising it or solving it. For most of it arises from a heart that is not prepared enough for evils, and especially not for death. How vainly miserable persons believe that they can evade death with flight! If it were otherwise, they would neither still be anxious regarding flight nor would the flight on this score be certain, even if they were to withdraw also. In fact, flight chiefly should be estimated as from the heart—as much as dread agitates it, prudence does not moderate it. Take an obvious example from a soldier. Ask him whether it would be licit to flee. They will all exclaim, "Not in the least!" But ask whether sometimes it is licit to withdraw. And ask if it is sometimes licit for the commander himself to withdraw, for this often belongs to prudence and to justice. So also you should consult the circumstances for yourself and your own. For just as it is fitting that a soldier is always to have a brave heart, so it is fitting for a Christian because he also is a soldier, and he has many and more serious reasons for fortitude than anyone else. But fortitude tames and expels terror. And those redeemed by Christ are faithful to him to the end, so that they would serve God without fear[42] (Luke 1:74). But as it is not licit for a soldier to withdraw or in any way desert their station, so it is not permitted for a Christian to turn aside from evils or the plague with loss to their necessary calling.

How to Avoid the Plague

Previously we distinguished between shunning the plague, an infected place, and persons, for when we are laid low by the plague it does not lurk

---

40. Gk. τόν τὸ κράτος ἔχοντα τοῦ θανάτου
41. Gk. διὰ παντὸς τοῦ ζῆν ἔνοχοι ἦσαν δουλείας
42. Gk. ἀφόβως

in the aether or stroll about, but we observe that it is evident either in a certain place or in persons. Moreover, we draw these conclusions:

Conclusion 1: It is not licit to desert a place, even though it is touched with the plague, to which you have been bound by a necessary bond of your vocation; in the same way either to a person or to people or an agent for a society. For example, you must defend the city, a castle, or a manor when the plague has already invaded it or afterwards; you cannot abandon them at your pleasure. Or without respect to the place, if the army, the people, the church, your family should remain in place when the plague falls upon them, indeed as it is not licit for soldiers to abandon [their post], then it is also not licit for magistrates to abandon their subjects, ministers their Church, teachers their schools, or parents their families, all of whom must stay, and that for the duration, in their stations in which societies each are bound to their duty, to that which they are called. On the other hand, if you are clearly free and have your own right and are not bound more to one place than another so that the locality, the people, or a society there could bear your absence without any loss of what you would be otherwise obligated to render, it is then right to withdraw; just as it is right to withdraw from an unsafe lodging to another safer and healthier one, and from one tenement to another, then why could you not also go to another city where changing location therefore grants a change of health? Nor does any reason compel you to live in a less clean place. And then why shouldn't those who seek their sustenance by their manual labor, when they are deprived of means by a plague and they are compelled to leave and endure life elsewhere, find work so that they might sustain themselves and their family?

Conclusion 2: Something similar must be said regarding whether persons infected with plague are to be abandoned or not. Of course, when you are bound to them by that necessity of blood, friendship, or office, so that they cannot manage without you and without your necessary support, assuredly one must remain and do for them what you would want done for yourself. Otherwise, if they should not miss your presence or assistance as necessary, and others would be adequately available, so that your assistance would be unnecessary or superfluous, it is licit for you to depart.

Now at last let us proceed to the decision of the proposed question. We answer that it is licit to withdraw in time of plague, with three precautions or distinctions; one toward God, one toward your soul, and [one toward] the necessary calling of life. That is, it is not licit to withdraw if you think that you can or must escape from God, his hand, or his judgment, or if it would be licit for you to withdraw yourself or furtively remove yourself from it. Yet it is apparent that sometimes this is the perverse and wicked persuasion of many. Next, one must not leave with a fearful heart, for that departure could not be approved of at all. Such a heart by no means would lack sin and it is contrary to Christian fortitude and fearlessness.[43] Finally, where a necessary vocation binds you to a place, such that you would be bound to it not by your choice but by another's will—like a servant, a handmaiden, a soldier, a pastor, and so forth—[it is by no means licit to withdraw] without the consent of those by whom you have been called to that place and to that province. Besides for just causes, it is by no means licit at all for servants to leave their household, soldiers their city or army, pastors their congregations, and so forth, or to desert one's office due to danger. On the contrary, if you did not hold a wicked intent to flee God, or have a wicked fear, or were not shirking your necessary calling, I do not see how it would not be licit to withdraw and turn aside from a place blasted with plague. I say "*would* be licit" for it must not be thought that you must withdraw or that you must be said to tempt God if, without any recklessness of heart, but the obligatory reverence for God and his hand, and from your contentment with your condition, you were to remain. Not at all! For many people with no need for restraint, as certainly must be taught from this case, do not sin. Yet it would have been far healthier to remain in that place, with many valid arguments that lead toward and promote godliness, for those who would appear to have also abandoned with that place godliness and their best opportunity of being converted and being saved.

In this regard some things also must be prescribed to those who depart so that they do not sin under pretext more willingly or easily. Namely, we will treat the case of conscience: 1) lest they would be led away for the sake of their desire, namely to this end—because there is no occasion for excessive drinking, reveling, and whatever kind of carnal pursuits there may be in their [current] pestiferous place,[44] so they would seek out another place just in case some bit of their flesh and carnal desires should be lost—which is entirely profane and opposed to God, who calls a person who has been notorious for this through these sorts of calamities to a better life and to salvation. 2) What is more, although you may depart, it is nevertheless necessary that you remain downcast. By no means are you less liable to those

---

43. Gk. ἀφοβίαι
44. Lat., Gk. *locus*, λοιμικος

common ills and other ones. You should humble yourself just as much as if you were there present; indeed more so, lest you think yourself immune to them and safe from them. 3) And at the same time you should assist brethren, fellow citizens, and friends, albeit in whatever way you can—in prayers, counsel, and alms—and not leave them destitute.

"Certainly, this is a similar case to flight or withdrawal in persecution." To which we answer no differently than this: That you should not fear to suffer for God and for the truth, nor should you persuade yourself otherwise—that you can and ought to shun God and his hand—nor should you desert your calling. I do not oppose that it is not licit to withdraw in that case, but otherwise I deny the point. Yet, it does no harm by any means either to those who remain or those who we read offered themselves to persecution and martyrdom. Consider how the church refers to Polycarp of Smyrna from Eusebius, bk. 4, ch. 14, who, after some time of prayer and counsel with the brethren,[45] foiled the plots of his enemies and, finally in a room from which he could have also easily fled to other residences, did not want to leave, but freely walked into the path of his persecutors. Having first humanely received them like guests at table, he handed himself over with a pleasant and steadfast heart. And many such instances are present from any time in the Church.

Certainly, Tertullian was of the opinion that it must not be fled at all. For this reason, when asked by Fabius on the matter above (he calls it a problem), he wrote the book *On Flight in Persecution*, wherein, because persecution is inflicted by God and results in the good of the Church, he absolutely denied that it is to be fled in any circumstance. "Therefore, if it is established," he says, "from whom persecution happens, we can now enter into and answer your question from the very first, that there is no fleeing in persecution. For if persecution happens by God, it will have to be in no way fled because it happens by God. This depends upon a twofold reason, since what happens by God can neither be avoided, nor could it be escaped."[46] But if this argument were to obtain then nothing in the nature of things—however evil, outlawed, or horrendous—would be licit to avoid, because whatever it is has come to pass by God as its supreme cause and moderator. And it would not be licit even [to act] as once happened in the prophets with David, Elijah, and Elisha, or with the apostles and other

---

45. Gk. ὑπὸ τῆς τῶν ἀδελφῶν διαθέσεως καὶ στοργῆς ἐκβεβιασμένος; Eusebius, *Ecclesiastical History*, bk. 4, ch. 14 in *NPNF2* 1:187–188.
46. Tertullian, *On flight in Persecution* (*De Fuga in Persecutione*) in *ANF* 4:118

Christians who turned aside and avoided the fury of their adversaries as well as the treachery and plots which they prepared for them. Because if the author had intended only this, that there is no fleeing in persecution—as if either flight were a necessary remedy or the only one, or everywhere and in every way flight had to test all either from an evil fear, "for a veil of fearfulness" as he said—no one would still be unbroken by it, much less "that it would be our lot to stand under the will of God than to flee under our own" as he also says splendidly.[47] But Christians, with few objecting, also fled persecutions in such a way that their faith and conscience were unharmed—provided that they did not refuse the gravest martyrdoms when necessary, nor give up their Scriptures, or sin—and not in such a way that Tertullian's book was valued or held as a rule. It is not at all worth mentioning [that he endorsed] the Montanist Paraclete and Enthusiasm, and Jerome counted that book among those which Tertullian composed against the Church.[48]

The great Athanasius, when he fled the treachery and assaults of the Arians, and therefore was rebuked by the Arians for his cowardice and fearfulness, wrote an *Apology* for himself and for his flight, wherein he learnedly and solidly shows how in such a case it would be licit to withdraw and frustrate the intentions and fury of one's persecutors. The Arians, with Syrianus leading them, stormed into the sanctuary at night with five thousand soldiers, brandishing swords, spears, and clubs, looking for Athanasius while he was keeping watch in prayer, not terrified at all. He was determined not to desert his people and sat, remaining in the episcopal throne, commanding the deacon to recite a psalm, the people to respond "for his mercy endures forever," and then for the people to leave. The people refused to leave their bishop abandoned to the hands of their enemies, and they all shouted, as much from the clergy as from the people, for him to leave and that he should sneak away first. He, however, refused to withdraw until everyone left before him. Wherefore while some were departing others of the monks and clergy came to him, grabbed him, and led him out safe and sound in their midst past the mob of soldiers. And then he says, "Since divine providence miraculously delivered us from this danger in this way, who can justly blame me because we did not give ourselves up into the hands of those that sought us, nor go back to present

---

47. Tertullian, *On Flight* in *ANF* 4:119
48. Cf. Jerome, "53 Tertullian," *Lives of Illustrious Men* (*De Viris Illustribus*) in *NPNF2* 3:373.

ourselves to them? This would have clearly been ingratitude to the Lord, to act against his commandment and contradict the practice of the saints."[49]

In that excerpt of his *Apology*, he encompassed most elegantly nearly all that could be said on this case. But as we made a distinction in the beginning of this question regarding a fearfulness of heart in flight, which must always be disapproved of, so also he held it as an outrage that the Arians therefore reproached him for timidity and cowardice.[50] He says that he fled so that at the time when he perceived the divine will that demanded of him a violent death or martyrdom, he was prepared not to flee and to offer himself with the calmest heart. By what reason he responds to those who said he did this:

> Wherefore the saints (as has been mentioned) who fled hid themselves and were reserved for a time like doctors until needed by the sick. But to the rest and to all people generally is set forth the law that they should flee when they are sought with persecutions and hide themselves while they are searched for, and they ought not to be rash and reckless in tempting the Lord, but wait (as I have said) until a definite time of dying should come or the Judge would decide something regarding them which seems right to him. But yet he wills that we should always be prepared, that either when the time calls or when they are apprehended we would contend for the Church even to the point of death. This law the blessed martyrs also observed in times of persecutions. And these same, although they were in hiding, fortified themselves. Because if some of them were discovered by their persecutors they were not taken due to recklessness, but everywhere among them all, they professed that their readiness and their offering were accomplished by the Holy Spirit."[51]

All well and good, because although he may settle an apology for flight or withdrawal, yet he would not judge rashly about those who are read to have offered themselves at some point to their persecutors, thinking that we must state from fairness in such a way that they are moved by a singular instigation of the Spirit rather than that they acted in this way with vain imprudence or recklessness. His predecessor, Peter of Alexandria, had

---

49. Athanasius, *Defense for his Flight (Apologia pro fuga)*, ch. 25, *NPNF2* 4:264.
50. Gk. δειλία
51. Athanasius, *Defense*, ch. 22, *NPNF2* 4:263

answered exceedingly differently in his penitential canons, Canon 9, with those who freely leap to the contest or to meet martyrdom; that we also must communicate with them because they claimed to have come to it in the name of Christ, although he says that they did not pay enough attention to his words that they must not enter into trial, and other warnings or examples which he adduces there as a just reason to turn from persecutions and evils.[52] Athanasius detested timidity and the flight that follows from it, but he also does well in detesting the other side—temerity. These are two extremes in this matter, and hence both must be guarded against. For it is not that you should fear evils excessively, or that you should bear them unadvisedly and to no purpose: "For they did not flee out of fear. May it never be!"[53] For they did not flee out of fear, he says of the saints who sometimes looked out for themselves with flight, "May it never be! Rather they considered flight as a wrestling match and meditation against death. These two things ought to be observed equally, and certainly with counsel—that they did not cast themselves into dangers nor with the crime of cowardice, as they abhorred cowardice, timidity, and the hardships of exile as more grave than death."[54] Nay, as we said previously he also prefers to call first his flight and then that of the saints an ἀναχώρησις, a withdrawal, although it is commonly employed even as the term for flight, for turning aside ill-will towards flight.[55] Speaking about others, he says, "For they did not institute withdrawal through a cowardly heart, but rather that they might teach a more intentional training. Neither were they condemned for their flight nor were they therefore accused of fearfulness."[56] Regarding himself, near the end he says, "And certainly that was the reason for our withdrawal."[57] For which he argued in this way among other things, "If they would scorn those who hide themselves, while they are sought after for death, and slander those who flee their persecutors, what, I ask, will they do when they see Jacob fleeing from his brother Esau—'Are you fleeing?'

---

52. See Peter of Alexandria, *The Canonical Epistle*, canon 9 in *ANF* 6:273
53. Gk. οὐ γὰρ δὴ διὰ δειλίαν ἔφευγον. Μὴ γένοιτο!
54. Athanasius, *Defense* ch. 17, *NPNF2* 4:261
55. Lat. *fugacitas*
56. Hoornbeeck's Gk. "οὐ δὲ γὰρ ἀντὶ ῥαθυμίας εἶχον τὴν ἀναχώρησιν, ἀλλὰ καὶ μείζονα τότε τὸν τόνον τῆς ἀσκήσεως ἐπέτεινον, οὐδὲ κατεγινώσκοντο φεύγοντες, οὐδὲ κατηγοροῦντο δειλίας παρὰ τοιούτων." Hoornbeek's Lat. "*neque enim per animi ignaviam secessionem instituerunt, quin potius ut se intentiori traderent ascesi, neque fugacitatis condemnabantur, neque timiditatis propterea accusabantur.*"
57. Gk. "Καὶ γὰρ τοιοῦτος ὁ τρόπος τῆς ἀναχωρήσεως ἡμῶν γέγονε." Lat. "*Atque illa quidem ratio fuit secessionis nostrae.*"

And Moses withdrawing to the Midianites from fear of Pharaoh—'Do you withdraw?'"[58] Fleeing, φυγὴ, is simply withdrawal, ἀναχώρησις, to him. "Or what will those who blabber on in this way answer about David who fled his own house from the pursuers Saul sent to kill him, and for hiding in a cave and changing his countenance, until he might escape Abimelech and escape his plots? Or what will those say, who are ready to say anything, if they should see the great Elijah ἐπικαλούμενον μὲν τὸν Θεὸν καὶ νεκρὸν ἐγείραντα," which is not, as the version of Pieter Nanninck has it, *Deum nominatum et mortuos excitantem*,[59] "God having been named and raising the dead;" but instead it should be *calling upon God and raising the dead*, hiding himself from Ahab, and fleeing from the threats of Jezebel—at which time even the sons of the prophet who were sought for slaughter hid in caves with Obadiah's assistance? Perhaps they have not read something of them as it is too outdated, or do they have no remembrance of the things mentioned in the Gospels? But then what? Are they ignorant of this one thing, that the disciples also sought retreats and hiding places from fear of the Jews? And Paul at Damascus escaped from the governor's hands in a basket, while he was sought by the prefect of his clan. With what mind, I ask, do they read those things about the saints? Or can they reveal then the pretext for their recklessness, if they would argue against God's will, and thoroughly slander the holy Scriptures?[60] But he likewise proffers examples from Christ, when he did not act any differently, and either fled Herod, or Archelaus, or the rest of the Jews as is read in the sacred history of the Evangelists. From which he responded abundantly to the slanders of the Arians regarding flight or withdrawal. His action was commended first by others and then later by Augustine, in his epistle to Honoratus.[61]

Nazianzus refers to Marcus Arethusius, the Stylite because it was not from cowardice (as Pirckheimer incorrectly translated it at first as *ob animi pusillanimitatem*, "on account of his faintheartedness," when in Greek it is οὐ δι᾽ ἀνανδρίαν μᾶλλον, ἢ φεύγειν ἐκ πόλεως εἰς πόλιν κελεύουσαν ἐντολήν: prudence, on account of the command saying that he must flee from city to city to avoid the fury of the Gentiles whose temples and idols he had

---

58. Athanasius, *Defense*, ch. 10, *ANF* 6:258
59. Athanasius, *Opera Omnia*, ed. Pieter Nanninck (Nannius) (Basil: Froben, 1556), 325.
60. Athanasius, *Defense*, ch. 10, *ANF* 6:258–659.
61. Augustine, Letter 228 in *NPNF1* 1:577–581.

demolished.⁶² But seeing that subsequently some took it as a bad example and fell away, but others rushed into dangers, he took counsel—which Nazianzus praised—took counsel and pursued it,⁶³ which is why he returned from flight and rejoiced to hand himself over to the infuriated people and to his persecutors; and so he became a martyr of Christ, ἀθλητὴς ἐθελοντὴς, a voluntary contender, although not so to other worthless people who interpret it more as περιφρόνησιν ἢ ἀνδρείαν, imprudence than fortitude. In this and similar cases of others offering themselves from a good heartfelt zeal into the danger of persecution, plague, or similar things, that saying of Athanasius must be applied, that one must believe there is the movement of a good spirit in them, so that we would not judge something rashly.

Clement, who is called the Roman in book five of the *Apostolic Constitutions*, ch. 7, teaches that a believer must not expose himself to dangers, nor fear due to cowardice, but flee cautiously and, if he falls in a trial, contend to restore his crown. Such is an argument of the chapter, but of himself he speaks in this way: "Wherefore we should not be exceedingly eager, nor fall headfirst into dangers, for the Lord says, 'Pray that you would not enter into temptation. Indeed the Spirit is willing but the flesh is weak,' so that if the time comes, we would not befoul our profession with cowardice."⁶⁴ And so in this business, whether one treats of flight in persecution or plague, one must answer in the same way to both questions. And what has been said there so appositely can be applied here: beware of recklessness so that you would not rush into dangers with no pressing necessity; nor also should you dread when you are even called to undergo death.

Hence there is what that most reverend man, George Abbot, the archbishop of Canterbury, wrote in his *Explanation of Six Illustrious Questions*, which Abraham Scultetus had reprinted in Germany. In question five, Abbot conjoined both, "On flight in persecution or plague" where his determination still may not satisfy a doubt.⁶⁵ In the whole matter, which he thinks he solves, there is only the distinction of persons. He pronounces one way on ministers and another on the laity. It is by no means licit for

---

62. See Gregory Nazianzus, *Oratio IV*, chs. 88–89 in *PG* 35:618–622, esp. 618; see idem, *D. Gregorii Nazianzeni Orationes XXX*, ed. Willibald Pirckheimer (Basil: Officina Frobeniana, 1531), 95; idem et al., *Julian the Emperor: Containing Gregory Nazianzen's Two Invectives and Libanius' Monody with Julian's Extant Theosophical Works*, trans. C. W. King (London: George Bell & Sons, 1888), 55–59.

63. Gk. Βουλὴν ἀρίστην τὲ καὶ φιλοσοφωτάτην

64. Hoornbeeck is paraphrasing *Apostolicarum constitutionum et catholicae doctrinae Clementis Romani Libri VIII* (Antwerp: Christophorus Plantin, 1578), 60–63.

65. Abbot, "On flight in persecution or plague." See page 274 in this volume.

a minister to flee either in persecution or plague, but certainly so for the laity. "As a summary, which embraces everything that has been said, as it is licit for a layman to flee in persecution, so also for a woman or a youth, because they will not render an account for other souls. But a minister must be expected to remain if he were to have a pastoral care, and against his own person there is not instituted a persecution when there are many pastors. But if this be so, then he can transfer the common care to the rest of the ministers and leave for a time."[66] And, regarding flight of plague, he says that for laity it is licit but not at all for a minister. Notwithstanding, the cases can depend on whether it is a time of persecution or in time of plague [to decide whether] it is or is not licit for the laity to flee. The case given is by no means of a kind in which his presence, duty, and assistance would be necessary; and to abandon one's neighbor, to desert one's vocation, is contrary to charity and justice. In a case of this sort many people can immediately imagine by what bonds of blood, friendship, and calling which we posed above that some people are obligated to others, which is beyond the standing and case of a minister and whatever a minister ought not to flee that arise from his calling, wherein he is bound to the Church. But there are other callings for other people, whereby they are daily obligated in the same way to other things. Therefore I prefer to search for a decision on the proposed question of withdrawal by reason of one's calling rather than simply from the [distinction] of persons.

Peter Martyr, besides in his *Common Places*, class 3, ch. 12, wrote a long letter on this matter, the summary of which he renders at this point: "Therefore flight is granted, but with this law, that we do not transgress the commandments of God by flight. The sum of which depends upon two items, that we pursue what is owed to God and our neighbor with due godliness and love."[67] That is the best rule and must be carefully observed!

Theologians everywhere love to follow Augustine here in his letter 180, to Honoratus, whose footprints Abbot neatly held to in his *Response* and as Aretius did also in his *Problematic Topics*, no. 89, "On flight."[68] But Augustine, when consulted on flight in a time of imminent danger and

66. Ibid.
67. Peter Martyr Vermigli (1499–1562), *Loci Communes*, 11th ed. (Geneva: Pierre Aubert, 1624), class III, ch. 12, §23, p465; for the entire treatment *"De Fuga"*, see §§22–31, pp. 464–467.
68. George Abbot, §16 in *Explicatio Sex Illustrium Quaestionum* (Frankfurt: Jonah Rosa, 1616), 146; see page 274 in this volume; Benedict Marti (Benedictus Aretius, 1505–1574), *SS. Theologiae Problemata hoc est, Loci Communes Christianae Religionis Methodice Explicati*, (Geneva: Isayas le Preux, 1617), 502–510.

persecution, answers, "Neither must they be prohibited who desire to travel to secure places if they can, nor must the bonds of our ministry, by which the love of Christ constrains us lest we desert the churches we must serve, be ruptured."[69] Thus he wanted all ministers to remain for some church has to survive, or at least some faithful upon whom they could and must bestow the holy things for the sake of the office.

Melanchthon in his *Theological Counsels*, part 1, page 664, in the time of the Germanic war in the year 1547 did not lightly and according to his own opinion say to Johann Mathesius, "Now I come to your chief question: If your magistrates do not expel you, I think you must remain in your station and your church."[70] And Franciscus Junius—in a disputation on the ecclesiastical ministry held in our academy at Leiden in 1600, with Guilielmus Rivet as respondent—set forth this as a corollary: "Flight from evident danger is not contrary to the office of a pastor, provided it is an extrinsic forcing into flight (with the good favor, counsel, or approval of the sheep), for he holds an earnest affection for the sheep and, by the example of Paul, in spirit is with them."[71] Note well that it is with the good favor of the sheep—it is not that he deserts them in flight and leaves them destitute.

Claude D'Espence, the Paris theologian, in his *Digressions on 1 Timothy*, bk. 3, ch. 19, after he had spoken about flight in persecution, introduces another dissertation on the same topic but in the time and risk of plague, and so the topics cohere amongst themselves and are expedited in a similar way. Likewise Alfonso Salmeron conjoins both in his *Commentary on the Gospel*, bk. 4, part 2, treatise 16.[72] In persecution the works of men intercede, and one must expressly beware of them. In plague, it is asked, namely is there an ordinary and mediate interposition of natural causes, and how could the corruption, infection, or ἀκρασία of these be cured and blunted? God also frequently conjoins both when he sets forth or inflicts his judgments. D'Espence distinguishes first between a free man, that he "licitly flees the imminent scourge of God—plague, famine, sword—so that

---

69. Augustine, Letter 228 in *NPNF1* 1:577

70. Philip Melanchthon, *Consilia sive Iudicia Theologica itemque Responsiones* 2 vols. (Neustadt: Wilhelm Harnisius, 1600), 1:664–665; idem, *Epistolae*, 2 vols. (London, 1570–1574), 2:39–40; idem, Ep. 3647, *CR* 6:304–305.

71. François Du Jon (Franciscus Junius, 1545–1603), Disp. 48 "De Ministerio Ecclesiastico" in *Opera*, 2 vols. (Geneva: Pierre et Jacques Chouet, 1613), 1:2112

72. Alphonso Salmeron, S.J. (1515–1585), "Tractatus 16 De fuga in persecutione" in *Commentarii in Evangelicam Historiam et in Acta Apostolorum*, 16 vols. (Cologne: Hierat & Gymnicus, 1612–1615), 4:359–367, especially 353–367.

he could be of more benefit and that for a longer time to himself and others, or with some other good intention."[73] But then he also has this,

> There is another reason why one who from his station and office would have been bound to a burden requiring his presence and in the event of his flight or daily absence it would result in loss, scandal, or danger either to the community or his neighbor. For a bond whereby someone is bound to another, and such a special obligation that has bound by natural and divine law, neither the fear of death nor the just scourge of the Lord dissolves. From which basis, namely those officers and their assistants who have undertaken the procurement of another's safety, whether public or private, are obligated not to flee but to remain, to live with and die alongside the souls they have care of... and also those officers of cities or communities (whether seculars or religious)—superiors, judges, magistrates, pharmacists—anyone likewise in a rule, whether monastic or domestic, and who live together as one—whether spouses, parents, children, tutors, students, masters, servants, neighbors necessary to other neighbors, the one lacking another's works, those owing mutual aid to one another—in the moment of need one must not desert another. For we also must lay down our lives for the brethren (1 John 3), have care for our own (1 Tim. 5), and love our neighbors as ourselves (Matt. 22).[74]

He determines the matter exceedingly well. He is persuasive that there is absolutely no flight [from one's duty], and he does prove it; but so long as people have an account of God and their neighbor and would not desert their necessary calling, he says, "In time of plague, or in some other case due to shunning the danger of death, certainly it is licit for free people to flee. There is no flight to a country estate from one's office, or from anywhere dangerous; it is not even licit to flee unless they also deliberate and provide somewhere to go for others to whom they are obligated."[75] Then he wisely and piously admonishes first those fleeing and then those remaining in a direct oration, lest he would judge or despise either, or lest they would

---

73. Claude D'Espence (1511–1571), see chs 14–18 on various kinds of persecution, see ch. 19 on flight in time and danger of plague, in *In priorem D. Pauli Apostoli ad Timotheum Epistolam, Commentarii et Digressiones* (Paris: Michaelis Vascosanus, 1561) 350–362, 362–365 respectively, 362H especially.
74. D'Espence, *Digressiones*, 363B.
75. D'Espence, *Digressiones*, 364F.

justify or praise themselves. That this usually happens in this business is all too familiar and reckless.

> And so those who flee danger in abhorrence of death and acknowledge and examine the weakness of their love toward their neighbor do not defend or excuse themselves, nor do they consider themselves in any different way than in true repentance, or consider that they will not escape the wrath of a striking God without it. And they who remain and persist do not condemn the weak, but commend their flight more to divine mercy. And they consider themselves and in what cases they should remain amidst the dangers of plague, whether they should remain in recklessness, surrounded by divine wrath, or should remain in the destitution of necessary supplies for those who travel elsewhere; or, in confidence of divine protection, animated by a spirit of love, humbled in the sight of God, interceding his wrath prayerfully. So that they may serve their neighbors they mourn with those who mourn, and so forth. And in turn, they do not withdraw from these their necessary support, but those who remain should provide for those that remain after themselves and relinquish it."[76]

I have not seen anyone of this era or class of writers treat this argument and delimit it more carefully and prudently or treat the doubtful case more learnedly and wisely. However, Bellarmine (after the book on ecclesiastical writers, in the index of things explained about Holy Scripture, on the first letter to Timothy) mentions Claude D'Espence and adds, "But he should be read cautiously here."[77] Of course, this is because D'Espence seemed quite moderate towards us and our perspectives; because in the Colloquy of Poissy (1561), when commanded by the Cardinal of Lorraine[78] to deal with Beza, D'Espence was not ashamed to disavow [the Cardinal's policy] publicly, stating that he was always horrified by the punishments that were previously inflicted upon poor people due to their religion, which comment first Beza and then des Gallars reference in the *Commentary on the*

---

76. D'Espence, *Digressiones* 365C

77. Robert Bellarmine, *De Scriptoribus Ecclesiasticis cum adjunctis indicibus* (Brussels: Jean Leonard, 1719), fol. Gg3r, on 1 Tim. "Claudius Espencaeus, sed hic caute legendus;" idem, *Opera* (Paris: L. Vivès, 1870–1891), 12:481.

78. The politically and ecclesiastically influential Cardinal Charles de Lorraine (1524–1574), Duke of Chevreuse, of the House of Guise. His sister was Mary of Guise, the mother of Mary Stuart (1542–1587), the Roman Catholic Queen of Scots.

State of Religion and the Commonwealth in the Kingdom of France, part 1, at year 1561, page 131.⁷⁹ Of that passage, there is the most ample comment in Jacques-Auguste de Thou's *Histories*, bk. 28.⁸⁰ Of course, comments of this kind were the reason the dignity of the cardinalcy was kept back from him judicially⁸¹ in the year 1555 when he and Juan de las Casas were excluded from the number of the cardinals, but for far different reasons. The former at least because he had said during his preaching that the *Golden Legend* would have to be called the *Iron Legend*, which he was also compelled to recant publicly.⁸² The latter was excluded because in his youth he was said to have praised an unmentionably abominable practice in a poem,⁸³ thus de Thou in bk. 16.⁸⁴ Which is not as doubtful as the historian references it (with "he was said to have praised") as there are several examples of this sort that I have seen in the public library of Utrecht. Perhaps it is so in many libraries, because the poem is not so long and is commonly joined to other Italian works and poems under the title, *Il primo libro dell' opere Burlesche di Francesco Bernia* (Florence, 1548).

But what has been said shall be to the question of the proposed case regarding fleeing or shunning the plague according to the three conditions

---

79. This oration of Beza's can be found in Jean de Serres, *Commentarii de statu religionis e reipublicae in regno Galliae*, 5 vols. (Geneva: 1571–1590), 1:127v–141r, esp. 1:131v. Beza: "For if you believe that last opinion, one side can in no way stop unless there is the total destruction and ruin of the other side, which is too inhuman to even think, and too horrible and cruel to do." For D'Espence's reported remark in Serres, see 1:163r: "D'Espence, who prefaced himself stating that he had long wished for the opportunity to confer together, says that he had always utterly abhorred those cruel punishments employed against those who embraced this religion."

80. A direct citation of the Latin commentary by Jacques-Auguste de Thou (Thuanus, 1533–1617), *Historiae Sui Temporis*, 6 vols. (Paris: Ambrose et Jerome Drouart, 1606–1614), 2:37; 551; idem, *Jac. Augusti Thuani Historiarum sui Temporis*, 7 vols. (London: Samuel Buckley, 1733), bk. 28, §12, 2:123; idem, *Histoire Universelle*, French trans. Le Beau, 16 vols. (London: 1734), 4:94. While the 1604–1619 Drouart Latin edition is the first edition, the 1733 Buckley Latin edition is the most critical and arranged with an easier apparatus for citation.

81. *abjudicata*: to be deprived of an office by a judicial action. D'Espence was censured several times by the Sorbonne, cf. Charles Dubray, "Claude D'Espence" in *The Catholic Encyclopedia* (New York: R. Appleton Co., 1909).

82. D'Espence was critiquing the *Legenda Aurea* as unreliable and mythical accounts of the saints. By the sixteenth century there were translations into most European languages. Originally a manuscript compilation by Jacobus de Voragine of Genoa in 1275, this work is sometimes known in English as *The Golden Legend* or *The Lives of the Saints* due to William Caxton's translation in 1483. For a modern translation, Jacobus de Voragine, *The Golden Legend: Readings on the Saints*, trans. W. G. Ryan, 2 vols. (Princeton: Princeton University Press, 1993).

83. Lat. *rem nefandam*

84. See *Historiarum*, bk. 16, §7, 1:551. There is an incomplete English translation of de Thou's *Historiarum*, entitled, *Monsieur de Thou's History of His Own Time*, trans. B. Wilson, 2 vols. (London: 1730), 2:65.

or cautions that we gave: 1) Let us not flee from a fearfulness of heart or dread of adversity, disease, or at last death. For the natural leading and instinct exists so that we would certainly fear evils and, to that extent, this is not disapproved of in the natural sphere of course, as our nature is affected by ills. But at the same time nature knows that it must be ruled by a higher spirit; that is, let us not fear evils only, solely, or chiefly, but the Spirit of God. And our faith should so restrain and sanctify that fear that faith would rule the person, not only his nature, so that from a glimpse of divine providence and divine love, although placed in the greatest evils, he even knows not to fear: "Do not fear what you are about to suffer,"[85] (Rev. 2:10), and Isaiah 43:1–2, "Do not fear, even when you pass through the water, I will be with you." That is, you are so safe and secure in divine providence that you do not countenance the presence of any evils and are not susceptible to them; not that you absolutely do not feel them, at least not according to your nature, but that you do not feel them comparatively and according to your spirit, to God. With only this in view, you would do nothing from recklessness or a mere contempt of soul. It belongs to courage, and preeminently to a Christian one, that proves itself as it drives out fear; and it does not take to flight out of fearfulness. For these are the words of Augustine: "But by no means is this to be done when there is a common danger. And what must be feared more, lest it should be believed that anyone doing this," (that is, so that one would flee), "is not doing so by a desire of regarding others, but by a fear of their own dying, which would do more harm [now] by their example of fleeing than would be offered by their service of living [in the future]."[86] 2) The other condition was that no one would allow themselves to intend to flee from God and his hand or judgments, which have been merited or caused by their own sins no less than those of others. Psalm 139:7, "Where will I go from your Spirit? Or to where shall I flee from your presence?" 3) Let no one desert a necessary calling to which God, people, duty, and conscience have bound him, which Augustine said are to be impeded by certain necessities. For it is not just or fair that the church or commonwealth should suffer any loss, or that we would place our private convenience or fear before public needs. In fact, without any vice-based fear or unbelief—of course it belongs to unbelief to want to depart from God and withdraw from him—anyone

---

85. Gk. μηδὲν φοβοῦ ἃ μέλλεις πάσχειν
86. Augustine to Honoratus, *Ep.* 228, §10 in *NPNF1* 1:579.

who is without a necessary calling, if he should desire to avoid or withdraw from a place at risk and infected with plague, cannot be blamed. It is not because he ought to withdraw, but because it is licit for him to do so. "Certainly it is licit for free people to flee, but it would be better not to flee," said D'Espence.[87] Indeed, [this is true] if in fact fleeing did not mark someone out or prove them to have a fearful heart. In this case flight must be done prudently and bravely, with no recklessness or lack of consideration. In the academy of Wittenberg, when the plague was prowling about in 1566, a public announcement by the rector in the time of Veit Winsheim[88] was published to the students in the name and by the command of the elector on August 11. It said the elector willed that they were to flee even neighboring towns (so the bulletin names it in the *Wittenberg Bulletins*, vol. 7) infected with plague and suspected places in this town, which are few, lest the seeds or pestilential miasma,[89] which have been restrained by the singular goodness of God, propagate and spread, with your negligence excepted.[90] Again, around September 12 of the same year[91] and by the same rector at the time when the plague was spread more broadly throughout the city and homes, there was this form of public warning to the students:

> The condition of all professors and students in the academy at this time are not the same. Certain professors are farther removed from infected places at this point and, by God's blessing, are sufficiently steadfast in heart and present. The contagion presses certain people that have been surrounded on all sides and enclosed in a most hazardous way, and of these some have large families with a great number of young children. Therefore, because we would find no place in our vicinity open and free from contagion for a modest assembly that could render some safe or convenient haven or refuge through winter, which is now already

---

87. D'Espence, *Digressiones*, 364F
88. Veit Winsheim (Vitus Winshemius, 1501–1570) was a German rhetorician, philologist and medical doctor known primarily for his orations and studies on Thucydides, Sophocles, and Demosthenes. He also wrote a work on ancient medical views of Galen.
89. Gk. μιάσματα λοιμώδη
90. The *Programmatum Wittenbergensium* have not been located in the primary or secondary literature.
91. *Pridie Idus Septembris*: lit. "On the day before the ides of September". The ides are the 13th of the month on the Roman calendar, with the exception of March, May, July, and October, in which it is the 15th.

close at hand;[92] and neither our purse nor yours would bear long trips; and there is hope that a savage winter would burst and inhibit the savagery of this rampaging evil; it seemed good to us that this homeland of our academy must not be entirely abandoned. And so even if some, upon whom the dangers press severely, transfer their families, yet it has been decided for the rest to remain and continue customary operations. Also, of those who withdraw their families, some within a few days and the rest when the [vernal] equinox is past, will see what hope the beginnings of winter would show; whether it [the contagion] has advanced or at that point been turned back. For we will not cast aside all hope at once regarding our academy with the arms themselves,[93] but confident of the divine assistance and protection, we will do the duties of our calling. For in him we live, move, and have our being. He is our life and our length of days. We belong to him whether we live or die. Let us not doubt that [he] will take care of any of us serving faithfully to the glory of God and the church in one's calling. But also, you scholastics are different. And thus if any are horrified by the present dangers with more downcast hearts, we do not want them to await here the outcome of their separation from their parents both with sadness and anxiety. If any want to hear their preceptors teaching again with more strengthened hearts, they will not be absent from the public lectures until extreme necessity compels both conjointly and individually to seek safer places. But we warn these not to cast themselves into dangers by carelessness or unnecessary duties. For if any will be infected, all necessary things which pertain to medication and cure has been carefully provisioned in our hospital. And those feeling the beginnings of infection, they should quickly indicate it. For we have learned that remedies applied in a timely fashion are effective and save many. Nor will anyone lack our faith, counsel, and our works.

Finally, when a given house of the academic community would be corrupted by the plague [they moved to] other houses, and when the prior household had been sent away, they moved another to the present situation, which was indicated again in a bulletin from November 9. But what they say about the individual hospital of students was exceedingly prudent,

---

92. Lat. *prae foribus est*: lit. "before the doors"
93. "To cast aside one's arms" was to forsake or abandon one's post; it was to desert the army.

lest they did not also look out for students infected and sick with the plague adequately. That was the custom in the Wittenberg Academy at the time for more than twenty years, so that not in the public hospital of the city, but in a building bought for this purpose by the senate of the Academy they might separate and care for their scholars afflicted either with the plague or another disease. By three decrees in separate, a collection from the students was established for bearing the costs of the academic hospital. That council is not at all to be disapproved of, especially when a common board and community was established for students, such as at the Wittenberg Academy and others, not insofar as it was for the poorer students, but also for any other students. However, it is right that it looks after each one in a timely fashion, especially for those who in time of plague are compelled to stay or want to stay in place [at school]. Because what is present here moderates this entire business with charity and prudence, bravely and in a Christian fashion. Some remain, others depart; "let each person be fully convinced in his own mind" (Rom. 14:5).[94] Between fearfulness and recklessness, a middle way must be held. So also Franciscus Junius determined in thesis 10 of his disputation "On the Christian Life" on June 16, 1600, with Daniel Couppé as respondent:

> However, when believers must do that, so that they may glorify his name either through death or through life, it is for them to discern the means of shining forth his glory. So we must leave the end of death and life to his choice of death so that they would not recklessly decide upon their own death in the custom of people devoid of true religion, nor would they dread it more than what is right, but hold the middle position, which Paul demonstrates in 1 Corinthians 5 and Romans 8, to go quickly to hasten death not because they wanted to strip [off this life] but because they desire to be clothed [with an eternal one].[95]

Thus we have solved the first question regarding flight from plague and, in treating that one—where up until this point the chief weight of

---

94. Gk. ἕκαστος ἐν τῷ ἰδίῳ νοῒ πληροφορείσθω
95. Junius, *Theses Theologicae*, Disp. 37, *Opera* (1613), 1:2081; cf. Franciscus Junius (praes.) and Daniel Couppé (Danieal Couppaeus, fl. 1599, resp.), *Theses Theologicae De Vita Christiana* (Leiden: J. Patius, 1599), 8 pages. There is one copy of the 1599 edition, held in the Bibliothèque Nationale de France; This disputation also appears in F. Junius, F. Gomarus, A. Walaeus, G. Coddaeus, and J. Bruno, *Compendium Theologiae Thesibus in Academia Lugduno-Bat. Ordine . . . ab anno 1598 usq[ue] ad annum 1605 concinnatum* (Hanover: Antonius, 1611).

that prior question has been situated—we have at the same time solved the second and third questions: how it is necessary for the heart to await an imminent affliction and plague bravely, and likewise how to receive and endure a present affliction. Fourth there follows a question regarding our duties towards those suffering from the plague and, at last, fifth, the necessary duties towards those who have passed.

Duties toward those suffering from the plague

These duties belong to different kinds and the duties vary. But we have spoken of the necessary ones and, of course, others are optional;[96] the latter can be rendered, the former must be. And the present question regards the former ones. For we are not inquiring now about what is licit for someone to do, but what must be done and what someone is obligated to do. The necessity [to act] rests upon one's duty, which on account of the foundation of a triple bond of blood, friendship, and office, or of a duty strictly defined, displays the needs about which each person must judge regarding the necessity of their service and support. The duties of the three kinds meet a triple object: one must care especially for the sick person's soul, then attend to the disease, and then prepare them for what to endure in the remaining amount of their life. The first belongs to ministers, to which are added comforters;[97] the second to doctors and surgeons; and the last commonly to male and female nurses.[98] And since they could also be provided and cared for either by their own when sick, or by another through alms and the public [treasury], here the work of deacons, almoners, and the public hospital is required. However, since many things could be asked here, we set aside some things on account of their variability,[99] and others we commit to each one's prudence. But what do you make of doctors? Nicolaus Clemanges (you know the one who, in his letter XXIV to Johannes de Monstrolio,[100] wanted it believed that he could discern contagious places and those infected with plague by his own sense of smell, and that he could find them) asked in another letter, namely XXVII, why doctors, who both do nothing for or are of little use to the sick, should not withdraw and go

---

96. Lat. *libera*
97. Lat. *Consolatores*, Gk. Παράκλητοι
98. Lat. *auxiliatores* and *auxiliatrices*
99. *Levitas*: lit. lightness; moveability; inconstancy
100. Nicolaus Clemanges, Ep. XXIV in *Opera Omnia* (Leiden: Ludovicus Elzevir et Henricus Laurentius, 1613), 90–92.

far away when they would remain with tremendous risk to themselves?[101] And regarding his own maternal uncle—who lived in a city that the plague blasted for a long time, and who at last also died because [Clemanges] was released from the grave penalties of his own counsel, although both a doctor and one who had located his uncle's hope of help in himself alone—surely Clemanges declared [his views] exceedingly recklessly and in a way that was not theologically or humanely adequate.

But regarding ministers of the Word, the more common question is whether it is licit for them to withdraw in such a time and in such a place? It is totally impermissible [for a minister] to withdraw himself from his ministry—to desert his office, throw down his arms, and desert the sheep—without the consultation and request of the Church.

The second question is whether he can withdraw himself, not totally from the ministry, but from a specific function, namely visiting those laid low by the plague. It cannot be said otherwise that part of the minister's office is the visitation of the sick and comforting them. Now, due to the danger, which adheres in this storm to the part of the sick, and due to the contagion, in case ministers or others would be infected, or their ministry to the healthy part in the church would be deficient, it is asked whether ministers could entirely remove this [function] from themselves as something alien or inopportune, so that they would not be present with the sick and comfort them. We certainly think that it is not at all licit for ministers to either omit some part of their duty due to danger (as if the ministry will include nothing but the pleasant and danger-free,[102] contrary to the Apostle in 2 Corinthians 11:26, "dangers in the city,"[103] and dangers[104] [everywhere], and in 1 Corinthians 15:30, "why are we in danger every hour?")[105] or to think it licit for them to withdraw and deny their service as if it is at their own choice and not by the judgment of the Church. We know that elsewhere when a plague violently attacks—such as in the Genevan Church—doctors, surgeons, and some delegated from the college of pastors are chosen by lot who assist those infected with plague according to the method of their office. I think that can certainly be observed where the plague results in no great carnage and fewer have been infected and

---

101. Clemanges, Ep. XXVII, *Opera*, 95–101.
102. Gk. ἀκίνδυνον
103. Gk. κινδύνοις ἐν πόλει
104. Gk. κινδύνοις
105. Gk. κινδυνεύομεν πᾶσαν ὥραν

where as many as have been infected can be assisted by those delegated. But where the plague savages more fiercely and the entire city is ablaze with it so that scarcely a district, street, or family is uninjured, where it spreads more broadly even than a fire, and the people are affected greater than what could be assisted by some delegates from the number of pastors, as happened sometimes in our city, I think it is then more than sufficient to commit the matter to the care and prudence of individual ministers assisted by comforters, as many as is necessary for that storm, so that in this way they would meet [the needs] and the duties of comforting in their own districts for as long as the present necessity demanded. This is not to say that ministers should be compelled to visit all the sick, which is impossible, nor that ministers should deny their service to all, especially to those earnestly seeking and gasping for it, which would be inhumane; just as they could not either refuse their closest friends or deny themselves in such a case from their own families. Possidius,[106] on Augustine, book 1, chapter 27 says, "And if perhaps he was requested by the sick to come for this purpose, that he would inquire of God for them in their presence and lay hands on them, he went without delay."[107] At the same time, prudence must be commended for all, first for those who call and send for a minister, and then for ministers themselves in their going. "Be not too zealous; moderation is best in all things."[108] Sometimes it is the case that the task can be handled by someone other than the minister; likewise, sometimes it is the case that the task cannot be handled either appropriately or decently by anyone but the minister. What is necessary in each case and what would be useful has to be discerned by conscience and prudence. To remove this entire task clearly and simply from ministers, as if they were privileged from right and duty, and that the task did not concern them, or that they could withdraw themselves at will, I do not approve of. Also it is shameful not to have anyone to support ministers with assistance, or not to allow other comforts in this case. Finally, one must have regard here to the disposition, necessity, and request of the church if she were to desire especially the present service of their pastors, so that those who are ministers—that is servants, not lords, of the church—would not leave their sheep destitute in their needs.

---

106. Lat., *Posidonius*, read *Possidius* to disambiguate from Possidius (d. circa 437) from Posidonius (c. 135 B.C. – 51 B.C.).

107. For a Latin-English text, see Possidius (c. 437), *Sancti Augustini Vita*, trans. H. T. Weiskotten (Princeton: Princeton University Press, 1919), 105–106. The translation rendered here is our own. Cf. idem, *Vita Sancti Augustini* in *PL* 32:56.

108. Gk. μηδὲν ἄγαν πάντων μέσ' ἄριστα. Theognis of Megara (ca. 540 BC), *Sententiae*, 335.

Nor do ministers show themselves faithful when the church testifies that she greatly lacked their service. This is the judgment and practice of the colleges of ministers in our present calamity.

"But," you say, "there is a danger threatening ministers when speaking with other people." As if in everyday afflictions it were necessary that we should be kept free from evils and risks instead of experiencing the same lot and condition of the church and our sheep? Esther 4:13–14, "Do not think in your heart as if in the house of the king you will escape what comes to all Jews. If you should remain silent in any way in this time, serenity and deliverance will come to the Jews from elsewhere. But in the meantime, you and your father's house will perish, and who knows whether for such a time as this you have come to the kingdom?"

"But," you say, "not all are endowed with that fortitude of heart whereby they could go and speak to those people." And yet one must strive towards that fortitude, not indulging oneself either in excessive fearfulness or failing to desire that such fearfulness would be cured and corrected. Cherishing, defending, or fighting on behalf of this vice and weakness of heart accomplishes nothing, much less commending or prescribing it, or casting down into fear other braver ministers by condemning them. Augustine: "However, it is important for those who have not been deceived in this matter by this error, but are nevertheless conquered by dread, to bravely contend against their fear, with the Lord having mercy on them and assisting them, lest graver ills without comparison, which must be feared much more than these, befall them. Let this happen where the love of God burns, that the desire for the world would not smoke. For love says, who is weak and I do not strengthen him?"[109]

Finally, you say "Perhaps those saved from danger could still be useful to many in this life." And who isn't? Nor do they so die or their service—one certainly does not die wrongly with this cost here paid, even if at risk to their life. They will eventually lose their life, of course, which they owe to God and to the Church, when it is to be laid down in this or that circumstance, nor are they certain of preserving their life outside of these duties. "If never, good; yet if at some point one must die, why not in this way?" responded that godly bishop to Augustine, who comforts him in his last [moments] with a hope of a longer life. "Blessed is that servant whom the Lord, when he comes, would find acting in this way" (Matt. 24:46). Likewise, in

---

109. See Possidius, *Vita Augustini*, bk. 1, ch. 30 in *PL* 32:62

the same letter Augustine says, "Let no one flee in such a way that in such great dangers the church would lack its necessary and obligatory ministry. No one may except himself because he seems to excel in some grace and, in so thinking, tells himself that his life is more valuable and therefore so is his flight. For anyone who thinks this without a doubt pleases himself, and yet, saying this, he displeases everyone else."[110] And regarding David, when he asked his advisers whether or not he should commit himself to the battle, "He accepted this from his own counselors who sought it. He did not presume. Otherwise he would have made many imitators of his cowardice who would believe that he did this not from consideration of its usefulness to others, but out of a great deal of fear."[111]

And what I have said about comforters or paracletes joined to the minister, could that also be understood of candidates for ministry? I leave this for others to investigate. There is no doubt that they would exercise themselves in this way and also that this experience would build a distinguished step[112] to a further promotion for whom it was granted. They would commend themselves ahead of their peers in an outstanding way.

In the ancient church there were people whom they called *Parabolani* (some called them *Parabolarii* and others *Paraboli*), people devoted to the service of the sick. The origin of the word is various and it also has various senses among different writers, with some deriving it from parables or sermons and preaching, which is the opinion of Francesco Accorso di Bagnolo, who understands *parabolani* to be medical doctors, and "the name is taken from this," he says, "because they had many parables, and when anyone is more talkative he is esteemed a more learned doctor in the common opinion."[113] Alciato refers to it in this way too, in his *Dispunctionum*, bk. 4, ch. 9.[114] For truly the jurists dispute about this due to the laws which occur regarding the *parabolani* in the Theodosian and Justinian Code.[115]

---

110. Possidius, *Vita Sancti Augustini*, 136–137.
111. Possidius, *Vita*, 132–133.
112. Gk. βαθμὸν
113. See the glossator, Francesco Accorso di Bagnolo (Accursius, c. 1182–1263) on bk. 1, title 3, "De Episcopis et Clericis," §XVII, note p, & §XVIII, note f in *Codex Dn. Iustiniani Sacratissimi Principis Accursii commentariis*... (Paris: Merlin, Desboys, & Nivellius, 1559), 63–64.
114. See the jurist, Andrea Alciato (1492–1550), *Paradoxorum ad pratum, libri sex, Dispunctionum, lib. IIII, De eo quod interest, liber unus, In tres libros Codicis, lib. III, Praetermissorum, lib. II, Declamatio, una, De Stip. Diuisionib. Commmentariolus* (Lyon: Sebastianus Gryphius, 1543), 160–161.
115. See *Codex Theodosianus*, lib. 16, title 2, leg. 43 in *Theodosiani Libri XVI cum constitutionibus sirmondianis et Leges Novellae ad Theodosianum*, ed. T. Mommsen and P. M. Meyer, 2 vols. (Berlin: Weidmann, 1905), 1:851

To *parabolize* on the *Capitula* of Charlemagne and his successors is to speak.[116] Whatever he thought, he parabolized, and did it; that is, Accorso said that it is from the Greek παραβολὴ. But the opinion of Alciato is different in that it was from certain plebeian *parabolani* who had been deputed to a servanthood either of the churches or of strangers or foreigners, and in a similar way to those enlisted for the soil,[117] so to speak, so that just like as it is not licit for the latter to leave from the cultivation of the fields, so it is not licit for the former to leave from their service to the sick who resided in the hospitals,[118] from παρα and βῶλος, which is taken to mean soil. But Hottomanus and others are better who think such things have been said from the danger to which they exposed themselves in the duty of the sick, in which they did not avoid the contagion of any disease, not even a pestilential one. So among the Greeks those are called παράβολα who cast themselves into the highest dangers, and a παράβολον ἔργον is a daring and dangerous deed; a παράβολον φάρμακον is a παράβολος, a daring, confident adventurer,[119] hence a παραβόλως adverbially means the same as audaciously and recklessly; from παραβάλλομαι, to be in danger, which is the same as παρακινδυνεύω and ῥεψοκινδυνῶ; see Julius Pollux, bk. 3, ch. 28 for περὶ του επικινδυνώδους, καὶ επικινδύνου παρακινδυνεύειν, παραβάλλεσθαι; see the Souda for παραβάλλευσθαι meaning πρὸς Κίνδυνον ῥίπτειν ἑαυτόν, which is "to cast oneself into danger."[120] But I think it is from this that the name of the *Paraboli* or *Parabolani*, together with others, is derived—primarily because of their condition of life and then their heart's daring[121] in casting themselves into dangers. This is also the opinion of Baronius, *Annales*, tome 5, at the year 416 near the end; the name derives from the Greek word παράβολος, "wherein is meant," he says, "a person who meets dangers head on, the sort who were thinking they would have charge of the care

---

116. On hospitals (*Nosochomia*) in Carolingian law, see *Capitularia Regum Francorum*, bk. 2, cap. 29, ed. A. Boretius and V. Krause, 2 vols. (Hannover: Bibliopolis Hahniana, 1883–1897), 1:420–421; *Karoli Magni et Ludovici pii Christianiss. Regum et Impp. Francorum Capitula sive leges Ecclesiasticae et civiles ab Ansegiso Abbate et Benedicto Levita collectae libris septem* (Paris: Guilelmus Pelé, 1640), 38–39.
117. *Adscriptitii glaebae*: Alciato, *Dispunctionum*, 161.
118. There is a Latin pun here on *ab agrorum cultura . . . a servitio aegrorum*: "from the cultivation of the fields . . . from the service of the sick"
119. Lat. *periclitator*
120. See "περὶ του επικινδυνώδους, καὶ επικινδύνου" 3.134 in Julius Pollux of Naucratis, *Onomasticon* (Ὀνομαστικόν), ed. Wilhelm Dindorf, 5 vols in 6 (Leipzig: Libraria Kuehniana, 1824), 1:173; For παραβάλλευσθαι πρὸς Κίνδυνον ῥίπτειν ἑαυτόν, see παραβάλλευσθαι in *Lexicon Suidae*, 3 vols. (Cambridge, 1705), 3:24, "παραβάλλευσθαι se in periculum conjicere."
121. Lat. *animi audaciam*

of every kind of sickness, even in time of plague."[122] The laws regarding the *parabolani* are found in the Theodosian Code on bishops and clergy in laws 42 and 43, from which were taken the Justinian Code, section 18 in the same title, "Of *Parabolani*, who are deputed for the purpose of caring for the pained bodies of the weak, we have commanded 600 to be established."[123] And it was their duty to be present with the sick, to care for them with whatever ministry and even medicine. For which reason they are said to care for pained bodies and to manage the experience of curing. A number of these seemed to have been sufficient for the city of Alexandria, for which reason sometimes factions and mobs were stirred up by the prefects, especially when a contention arose between the prefect and the bishop, such as existed in a past year between Orestes and Cyril. The occasion of that law was in bk. 17, "It pleases our clemency that the clergy would have nothing in common with public civil processes, or pertaining to its council,[124] to whose bodies they have not been connected. In addition to these, neither do we allow those who are called *parabolani* to any public spectacle, to a place of council, nor the license to undertake judgment; unless perhaps each, due to their own cases and needs, would come to a judge, either accusing someone in a suit or are themselves accused by someone or by a syndic ordained to the common cases belonging to their entire body, so that if any of them would violate these and is removed from the small Parabolani[125] and is subjected to a suitable punishment, he is never returned to the same responsibility."[126] This body, as we have seen, consisted of hundreds of people who were subject to the bishop and were constituted by him, for which reason they also easily followed his factions as others did as well, even contrary to the [imperial] prefects. But some were common Parabolani and others the honored,[127] and then there were the curial ones, which likewise were not subject to the bishop or dependent on him. For which reason in bk. 18 it states,

> We have commanded that for the *Parabolani*, who were deputed for caring for the pained bodies of the frail, six hundred would be estab-

---

122. See Cesare Baronio, 416 AD §XXXVIII "De Parabolanis Rescriptum Imperatoris," *Annales Ecclesiastici* (Venice: Laurentius Basilius et Antonius Tivanius, 1705–1712), 5:333
123. Cf. *Cod. Theod.* 16.2.42–43 (1905), 1:851,; *Justinian Codex*, bk. 1, title 3, §18, *Corpus Iuris Civilis*, 3 vols. (Krueger, 1888–1895), 3:20.
124. Lat. *curia*
125. *Brevibus parabolanis*
126. *Cod. Just.* 1.3.17 in *CJC* 3:20
127. Lat. *vulgares . . . honorati . . .*

lished; so that by the will of the most reverend man, the bishop of the city of Alexandria, regarding these who had previously and who according to custom [now] manage the task of caring, six hundred should be chosen for the care of this kind, of course with the honored and curial ones excepted. But if anyone must be taken from their natural lot, another will be enlisted in his place according to the will of the same priest (with the honored and curial *Parabolani* excepted), so that these six hundred would comply with the commands and directions of the most reverend man the priest and remain under his care. As to the rest, the form of a broad law included up until now must be maintained over these *Parabolani* (as has already been stated either regarding public spectacles, judicial processes, and other things).[128]

Therefore, those had been established by the bishop as overseers to care for the sick throughout the city, with whatever service, even medical, was needed. This is why many commentators call the *Expositores Parabolani* medical doctors, who are called by Modestinus *circuitores*, since those who bring help to the sick go around or throughout the city. And this is enough about the *Parabolani* of the ancients.

Excursus on Martyrdom through Plague

A question has been recently moved: ought they be considered martyrs, who—whether *Parabolani* or anyone else—with danger to their life, rendered any kind of a holy or bodily service to the sick (that is, to those suffering with the plague) and in doing so were corrupted by the disease and extinguished? The occasion for the controversy is a passage in a letter of Dionysius concerning the Alexandrian plague in Eusebius, bk. 7, ch. 22,[129] where he diligently explains how Christians managed the plague— that is, in a way far different from the Gentiles who, as one may reference in their own writings, fled it full of fear in any way they could as "a thing

---

128. *Cod. Just.* 1.3.18 in *CJC* 3:20
129. Lat. *lb. VII. cap. XVII*: see instead, Eusebius, *Ecclesiastical History*, bk. 7, ch. 22 in *NPNF2* 1:306–7, especially 7.22.8: "Truly the best of our brethren departed from life in this manner, including some presbyters and deacons and those of the people who had the highest reputation; so that this form of death, through the great godliness (πολλὴν εὐσέβειαν) and strong faith (πίστιν ἰσχυρὰν) it displayed, appears to lack no mark of martyrdom (μηδὲν ἀποδεῖν μαρτυρίου δοκεῖν)." For a critical Greek text of this letter see Dionysius of Alexandria (c. 191–264 AD), *The Letters and Other Remains of Dionysius of Alexandria*, ed. C. L. Feltoe (Cambridge: Cambridge University Press, 1904), 83.

more dreadful than any dread."[130] "But to us," he says, "it was not thought of in this way, but it was inflicted from heaven by God, to exercise our faith and to test[131] the endurance of our heart no less than other kinds of misfortunes,[132] which sometimes befell us."[133] Now, concerning how believers in this storm of circumstances conducted themselves towards one another and with what kind of love and duties they proceeded amongst themselves is worthwhile for us to hear:

> The majority of our brethren were inflamed with such an immense ardor of love and fraternal kindness, that they did not spare their life in the least, but firmly holding fast to each other, they zealously visited those who were oppressed by the disease without any concern for themselves or precaution applied, (that is, ἀφυλάκτως)[134] and ceaselessly ministered to them, serving them in Christ. And they left this life with them most joyfully infected with the contagion of others, even drawing the sickness from their neighbors to themselves and freely and kindly soothing their pains. Likewise, many who took care of the sick and restored others with their strength themselves died having drawn their death to themselves. And the common saying that always seemed a polite word of courtesy, they then made real in action, taking their departure as the others' 'offscouring.'[135] Therefore, easily the most outstanding of our brethren with respect to virtue sought their death in this manner. Not a few of which included presbyters, deacons, and some people who were greatly praised for their virtue; so that this kind of death, through the great godliness and strong faith it displayed, seemed to lack nothing of the splendor of martyrdom. And they also took the bodies of the saints in their open hands and placed them on their bosoms, closed their eyes and their mouths, and bore them away on their shoulders and laid them

---

130. Gk. πρᾶγμα φόβου τε παντὸς φοβερώτερον: Dionysius of Alexandria, *Letters*, 81; Cf. Eusebius, *History* in NPNF2 1:306.

131. Gk. γυμνάσιον δὲ καὶ δοκίμιον

132. Cf. Hoornbeek Lat., *incommodarum genera*, Dionysius of Alexandria, Gk. τῶν ἄλλων ἔλαττον.

133. Hoornbeek's Latin translation expands upon the Greek text here and elsewhere with several rhetorical flourishes. His Latin phrases *sed a Deo* and *coelitus inflictam* are interpretive inferences from the Greek text; cf. Dionysius, *Letters*, 82; Hoornbeek et al., *Variorum Tractatus Theologici de Peste*, 337.

134. Lat., Gk. *nulla sui cura aut cautione adhibita*, ἀφυλάκτως

135. Cf. Dionysius, *Letters*, 83n1. A common courteous greeting in Alexandria in the period was ἐγώ εἰμι περίψηνά σου, that is, "I am offscouring," which was effectively, "I am your obedient servant."

out decently; and they clung to them and embraced them as friends, they carefully washed them and prepared them for burial with garments. And shortly afterwards they too received like treatment, for the survivors were continually following those who had gone before them. But the heathen did all these things quite differently. For they deserted those who began to become sick, and abandoned their dearest friends, tossed them out into the streets when they were half dead, and left the dead like refuse, unburied to be mutilated by the dogs.[136] They shunned any participation or fellowship with death, which still, even with all their seeking out countless precautions, in no way could they escape.[137]

The same historian references similar things in the time of the plague under Maximinus in bk. 9 ch. 7.[138]

This passage is noteworthy because it displays the illustrious love of the early Christians towards each other, towards the afflicted, the sick, and the dead, and their genuine[139] and constant duties that are so worthily read and observed; and other such excerpts incline even more against the contrary view. People are more accustomed to avidly identify these passages than to avidly lay hold of and follow them. But let us note: 1) that from this part the author describes true Christians and those duties that it was proper and decent for them to do; 2) but the contrary he lays down and observes in the heathen, first because it concerns an excessive dread of evil and the plague, and then of what are the duties of love are; 3) and that indeed the reason for the distinction derives from love, or a contempt of life and death, because Christians do not consider life so precious or death such loss; but the heathen most vehemently turn aside from these, the participation and fellowship of death;[140] 4) yet however they may fear and flee, they contract it, "even with all their seeking out countless precautions;"[141] 5) but due to those duties of godliness and charity, it especially commends these Christians and among them, those who excel still more than others; he calls them, "the majority of our brethren"

---

136. Hoornbeek adds to the Greek with his Latin translation, *canibus exponere dilanianda*
137. Cf. Eusebius, *History* in *NPNF2* 1:307
138. Eusebius, *Ecclesiastical History*, bk. 9, ch. 7 in *NPNF2* 1:360–361
139. Lat. *infucata*: lit. "unvarnished, unpainted"
140. Gk. διάδοσιν καὶ κοινωνίαν
141. Gk. καὶ πολλὰ μηχανωμένοις ἐκκλῖναι ῥᾴδιον

and "some people who were exceedingly praiseworthy;"[142] 6) and not just from the common people, but also presbyters and deacons; 7) he mentions the duties of godliness first towards the sick and then the dead; 8) and finally even extols it as a kind of martyrdom, , that is, "this kind of death, through the great godliness and strong faith it displayed, seemed to lack nothing of the splendor of martyrdom."[143] Hence that question on martyrdom through plague: whether one who, from the love and duties rendered to people suffering from the plague, dies—even perhaps from contracting that contagion—ought to be placed on the roll of the martyrs just as the one who dies on account of the faith is a true martyr? Certainly, the occasion for the controversy has been seen in that passage in Eusebius, but all the force and strength that attends it is from the Roman martyrology wherein those Alexandrians entered in and are celebrated as martyrs on February 28: "The remembrance of the most holy presbyters, deacons, and very many others of Alexandria who, in the time of Emperor Valerian, when the plague was most savagely prowling about, ministered to those suffering with the disease, most freely met death, and whom it was customary to venerate as martyrs for their religious faith of the godly."[144] Because if you will say it is erroneous and therefore the faith and religion of the Roman Church, you must see where these things tend. And so we see that question was moved and thrived among only the papists from the time Theophilus Raynaud, a Jesuit, began to dispute in favor of a martyrdom through plague, in a singular work written for this purpose, *On Martyrdom through Plague*, and whom Filiberto Marchini follows in his treatise, *On the Divine War*, or on plague, which he calls a war inflicted by God upon man. Next follows Cornelius à Lapide in his commentary on Hosea, chapter eleven at the end, where he writes in this way: "Finally, ahead of the rest of the martyrs of the Church, he numbers those who minister to those suffering the disease out of love, who stand by the same sick and die. There is an outstanding example in the *Roman Martyrology* on the day, February 28."[145] But the treatises of Raynaud's and Marchini's on the martyrdom of plague were publicly condemned by a decree of the cardinals, and it was placed on the *Index of prohibited books* under

---

142. Gk. ἀρίστους τῶν ἀδελφῶν. Καὶ τοὺς ἀπὸ τοῦ, λαοῦ λίαν ἐπαινουμένους

143. Gk. ὡς καὶ τοῦ θανάτου τοῦτο τὸ εἶδος διὰ πολλὴν εὐσέβειαν καὶ πίστιν ἰσχυρὰν γινόμενον, μηδὲν ἀποδεῖν μαρτυρίου δοκεῖν

144. Cesare Baronio, *Martyrologium Romanum* (Cologne: Ioannes Gymnicus, 1603), 148

145. Cornelius à Lapide, *Commentaria in Duodecim Prophetas Minores* (Venice: Hieronymus Albrizzi, 1703), 135; cf. Baronio, *Martyrologium Romanum* (1603), 148

Innocent X in the year 1647, on the eleventh of March, where in the *Catalogue* of prohibited books it says,

> The theological disquisition of Theophilus Raynaud compared the improper martyrdom through plague to the one commonly called proper. It belongs to the same [category] of popular error discussed regarding communion on behalf of the dead. A taste of the work, which is entitled *Spiritualia Heteroclita et anomalia pietatis*, of Filiberto Marchini of Novara, regarding the sacrament of orders, must absolutely [be prohibited] until it is corrected. Of the same error is his *Divine War effusively and diligently explained*, [and it is prohibited] until it is corrected.[146]

And against their opinion Tomás Hurtado of Toledo has disputed broadly in his book *Resolutions on the True Martyrdom of Faith*, resolution 62; but in fact, several of the reasons with which he opposes them are often quite inane.[147]

But it is amazing to see with what arguments Raynaud and Marchini fight in favor of their opinion, not only so that they may prove that martyrdom of plague is a real term, but also how it exceeds the martyrdom of faith. Of course they distinguish martyrdom into one of faith, which is the common and general one as approved by all, as when someone is killed for the sake of the faith, and another martyrdom of love or mercy, which kind they consider occurs through plague.

The passages of Scripture that they bring forward are the ones that command believers to lay down their lives for their brethren, especially in 1 John 3:16. Then they supply the reasons why the excellence of this martyrdom surpasses the martyrdom of faith. In the latter it seems there is some compulsion, for those martyrs are compelled to it by persecutors or tyrants, but in the former one runs to death only freely. In the martyrdom of faith there intercedes some sin of the persecutors; in the martyrdom of love there

---

146. Raynaud's work was condemned on December 18, 1646; cf. "Theophilus Raynaudus," *Index Librorum Prohibitorum* (Rome: The Vatican, 1946); "De martyrio per pestem, ad martyrium improprium et proprium vulgare comparato, disquisitio theologica." Four of Raynaud's other works would be banned successively in 1646, 1658, 1659, 1671.

147. Tomás Hurtado, O.P. (1589–1659), *Resolutiones Orthodoxo-Morales, Scholasticae, Historicae de vero, unico, proprio et Catholico Martyrio Fidei, Sanguine Sanctorum violenter effuso, rubricato adversus quorundam καινολογίαν de proprio Martyrio Charitatis et Misericordiae* (Cologne: Cornelius ab Egmond et Socios, 1655), 275–289.

is no sin of anyone. In the one of love there seems to be a greater conformity and likeness to the passion of Christ than the other, because Christ was free when he willed to lay down his life or not. And thus those martyrs of the plague, with no one driving them to do so, freely pour out their life and seem to meet death more for the wellbeing of their neighbor than the other martyrs of faith. Also, they live in danger of death longer, which danger the martyrs of faith resolve more quickly. The martyrdom of faith would become necessary given that the objective of the other party is the denial of Christ, the most serious sin, and must be entirely avoided; in the martyrdom of plague, with no such objective from an opposing sin, no one is compelled to it; but when one could perhaps turn away without sin, nevertheless the martyr does not will to do so. For which reason this martyrdom is a more excellent degree of love than the other. And even those plague-martyrs die for the faith, namely in faith, hope, and patience of the divine promises and eternal life, and not only for the faith but also for their brethren.

By these and other similar quibbles they at least prove the outstanding virtue in those who die in this way from the plague; nevertheless they are still not properly called martyrs. And there is no lack of anything in true martyrs that results in the singular and highest commendation of this virtue. But the question is about true martyrdom, that is, not martyrdom improperly and by similarity, or a certain analogy, properly speaking. But martyrdom is what anyone suffers for the confession of the truth in a violent death by tyrants or persecutors, sentenced against them only out of hatred for the truth. It is not when someone dies by a natural or common death not inflicted by people or by force, and for some other cause than a testimony of the truth. Metaphorically, so that one may speak of a martyr or martyrdom where someone has suffered something for a good cause or for a good goal, there is no difficulty at all, and that writers of all kinds frequently speak in this way has been noted. But that does not have any bearing on this controversy, which is about "martyr" by its real name and speaking specifically. Chrysostom did call someone a martyr, but he did so not specifically, but rhetorically more than properly. Speaking of one also who endured adversities patiently and blesses God, he said "Nothing is more holy than this tongue that gives thanks to God in adversities. It certainly is not less holy than the tongue of the martyrs; both equally are crowned" (Hom. 8 on Col.).[148] And thus, in the letter of Dionysius, the

---

148. Chrysostom, "Homilies on Colossians, Col. 3:5–7" in *NPNF1* 13:298

martyrs of Alexandria are not properly called martyrs, but their death was very similar to martyrdom; "It seems that it was no different from martyrdom."[149] And in the Roman martyrology, it customarily venerated them as martyrs who had the religious faith of the godly. "As martyrs," but not as real ones properly speaking. In this sense Gabriel Vázquez, on part III of Thomas, disputation 153, ch. 3 from Durandus, says that martyrdom not only has an efficacy from love, which it necessarily requires, but from the cause of suffering, and in conformation (I prefer to read it this way rather than *confirmatio*) to the passion of Christ. "For if out of love," he says, "someone offers himself to death in order to free someone from death or from sickness, he will not be a martyr, although he does die from love. But he must suffer for the sake of Christ at the hands of a tyrant, and not only must he suffer and make his confession from love before the tyrant, but he also must in fact die, and in this way be conformed to the death of Christ himself."[150]

In whatever way the case comes down on this matter, in my opinion at least, Theophilus Raynaud and Filiberto Marchini, who follows him, have erred in what they commented and [in how] they viewed the martyrdom of plague. Nevertheless, on this point, when they said that helping those infected with plague is an act of fortitude, they did not err at all. And on this point they must not be thrashed by their adversaries, among whom the chief is Tomás Hurtado, who throughout his work does not dispute against them wisely or fruitfully enough. Certainly he did not do this in Resolution 6, when he openly and prolixly denies that serving those infected with plague in an epidemic is an act properly elicited from fortitude.[151] And why not? Because it is an act of friendship and love? As if those were opposed! Cannot fortitude and love be exercised at the same time in the same act? "The act is not properly speaking elicited from ethical fortitude unless it is ordered by a tyrant or potentate in hatred of some truth." But he should prove this. It is certainly so in the case of martyrdom, but we are not debating for this now, simply for fortitude. It is not as if fortitude would have no place unless against tyrants or in persecutions, and it is of no use in intrepidly facing other evils. "Where there is no combat or

---

149. Gk. μηδὲν ἀποδεῖν μαρτυρίου δοκεῖν; Lat. *videri nihil abfuisse a martyrio*: lit. "it seemed far from martyrdom by nothing"

150. Gabriel Vázquez (c. 1549–1604), *Commentaria ac Disputationes in Tertiam Partem S. Thomae*, 2 vols. (Ingolstadt: Officina Typographica Ederiana, 1612), 2:481.

151. Hurtado, "Resolutio VI: Utrum sit actus proprius elicitus a fortitudine Ethica in servire peste et epidemia infectis", *Resolutiones*, 5–7

battle," he says, "in which death is condemned and there is a mean between fear and confidence, there cannot be a formal object of ethical fortitude."[152] What? Can death and the dangers of death be condemned only in combat or battle, and not also in plague? Is not the mean between fear and audacity constituted here in the heart? There is a battle and combat of the heart in all dangers anyone enters. Therefore, here also there is an object of fortitude.

Thomas is not the one that he should appeal to. Among other passages in him, here is a very evident one at hand, which is in *Summa Theologica*, IIaIIae question 123, article 5:

> Therefore it pertains to fortitude to show a strength of heart against the dangers of death, not only which threaten in a general war, but also which threaten in single combat, which can be called by the common term war. And second this must be granted, that fortitude properly speaking is not only with regard to dangers of death that occur in war, but also with regard to dangers of any kind of death a person can undergo on account of virtue. For example, when someone does not fail to accommodate a sick friend out of fear of a deadly infection or does not fail to go on a trip for the purpose of accomplishing some godly business due to a fear of shipwreck or brigands."[153]

Unless perhaps this whole dispute will be about the term more than about the substance, just as our adversary takes [a definition of] fortitude or distinguishes between an ethical fortitude and a supernatural one, or between fortitude and magnanimity, or between a primary act of fortitude and a secondary one. For elsewhere in resolution 11, Hurtado speaks in this way,

> I think that even those who, in time of epidemic or contagion, are kindled by love of neighbor for God's sake to condemn death and its gravest dangers, not only are brave with a supernatural fortitude but are also magnanimous, if it would give them strength in relation to the magnitude of the danger, just as is evident from what has been said. Now in fact they do moderate the fear of death and meet its dangers insofar as they are moved from the magnitude of the good hoped for themselves to bear the contagion. They are therefore the bravest and

---

152. Hurtado, *Resolutiones*, 6
153. Thomas, *ST*, IIaIIae q. 123, art. 5

most magnanimous, for they condemn what they dread and what is terrible. Wherefore, without a doubt they have the secondary act of fortitude, according to what we have said above.[154]

In fact, fortitude is a virtue that intrepidly faces any dangers and does so with reason. In this way, it seems to me that it can be defined easily and includes the points that are usually argued here in various ways. The object shows its evil but also its sorrow too, and not just any kind, for no one shows fortitude in a light matter that must be condemned, but in a weighty one, and that of most weight—namely death and the dangers of death. This object of fortitude is external and removed; and since in the soul nothing has sway except through internal affections and *pathos*,[155] as Cicero explains diseases, fortitude is occupied first and foremost in the things that moderate those. Moreover, there are two extremes[156] of affections: in deficit, fear or timidity; in excess, audacity or temerity. And between these means lies fortitude, which prevents the soul from both extremes. Chiefly, I say, this fortitude is concerned with timidity, insofar as it is more inimical and contrary to itself; but properly, audacity seems more suited to it, in which it sees something of itself. But fortitude sees nothing of itself in fear, for which reason it restrains the former and moderates the latter, and in the definition of it I think another notion must be injected: *intrepidity*. I have said "facing" because fortitude is turned more towards imminent and future things, whereas patience is occupied with the present. But it is evident that first comes fortitude and then patience. So then in Scripture; in Colossians 1:11, being strengthened with all fortitude, for all patience and longsuffering,[157] which he called, acting like men,[158] in 1 Corinthians 16:13. Cicero in his *Tusculan Disputations*, bk. 2, ch. 18: "Fortitude is proper to a man especially, whose two greatest duties are a contempt of death and pain."[159] But of facing it "with reason" as distinguished from temerity, which rushes into dangers with a vain and blind impetuousness and not from reason, and audacity, which rushes blindly into danger without the watchful judgment of reason but with the contempt of it.

154. Hurtado, *Resolutiones*, 28.
155. Gk. πάθη < πάθος has come into English with a somewhat narrower meaning than the Greek, which carries the meaning here of "passion" or "emotion."
156. Gk. ἀκρότητες
157. Gk. ἐν πάσῃ δυνάμει δυναμούμενοι . . εἰς πᾶσαν ὑπομονὴν
158. Gk. ἀνδρίζεσθε
159. See Cicero, *Tusculan Disputations* in *LCL* 141:194–195

The difficult question is whether it ought to belong to virtue that you would go towards death to save another from the danger of it, or to serve another person infected with plague with an equally certain danger of death? The difficulty comes in at this point: to what extent and how far must we expose our life for the life and convenience of others? The question is not *whether* we are obligated simply to help others, but to what *extent*—with equal risk to ourselves? So that we may save others from a disease and from death when there is the same danger for the one rushing in? Some things need to be distinguished, for no one should explain this as an ambiguous and utterly obscure matter or question without careful and solid distinctions, which are like lights in a dark hall.[160] First the danger ought to be distinguished between an *evident* danger—and certainly, as much as one can, it is licit to judge whether it is a morally certain one—and a danger that is considered *probable* and contingent. Or, it ought to be distinguished between a grave and a most grave one. Next, the one whom we serve is regarded either only as a *human being*, connected to us or strongly attached to us by no other rationale; or as a familiar friend; or even as a believer and Christian, that is as one equal to us; or as a superior, to whom we otherwise owe many things, whether on private terms (such as to parents and siblings) or publicly (such as to the church and to the magistrate). Certainly we do not owe equal things to all of those, but several or greater ones to some than to others. Finally, we intend the good of our neighbor, either only a bodily good or even a spiritual and eternal good. Hence, we conclude now thus:

Conclusion 1: In actions and duties of love a ranking[161] must be preserved, first of things and then of persons, so that at every point the lesser gives way to those more weighty and worthy. For love is neither blind nor does it act recklessly, such that it does not listen to reason, but ordinarily must [be guided] by it to the best good.

Here the ranking of things is ordered so that things and goods lead to life, both bodily and spiritual ones, according to Christ's words in Matthew 16:26: "For what does it profit a man if he should gain the whole world, but lose his own soul?" The ranking of persons so that an equal neighbor yields to you, and you both to God—from the force of that rule in Matthew 22:37–39 that you shall love God above all things and your neighbor as

---

160. *faculae*: the metaphor is like wall sconces that punctuate a dark path, or carriage lights for driving at night

161. Lat. *ordo*

yourself—is constructed like a triangle of love. At the apex is God, placed above all and who alone holds that place without peer. At the base are ourselves and our neighbor on an equal level, except that we hold one angle and our neighbor the other. Therefore, in a trial and in a doubt where it is then asked which one either must yield or pay the cost to the other, it becomes evident from this schematic. But because it is about serving others with a risk to one's life, it must be considered and explained more broadly.

Conclusion 2: We owe more and therefore must expend more, even with danger of life, to parents than to others, to believers more than to outsiders, to the church, the magistrate, and the commonwealth than to private persons. That is, to die for our country and for our brethren. First John 3:16, "And we must lay down our lives for the brethren;" John 15:13, "Greater love has no one than this, that he lays down his life for his friends;" Romans 5:7, "For hardly will someone die for a righteous man, but perhaps for a good man someone would dare to die;" Galatians 6:10, "Let us do good to all, but especially to the household of faith;" 1 Samuel 18:33, "O Absalom, would that I had died instead of you!" The matter itself sufficiently describes that death is not to be faced in every case, everywhere, or for any reason. Regarding this, one must see in what follows whether and when it is licit, or to what extent we would be obligated.

Conclusion 3: We must face a *probable* danger in order to rescue another from an *evident* and gravest kind of danger.

Conclusion 4: We are compelled to undergo an evident danger for the sake of others when the purpose of our office demands it, such as in war, fire, and similar applicable cases that are incumbent upon people ordained and called to those crises.

Conclusion 5: Even outside the purpose of our individual office, when you see a noteworthy, great, and necessary good that would result to the greater glory of God and to either the wellbeing of the church or the commonwealth, or to another person's salvation, for whose sake you expose yourself to danger—if it is evident that it is far more necessary and advantageous for those to benefit, then it is licit to undergo evident danger. And certainly you must only have regard for that goal of the good in facing the danger.

Conclusion 6: Whether in the case of friendship specifically and evidence of it, not for any other ulterior goal that demands it, as we have taught, it would be right to put one's life in evident danger so that you would save the life of your friend. This question is exceedingly complicated. Of course, you would be a peer and equal in every condition, and you would not be obligated by duty or calling to bring assistance; and the danger is both evident and certain that your friend would die unless you would assist with the certain (that is, morally speaking) danger, and so you hurry with that intention of heart to save. Then it is asked if it would be licit for you or if you would also be obligated to expose yourself to that evident danger, even to the point of death, in order to save another? And so, ought this to be interpreted in such a way that dying for your friends is dying for the brethren? Let us pose an example: In a common shipwreck you might escape [death] by laying hold of a nearby plank; or does it belong to virtue or acting well for you to extend it to your friend, with a certain and evident danger to your own life? Similarly, in a common famine you have bread with which you may sustain yourself or him; do you hand the bread over to your friend, with the greatest hazard to yourself, so that you namely save your friend instead? The opinions of the doctors differ. There are those who affirm [that you do], such as Filiberto Marchini—for that case pertains to the treatment of this question in part 1, chapter 12, in his *Divine War, or the time of plague*—and several whom Marchini claims in favor of his opinion; anyone who approves of those acclaimed examples of the ancients where someone died joyfully for the sake of another (see Lessius, Bañez, and others).[162] Petrus Navarra denies the question in *On Restitution*, book 2, chapter 3, as does Bonaventure, Durandus, Paludanus, and other scholastics in bk. 3, distinction 29.[163] Still others distinguish the question, such as Pedro de Lorca, the Spaniard, in disputation 28, so that one may expose oneself to danger for the life of another whenever it is a work of outstanding fortitude and is *owed*, such as if it were laid down for the commonwealth; or whenever it is praiseworthy but *not owed*, such as if for a father or friend, with whom there is an intervening, great, and virtuous friendship. But whenever it is not praiseworthy but inordinate—such as if done for any

---

162. Filiberto Marchino, *Belli Divini, sive Pestilentis Temporis* (Florence: Typographia Sermartelliana, 1633), 34–38; Leonardus Lessius S.J. (1554–1623), *De Justitia et Jure* (1605), ch. 6 dub. 6 num. 30; Bañez.

163. Petrus Navarra, bk. 2 ch. 3 dub. 3, nos. 41–60, *De Restitutione in Foro Conscientiae*, 2 vols. (Toledo: Pedro Rodrigo, 1595–1597), 1:327–338; Bonaventura (1221–1274), bk. 3 d. 29 q. 3, *Commentaria in Quatuor Libros Sententiarum* in *Opera* (Quaracchi, 1882), 3:643–645; Durandus of Pourçain (1230–1296), bk. 4. dist. 17, q. 6, *In Quatuor Libros Sententiarum Quaestionum Resolutiones* (Lyon: Gulielmus Rouillius, 1563), fols. 294r–v; Pierre de Palude O.P. (Paludanus, 1277–1342), bk. 4 d. 15, q. 3. art. 2 concl. 3, *Scriptum in Quartum Sententiarum Petri Lombardi* (Venice, 1493), fols. 68v–69r; cf. Marchino, *Belli Divini*, p34, §1; note Marchino's quote of Bonaventure is correct, but his citation is not, and has been corrected here.

other person in a way one judges as an imprudent and prodigal outpouring that could not be excused from fault, as if someone were to hand over all one's property to an unknown person—it would be considered manifestly stupid and wasteful.[164] Cornelius à Lapide on 1 John 3:16 says, "A friend is not obligated to expose his life [to danger] for the life of a friend. For this is loving a neighbor, not as oneself, but more than oneself, which exceeds the rule of the doctrine.[165] Augustine says in his book, *On Lying*, chapter 6, 'yet if someone would expose [themselves to danger], he would act in a praiseworthy manner, for he would expose his life for righteousness and for the good of the virtue of friendship.'"[166] Sylvius on IIaIIae q. 26, art. 4 distinguishes exposing one's life to danger on behalf of another in three ways: either as our life is exposed for the life of a precisely equal friend, and must not be regarded as anything other than a life for a life; or second, when a life is regarded as a righteous life of a moral friendship, and as that alone; or third, if it is regarded as a good of Christian charity for the spiritual wellbeing of our neighbor.[167] For the first way, he denies that it is licit, but contrary to the inclination of a true and correct natural love to estimate another's life as more than one's own. The second he concedes is among the heathen, where one's own life was not laid down precisely for the life of a friend, but it was a natural righteousness of moral virtue, which they acknowledged as the only one. But among Christians that is illicit, partly because Christians are obligated to regard something other than only the natural righteousness of moral virtue, and partly because it is inordinate to

---

164. Pedro de Lorca, O. Cist. (Petrus Hispanus, 1561-1612), *Commentaria et Disputationes in Secundam Secundae Diui Thomae tomus iste tres continet sectiones, primam de fide, alteram de spe, tertiam de charitate* (Madrid: Luis Sanchez, 1614), 714–717. Cf. Thomas Aquinas, *ST* II^aII^{ae} qu. 26, art 5 "Whether someone ought to love his neighbor more than his own body?" response to objection 3, "The care of one's own body is an imminent concern for every person, but his neighbor's welfare is not his imminent concern, unless perhaps in an emergency. And so there is not necessity from love that a person expose their own body [to danger] for their neighbor's welfare, unless in an emergency because he is obligated to provide for his welfare. But that someone freely offers himself for this purpose pertains to the perfection of love." Lorca's disputation is a sixty-section response to the loc. cit. in Thomas and an attempt to reconcile that view with 1 Corinthians 13:5, "Love seeks not its own," divided into three *membra*. The second *membrum*, "when would we be obligated to prefer the spiritual good of our neighbor to our bodily good" (§§XXVI–XLII) is Hoornbeeck's primary focus here.

165. Cornelius à Lapide, *Commentaria in Acta Apostolorum, Epistolas Canonicas, et Apocalypsin* (Paris: George Josse, 1648), 460.

166. Augustine, *On Lying (De Mendacio)* in *NPNF1* 3:457–480; cf. Marchino, *Belli Divini*, p. 34, §2, p. 37, §19.

167. Franciscus Sylvius, *Commentarii in totam Secundam Secundae S. Thomae Aquinatis* in *Opera Omnia*, 6 vols. (Antwerp: Joannes Baptista Verdussen, 1697–1698), 3:152–155.

deprive oneself of the advantage of advancing in spiritual goods for only a righteousness of a natural moral order. The third way he thinks is entirely licit—to expose one's own life for the life of an equal neighbor when it is ordered to his or someone else's eternal salvation. Or, he says, if it should be done from a love of Christian virtue and for the example of others, or if the one on behalf of whose life this is done is in a state of damnation, but the other one is confident he is in a good state. So also Becanus in his *Summary of Scholastic Theology*, vol. 3, ch. 19, q. 2, and Azor in his *Moral Instructions* tome 2, bk. 12, ch. 4, q 2. think that it is licit but that it is not commanded to pour out one's life for a friend from the sole motive of friendship.[168] Certainly, I think that one must entirely disapprove of bringing your life into a present and evident danger for another of an equal condition and to whom you have not been bound by reason of a duty, for only moral friendship. It is another thing though, if in addition you regard their spiritual good, and then lay down your life for the brethren, friends, or even others; then duty requires it. And so I think it must be explained in this way: regarding the laying down of one's life for the brethren, no one is bound and obligated to do it unless the necessity and outcome of the circumstance demands it, as if it is to his profit and eternal salvation; in which sense that rule in 1 John 3:16 is interpreted by Peter Martyr Vermigli in his letter *On Flight in Persecution*, also cited previously, and William Ames in his *Cases of Conscience*, bk. 5, ch. 7.[169] If only for the sake of displaying some virtue—even a Christian one—or love, I do not think it is licit unless the necessity of salvation would demand and urge it. And those who recount that this was done only from some joy of the soul and as if from friendship, as in such examples of the heathen and from Valerius Maximus that are adduced here, [see that] such things do not happen among the Christians. Besides, what they did from only some *moral* virtue and with regard for that easily runs toward either some vain captivation with a little bit of glory or even a madness, so that they would even die *with* their friend rather than *for* him; certainly, with what we possess of our own life and gifts, it seems best that prodigality must not be praised. Therefore, to be sure, I cannot praise those things according to the Law of God and our religion. The other thing is that

---

168. Martin Becanus, S.J. (1563–1624), tomus 3, secundae partis pars II, [Tract. 1, ch. 19], q. 2, no. 18, *Summa Theologiae Scholasticae*, 6 vols. (Lyon: Nicolai Gay, 1644–1645), 3:432; Juan Azor, S.J. (Azorius, 1536–1603), tom. 2 bk. 12, ch. 4, q. 2, *Institutiones Morales* (Cologne: Antonius Hierat, 1608–1618), 2:1707–1714, esp. 1707.

169. William Ames, *Conscience with the Powers and Cases thereof* (London: 1643), 131.

although it is made acceptable (although sometimes it is not) by popular or political applause, and by the vain praises and applause of men for such an action, we do not see it as something licit from the prescript of religion and of Christ. Therefore, you are not *obligated*, with such a great or evident danger, to assist another who is your equal beyond the necessity of your office and calling.

Thomas, in a similar case (for the same thing can be applied throughout) in *Summa Theologica*, IIaIIae, q. 32, art. 6, which asks whether someone must give alms from what one needs, answers:

> Something is spoken of as necessary in two ways: in one way, because without it something is impossible, and alms must not be given at all from what is so necessary. For instance, if a man found himself in the very moment of necessity and had only enough to support himself and his children, or others dependent upon him, were he to give what he needs away in alms he would take away from his life and his dependents. But I say this, that unless perhaps such a case is imminent, whereby he would deprive himself of his necessities, a man might help a great personage and supporter of the Church or Commonwealth, since it would be a praiseworthy act to endanger one's life and the lives of those who are under our charge for the delivery of such a person, since the common good ought to be preferred to one's own good.[170]

This is entirely in accordance with our mind and opinion. In necessary and evident danger it is not the life of another person, with whom we are equals, that is to be preferred to our own. And the moment of danger must not be faced with a free motion of the heart, outside the office and necessity of our calling, whenever the name is pretended for friendship; [but only] where there is nothing else more grave [at stake] than eternal salvation or the wellbeing of many. For I do not think that the life of another must be assisted when there is equal danger to our own.

Conclusion 7: Finally, by applying the previous things to the present case of the contagion of plague there is certainly a *probable* and contingent danger, but not an evident and most serious one. And therefore no one must be restrained from bringing help here who are called to this by any reason of their office, or offering extraordinary usefulness; and one may assist a

---

170. Thomas Aquinas, *ST* II^{a}II^{ae} qu. 32, art. 6.

person struggling with some danger to their life since, as we have seen, it is not even licit to turn away from evident danger for the one bearing an office in this way, which is by no means less or not so certain or universal, which sort of case this is. Friedrich Balduinus, in his *Cases of Conscience*, bk. 4, ch. 17, explaining 1 John 3:16 regarding which cases would it be licit to pour out one's life for another, concedes this in his third point: "[it is licit] when someone exposes their bodily life to danger for the sake of the spiritual life of another, so that someone is present with the infected in time of plague to comfort them, and presents the holy nourishment of the soul."[171] This is better than what he counseled in chapter 9, case 6: "In order that the pastor may visit a sick person, he should command that the sick person is carried out of his sickroom into a sunny place and, the pastor himself positioned upwind, he should hear the sick person's confession and extend to him the holy supper. The remaining pertinent things for this act should be pursued, so that there will be less danger of infection."[172] William Ames in his *Cases of Conscience*, bk. 5, ch. 7: "Even in extreme necessity every person of a common condition (but it is especially for the one upon whom such an office is singularly incumbent) is bound to expose his life to a probable danger, to impede the certain death of another. For the certain death of another is a greater evil than his own uncertain one. So then it is not licit for a pastor in time of plague or persecution to desert the Church, unless perhaps there may be a suitable other person who undertakes that care."[173] That last part is taken with [too] great precaution and can be taken with a grain of salt. Johann Gerhard in his *Loci Communes*, vol. 6, "On the Minister of the Church," page 334 and §290:

> Whether it is licit for a minister of the church to flee in time of plague? We deny it. Certain people add this limitation, that it is licit for ministers of the Church to seek a retirement in time of plague, if they may substitute others in their place who would fulfill the parts of their ecclesiastical office with no less dexterity, diligence, and faith than themselves. But one must diligently take care lest scandal would be offered to the weak—which hardly can be done in advance—if they who light the way for the rest by their own example should flee in time of plague.

---

171. Friedrich Balduinus, bk. 4, ch. 17, case 8, *Tractatus . . . Casibus nimirum Conscientiae* (Frankfurt: Caspar Wachtler, 1654), 941.
172. Balduinus, *Tractatus*, bk. 4, ch. 9, case 6, p818.
173. William Ames, *Conscience with the Powers and Cases thereof* (London: 1643), 131.

And it was right to exhort them to faith, love, patience, and kindness even if they should substitute another in their place.[174]

Melchior Sylvester follows Gerhard in his book *The Conscientious Pastor*, class 1, q. 14,[175] and so does Benedictus Carpzovius in book 1 of *Consistorial Definitions*, title 5, definition 72:

> But what about in time of plague, could then at least the superintendent or another minister of the church take himself and remain elsewhere for a time? Certainly not: 1) Because the hearers or parishioners during this time would then lack especially his works and ministry, whereby they are admonished to repentance and informed about their blessed departure from this life. 2) This cannot happen without scandal, for their departure argues for a lack of confidence in the divine promises: "evil will not come near you" (Ps. 91:7), "the hairs of your head are all numbered" (Matt. 10:30), and "I will not leave you nor forsake you" (Heb. 13:5).[176]

And he adds in the same sentence the rescript of the Elector of Saxony on September 9, 1633 to the superintendent and senate of Lubenwerden. When the pastor of the infected locale died, and with the ministerial position then vacant either in the countryside or in some other place, the neighboring ministers could not come to fulfill the care of that vacant church. Then from the electoral rescript of November 11, 1631 he shows first the decrees of the highest consistory, definition 165. But, in the meantime, so the church would not be missing any office, the sick of that place wanted it to be administered by a Catechizer, or the holy duties to be administered by another to be provided quickly as the new pastor of the church.

Necessary duties towards those who have passed

All these things concern the duties that must be rendered to the sick or to those infected with plague; the summary of which at this point is that we

---

174. Johann Gerhard (1582-1637), *Theological Commonplaces: On the Ministry II*, trans. R. J. Dinda, eds. B. T. G. Mayes and H. R. Curtis (St. Louis, MO.: Concordia Publishing House, 2012), §290; idem, *Loci Theologici* 9 vols. (Frankfurt, Hamburg: Bibliopolae Hamburgensis,1657), 6:170-171.

175. Melchior Sylvester Eckhard, *Pastor Conscientiosus, hoc est, variae quaestiones, de casibus et rebus dubiis, ministri personam propius tangentibus* (Ulm: Balthasar Kühn, 1651), 30-32.

176. Benedictus Carpzovius (1595-1666), *Jurispendentia Ecclesiastica seu Consistorialis Rerum et Queastionum . . . Definitiones* (Leipzig: Timothy Ritzsch, 1655) 87-88.

may act everywhere *bravely* and *prudently*, never in an un-Christian way towards others, but rather in such a way that we want done for us. For which reason how we must conduct ourselves toward the dead is likewise apparent, either as they are dying, or as their bodies are about to be buried, or moderating the weeping upon their departure. Concerning this I will refrain repeating what is customarily said in the theological commonplaces; if I would pursue it again, I would not be able to contain myself within the present argument. Yet, the chapters of meditations and our duties which they consider—those have to be fixed and noted here, and also what arguments they make. And this has already been noted and observed by many, that everywhere people are dying from the plague they are dying in a more devotedly and holy fashion compared to every other kind of disease or death; this in fact is the good of death, which in itself alone is evil. Among the ancients Ambrose wrote about this. D'Espence said, "Because it has been appointed for men once to die (Hebrews 9), do not refer to eternal felicity until you should have lived well, and to that degree you will die blessedly; with the singular blessing of God, dying with plague as very many have done, composed in heart and mind, undiminished in sense and reason, and hence to depart as one returning to the Lord."[177] However, regarding what he says about the constancy of mind, we are not ignorant of the vehemence and sudden heat of fevers that disturb the mind, at least for a time. At the same time—because we know much has been agitated about this—when anyone dies with such a strong confusion of their mind and alienation from it, the rest of their life having been sober and godly, ought their lesser condition be considered and thus certainty of their salvation be less? We deny it. Since in regarding a person, one must not be judged more by their last end or act than by their entire life, and still less by what he does in some evil that he suffers. Hence, because he lacks some salted wafer, which otherwise he could take with a healthy and whole mind, he will not certainly lack the salvation promised to believers; and furthermore the kindnesses of God are irrevocable.[178]

Franciscus Junius, in his *Explanation of Two Hundred Questions,* q. 23, asks, "What judgment ought to be made regarding the spirits of those who either are extinguished in a frenzy or suddenly are removed from life in the midst of some evil deed, without any sign of repentance?" He answers,

---

177. D'Espence, *Opera Omnia,* (Paris: Claude Morel, 1619), 253.
178. Gk. ἀμεταμελήτοις Cf. Rom. 11:29

Two thing must be considered in this question: 1) it is necessary to suspend our judgment regarding repentance, and 2) the condition of those who suddenly die must be distinguished. The former is absolutely necessary, namely that we would suspend our judgment, for repentance is placed at least first in the internal sense and motion, and next in the meaning of the motion, whether public or private, which they call a confession.[179] A judgment cannot be made rashly and contrary to kindness regarding those who die suddenly, although with no sign given of repentance. Yet if that is granted, it does not have to be retracted, as it is a matter only God knows. The declaration of Scripture is certain: the impenitent are assigned to death, but formally repentance is an interior thing and (to use the words of Ambrose) God sees one way, and man another. The former looks on the heart, the latter on the exterior; therefore, we say it is necessary for us to suspend judgment. However, in the condition of persons, about which is treated, a distinction must be posed. For the reason that there is one who dies in weakness, and another who dies in the plague: the insane, the comatose, and similar sorts who struggle with infirmity, which evil God does not impute to them, just as we read in the history of the Gospel; when the mother-in-law of Peter labored with a burning fever, Christ rebuked the fever, but not the woman. And so then it cannot be doubted that for those whom weakness destroys (if they were believers previously) God gives grace without accounting of that infirmity. But regarding those who are slain in the very act of sin,[180] their reason is as those who die impenitent, which is the same reason that they have no share in eternal life. But because this only is posited, it does not evidence repentance from any sign that in turn must be posited. Therefore, judgment regarding these about whose repentance is not evident to us must be left to God, and so our judgement regarding them must be suspended, even as we are taught from their example that at any hour we must be prepared for leaving from this life.[181]

Finally, regarding the burial of cadavers, especially in a time and place of pestilential contagion, I have decided to say, for the purpose of confirming

---

179. Gk. ἐξομολόγησιν
180. Lat. *in flagrante delicto*
181. *Explicatione Quaestionum CC MS.* Qu. XXIII: This work is not extant in his printed works or *Opera*. Given the usage of "MS.," this is probably a manuscript.

the view of the brilliant Dr. Rivet, that they must be moved out to anywhere else than our temples. Of the first instance of that custom, in which the dead began to be brought into the temples and buried there, I have spoken in the book on *Euthanasia* in Dutch, chapter 7, at the beginning, as well as of the beginnings and progress of digging [the grave]. But at the lowering, which I see firsthand, I pass by as I anticipate prolixity on it.

Nothing now at last remains, other than fervent prayers to ask God that he would soften and take it away the present calamity which gave the reason for this writing, that we would acknowledge our sins and confess that the plague is a worthy and fitting outcome,[182] as the Greeks say in that very prayer, which they customarily recite in such a tempest in the *Euchologion*, called a prayer "for the plague of mortality."[183] Cyprian called it "the mortality" in a little book that he wrote on the occasion of the plague, which we noted above. There we read these most worthy words, with which we will finish, "Many of our people die in this mortality; that is, many of our people are liberated from this world. This mortality, just as it is a plague to Jews and Gentiles, and enemies of Christ, so it is a departure to salvation to God's servants."[184] Of course, he had learned this from Tertullian his preceptor, because Tertullian wrote in book 1, chapter 7, of *To his Wife*, "I encourage you to think over this, that no one is led out of this age except by the will of God, if not even a leaf will fall from a tree apart from his will. Likewise, it is necessary that the one who brought us into the world is the same one who will also lead us out."[185]

FINIS.

---

182. Gk. τὸ κατάλληλον ἀποτέλεσμα
183. Gk. εἰς τὴν πληγὴν τοῦ θανατικοῦ; cf. There are at least five prayers that include this Greek phrase (translated by the Latin *oratio in mortalitatis plagam*) or a similar one in *Εὐχολογιον, id est, rituale Graecorum* (Paris: Simeon Piget, 1647), 796–805.
184. See page 323 in this volume.
185. Tertullian, *To His Wife* in *ANF* 4:43.

Part II
++++

Reformation and Post-Reformation Plague Writings

5

Plague Hymn

INTRODUCTION

Huldrych Zwingli (b. 1484) was not in Zurich when plague struck the city in August 1519. Only months into his new appointment as the *Leutpriester* ("People's Priest") of Zurich's Grossmünster, the Swiss pastor was already exhausted from his labors and enjoying a much-needed rest sixty miles away at the mineral springs in Bad Pfäfers. When he received news of the outbreak, however, Zwingli immediately returned to his post to shepherd Christ's flock through what would be a season of intense trial, suffering, and loss. The plague, which lasted until February 1520, devastated Zurich, killing a quarter of the city's population, including Zwingli's brother Andreas. In September 1519, Zwingli himself contracted the illness and was brought very near to death. His recovery was slow, and towards the end he composed (or maybe completed) his famous *Pestlied* ("Plague Hymn") as a testimony to God's sovereign care and provision for him in his affliction.

Drawing inspiration from Psalm 18, Zwingli's poem rehearses the stages of his crisis and deliverance. In stanza one he describes the onset of the illness, in stanza two the growing intensity of his suffering and near-death experience, and in stanza three his joy and thanksgiving for his unexpected recovery and for the opportunity to live another day in service to God. As marvelous as the poet's experience is, however, *Pestlied* is not primarily about Zwingli the sufferer; rather it is about God the Savior. God is the principal actor throughout. God protects the vulnerable (*I think Death is at the door, Stand before me, Christ*); God heals the wounded (*Take out the dart, Which wounds me*); God consoles the sorrowful (*Come to me then, With Thy grace, O my only consolation!*); God fights for the weak (*Therefore is it time, That thou my fight Conductest hereafter*); God saves the sinful ([Thy grace] *will surely save Everyone, who His heart's desire And hopes sets on Thee*). The speaker, by contrast, is largely passive. His faculties increasingly fail him (*My tongue is dumb, It cannot speak a word. My senses are blighted*). In his weakness and helplessness, the poet is left with nothing but his faith in Christ, and the chief expression of that faith, namely prayer. But, perhaps surprisingly, this faith is sufficient for the needs of the day. In the midst of the encroaching darkness, intense pain, and specter of death, the speaker finds consolation, peace, and even joy in knowing that his life is in the hands of a God who is sovereign and who, having triumphed over Death in his risen Son, is able to deliver from the same those who belong to him.

Zwingli's joy in his recovery is somewhat attenuated, however, by the knowledge that one day he will again suffer greatly and *not* recover: "Although I must The punishment of death Sometime endure, Perhaps with greater anguish Than would now have Happened, Lord!" Death is inevitable.[1] Thus, Zwingli's assurance is found not in his recovery from his particular, momentary affliction, or, in fact, in any remedy this world can offer. Zwingli's sure hope for resisting the attacks of the Devil and for overcoming the finality and curse of Death is found in God himself. God, he discovers in new and powerful ways through his experience, is the only refuge and strength for the weak and sin-weary soul. Like Paul who learned how to be brought low and how to abound (Phil. 4:12), Zwingli learns to despise both "gain and loss" for the surpassing worth of knowing the consolation of God's grace toward him in Christ.

Zwingli would emerge from this crisis a changed man. Numerous biographers have noted the profound and formative influence this illness had on the reformer's life and ministry. One scholar remarks, "As a consequence the thirty-six year-old priest began to emphasize more strongly both human sinfulness and salvation through God's grace alone."[2] This renewed emphasis on God's grace as the only and sure hope for sinners shines forth clearly in Zwingli's final stanza where he declares, "Since I came. So near; So will I still. The spite and boasting. Of this world. Bear joyfully for the sake of the reward. By Thy help, Without which nothing can be perfect."

Shortly after its composition, *Pestlied* entered the church's hymnic tradition and, having since been adapted and translated into numerous languages, remains in use to this day. Its popularity is probably not attributable to the greatness of Zwingli as a poet, but rather to the greatness of

---

1. Zwingli would die on the battlefield in the Second Kappel War on October 11, 1531.
2. Emidio Campi, "The Reformation in Zurich," in *A Companion to the Swiss Reformation*, ed. Amy Nelson Burnett and Emidio Campi (Leiden: Brill, 2016), 69.

God as a Savior of sinners, whose grace is so powerfully, poignantly, and memorably set on display in these verses.

"A Christian Song Written by Huldreich Zwingli When He was Attacked by the Pestilence" (Ein chritenlich gsang, gestalt durch H. Z., als er mit pestilentz angriffen ward). Translation reprinted with notes from Samuel Macauley Jackson, *Huldreich Zwingli: The Reformer of German Switzerland 1484-1531*, second edition, revised (New York: G. P. Putnam's Sons, 1903), 132-4.

Plague Hymn ("Pestlied")[3]
Huldrych Zwingli
Translated by Samuel Macauley Jackson

I.—At the Beginning of the Illness.

Help, Lord God, help
In this trouble!
I think Death is at the door.
Stand before[4] me, Christ;
For Thou hast overcome him!
To Thee I Cry:
If it is Thy will,
Take out the dart,
Which wounds me
Nor lets me have an hour's
Rest or repose!
Will'st Thou however
That Death take me

---

3. Commenting on other English translations, the latter of which is still widely circulated today, Jackson writes, "the poetical version given in the English translation of Merle D'Aubigné's *History of the Reformation* (ed. Edinburgh: Oliver & Boyd, 1853, ii, 466 sqq), and the better one in Schaff's *History of the Christian Church* (vii., 44-46, with the original text) represent the original form to some extent, but they do not give all the lines and are paraphrastic. In order to enable the reader to have the entire poem and the exact meaning of the author, it is here given in literal prose translation, line by line, as far as the idiom admits." Ibid., 132–33, n. 5.

4. In the sense of "protect."

In the midst of my days,
So let it be!
Do what Thou wilt;
Me nothing lacks.[5]
Thy vessel am I;
To make or break altogether.
For, if Thou takest away
My spirit
From this earth,
Thou dost it, that it[6] may not grow worse,
Nor spot
The pious lives and ways of others.

II.—In the Midst of his Illness.

Console me, Lord God, console me!
The illness increases,
Pain and fear seize
My soul and body.
Come to me then,
With Thy grace, O my only consolation!
It[7] will surely save
Everyone, who
His heart's desire
And hopes sets
On Thee, and who besides
Despises all gain and loss.
Now all is up.
My tongue is dumb,
It cannot speak a word.
My senses are all blighted.
Therefore is it time
That thou my fight
Conductest hereafter;
Since I am not

---

5. The words may also mean equally well, "nothing shall be too much for me."
6. "It," i.e., my spirit.
7. "It," i.e., Thy grace.

So strong, that I
Can bravely
Make resistance
To the Devil's wiles and treacherous hand.
Still will my spirit
Constantly abide by Thee, however he rages.

III.—During Convalescence.

Sound, Lord God, sound!
I think I am
Already coming back.[8]
Yes, if it please Thee,
That no spark of sin
Rule me longer on earth.
Then my lips must
They praise and teaching
Bespeak more
Than ever before,
However it may go,
In simplicity and with no danger.
Although I must
The punishment of death
Sometime endure,
Perhaps with greater anguish
Than would now have
Happened,[9] Lord!
Since I came
So near;[10]
So will I still
The spite and boasting
Of this world
Bear joyfully for the sake of the reward
By Thy help,
Without which nothing can be perfect.

8. I.e., to health, to myself.
9. I.e., if I had died this time.
10. I.e., to death's door.

6

Whether One May Flee from a Deadly Plague

Introduction

Martin Luther (b. 1483) probably needs little by way of introduction to readers of this volume. Unquestionably the central figure of the protestant reformation of the sixteenth century, Luther worked tirelessly to reform the church according to the word of God and to return the church to the same word as her ultimate authority. Even during his lifetime, Luther's thought and theology spread to the far corners of Europe and beyond. As a consequence, his guidance was frequently sought on issues ranging from the theological to the political. The letter that follows, written to pastor Johann Hess of Breslau (though intended for wider circulation), is Luther's response to one such inquiry—whether one may flee a deadly plague.

It is important to note that the counsel and instruction Luther offers in this letter is far from theoretical. Between the time he began writing the letter (late July, 1527) and the time he finished (early November 1527 at the latest), a plague had struck the city of Wittenberg (August 2, 1527). For the safety of her students and professors, the University of Wittenberg was relocated, first to Jena and then to Schlieben, until the plague passed. However, against the wishes of Elector John and the urgings of his friends, Luther decided to remain in Wittenberg along with his friend Bugenhagen to provide spiritual care to the sick, the dying, and the fearful citizens of the city.[1] The dark days that ensued are described by one scholar as follows: "By August 19 there were eighteen deaths; the wife of the mayor, Tilo Dene, died almost in Luther's arms; his own wife was pregnant and two women were sick in his own house; his little son Hans refused to eat for three days; chaplain George Rörer's wife, also pregnant, took sick and lost both her

---

1. *Luther's Works* 43, edited by Gustav K. Wiencke (Philadelphia: Fortress Press, 1968), 115.

baby and her life; Bugenhagen and his family then moved into Luther's house for mutual encouragement."[2] Furthermore, "the people around Luther heard how a Dominican in Leipzig had, early in September, mocked the way the Wittenbergers had run away from the plague."[3] Luther, who only months before was beset with severe depression, describes the desperate situation in a letter to his friend Amsdorf with words which are at the same time sober and yet full of hope: "So there are battles without and terrors within, and really grim ones; Christ is punishing us. It is a comfort that we can confront Satan's fury with the word of God, which we have and which saves souls even if that one should devour our bodies. Commend us to the brethren and yourself to pray for us that we may endure bravely under the hand of the Lord and overcome the power and cunning of Satan, be it through dying or living. Amen."[4] It was in the midst of these uncertain and disorienting days, surrounding by death and tempted to despair, that Luther composed his open letter to pastor Hess.

Luther's parameters for flight are somewhat unsurprising, and are, in their broad contours, echoed in the other pieces included in this volume. Those who in God's providence hold office, whether secular ("mayors, judges and the like") or sacred ("preachers and pastors"), may not flee a plague as they have a divinely appointed duty to perform for the good of the community. An exception may be made however where a capable substitute can be found to fulfill these essential functions. For those who do not hold office however, Luther says, fleeing or remaining is a matter of faith: "If someone is sufficiently bold and strong in his faith, let him stay in God's name; that is certainly no sin. If someone is weak and fearful, let him flee in God's name as long as he does not neglect his duty toward his neighbor." There are, however, dangers to be avoided on both sides. Those who remain must be careful not to tempt God by acting carelessly regarding their own health by, for example, not taking appropriate precautions or by unnecessarily exposing themselves to the contagion. To do so would, in effect, be to commit suicide.

On the other hand, those who flee must be careful that they are not giving into an ungodly fear of death and perhaps neglecting their God-given duties to care for their neighbors. To these Luther, somewhat pointedly, counsels courage born of faith in Christ and the promises of the gospel. He

2. Ibid., 116.
3. Ibid.
4. Ibid.

says, "Shame and more shame on you, you out-and-out unbeliever, for despising such great comfort and letting yourself become more frightened by some small boil or some uncertain danger than emboldened by such sure and faithful promises of God! What would it avail you if all physicians and the entire world were at your service, but God were not present? Again, what harm could overtake you if the whole world were to desert you and no physician would remain with you, but God would abide with you with his assurance?"

The central principle animating all of Luther's guidance is love. As horrible as death by plague is, there is a much greater evil to be feared and fled, namely the evil of not loving God and not loving one's neighbor. To love God, for Luther, is to love neighbor. He writes, "We can be sure that God's punishment has come upon us, not only to chastise us for our sins but also to test our faith and love—our faith in that we may see and experience how we should act toward God; our love in that we may recognize how we should act toward our neighbor." At times, the most God-honoring and neighbor-loving course of action is fleeing danger that your life might be preserved and so that you might be in a better position to help others do the same. In this case, flight is not optional, but obligatory. At other times, the course most honoring to God and loving to neighbor may be to stay in harm's way in order to care for those in need physically or spiritually, or to maintain the basic functions of society that promote order and health. Thus, Luther writes, "Yes, no one should dare leave his neighbor unless there are others who will take care of the sick in their stead and nurse them. In such cases we must respect the word of Christ, 'I was sick and you did not visit me...' (Matt 25:41–46). According to this passage we are bound to each other in such a way that no one may forsake the other in his distress but is obliged to assist and help him as he himself would like to be helped."

Often working against acts of love is fear, an emotion no doubt painfully familiar to every Wittenberger at the time. Yet Luther vividly describes fear as a tool of the devil who delights in "making us deathly afraid, worried, and apprehensive so that we should regard dying as horrible and have no rest or peace all through our life." In answer to the devil's temptations, Luther, in his inimitable way, arms Christians with a response which unsurprisingly begins with a taunt: "Get away, you devil, with your terrors! Just because you hate it, I'll spite you by going the more quickly to help my sick neighbor," and which in turn gives way to soaring expressions of confidence in Christ's finished work and courage in the face of unimaginable danger:

> If Christ shed his blood for me and died for me, why should I not expose myself to some small dangers for his sake and disregard this feeble plague? If you can terrorize, Christ can strengthen me. If you can kill, Christ can give life. If you have poison in your fangs, Christ has far greater medicine. Should not my dear Christ, with his precepts, his kindness, and all his encouragement, be more important in my spirit than you, roguish devil, with your false terrors in my weak flesh? God forbid! Get away, devil. Here is Christ and here am I, his servant in this work. Let Christ prevail! Amen.

Amen indeed.

Martin Luther, *Luther's Works, Vol. 43: Devotional Writings II*, ed. Jaroslav Jan Pelikan, Hilton C. Oswald, and Helmut T. Lehmann, vol. 43 (Philadelphia: Fortress Press, 1999), 119–38.

Whether One May Flee From A Deadly Plague
Martin Luther
Translated by Carl J. Schindler

To the Reverend Doctor Johann Hess, pastor at Breslau, and to his fellow-servants of the gospel of Jesus Christ (1527 A.D.):

Grace and peace from God our Father and our Lord Jesus Christ. Your letter, sent to me at Wittenberg, was received some time ago. You wish to know whether it is proper for a Christian to run away from a deadly plague. I should have answered long ago, but God has for some time disciplined and scourged me so severely that I have been unable to do much reading or writing. Furthermore, it occurred to me that God, the merciful Father, has endowed you so richly with wisdom and truth in Christ that you yourself should be well qualified to decide this matter or even weightier problems in his Spirit and grace without our assistance.

But now that you keep on writing to me and have, so to speak, humbled yourself in requesting our view on this matter so that, as St. Paul repeatedly teaches, we may always agree with one another and be of one mind (1 Cor. 1:10; 2 Cor. 13:11; Phil. 2:2). Therefore we here give you our opinion as far as God grants us to understand and perceive. This we would humbly submit to your judgment and to that of all devout Christians for them, as is proper, to come to their own decision and conclusion. Since the rumor of death is to be heard in these and many other parts also, we have permitted these instructions of ours to be printed because others might also want to make use of them.

To begin with, some people are of the firm opinion that one need not and should not run away from a deadly plague. Rather, since death is God's punishment, which he sends upon us for our sins, we must submit to God and with a true and firm faith patiently await our punishment. They look upon running away as an outright wrong and as lack of belief in God. Others take the position that one may properly flee, particularly if one holds no public office.

I cannot censure the former for their excellent decision. They uphold a good cause, namely, a strong faith in God, and deserve commendation because they desire every Christian to hold to a strong, firm faith. It takes more than a milk faith to await a death before which most of the saints themselves have been and still are in dread. Who would not acclaim these earnest people to whom death is a little thing? They willingly accept God's chastisement, doing so without tempting God, as we shall hear later on.

Since it is generally true of Christians that few are strong and many are weak, one simply cannot place the same burden upon everyone. A person who has a strong faith can drink poison and suffer no harm, Mark 16:18, while one who has a weak faith would thereby drink to his death. Peter could walk upon the water because he was strong in faith. When he began to doubt and his faith weakened, he sank and almost drowned. When a strong man travels with a weak man, he must restrain himself so as not to walk at a speed proportionate to his strength lest he set a killing pace for his weak companion. Christ does not want his weak ones to be abandoned, as St. Paul teaches in Romans 15:1 and 1 Corinthians 12:22. To put it briefly and concisely, running away from death may happen in one of two ways. First, it may happen in disobedience to God's word and command. For instance, in the case of a man who is imprisoned for the sake of God's word and who, to escape death, denies and repudiates God's word. In such a situation everyone has Christ's plain mandate and command not to flee but rather to suffer death, as he says, "Whoever denies me before men, I will also deny before my Father who is in heaven" and "Do not fear those who kill the body but cannot kill the soul," Matthew 10:28, 33.

Those who are engaged in a spiritual ministry such as preachers and pastors must likewise remain steadfast before the peril of death. We have a plain command from Christ, "A good shepherd lays down his life for the sheep but the hireling sees the wolf coming and flees" (John 10:11). For when people are dying, they most need a spiritual ministry which strengthens and comforts their consciences by word and sacrament and in faith overcomes death. However, where enough preachers are available in one locality and they agree to encourage the other clergy to leave in order not to expose themselves needlessly to danger, I do not consider such conduct sinful because spiritual services are provided for and because they would have been ready and willing to stay if it had been necessary. We read that St. Athanasius fled from his church that his life might be spared because many others were there to administer his office. Similarly, the brethren in Damascus lowered Paul in a basket over the wall to make it possible for him to escape, Acts 9:25. And also in Acts 19:30. Paul allowed himself to be kept from risking danger in the marketplace because it was not essential for him to do so.

Accordingly, all those in public office such as mayors, judges, and the like are under obligation to remain. This, too, is God's word, which institutes secular authority and commands that town and country be ruled, protected, and preserved, as St. Paul teaches in Romans 13:4, "The governing authorities are God's ministers for your own good." To abandon an entire community which one has been called to govern and to leave it without official or government, exposed to all kinds of danger such as fires, murder, riots, and every imaginable disaster is a great sin. It is the kind of disaster the devil would like to instigate wherever there is no law and order. St. Paul says, "Anyone who does not provide for his own family denies the faith and is worse than an unbeliever" (1 Tim. 5:8). On the other hand, if in great weakness they flee but provide capable substitutes to make sure that the community is well governed and protected, as we previously indicated, and if they continually and carefully supervise them [i.e., the substitutes], all that would be proper.

What applies to these two offices [church and state] should also apply to persons who stand in a relationship of service or duty toward one another. A servant should not leave his master nor a maid her mistress except with the knowledge and permission of master or mistress. Again, a master should not desert his servant or a lady her maid unless suitable provision for their care has been made somewhere. In all these matters it is a divine command that servants and maids should render obedience and by the same token masters and ladies should take care of their servants. Likewise, fathers and mothers are bound by God's law to serve and help their children, and children their fathers and mothers. Likewise, paid public servants such as city physicians, city clerks and constables, or whatever their titles, should not flee unless they furnish capable substitutes who are acceptable to their employer.

In the case of children who are orphaned, guardians or close friends are under obligation either to stay with them or to arrange diligently for other nursing care for their sick friends. Yes, no one should dare leave his neighbor unless there are others who will take care of the sick in their stead and nurse them. In such cases we must respect the word of Christ, "I was sick and you did not visit me. . ." (Matt. 25:41–46). According to this passage we are bound to each other in such a way that no one may forsake the other in his distress but is obliged to assist and help him as he himself would like to be helped.

Where no such emergency exists and where enough people are available for nursing and taking care of the sick, and where, voluntarily or by orders, those who are weak in faith make provision so that there is no need for additional helpers, or where the sick do not want them and have refused their services, I judge that they have an equal choice either to flee or to remain. If someone is sufficiently bold and strong in his faith, let him stay in God's name; that is certainly no sin. If someone is weak and fearful, let him flee in God's name as long as he does not neglect his duty toward his neighbor but has made adequate provision for others to provide nursing care. To flee from death and to save one's life is a natural tendency, implanted by God and not forbidden unless it be against God and neighbor, as St. Paul says in Ephesians 5:29, "No man ever hates his own flesh, but nourishes and cherishes it." It is even commanded that every man should as much as possible preserve body and life and not neglect them, as St. Paul says in 1 Corinthians 12:21–26 that God has so ordered the members of the body that each one cares and works for the other.

It is not forbidden but rather commanded that by the sweat of our brow we should seek our daily food, clothing, and all we need and avoid destruction and disaster whenever we can, as long as we do so without detracting from our love and duty toward our neighbor. How much more appropriate it is therefore to seek to preserve life and avoid death if this can be done without harm to our neighbor, inasmuch as life is more than food and clothing, as Christ himself says in Matthew 6:25. If someone is so strong in faith, however, that he can willingly suffer nakedness, hunger, and want without tempting God and not trying to escape, although he could do so, let him continue that way, but let him not condemn those who will not or cannot do the same.

Examples in Holy Scripture abundantly prove that to flee from death is not wrong in itself. Abraham was a great saint but he feared death and escaped it by pretending that his wife, Sarah, was his sister. Because he did so without neglecting or adversely affecting his neighbor, it was not counted as a sin against him. His son, Isaac, did likewise. Jacob also fled from his brother Esau to avoid death at his hands. Likewise, David fled from Saul, and from Absalom. The prophet Uriah escaped from King Jehoiakim and fled into Egypt. The valiant prophet, Elijah, 1 Kings 19:3, had destroyed all the prophets of Baal by his great faith, but afterward, when Queen Jezebel threatened him, he became afraid and fled into the desert. Before that, Moses fled into the land of Midian when the king searched for him in Egypt. Many others have done likewise. All of them fled from death when it was possible and saved their lives, yet without depriving their neighbors of anything but first meeting their obligations toward them.

Yes, you may reply, but these examples do not refer to dying by pestilence but to death under persecution. Answer: Death is death, no matter how it occurs. According to Holy Scripture God sent his four scourges: pestilence, famine, sword, and wild beasts. If it is permissible to flee from one or the other in clear conscience, why not from all four? Our examples demonstrate how the holy fathers escaped from the sword; it is quite evident that Abraham, Isaac, and Jacob fled from the other scourge, namely, hunger and death, when they went to Egypt to escape famine, as we are told in Genesis 40–47. Likewise, why should one not run away from wild beasts? I hear people say, "If war or the Turks come, one should not flee from his village or town but stay and await God's punishment by the sword." That is quite true; let him who has a strong faith wait for his death, but he should not condemn those who take flight.

By such reasoning, when a house is on fire, no one should run outside or rush to help because such a fire is also a punishment from God. Anyone who falls into deep water dare not save himself by swimming but must surrender to the water as to a divine punishment. Very well, do so if you can but do not tempt God, and allow others to do as much as they are capable of doing. Likewise, if someone breaks a leg, is wounded or bitten, he should not seek medical aid but say, "It is God's punishment. I shall bear it until it heals by itself." Freezing weather and winter are also God's punishment and can cause death. Why run to get inside or near a fire? Be strong and stay outside until it becomes warm again. We should then need no apothecaries or drugs or physicians because all illnesses are punishment from God. Hunger and thirst are also great punishments and torture. Why do you eat and drink instead of letting yourself be punished until hunger and thirst stop of themselves? Ultimately such talk will lead to the point where we abbreviate the Lord's Prayer and no longer pray, "deliver us from evil, Amen," since we would have to stop praying to be saved from hell and stop seeking to escape it. It, too, is God's punishment as is every kind of evil. Where would all this end?

From what has been said we derive this guidance: We must pray against every form of evil and guard against it to the best of our ability in order not to act contrary to God, as was previously explained. If it be God's will that evil come upon us and destroy us, none of our precautions will help us. Everybody must take this to heart: first of all, if he feels bound to remain where death rages in order to serve his neighbor, let him commend himself to God and say, "Lord, I am in thy hands; thou hast kept me here; thy will be done. I am thy lowly creature. Thou canst kill me or preserve me in this pestilence in the same way as if I were in fire, water, drought, or any other danger." If a man is free, however, and can escape, let him commend himself and say, "Lord God, I am weak and fearful. Therefore I am running away from evil and am doing what I can to protect myself against it. I am nevertheless in thy hands in this danger as in any other which might overtake me. Thy will be done. My flight alone will not succeed of itself because calamity and harm are everywhere. Moreover, the devil never sleeps. He is a murderer from the beginning (John 8:44) and tries everywhere to instigate murder and misfortune."

In the same way we must and we owe it to our neighbor to accord him the same treatment in other troubles and perils, also. If his house is on fire, love compels me to run to help him extinguish the flames. If there are enough other people around to put the fire out, I may either go home or remain to help. If he falls into the water or into a pit I dare not turn away but must hurry to help him as best I can. If there are others to do it,

I am released. If I see that he is hungry or thirsty, I cannot ignore him but must offer food and drink, not considering whether I would risk impoverishing myself by doing so. A man who will not help or support others unless he can do so without affecting his safety or his property will never help his neighbor. He will always reckon with the possibility that doing so will bring some disadvantage and damage, danger and loss. No neighbor can live alongside another without risk to his safety, property, wife, or child. He must run the risk that fire or some other accident will start in the neighbor's house and destroy him bodily or deprive him of his goods, wife, children, and all he has.

Anyone who does not do that for his neighbor, but forsakes him and leaves him to his misfortune, becomes a murderer in the sight of God, as St. John states in his epistles, "Whoever does not love his brother is a murderer," and again, "If anyone has the world's goods, and sees his brother in need [yet closes his heart against him], how does God's love abide in him?" (1 John 3:15, 17). That is also one of the sins which God attributed to the city of Sodom when he speaks through the prophet Ezekiel 16:49, "Behold, this was the guilt of your sister Sodom: she and her daughters had pride, surfeit of food, and prosperous ease, but did not aid the poor and needy." Christ, therefore, will condemn them as murderers on the Last Day when he will say, "I was sick and you did not visit me" (Matt. 25:43). If that shall be the judgment upon those who have failed to visit the sick and needy or to offer them relief, what will become of those who abandoned them and let them lie there like dogs and pigs? Yes, how will they fare who rob the poor of the little they have and plague them in all kinds of ways? That is what the tyrants do to the poor who accept the gospel. But let that be; they have their condemnation.

It would be well, where there is such an efficient government in cities and states, to maintain municipal homes and hospitals staffed with people to take care of the sick so that patients from private homes can be sent there—as was the intent and purpose of our forefathers with so many pious bequests, hospices, hospitals, and infirmaries so that it should not be necessary for every citizen to maintain a hospital in his own home. That would indeed be a fine, commendable, and Christian arrangement to which everyone should offer generous help and contributions, particularly the government. Where there are no such institutions—and they exist in only a few places—we must give hospital care and be nurses for one another in any extremity or risk the loss of salvation and the grace of God. Thus it is written in God's word and command, "Love your neighbor as yourself," and in Matthew 7:12, "So whatever you wish that men would do to you, do so to them."

Now if a deadly epidemic strikes, we should stay where we are, make our preparations, and take courage in the fact that we are mutually bound together (as previously indicated) so that we cannot desert one another or flee from one another. First, we can be sure that God's punishment has come upon us, not only to chastise us for our sins but also to test our faith and love—our faith in that we may see and experience how we should act toward God; our love in that we may recognize how we should act toward our neighbor. I am of the opinion that all the epidemics, like any plague, are spread among the people by evil spirits who poison the air or exhale a pestilential breath which puts a deadly poison into the flesh. Nevertheless, this is God's decree and punishment to which we must patiently submit and serve our neighbor, risking our lives in this manner as St. John teaches, "If Christ laid down his life for us, we ought to lay down our lives for the brethren" (1 John 3:16).

When anyone is overcome by horror and repugnance in the presence of a sick person he should take courage and strength in the firm assurance that it is the devil who stirs up such abhorrence, fear, and loathing in his heart. He is such a bitter, knavish devil that he not only unceasingly tries to slay and kill, but also takes delight in making us deathly afraid, worried, and apprehensive so that we should regard dying as horrible and have no rest or peace all through our life. And so the devil would excrete us out of this life as he tries to make us despair of God, become unwilling and unprepared to die, and, under the stormy and dark sky of fear and anxiety, make us forget and lose Christ, our light and life, and desert our neighbor in his troubles. We would sin thereby against God and man; that would be the devil's glory and delight. Because we know that it is the devil's game to induce such fear and dread, we should in turn minimize it, take such courage as to spite and annoy him, and send those terrors right back to him. And we should arm ourselves with this answer to the devil:

"Get away, you devil, with your terrors! Just because you hate it, I'll spite you by going the more quickly to help my sick neighbor. I'll pay no attention to you: I've got two heavy blows to use against you: the first one is that I know that helping my neighbor is a deed well-pleasing to God and all the angels; by this deed I do God's will and render true service and obedience to him. All the more so because if you hate it so and are so strongly opposed to it, it must be particularly acceptable to God. I'd do this readily and gladly if I could please only one angel who might look with delight on it. But now that it pleases my Lord Jesus Christ and the whole heavenly host because it is the will and command of God, my Father, then how could any fear of you cause me to spoil such joy in heaven or such delight for my Lord? Or how could I, by flattering you, give you and your devils in hell reason to mock and laugh at me? No, you'll not have the last word! If Christ shed his blood for me and died for me, why should I not expose myself to some small dangers for his sake and disregard this feeble plague? If you can terrorize, Christ can strengthen me. If you can kill, Christ can give life. If you have poison in your fangs, Christ has far greater medicine. Should not my dear Christ, with his precepts, his kindness, and all his encouragement, be more important in my spirit than you, roguish devil, with your false terrors in my weak flesh? God forbid! Get away, devil. Here is Christ and here am I, his servant in this work. Let Christ prevail! Amen."

The second blow against the devil is God's mighty promise by which he encourages those who minister to the needy. He says in Psalm 41:1–3, "Blessed is he who considers the poor. The Lord will deliver him in the day of trouble. The Lord will protect him and keep him alive; the Lord will bless him on earth and not give him up to the will of his enemies. The Lord will sustain him on his sickbed. In his illness he will heal all his infirmities." Are not these glorious and mighty promises of God heaped up upon those who minister to the needy? What should terrorize us or frighten us away from such great and divine comfort? The service we can render to the needy is indeed such a small thing in comparison with God's promises and rewards that St. Paul says to Timothy, "Godliness is of value in every way, and it holds promise both for the present life and for the life to come" (1 Tim. 4:8). Godliness is nothing else but service to God. Service to God is indeed service to our neighbor. It is proved by experience that those who nurse the sick with love, devotion, and sincerity are generally protected. Though they are poisoned, they are not harmed. As the psalm says, "in his illness you heal all his infirmities" (Ps. 41:3), that is, you change his bed of sickness into a bed of health. A person who attends a patient because of greed, or with the expectation of an inheritance or some personal advantage in such services, should not be surprised if eventually he is infected, disfigured, or even dies before he comes into possession of that estate or inheritance.

But whoever serves the sick for the sake of God's gracious promise, though he may accept a suitable reward to which he is entitled, inasmuch as every laborer is worthy of his hire—whoever does so has the great assurance that he shall in turn be cared for. God himself shall be his attendant and his physician, too. What an attendant he is! What a physician! Friend, what are all the physicians, apothecaries, and attendants in comparison to God? Should that not encourage one to go and serve a sick person, even though he might have as many contagious boils on him as hairs on his body, and though he might be bent double carrying a hundred plague-ridden bodies! What do all kinds of pestilence or devils mean over against God, who binds and obliges himself to be our attendant and physician? Shame and more shame on you, you out-and-out unbeliever, for despising such great comfort and letting yourself become more frightened by some small boil or some uncertain danger than emboldened by such sure and faithful promises of God! What would it avail you if all physicians and the entire world were at your service, but God were not present? Again, what harm could overtake you if the whole world were to desert you and no physician would remain with you, but God would abide with you with his assurance? Do you not know that you are surrounded as by thousands of angels who watch over you in such a way that you can indeed trample upon the plague, as it is written in Psalm 91:11–13, "He has given his angels charge of you to guard you in all your ways. On their hands they will bear you up lest you dash your foot against a stone. You will tread upon the lion and the adder, and trample the young lion and the serpent under foot."

Therefore, dear friends, let us not become so desperate as to desert our own whom we are duty-bound to help and flee in such a cowardly way from the terror of the devil, or allow him the joy of mocking us and vexing and distressing God and all his angels. For it is certainly true that he who despises such great promises and commands of God and leaves his own people destitute, violates all of God's laws and is guilty of the murder of his neighbor whom he abandons. I fear that in such a case God's promise will be reversed and changed into horrible threats and the psalm will then read this way against them: "Accursed is he who does not provide for the needy but escapes and forsakes them. The Lord in turn will not spare him in evil days but will flee from him and desert him, The Lord will not preserve him and keep him alive and will not prosper him on earth but will deliver him into the hands of his enemies. The Lord will not refresh him on his sickbed nor take him from the couch of his illness." For "the measure you give will be the measure you get" (Matt. 7:2). Nothing else can come of it. It is terrible to hear this, more terrible to be waiting for this to happen, most terrible to experience it. What else can happen if God withdraws his hand and forsakes us except sheer devilment and every kind of evil? It cannot be otherwise if, against God's command, one abandons his neighbor. This fate will surely overtake anyone of this sort, unless he sincerely repents.

This I well know, that if it were Christ or his mother who were laid low by illness, everybody would be so solicitous and would gladly become a servant or helper. Everyone would want to be bold and fearless; nobody would flee but everyone would come running. And yet they don't hear what Christ himself says, "As you did to one of the least, you did it to me" (Matt. 25:40). When he speaks of the greatest commandment he says, "The other commandment is like unto it, you shall love your neighbor as yourself" (Matt. 22:39). There you hear that the command to love your neighbor is equal to the greatest commandment to love God, and that what you do or fail to do for your neighbor means doing the same to God. If you wish to serve Christ and to wait on him, very well, you have your sick neighbor close at hand. Go to him and serve him, and you will surely find Christ in him, not outwardly but in his word. If you do not wish or care to serve your neighbor you can be sure that if Christ lay there instead you would not do so either and would let him lie there. Those are nothing but illusions on your part which puff you up with vain pride, namely, that you would really serve Christ if he were there in person. Those are nothing but lies; whoever wants to serve Christ in person would surely serve his neighbor as well. This is said as an admonition and encouragement against fear and a disgraceful flight to which the devil would tempt us so that we would disregard God's command in our dealings with our neighbor and so we would fall into sin on the left hand.

Others sin on the right hand. They are much too rash and reckless, tempting God and disregarding everything which might counteract death and the plague. They disdain the use of medicines; they do not avoid places and persons infected by the plague, but lightheartedly make sport of it and wish to prove how independent they are. They say that it is God's punishment; if he wants to protect them he can do so without medicines or our carefulness. This is not trusting God but tempting him. God has created medicines and provided us with intelligence to guard and take good care of the body so that we can live in good health.

If one makes no use of intelligence or medicine when he could do so without detriment to his neighbor, such a person injures his body and must beware lest he become a suicide in God's eyes. By the same reasoning a person might forego eating and drinking, clothing and shelter, and boldly proclaim his faith that if God wanted to preserve him from starvation and cold, he could do so without food and clothing. Actually that would be suicide. It is even more shameful for a person to pay no heed to his own body and to fail to protect it against the plague the best he is able, and then to infect and poison others who might have remained alive if he had taken care of his body as he should have. He is thus responsible before God for his neighbor's death and is a murderer many times over. Indeed, such people behave as though a house were burning in the city and nobody were trying to put the fire out. Instead they give leeway to the flames so that the whole city is consumed, saying that if God so willed, he could save the city without water to quench the fire.

No, my dear friends, that is no good. Use medicine; take potions which can help you; fumigate house, yard, and street; shun persons and places wherever your neighbor does not need your presence or has recovered, and act like a man who wants to help put out the burning city. What else is the epidemic but a fire which instead of consuming wood and straw devours life and body? You ought to think this way: "Very well, by God's decree the enemy has sent us poison and deadly offal. Therefore I shall ask God mercifully to protect us. Then I shall fumigate, help purify the air, administer medicine, and take it. I shall avoid places and persons where my presence is not needed in order not to become contaminated and thus perchance infect and pollute others, and so cause their death as a result of my negligence. If God should wish to take me, he will surely find me and I have done what he has expected of me and so I am not responsible for either my own death or the death of others. If my neighbor needs me, however, I shall not avoid place or person but will go freely, as stated above. See, this is such a God-fearing faith because it is neither brash nor foolhardy and does not tempt God.

Moreover, he who has contracted the disease and recovered should keep away from others and not admit them into his presence unless it be necessary. Though one should aid him in his time of need, as previously pointed out, he in turn should, after his recovery, so act toward others that no one becomes unnecessarily endangered on his account and so cause another's death. "Whoever loves danger," says the wise man, "will perish by it" (Ecclus. 3:26). If the people in a city were to show themselves bold in their faith when a neighbor's need so demands, and cautious when no emergency exists, and if everyone would help ward off contagion as best he can, then the death toll would indeed be moderate. But if some are too panicky and desert their neighbors in their plight, and if some are so foolish as not to take precautions but aggravate the contagion, then the devil has a heyday and many will die. On both counts this is a grievous offense to God and to man—here it is tempting God; there it is bringing man into despair. Then the one who flees, the devil will pursue; the one who stays behind, the devil will hold captive so that no one escapes him.

Some are even worse than that. They keep it secret that they have the disease and go among others in the belief that by contaminating and poisoning others they can rid themselves of the plague and so recover. With this idea they enter streets and homes, trying to saddle children or servants with the disease and thus save themselves. I certainly believe that this is the devil's doing, who helps turn the wheel of fate to make this happen. I have been told that some are so incredibly vicious that they circulate among people and enter homes because they are sorry that the plague has not reached that far and wish to carry it in, as though it were a prank like putting lice into fur garments or flies into someone's living room. I do not know whether I should believe this; if it is true, I do not know whether we Germans are not really devils instead of human beings. It must be admitted that there are some extremely coarse and wicked people. The devil is never idle. My advice is that if any such persons are discovered, the judge should take them by the ear and turn them over to Master Jack, the hangman, as outright and deliberate murderers. What else are such people but assassins in our town? Here and there an assassin will jab a knife through someone and no one can find the culprit. So these folk infect a child here, a woman there, and can never be caught. They go on laughing as though they had accomplished something. Where this is the case, it would be better to live among wild beasts than with such murderers. I do not know how to preach to such killers. They pay no heed. I appeal to the authorities to take charge and turn them over to the help and advice not of physicians, but of Master Jack, the hangman.

If in the Old Testament God himself ordered lepers to be banished from the community and compelled to live outside the city to prevent contamination (Leviticus 13–14), we must do the same with this dangerous pestilence so that anyone who becomes infected will stay away from other persons, or allow himself to be taken away and given speedy help with medicine. Under such circumstances it is our duty to assist such a person and not forsake him in his plight, as I have repeatedly pointed out before.

Then the poison is stopped in time, which benefits not only the individual but also the whole community, which might be contaminated if one person is permitted to infect others. Our plague here in Wittenberg has been caused by nothing but filth. The air, thank God, is still clean and pure, but some few have been contaminated because of the laziness or recklessness of some. So the devil enjoys himself at the terror and flight which he causes among us. May God thwart him! Amen.

This is what we think and conclude on this subject of fleeing from death by the plague. If you are of a different opinion, may God enlighten you. Amen.

Because this letter will go out in print for people to read, I regard it useful to add some brief instructions on how one should care and provide for the soul in time of death. We have done this orally from the pulpit, and still do so every day in fulfillment of the ministry to which we have been called as pastors.

First, one must admonish the people to attend church and listen to the sermon so that they learn through God's word how to live and how to die. It must be noted that those who are so uncouth and wicked as to despise God's word while they are in good health should be left unattended when they are sick unless they demonstrate their remorse and repentance with great earnestness, tears, and lamentation. A person who wants to live like a heathen or a dog and does not publicly repent should not expect us to administer the sacrament to him or have us count him a Christian. Let him die as he has lived because we shall not throw pearls before swine nor give to dogs what is holy (Matt. 7:6). Sad to say, there are many churlish, hardened ruffians who do not care for their souls when they live or when they die. They simply lie down and die like unthinking hulks.

Second, everyone should prepare in time and get ready for death by going to confession and taking the sacrament once every week or fortnight. He should become reconciled with his neighbor and make his will so that if the Lord knocks and he departs before a pastor or chaplain can arrive, he has provided for his soul, has left nothing undone, and has committed himself to God. When there are many fatalities and only two or three pastors on duty, it is impossible to visit everyone, to give instruction, and to teach each one what a Christian ought to know in the anguish of death. Those who have been careless and negligent in these matters must account for themselves. That is their own fault. After all, we cannot set up a private pulpit and altar daily at their bedside simply because they have despised the public pulpit and altar to which God has summoned and called them.

Third, if someone wants the chaplain or pastor to come, let the sick person send word in time to call him and let him do so early enough while he is still in his right mind before the illness overwhelms the patient. The reason I say this is that some are so negligent that they make no request and send no message until the soul is perched for flight on the tip of their tongues and they are no longer rational or able to speak. Then we are told, "Dear Sir, say the very best you can to him," etc. But earlier, when the illness first began, they wanted no visit from the pastor, but would say, "Oh, there's no need. I hope he'll get better." What should a diligent pastor do with such people who neglect both body and soul? They live and die like beasts in the field. They want us to teach them the gospel at the last minute and administer the sacrament to them as they were accustomed to it under the papacy when nobody asked whether they believed or understood the gospel but just stuffed the sacrament down their throats as if into a bread bag.

This won't do. If someone cannot talk or indicate by a sign that he believes, understands, and desires the sacrament—particularly if he has willfully neglected it—we will not give it to him just anytime he asks for it. We have been commanded not to offer the holy sacrament to unbelievers but rather to believers who can state and confess their faith. Let the others alone in their unbelief; we are guiltless because we have not been slothful in preaching, teaching, exhortation, consolation, visitation, or in anything else that pertains to our ministry and office. This, in brief, is our instruction and what we practice here. We do not write this for you in Breslau, because Christ is with you and without our aid he will amply instruct you and supply your needs with his own ointment. To him be praise and honor together with God the Father and the Holy Spirit, world without end. Amen.

Because we have come upon the subject of death, I cannot refrain from saying something about burials. First of all, I leave it to the doctors of medicine and others with greater experience than mine in such matters to decide whether it is dangerous to maintain cemeteries within the city limits. I do not know and do not claim to understand whether vapors and mists arise out of graves to pollute the air. If this were so my previously stated warnings constitute ample reason to locate cemeteries outside the city. As we have learned, all of us have the responsibility of warding off this poison to the best of our ability because God has commanded us to care for the body, to protect and nurse it so that we are not exposed needlessly. In an emergency, however, we must be bold enough to risk our health if that is necessary. Thus we should be ready for both—to live and to die according to God's will. For "none of us lives to himself and none of us dies to himself," as St. Paul says, Romans 14:7.

It is very well known that the custom in antiquity, both among Jews and pagans, among saints and sinners, was to bury the dead outside the city. Those people were just as prudent as we claim to be ourselves. This is also evident in St. Luke's Gospel, when Christ raised from the dead the widow's son at the gates of Nain (for the text of Luke 7:12 states, "He was being carried out of the city to the grave and a large crowd from the city was with her"). In that country it was the practice to bury the dead outside the town.

Christs tomb, also, was prepared outside the city. Abraham, too, bought a burial plot in the field of Ephron near the double cave where all the patriarchs wished to be buried. The Latin therefore employs the term efferi, that is, "to carry out," by which we mean "carry to the grave." They not only carried the dead out but also burned them to powder to keep the air as pure as possible.

My advice, therefore, is to follow these examples and to bury the dead outside the town. Not only necessity but piety and decency should induce us to provide a public burial ground outside the town, that is, our town of Wittenberg.

A cemetery rightfully ought to be a fine quiet place, removed from all other localities, to which one can go and reverently meditate upon death, the Last Judgment, the resurrection, and say one's prayers. Such a place should properly be a decent, hallowed place, to be entered with trepidation and reverence because doubtlessly some saints rest there. It might even be arranged to have religious pictures and portraits painted on the walls.

But our cemetery, what is it like? Four or five alleys, two or three marketplaces, with the result that no place in the whole town is busier or noisier than the cemetery. People and cattle roam over it at any time, night and day. Everyone has a door or pathway to it from his house and all sorts of things take place there, probably even some that are not fit to be mentioned. This totally destroys respect and reverence for the graves, and people think no more about walking across it than if it were a burial ground for executed criminals. Not even the Turk would dishonor the place the way we do. And yet a cemetery should inspire us to devout thoughts, to the contemplation of death and the resurrection, and to respect for the saints who rest there. How can that be done at such a common place through which everyone must walk and into which every man's door opens? If a cemetery is to have some dignity, I would rather be put to rest in the Elbe or in the forest. If a graveyard were located at a quiet, remote spot where no one could make a path through it, it would be a spiritual, proper, and holy sight and could be so arranged that it would inspire devotion in those who go there. That would be my advice. Follow it, who so wishes. If anyone knows better, let him go ahead. I am no man's master.

In closing, we admonish and plead with you in Christ's name to help us with your prayers to God so that we may do battle with word and precept against the real and spiritual pestilence of Satan in his wickedness with which he now poisons and defiles the world. That is, particularly against those who blaspheme the sacrament, though there are other sectarians also. Satan is infuriated and perhaps he feels that the day of Christ is at hand. That is why he raves so fiercely and tries through the enthusiasts to rob us of the Savior, Jesus Christ. Under the papacy Satan was simply "flesh" so that even a monk's cap had to be regarded as sacred. Now he is nothing more than sheer "spirit" and Christ's flesh and word are no longer supposed to mean anything. They made an answer to my treatise long ago, but I am surprised that it has not yet reached me at Wittenberg. [When it does] I shall, God willing, answer them once again and let the matter drop. I can see that they will only become worse. They are like a bedbug which itself has a foul smell, but the harder you rub to crush it, the more it stinks. I hope that I've written enough in this pamphlet for those who can be saved so that—God be praised—many may thereby be snatched from their jaws and many more may be strengthened and confirmed in the truth. May Christ our Lord and Savior preserve us all in pure faith and fervent love, unspotted and pure until his day. Amen. Pray for me, a poor sinner.

7

The Merciful Hands of the Lord

Introduction

Ludwig Lavater (b. 1527) faithfully served as a preacher and archdeacon at the Grössmunster church in Zürich for thirty-six years, until his death in 1586.[1] Alongside Heinrich Bullinger, Lavater played an important role in the stabilization and reception of Huldrych Zwingli's insights in Zürich during the period between the tragedy of the battle of Kappel and Zwingli's martial death in 1531 and the death of Bullinger, Zwingli's successor, in 1575. This, perhaps, was his most lasting contribution to the progress of the Reformation, the development of Reformed liturgy, and church polity.[2] How did he accomplish this?

First, in his day Lavater was known as a concise preacher. His close friend and biographer, Johann Wilhelm Stucki, remarked,

> [Lavater's] sermons were prepared without paint or pigment, not for ostentation, but edification, that is, for the benefit of his hearers, adapted first to the sense and understanding of the lettered and the unlettered, and most of all, in doctrine and comfort... He applied an

---

1. For Johann Guilelmus Stucki's account of the life of Ludwig Lavater, see Ludwig Lavater, *Nehemias, liber Nehemiae, qui et secundus Ezrae dicitur, homilis LVIII* (Zürich: Officina Froschoviana, 1586), fols. α2r–ε1v. For a modern account of his father, Hans Rudolf Lavater, see Heinzpeter Stucki, "Bürgermeister Hans Rudolf Lavater, 1492–1557: ein Politiker der Reformationszeit" in *Züricher Beiträge zur Reformationsgeschichte*, vol. 3 (Zürich: Theologischer Verlag, 1973). For biographical and bibliographical listings, see Hans Ulrich Bächtold, "Ludwig Lavater" in *Historisches Lexicon der Schweiz*, version 11/20/2008, https://hls-dss.ch/de/articles/010728/2008-11-20/, consulted on 6/15/2021; Georg von Wyß, "Ludwig Lavater" in *Allgemeine Deutsche Bibliogrphie* (1883), 18:83–84. For an English account of Lavater and early modern biography, see Irena Backus, *Life Writing in Reformation Europe: Lives of Reformers by Friends, Disciples, and Foes* (Ashgate: Aldershot, 2008), 111–116.

2. See Luca Baschera, Bruce Gordon, and Christian Moser, "Emulating the Past and Creating the Present: Reformation and the Use of Historical and Theological Models in Zurich in the Sixteenth Century" in *Following Zwingli*, 15–22.

order and method that was so outstanding (which I need not add) that even his entire sermon could easily be understood and memorized by any person not entirely dull and dimwitted.³

Lavater "did not only blaze with his own ardent zeal to preach, but he also most eagerly listened to the sacred sermons of other ministers, although sometimes they were far more inferior in their [level of] teaching (so great and so ardent was his zeal and love of holy things)."⁴ It was through this constant zeal and attentiveness to a range of sermons and theological writings that Lavater credited his theological advance to stalwarts in Zurich such as the professor of New Testament, Heinrich Bullinger (1504–1575); professor of Greek and Hebrew, Konrad Pellikan (1478–1556); professors of Old Testament, Theodor Bibliander (1506–1564), Peter Martyr Vermigli (1499–1562), Josias Simler (1530–1576), and Johann Wolf (1521–1572). It was in interaction with them that Lavater grew, even though he was a scholar trained in his own right at Kappel, Zurich, Strassburg, Paris, and Lausanne.

Second, he accomplished this through his publications. Although Lavater is little known today in popular writings, in the sixteenth century "he was the third most productive author in his city, ranked after Heinrich Bullinger and Rudolf Gwalther."⁵ Furthermore, Lavater coupled learned brevity with simplicity in his writing as well. Stucki reported that "just as his sermons delivered orally in vivid speech, were approved of especially by the most learned men, so also his writings were commended for their brevity, clarity, godliness, and erudition."⁶ His publications were well received not just in his homeland of Switzerland but also among other places in England, especially among disciples of Vermigli such as John Jewel (1522–1571).⁷

---

3. See Ludwig Lavater, *Nehemias, liber Nehemiae, qui et secundus Ezrae dicitur, homilis LVIII* (Zürich: Officina Froschoviana, 1586), γ1v. Cf. Irena Backus has translated the same Latin quote in *Life Writing in Reformation Europe: Lives of Reformers by Friends, Disciples, and Foes* (Ashgate: Aldershot, 2008), 114. While an excellent translation, the one offered here differs on several minor points of nuance. Backus summarizes Stucki's emphases in his biography of Lavater as an exemplar "embodying all the virtues of a good pastor," 116.

4. Lavater, *Nehemias*, fol. γ2r.

5. See Christian Moser, "A Mirror of Virtue: Commentaries on the Book of Ruth in Sixteenth-century Zurich" in *Following Zwingli: Applying the Past in Reformation Zurich*, ed. L. Baschera and B. Gordon (Routledge: London, 2014), 124.

6. Lavater, *Nehemias*, fol. γ3v; this Latin portion is cited but not translated in Backus, *Life Writing*, 115n55.

7. Lavater, *Nehemias*, fols. γ3v–γ4r; cf. Backus, *Following Zwingli*, 115nn56–57.

Third, Ludwig Lavater's pastoral care cannot be overlooked. We are told by Stucki, the biographer and family friend of both Ludwig and his father, Hans Rudolf Lavater (1492–1557), that Hans was a godly soldier, politician, and firm supporter of the Reformation in Zürich, and thus a political stalwart for the cause of the Reformation throughout Switzerland until his death.[8] Where Hans had served Switzerland politically, Ludwig served Zurich pastorally. Stucki reported that Ludwig served as a clear image and model since "examples of nearly all the virtues could be drawn from him." Full of "fatherly wisdom and prudence" whether in public or private, politics or church matters, he was candid, sincere, frank, a lover of truth, patient, frugal, and temperate.[9] With humanity and liberality, Lavater was quick to succor the needs of the poor and destitute with food, drink, and clothing while he himself refrained from all luxury and drunkenness. Not only was he a friend of the poor and needy at home, but he was also compassionate towards the straits of refugees and travelers, "especially to those who had abandoned their homeland for the cause of the true religion, who were compelled to flee for asylum and safe refuge to us, such as the English, the Italians, and the French."[10]

It is on the topic and practice of plague where we see these three strands of Lavater's pastoral service converge. His sermons on plague were printed and published in both German and Latin and included at various points in his commentaries.[11] Stucki notes, regarding Lavater's sense of Christian charity, that he was mindful of the sick and suffering: "whether called or not he very freely visited any sick, and especially those close to death, and comforting them with godly sermons, he looked out for their salvation in an outstanding way."[12] Below is a sample of his sermon and comments on 1 Chronicles 21 in relation to the question of the plague. Not only does Lavater consider the question of God's sovereignty over the plague and the relationship between suffering, sin, and repentance, but he considers the role of a godly pastor and the duties of a godly king in the face of a plague.

---

8. Lavater, *Nehemias*, fols. α2r– α3v.
9. Lavater, *Nehemias*, fol. γ4v.
10. Lavater, *Nehemias*, fol. δ1r.
11. Lavater, *Von der Pestilenz, zwo Predginen die ein vom Ursprung der Pestilenz, wohar die sye, item warumb sy regiere unnd wie man sich darinnen halten sölle die ander dess säligen Bischoffs und Martyrers Cypriani von jm zuo Carthago* (Zurcih: Christoffel Froschouwer, 1564); idem, *De Pestilentia concio Ludovici Lavateri . . . edita Joannis Pontisellae* (Zurich, 1586); idem, *In libros Paralipomenon sive Chronicorum . . . Commentarius* (Zurich: Christophorus Froschouer, 1573), fols. 76v–80r
12. Lavater, *Nehemias*, fol. δ1r.

Furthermore, in David's repentance and desire to take the trouble of Israel and Judah upon himself, Lavater points to the model of the best pastor, that shepherd of the sheep, Jesus Christ, of whom David is a type.

Ludwig Lavater, *In libros Paralipomenon sive Chronicorum . . . Commentarius* (Zurich: Christophorus Froschouer, 1573), fols. 76v–80r

The Merciful Hands of the Lord
Commentary and a Brief Excursus on Plague from 1 Chronicles 21:9–15

Ludwig Lavater
Translated by Todd M. Rester

And so Jehovah spoke to Gad, David's seer, saying, "Go and say to David saying, 'Thus said the Lord, Three things I stretch out upon you, choose for yourself one of them that I may do it to you.'" And so Gad came to David and said to him, "Thus said Jehovah, 'Choose for yourself: either three years of famine, three months of you being devoured by the face of your enemies, even while the sword of your enemies attacks you, or three days of the sword of the Lord, and the plague will prowl through your land, and the Angel of Jehovah will devastate throughout the whole territory of Israel. Now choose, and see what word I should respond to the one who sent me.'" (1 Chron. 21:9–12)

The third part of this passage treats of the penalty with which the Lord afflicted David and the people. Why he chastised the people will follow in its own topic. God, through Gad, answers and counsels David. In Samuel [2 Sam. 24:11], it is said that the Word of the Lord was brought to David when he rose with the morning (for we gather from Psalm 6 that at night he deplored his miseries). He calls him a seer, for those who were at a later time called prophets were called seers from the most ancient of times (1 Sam. 9[:9]). Now kings had their own prophets who diligently exhorted them to the study of virtue and called them back from vices. [But] today, kings have their own priests (*sacrificuli*) and, as they also call them, chaplains, who very frequently flatter them and instill in them a hatred of true religion. It must be praised in David that he had [Gad] in his court whom he had as a companion in his exile, and that in times of flourishing he did not forget his old friends. For the purpose of our comfort, it is relevant that God immediately and in a familiar way deigned to speak through the prophet to David. Even good men do not deign to speak for a time with those that offended them. God, however, immediately answers those who cry out to him from their hearts and receives them in grace. He did not delay the comfort any longer than David, when he was carefree, had put off his repentance. For it was nine months and twenty days before those who had taken a census of the people had returned home. But even if God delays for some time he does not do this because he has forgotten about us, but in order that we would more fervently pray. We have an example in the Canaanite woman in Matthew 15. To us he does not send an angel or the prophets, as he did with the ancients, but he sends those whom he has ordained to this [office], and he sends the power of the Holy Spirit. Certainly, the prophet discusses with David the punishment that had to be inflicted upon him; but it must be believed that, in the custom of the ancient prophets, [Gad] also applied comfort to him. Approaching him in good faith, Gad explained the mandates with no delay interposed. Gad was familiar with the king, so neither in word nor deed did he want to cast David into mourning, but with God commanding him, he did his duty. He did not dodge, saying, "Supply another to go to him," or "David did not want to listen to Joab and the leaders of the army, how much less will he listen to me!" And so let first all other pastors and then court preachers (*aulici concionatores*) learn that they should execute their office without delay or fear when matters require. For if human reasoning must be listened to, we would never do what we ought; the outcome must be left to God. But the nature of their office is set forth in the holy Scriptures elsewhere. Also magistrates, heads of households, school administrators, and others should faithfully perform what God has commanded them. We also have an example of this in what Amos says in chapter 3: "The Lord does not inflict any evil other than what he reveals previously to his servants." Noah declared the Flood in advance, Lot the destruction of the inhabitants of Sodom, Moses that of the Egyptians, many prophets the exile of the inhabitants of Israel and Judah, and so forth.

Gad employs the prefatory formula customary of the prophets, "Thus said the Lord," so that David would understand that the word set forth to him did not belong to man but to God. We too must listen to the reading of the prophets and apostles as if none other than God himself were speaking to us from heaven: "Give David the option that he would choose either three years of famine, three months of hostile persecution wherein no one would be safe, or three days of pestilence." In Samuel [2 Sam. 21], mention is made of seven years of famine and in this passage three, but this is easy to reconcile. It must be said that to the three years of famine due to the slaughter of the Gibeonites, three more are added. And since [the land] would be barren in the sixth year up to that point due to drought and the farming interrupted, the seventh year would also remain barren. Certainly, the option of penalties was given to him, but these penalties were not trivial, for famine includes frost, hail, drought, war, sedition, pillaging of property, plague, various incurable diseases, and so forth.

We gather from this passage what the fruits of sin are, namely public and private calamities. Moreover, these three things—namely famine, war, and plague—are God's chief scourges with which people who must be chastised due to their sins are threatened in the Law and the Prophets. Add to these evil beasts, about which we have noted several things in our commentaries on Ezekiel the prophet.[13] However, because these do not prowl about apart from being governed by God, this shows what option God grants him. For unless these choices David might have chosen rested in the power of God, David's choice would not have happened, but something different would have come about.

We deduce this also: that even though we may be penitent and God responds to us in grace, we may yet at the same time be afflicted with penalties. Previously David repented, and [God] answered by Nathan that his sins were forgiven but that David must be chastised, even though the punishments were mitigated. Emperor Maurice repented and, despite having converted, he sustained temporal punishments.[14] Moreover, God disciplines his own with penalties so that they, and others, would acknowledge that he truly is angered by sins, and so that those led away from evils,

---

13. Cf. Ludwig Lavater, from "Homilia XVI" in *Propheta Ezechiel ... homiliis seu commentariis expositus* (Geneva: Jean Crespin, 1571), fol. 26r—26v.

14. E.g. For a Greek-Latin text, see Theophanes the Confessor, "Anno Mundi 6094" *Chronographia*, vol 1 of 2 in *Corpus Scriptorum Historiae Byzantinae*, 50 vols. (Bonn: Niebuhr & Bekker, 1828–1897), 43:439–440.

and others, would more diligently beware of sins. For these disciplines are far different from the punishments of the wicked.[15] By no means must it be thought that the penalties with which we may be disciplined are satisfactions for our sins. But even if God does not always bring a temporal punishment to bear, he always brings to bear an eternal one, because what Jeremiah 18 says—"If some people were to repent, I also would repent"—must be understood regarding eternal salvation and destruction, and not generally.

It must be added to these points that if with regard to our commonwealth we desire safety, then princes and people ought to take heed to themselves of those sins that bring destruction upon commonwealths. It must also be specially noted that it would turn out badly for people if they would spurn profitable counsel. Joab and the other warlords gave good advice to David, that he should not number the people, and they brought forward grave consequences. But David remained stuck in his opinion. Therefore, God punished his stubbornness with a plague. First others and then especially youths who are not yet experienced in counsel should heed those who rightly warn them, lest in the end they are compelled to say, "Why, O wretch, did I condemn the voice of my parents, my relations, and my teachers?" Solomon, to deter youth from harlotry, employs this argument before all others in Proverbs 5; lest, when harlots have consumed your wealth and life, you would deplore your miserable condition with a final wailing and crying.

Gad orders David to see and consider what response he would now give to God who had sent him. For God not only orders David to declare his desire but wants to hear a response from him. Let each person now consider how they would answer God for themselves when an account of their duty is demanded from them. What would that person do in the fatal hour and on the last day according to the parable of Matthew 25, regarding those who had received talents from their lord? Or in Ezekiel 23 when he would require the blood of those perishing from the hand of the watchman?

> And David said to Gad, "I am in great distress!" Let me fall, I ask, into the hand of Jehovah (because his mercies are exceedingly great) and let me not fall into the hand of man." (1 Chron. 21:13)

---

15. To emphasize Lavater's distinction, the same word *poena* has been translated as "penalty" with respect to the righteous, but "punishment" with respect to the wicked. Lavater uses the same word, *poena*, for both.

David's response, which the prophet asks from him, is certainly brief, but it contains many things. Now just as we have in Gad an example for godly ministers who teach in courts (for that which God commanded, he proclaimed to the king), so in David an example of a good prince is set down in front of us. For he received and heard the prophet modestly, respecting him by whom Gad had been sent. He does not countenance his arrival shamefully or with annoyance. He does not say, "You think of yourself [too highly], man sent by God, when you come at your pleasure, you who [must] labor with greater troubles than I do!" Rather, he listens to him no less attentively than if God himself is speaking. How may princes are there today who want to hear nothing from their [advisors] besides what is pleasing to them? They certainly say that they love God's Word, but if anyone brings something to them that conflicts with their inclinations, they are immediately ablaze, and remove [the offenders] from their positions. The blessed Ambrose said, regarding Emperor Theodosius, "I loved that man who approves more of the one who argues with him than the one who flatters him."[16] O our Good God, how rare are such princes! But that should not seem amazing to us when not even townsmen[17] and farmers want to be rebuked by pastors. They immediately say, "Who is this preacher? Of what quality is he? Of what quality is his family?" In diseases of the body, we gladly employ the works of an experienced doctor, although he may be burdened with his own vices. Many even implore the assistance of Jewish doctors. There are some who say (albeit impiously) that they would use the works of the devil if they knew it would restore them to health. But in the meantime, in diseases of the soul they do not want to endure preachers who are liable to some vice. Also in other ills it is enough for us if we are simply delivered—such as in the case of shipwrecks, wartime dangers, and so forth. For someone would be stupid if they did not want to be rescued from the water, did not want to leave prison, or did not accept food and clothing unless it were by a person preeminent in many virtues. Nevertheless, some people, and especially the Anabaptists, think this way. But people should not condemn ministers who struggle with a number of their own vices. However, the magistrate

---

16. Ambrose of Milan, *De Obitu Theodosii Oratio*, ch.34 in PL 396; idem, *Ambrose of Milan: Political Letters and Speeches*, trans. J. H. W. G. Liebeschuetz and C. Hill (Liverpool: Liverpool University Press, 2005), 193.

17. Lat. *Cives*, probably standing in for the German and Swiss-German, *burgher*.

should restrain those [ministers] liable to evident crimes and bring them into order.

But what does David say? *I am in great distress!* He saw that it was a dangerous choice, for famine, war, and pestilence bring with them many evils; and so he was distressed and disturbed. David would have taken heed to all these things if, at the beginning, had he followed the advice of his princes and not numbered the people. Many could avoid many ills today if they would follow profitable advice, but because they do not they cast themselves into such great ills that they do not know which way they should turn. But [when] our affairs are such, one must not despair of God's grace. No matter how much circumstances [seem] desperate, at this point they must be moderated with good advice, lest along with the goods of the body and external goods lost we would also cast aside the goods of the soul. David said, "Let me fall into the hand of God." He calls the plague "the hand," that is, the work of God, because in a plague God acts by himself. He does not use the works of men. Certainly famine and war are the hand of God, but in those cases God uses the hands of wicked men—moneylenders, leading citizens,[18] greedy soldiers—who raise the price of goods, who trample on, rip apart, and burn everything. David does not choose that plague in which he would have suffered less for himself, but that one which was equal to all. Had a famine arose, many could have a hope to enrich themselves; in war many could have hope in their weapons, their strength, and their fortifications. But in a plague help can be hoped for from nowhere else than from God. Therefore, we see how religious David was, and how much he loved people. Who does not see how few today are so affected? Many want everyone to perish provided that they themselves survive; with others exposed to danger, they look out only for themselves. Indeed, a base ignoble person fears nothing more than plague, although they all acknowledge that it is lighter than other penalties. David adds the reason why he chose the plague: because the mercies of God are many. He says few words about it in this passage, but in Psalm 103 he explains with many more: "For as high as the heavens are above the earth, so great is his kindness towards those who fear him. And as far as is the east is from the west,[19] so far does he remove our sins from us. And as a father

---

18. Lat. *monopoli* from Gk. μονοπολοι
19. Lat. *quam longe distat ortus solis ab occasu*: lit. "as far distance as the rising of the sun is from its setting"

pities his children, so the Lord pities those that fear him." And so forth (Ps. 103:11–13ff). Many thoughts and many examples demonstrate the immeasurable mercy of God towards us. God declares his mercy in the calamities of war and famine, but frequently we refer to these as brought about by men, which are in fact inflicted by God. If we are delivered from wars, we say that the enemies could have advanced farther, but they were mindful of human causes and similar things. If we are delivered from famine, we praise the liberality of others and the labors of those cultivating the earth and similar things.

When he says, "But let me not fall into the hand of man," David is speaking about a hostile pursuit and hunger. It is not because he would not fall into the hand of God with those [enemies] prowling about, but because regarding the plague, in which the works of men are not employed, it is more conspicuously God's hand. It must not be thought that David thought that men could ravage more than God wills, for he knew that God, who always restrains the furious currents of the sea, can restrain the minds of men. If God punishes by himself, his mercy is more apparent because he is concerned with our benefit (*utilitas*); but men indulge their own desires. Many times when God forgives our sins they still hold on to their hatred. In the cause of Saul and his son, David had experienced the cruelty of men. Susanna seems to have stated it the contrary way, for she preferred to fall into the hand of men rather than God's.[20] But this phrase is taken another way in that passage, for the sense is that she preferred to die than to offend God, about which see Peter Martyr [Vermigli] on 2 Samuel.[21]

But just as David leaves himself to the divine will, so we also ought to do, seeing that the matter cannot be any other way. For unless we do this we will not have a solid comfort. For wherever you turn you will find nothing besides anxiety or terror, and no escape. If you would consider yourself, you cannot stand if you implore the mercy of your enemies; they will allot you none. Therefore, you cannot do anything more useful than to cast yourself, with David, upon divine providence. In dangerous diseases many leave themselves to the will of the surgeons, for unless they would do this

---

20. Reference to the apocryphal addition to the book of Daniel named after its heroine Susanna (see Sus. 22–23).

21. See Peter Martyr Vermigli (1499–1562), *In duos libros Samuelis Prophetae... Commentarii*, 2nd ed. (Zurich: Christophorus Froschouerus, 1571), 321.

they would not receive their care. Why then do we not leave ourselves entirely to God, our most tender Father? David does not ask when the plague would begin or when it would prowl about, but all these things he leaves to God's choice, to whom nothing must be commanded.

> And so God gave a pestilence to Israel, and 70,000 men of Israel fell. And then God sent a certain angel to Jerusalem to destroy it, but when he was about to destroy it... (1 Chron. 21:14–15)

How the plague inflicted by God ravaged throughout the kingdom of Israel will be described briefly. It carried off 70,000 men. Whether children and women were also included makes no difference for us to know. 2 Samuel teaches that it raged from the morning until the time established. There it adds "from Dan to Beersheba," that is, throughout all the Israelite territory. By *Moed* some understand noon or evening of the third day, so that God chose one [day] instead of three days. According to this interpretation, if we should take it, we gather that God is so merciful that he deigns to be lenient and to mitigate the penalties we deserved if, like David, we turn to him with our whole heart. He did not carry off as many of the people as he could have, and he even spared David himself. Furthermore, regarding more recent times that are full of afflictions, Christ our Lord predicted in Matthew 24 that these must be cut short for the sake of the elect.

Next, we have the example of that rule in the Book of Wisdom, chapter 11, through which anyone who sins is punished by the same.[22] Certain persons, even as this was read, worshiped serpents and vile beasts, and so God inflicted upon them beasts, lions, bears, and serpents by whom they were killed. David committed adultery and perpetrated murder, and so his daughter Tamar was defiled; and Amnon's defilement resulted in his murder. Next followed the sedition advanced by Absalom, during which David's concubines were defiled and citizens were slaughtered. In this passage, David sins by numbering the people, and so the people are threatened with the plague. Solomon forsook God due to his foreign wives, and so the Israelites forsook him, which defection later produced first countless other evils and then civil wars. Today God also punishes debauchery and adultery with similar sins. Melanchthon in his writings once said that the sins

---

22. Wisdom of Solomon 11:15–16

of the seed are punished in the seed, that is, in the children.[23] Likewise, if any trust excessively in their children, sometimes they experience this very thing. Their hope must not be placed in them, but in God.

We gather from this how powerful God is and how easily he could punish those who rebel. For when the angel was sent, he brought down so many brave men who would have met any circumstance with unbroken courage in such a short time. It is certainly amazing how such small pustules can extinguish such a multitude of people. There is no counsel against God. The bravest nations cannot prevent the punishments of God the least bit. What is more contemptible than locusts, flies, hornets, and other insects? Yet God calls these little animals his brave host, and with these he broke the Egyptian king and other nations. No one can resist them if they should fly in troops; by no strength can they be driven off. Therefore, let us not attribute too much to ourselves, but let us subject ourselves to God Almighty.

It must also be observed that God employed the works of his good angels (although this ill could seem to have been bad) not only for the defense of his people, but also for inflicting punishments upon his enemies. The angel of the Lord slew the first born of the Egyptians.[24] The angel struck down the army of Sennacherib as it besieged Jerusalem.[25] The angels in Revelation pour out bowls of divine wrath against the Anti-Christians.[26]

ON THE PLAGUE

In this passage, certain things must be noted about the plague so that we may also think correctly about other penalties with which we are afflicted by God. The plague or pestilence (the ancients, as Nonius testifies, also called it *pestilitas*)[27] is a known disease, which sometimes prowls about in

---

23. For an example of this language, see the synodical oration Melanchthon wrote for prince George Anhalt and sent to him on June 10, 1549. Prince George delivered it on June 17, 1549. This oration can be found in CR 11:847–848; "Let us be moved by a fear of this punishment, because it is most true, in the offspring the sins of the seed are punished" (*in sobole puniri peccata seminis*), and also "Such examples are countless in the histories and many examples can be seen in daily life, because it is a most certain rule, in the seed and offspring are punished the outrages that occur by an abuse of the seed, because, since God has a chaste mind, is horribly angered by a violation of chastity." (*regula certissima est puniri in semine et sobole, delicta seminis abusu facta, quia Deus cum sit mens casta, horribiliter irascitur violationi castitatis*).
24. Exod. 12:29–32
25. 2 Kings 19:20–37; Isa. 37:21–38
26. Rev. 16
27. Nonius Marcellus, *De Compendiosa Doctrina*, 158; cf. "pestilitas" in *Nonius Marcellus' Dictionary of Republican Latin*, ed. W. M. Lindsay, 3 vols. (Oxford, 1901–1903).

one place—for there is a great amount of difference among the natures of places; some are salubrious, others pestilential—sometimes it roves over one whole region, and other times throughout the whole world. How atrocious that disease is the subject matter itself teaches. Those who are corrupted by it are twisted by the most serious fever, and many immediately begin to rave and rage. Some who were in the depth of the disease[28] cast themselves headlong from windows. Many depart from the living within a few days—in fact, some within a very few hours—and someone thought to be stronger than anyone is quite quickly extinguished. Parents often die with small children left behind, and so sometimes the entire commonwealth experiences a great loss by what is suffered by a few. Not a few people are deserted by their families when a plague is raging. Many who are afflicted with this disease for a long time are at last delivered, but they lose the power of their memory, their hearing, their sight, and their use of speech; and their body contracts [other] deficiencies.

But the plague does not prowl about so recklessly that by some vicissitude the plague follows upon health. Rather it is inflicted by God; no fewer or more die, none more quickly nor more slowly than God has established. For no ill rages about without God so permitting, willing, and governing. If a little sparrow, with our Savior himself as witness, does not fall haphazardly, much less beasts of burden and—due to whom all these things have been created—men. Plague is called in this passage "the hand of God" because it is inflicted by the one and only will of God. And in Samuel this plague is expressly said to have been inflicted by God. The option is given to David to choose between three penalties; therefore this plague does not rage recklessly or by a certain necessity of the stars. For the stars and other natural things await the will and command of God. I also do not deny that there are natural causes of plague: the constellations, the conjunctions of the planets, southern winds, putrefaction, and other things. But God is not bound at all to second causes. Know this: he does this for the benefit of repentance.

Yet, just as he inflicted other calamities, so God also inflicts plague. There are many testimonies to this in the Law and the Prophets. In 2 Samuel the cause of this plague is indicated, soon after the beginning of chapter 24, as the sin of the Israelite people. After peace returned, they had undoubtedly become more insolent. Moreover, these circumstances stir

---

28. Lat. *morbi gravitate*

us up and impel us to repentance, which consists in this: that we would acknowledge and confess our sins and embrace Christ by faith. In Amos 4 God must still be sought because they did not turn to him in war, famine, or plague. There are other causes of plague also. For God tests our faith and love, and so forth, through this plague.

But just exactly how we ought to conduct ourselves before, during, and after a plague, I will demonstrate next. It is of great importance to know this, for by one and the same exercise we will learn something also of what ought to be done in other calamities and how we ought to be adequately prepared for death. When a plague is raging, we ought not to be so disturbed and thrown into consternation, as if we had never heard about death, and as if God is not our God even in a plague or other penalties. To fear death is human, for we are not sticks and stones; only we ought not to be excessive about it. It must be considered that nothing happens to us apart from the providence of God, and, because he is our Lord and Father, it is right that we would submit to him and reverence him. One must marvel at the foolishness of those who do not want to receive letters, money or other articles from places in which the plague is raging, as if the plague resides in them.

Next, in time of plague especially one must be zealous for godliness and a holy life. One must diligently hear the word of God, lean upon him in prayers, be zealous in fasts, and be generous in alms. Those who flee holy assemblies so that they may not be corrupted by the plague; those who do not want to labor more fully, but day and night gorge themselves; those who have persuaded themselves that they will not die, or if they should see godly people die, want to ward off death with ungodliness, sin vigorously. If we are horrified at the punishment we should also be horrified by the cause of sin, that is, sins and crimes. However, there is no prohibition upon using preventative remedies,[29] such as when we kindle various odors by which the air is corrected and the poison is driven out, or when we observe a good diet. Many think that nothing is more useful than that they take flight immediately from pestilential places to salubrious ones, but one must see what an account of our duty demands. David and the elders did not plan flight for themselves but, clothed in sackcloth, they patiently awaited the hand of God. We must not abandon our station without God's authorization; a station in which we have been placed by him. But is not God present

---

29. Lat., Gk. *remediis*, προφυλακτικοῖς

everywhere? In the Law, Psalm 139, and Amos 3, the sin whereby the air is infected inheres in us. But in those places in which the plague ravages, was there not sometimes healthful air? At the same time, no one ought to expose themselves recklessly to danger and so tempt God. Yet those who visit the sick must not be said to tempt God, and so forth. For the Lord demands this from us, who can serve among ourselves no less than the Israelites once did among the Egyptians, upon whom he inflicted the same disease. But your duty is to care for those infected with the plague who belong to your household, so that they would not perish from either hunger or thirst. It is likewise your duty to visit your neighbors, relatives, and in-laws, and to be present for them and to comfort them. And if you yourself cannot conveniently do it, you ought to call ministers of the Word [to do so]. Also, familiar friends, servants, and maidservants must not be driven out of their houses unless they could be cared for sufficiently in public places. Likewise, the dead are not to be cast out into the streets or sewers, but honorably buried and mourned. Yet sensibility must be kept in mourning. Likewise, an honorable remembrance of the departed must be made. It is a great barbarity to deny hospitality to travelers coming from pestilential places. Likewise to eject citizens infected with the plague from the cities, and in so doing slay them with hunger and cold. Likewise to desert people closely connected to us, and so not even to be present with them when they are dying.

But whoever senses that they are already infected, or who gathers from obvious initial symptoms[30] that they are soon to be infected, ought to employ medicine, which is a gift of God. There are various potions, lozenges,[31] and powders that physicians say must be used; also the placement of plasters and the drawing of pestilential blood by cutting or cupping[32] are very often useful. At the same time, it must be known that medicine is uselessly applied if the blessing of God does not accompany it. But you shall commit yourself to the heavenly Father especially, who, on account of the merit of Christ, wills to be favorable to sinners; and you shall prescribe nothing to him. Because if you see that you are about to be called out of this life, think what you will leave behind and what you will acquire. You are leaving behind a corrupt world and a weak and miserable body, and you acquire eternal life. You will be led out from the poorest prison into a royal palace. Also, place other things before your eyes that would kindle in you the

---

30. Lat. *ex signis non obscuris . . . initiis*
31. Lat. *electarium*: a medicine that melts in one's mouth.
32. Lat. *scarificatione aut cucurbitulis*

desire of the next life. Likewise compose a testament, ordering all your affairs so that either your children or other people would not battle amongst themselves after your passing. Children and others must be exhorted to godliness and to a zeal for virtue; for those things pierce most deeply into their hearts which are heard from the death of a neighbor. Also, we must be gracious to those who serve us in diseases. For there are those who plan all things poorly. Finally, the fatal hour must be awaited patiently and the spirit is to be commended to God, because if the plague ceases or those snatched by this disease are revived, they should attribute it to God alone and that rightly, so that they would not fall into the same or a more serious disease on account of attributing this to medicine.

So let everyone serve God diligently in their vocation. For it often happens that when the plague has been endured people lead more dissolute lives than they did previously (especially those to whom a splendid inheritance has fallen), and they do not conduct themselves otherwise than as if they had now been unburdened from all ills. When you think you have escaped death, you are in fact closer to it than you ever were before. All of us must die, and that sooner than we think. Nothing is more stupid than to promise ourselves many years when it is uncertain whether we would survive tomorrow. As to the rest, how we ought to conduct ourselves in a plague, we know more fully from the example of David.

> Jehovah saw and he relented from the evil, and he said to the devastating angel, 'That is now enough, stay your hand.' But the angel was standing beside the field of Ornan the Jebusite. And David lifted up his eyes, and he saw the angel of Jehovah standing between heaven and earth, and he saw his sword was unsheathed in his hand, stretched out against Jerusalem, and so David and the elders, clothed in sackcloth, fell on their faces. And David said to God, "Did not I order the people numbered? And I—I am the one who did this terrible thing. But these sheep, what have they done? O Jehovah my God, I ask that your hand would be against me and against my father's house, and do not let the plague be against this your people. (1 Chron. 9:15–17)

The fourth part of this chapter contains how, when the plague had been endured, God turned toward David in grace. From this part, not only do we learn how famine, plague, wars, and other calamities do not cease before God has willed, but also how clement and merciful God is towards people. In Psalm 103 it is said that he is not angry forever, like certain people who after they have been offended scarcely—and not even scarcely—can be placated. God in his wrath, says Habakkuk 3, does not forget his mercy, and his love towards us surpasses that of a father's or mother's (Isa. 49; Ps. 30, 86; Ecclus. 2).

If anyone would take notice, he will see individual words placed in this passage that testify of God's love toward us: (1) "He said" and "the Lord saw," namely with the eyes of his mercy, when the angel was about to slay many. In Exodus it is said that he saw the afflictions of the Israelites.[33] In Psalm 94:9,[34] does the one who made eyes not see? (2) He is led by repentance. This is said in a human fashion about God because he does the same thing that the repentant do, that is, he did not proceed to inflict punishments. (3) With "That is enough," he witnesses with his words that he is setting aside his anger. (4) He commands [the angel] to rest from inflicting the plague, declaring by his deeds how benevolently he is affected toward his people. The angel did not cease until he was recalled. Elsewhere in words and deeds he also declares his love towards mankind.[35] At this point it is pertinent that he had mercy on the people and took away the penalty—and at a time earlier than David expected, for it is understood from the subsequent verses that he thought that plague would last longer. However, he is not merciful towards us in this way because he does not detest sin or because we possess some merits, but instead because we embrace Christ our mediator by faith. For this does not pertain to the wicked, but to those who have true repentance.

Regarding David, it is said that he saw the angel standing between heaven and earth, with a drawn sword that was directed against Jerusalem, "By the threshing floor of Ornan the Jebusite," about which we have more later. The angel struck fear into David, so that he would be more cautious later and beware of sins, and so that others also would see that this plague did not arise by happenstance, but by an angered God. David and the elders, when the angel appeared, fell on their faces, partly from fear and weakness (for it is said that David was shaking in his boots thoroughly)[36] and partly so that they may testify of their humility in contrast to the majesty of God. They did not prostrate themselves so that they might worship the angel; they

---

33. E.g. Exod. 3:7
34. Lavater: Psalm 33
35. Gk. φιλανθρωπίαν
36. Lat. *in calce enim dicitur Davidem valde perterritum fuisse*

knew that they must not worship anyone except God. They sin seriously who worship angels. In Revelation one reads that the angel did not want to be adored by John; how much less ought saints be worshiped.[37]

It is added that David and the elders were clothed in sackcloth. Sackcloth is made from a base kind of cloth and was not made for ostentation. Here it was the outfit of the penitent and mourning as we see throughout Scripture. That the heathen also employed sackcloth is evident in the history of Jonah. It is insufficient to take only the outfit of mourning, for it is necessary that the heart is contrite. In adverse circumstances it was a solemn external symbol to testify to one's grief. They sin who, in time of plague, war, and famine, do not set aside their fine clothing and do not guard themselves from drinking to the point of drunkenness and other sins. Moreover, it would be useful for a magistrate, like in this passage as David and the elders did, to lead the way for others in uprightness of life. The ardent prayers of David follow, from which we learn that in adverse circumstances we must pour out prayers for ourselves and others, and to be more inclined to greater prayers than to greater evils. Christ teaches the same thing in Luke 18, and likewise by his example in Matthew 26. Let us now look at the individual parts of these prayers:

1. David confesses before God and the elders his own sins: "Did not I order the people numbered? And I—I am the one who sinned, who did this terrible thing." He does not deny that he sinned and he does not make light of his sin, and he does not cast the cause of his sin upon others. When God inflicts punishments, let each person accuse I, not others. We will find many things in ourselves that are worthy of penalties. Even if we are not guilty of public crimes, we do little of what is demanded from us, nor do we do it in the way that we ought. In Daniel 9, he also numbered himself among those who had sinned, and so did other prophets.

2. He excused the people by saying, "But these sheep, what have they done?" It was not that they were free from the corruption of sin and the injury was done to them [regardless], but it was due to the numbering of the people. All people are worthy of eternal death unless God spares them due to the merit of Christ. "I," David says, "am their shepherd, so I must be punished because I sinned."

3. He takes to himself the punishment. He prays that God would afflict him and his family with the penalties. Again, David calls him his God,

---

37. Rev. 22:9

declaring his own confidence in him. Moreover, the injury is not against David's own because he wants his father's house to be struck. For through David they had been raised up to glory.

4. He begs that the hand of God would not be against the people, that is, that he would not chastise them further. He certainly did not want to teach that God *must* do something or prescribe something to him. But he expressed these words with forceful emotion. The godly accommodate their will to the will of God. Again, he calls the Israelites "the people of God."

In this passage is set before us the image of the best prince who loves his own people: he prays for them, and he asks that the punishment be diverted against himself, not against them. It must not be thought that he is acting out of hypocrisy. For thus Moses desired to be blotted out of the book of life.[38] He does not say "the loss will be small if several hundred peasants[39] perish, provided I am safe," but considers his account for them. Such princes are rare today. Perhaps there are not lacking princes who have a greater care for their game and hunting dogs than for their own subjects; who do not hesitate to skin the wretches with their enormous and innumerable demands. David is a type of Christ, who not only desired to die for his own but in fact did die for them—indeed, even for his enemies, so that he might reconcile them to God the Father.

Why did others die and not David?

From this passage this question arises: who would act so that David, who deserved this punishment as he himself acknowledged, would not be infected with the plague, but meanwhile other innocent people would perish? Would not God—when the Jews commonly blurted out this proverb: "our fathers ate the sour grape, but our teeth are set on edge" (Ezekiel 18)—deny that this is so? The soul, he says, who sinned shall itself die. The son will not bear the iniquity of the father, and the father will not bear the iniquity of the son. The righteousness of the righteous will be upon that person, and the ungodliness of the ungodly will be upon that person. By these words he shows that everyone will bear his own fault. If the father was ungodly and is therefore delivered to eternal damnation by God, this does not injure at all the son who lived a godly life and did not follow in the footsteps of his

---

38. Exod. 32:31–32
39. Lat. *rustici*

father. And just as the godliness of the father is useless to the son for eternal life unless he also is godly, so the son's sin is no hindrance to [the father], unless the father is also ungodly. But this seems to be adverse to what David confesses—that he sinned and not the people—and so he desired to draw the penalty to himself. It appears that due to his sin, so many thousands of people ought not to have died, but only the one who had sinned. But David survives and the rest are extinguished by the plague. Likewise in the Decalogue God says that he will seek the iniquity of the fathers in their children to the third and fourth generation.[40] We answer that God did not say that he would punish another's sin in the innocent, for he adds, "of those who hated me." But in this way the sin of the parents is said to be punished upon the children, that if they had cut off the sins of their fathers, their punishment could have been further stayed. Even if they would be worthy of punishment themselves, yet because they are punished to the third and fourth generations they must be worthy of it by their parents. If anyone should object that even infants die in their mother's womb, in their cradle, in earthquakes, the sackings of cities, and floods, we will answer that they are not even innocent before God for we are conceived in sin. But even if David's subjects did not sin with respect to the numbering of the people, yet they sinned in other matters, which is expressly said in 2 Samuel 24, that they abused the peace divinely granted to them and they were also ungrateful to God for his other kindnesses. Next, David did not bear his own sin irreverently. There is not only one kind of punishment with which God chastises his own. For even if he was not infected with the plague, yet he was gripped by the greatest grief by this penalty and by the angelic vision, as is said in the end of the chapter. He likewise lost many outstanding men and people dear to him. And how much like a cross it is to lose good and faithful friends is learned by experience. But that he did not suffer from the plague must be attributed to divine mercy. If some adversity was inflicted on the people due to his sins, they were also affected with many blessings due to his many virtues. Some distinguish among penalties: one they call temporal and bodily on this earth, and the other spiritual and eternal. This latter one is not inflicted on others, but the prior are. That is clear in the case of the sons and descendants of Saul and Ahab. For the sons paid for the fault of the father, and the father that of the son, as in the case of Eli. So subjects pay for those of their prince, as in this passage, and vice versa.

40. Exod. 20:4–6

8

The Work of Christ and the Christian's Duty

Introduction

In his last letter to Jerome Zanchi, dated August 29, 1563, John Calvin wrote: "When we have performed our duty, it remains for us to rest quietly in the decisions of God."[1] Both the performance of one's duty and the quiet resting in the decisions of God can be immensely difficult even in the best of times, and much of Zanchi's life was a far cry from the best of times. In fact, when Zanchi received Calvin's letter, his world was marked by extraordinary conflict and deep personal crisis as he was engaged in a theological controversy that would irreparably divide European Protestantism.

Jerome (or Girolamo) Zanchi was born on February 2, 1516 in Alzano, Italy to a well-educated family of lawyers, historians, and poets. After joining the Augustinian Canon in nearby Bergamo at the age of fifteen, Zanchi made his way to Lucca in 1541 where, at the Priory of San Frediano, he would meet Peter Martyr Vermigli. Through the influence of Vermigli, as well as through the writings of Bucer, Melanchthon, Bullinger, and Calvin, Zanchi embraced the theology of the reformation. In 1551, on account of the Inquisition, Zanchi would follow Vermigli and a growing diaspora of Italian refugees into a self-imposed exile, seeking freedom to preach and teach the word of God according to conscience.

In 1553 Zanchi was appointed to the theological faculty of the College of St. Thomas in Strasbourg (a position previously held by Vermigli himself) where for the next ten years he taught Old Testament. Here Zanchi would become engaged in increasingly polemical debates with the Lutherans over the Lord's Supper and predestination—debates which led him to leave his

---

1. Quoted in Joseph Tylenda, "Girolamo Zanchi and John Calvin: A Study in Discipleship as Seen Through Their Correspondence" in *Calvin Theological Journal* 10, no. 2 (November 1975): 136.

post in Strasbourg in 1563 and his post in Heidelberg in 1577 when Heidelberg University passed into Lutheran hands. Zanchi's position as a leading figure in the reformation movement was established during his tenure in Heidelberg where he succeeded Zacharius Ursinus as professor of theology in 1564. Here he would produce his most famous works, including *De tribus Elohim* (1572), *De natura Dei* (1577), and *De operibus Dei* (pub. 1591).

The piece which follows, however, comes from Zanchi's final tenure as professor of New Testament at Neustadt an der Haardt (1578–1590). It is an excerpt from his commentary on Philippians in which he briefly expounds the significance of Paul's commendation of Epaphroditus of whom he says, "for on account of the work of Christ he drew near to the point of death."

Zanchi's exposition is followed by an excursus in which he applies Paul's teaching to the question of whether one may flee the plague. The point of connection is obvious: how does one persist in the work of Christ even to the point of death, as Paul clearly teaches, in the context of the plague? Does Paul's teaching imply that ministers of the gospel must never flee the plague, for to do so is to abandon the work of Christ to which they have been called? Should pastors, as Zanchi put it, not be "prepared to suffer all things and die for Christ?" And is not flight evidence that one "desires to keep his own soul safe in the present" with the result that he shall surely lose it in the age to come?

These questions were not simply exercises in speculation or casuistry, but emerged both from Zanchi's own experience of the plague as well as his observations of others who sought to navigate these difficult decisions. In this vein, Zanchi relates the tragic events of Bullinger's experience who, after visiting a woman sick with the plague, became infected himself and inadvertently infected his wife and daughter as well. Though Bullinger recovered, both his wife and his daughter died.

Zanchi's own experience of the plague came between his tenures in Strasbourg and Heidelberg, when he pastored Italian refugees in Chiavenna. In 1564 a plague swept through the region, and Zanchi's city was virtually emptied through flight and death. Zanchi himself fled the city until the plague would abate, an action which, at the time, drew heavy criticism. Yet Zanchi understood, as one scholar put it, that "pastors were difficult to find, and those they had would have to be preserved for better days."[2]

2. Ibid., 138.

That Zanchi does not fundamentally disagree with Luther is evident from his closing paragraph:

> The main point? Two rocks must be steered clear of: stupid boldness and exceedingly vicious fear. On the first, one does those things that—while we fear nothing—would often lose ourselves and others. On the second it happens that as we would look to our own life, we would desert the work of Christ. Therefore, let us fear what can happen if we fail to avoid those evils. But let us be confident in the Lord and let us remain as steadfast as possible—even to the point of death—in our calling and in the work of Christ.

However, Zanchi's discussion may be read as a "Yes, but. . ." to Luther's famous letter. Yes, a pastor may be called to stay in harm's way to shepherd Christ's church through trials, but there may be mitigating factors which must be considered for the good of the whole church. There are questions like: Is the threat specific (e.g. the persecution of an individual) or general (e.g. plague or general persecution)? Is there a way that the minister might perform his duties to lessen the likelihood of infection? Are there some ministers whose lives are worth preserving more than others for the greater good of the church? As these questions suggest, the answer to "May a minister of the gospel flee the plague?" is not easy, simple, or straightforward. It requires great wisdom and sober reflection by the church and her leaders. Zanchi, for his part, believes the minister has a responsibility to care for the sick and dying, but also has a responsibility to the well and the living, beginning with those in his own home. Thus, for Zanchi it is not only licit but at times obligatory for Christians, even ministers, to flee from before a plague.

Zanchi lived much of his life as a double exile. He was an exile from his native Italy on account of his Reformed faith—a loss poignantly captured in his epitaph which reads: "Here lie the bones of the Italian Zanchi, who was exiled from his homeland for love of Christ." But perhaps even more profoundly, Zanchi endured countless trials, hardships, frustrations, disappointments, and griefs (including plague) common to the Christian life, each a reminder that this world was not his home. Through it all, the Italian reformer's life was marked by both a faithfulness to his duties—his duties as a Christian, a minister, and a professor—and a spirit of submission to the will of God as it was revealed in his word and, at times, in his hard providences.

Girolamo Zanchi, *In D. Pauli Apostoli Epistolas ad Philippenses, Colossenses, Thessalonicenses Commentarii* (Neustadt: Matthaeus Harnisius, 1595), 156–163.

The Work of Christ and the Christian's Duty
an Excerpt from an Exposition of Philippians 2:30

Jerome Zanchi
Translated by Todd M. Rester

> For on account of the work of Christ he drew near to the point of death, and did not consider his own life of any account (παραβουλευσάμενος τῇ ψυχῇ) so that he might supply what was lacking in your duty (λειτουργίας, ministry) towards me. (Phil. 2:30)

The Apostle had said two things in the prior verse: The first is specific to Epaphroditus, "[to] receive him in the Lord, with a common joy," namely just as a true and faithful minister of Christ, as he had described above. The other is general and regards all true ministers, saying "and those who are such, consider as precious."

Now what the Apostle had said about Epaphroditus, that he was worthy to be received with all joy in the Lord by the Philippians as a true minister of Christ, he confirms with the most obvious expression and duty of a faithful minister, saying "For on account of the work of Christ he drew near to the point of death. . ."

The summary of the matter is this: because you Philippians yoked yourself to him, Epaphroditus preferred the work of Christ to his own life; therefore, as a true minister of Christ he is worthy for you to receive him with all joy in the Lord. He proves the antecedent because on account of the work of Christ that needed to be perfected—"so that he would supply the defect of your duty towards me"—he drew near to the point of death and did not hold his own life of any account.

But what did the Apostle understand by the term "the work of Christ?" He calls the minister's entire office the work of Christ because the Philippians enjoined Epaphroditus for the purpose of what must be completed towards the Apostle. However, they enjoined him not only so that he would bring alms all the way to Rome, but also so that he might serve Paul, whom he was commissioned to diligently seek out, in all his necessities, whether in prison or outside of prison. And in this way this scholium[3] is to be understood.

Therefore, is not serving the holy saints of Christ the work of Christ, along with preaching the Word of Christ and administering his sacraments? And why are they works of Christ? As the scholia explains regarding the two causes: First, because those things are offered by the saints to Christ, according to that passage, "The one who receives you, receives me" (Matt. 10:40); and likewise, "what you did for one of the least of these my brethren, you have done for me" (Matt. 25:40). Second, because Christ commands this especially, namely that we cherish those who labor in the Word and suffer persecution for Christ with a certain special honor. Thus, the apostle says about Epaphroditus: "receive him in the Lord."

Nevertheless, there are those who take τὸ ἔργον τοῦ χριστοῦ to mean "the ministry," whereby the Apostle acted for Christ. In this case, this would be the sense: Epaphroditus came to Rome and served the Apostle all the way to the point of death, so that just as he served him in life, he promoted the Gospel through his ministry. For the promotion of the gospel through the ministry of Paul is the very work of Christ, to whom Epaphroditus drew near to serve even to the point of death. But we can join both senses: what Epaphroditus rendered and the goal to which he rendered it were works of Christ, for whose sake Epaphroditus drew near to the very point of death.

The phrase παραβουλευσάμενος τῇ ψυχῇ according to its meaning is properly "to thoroughly have a view to their own life." For he replaced the word "soul" with "life" in the custom of Holy Scripture. And παρα in the composition of the verb means "thoroughly," just as it also means παραλογίζεασμενος, "to thoroughly reason," from which is παραλογίζισμοί.

But what is it to thoroughly look to one's own life? Physically speaking, something done contrary to one's own health is to hold one's life as of no account, as one who exerts himself well beyond his strength, who is overly watchful, or even those who eat and drink to excess. Just as on the contrary, one is rightly said to look to oneself and one's own life who rightly handles

---

3. A *scholium* is a term for an inserted section of commentary on a particular topic or issue common among sixteenth century bible commentators. The *scholia* from a theologian's writings were frequently gathered into a handbook of theological topics or commonplaces *(loci communes)* for theology students.

all things for their own well-being, whether to recover it or preserve it. The Apostle speaks about Epaphroditus in this sense because his esteem for the work of Christ that he had undertaken to accomplish went beyond his own strength, more than he had labored for his own present life by serving Paul. Therefore, physically speaking, Epaphroditus looked to his own life poorly.

But speaking theologically, and in a Christian way, that man is said to look after his life poorly who, with Christ neglected and with the law of the Lord held in contempt, serves idols and indulges his own desires. For in this path one does not arrive at true life but undertakes a journey to eternal death. On the contrary the one who looks to himself well, who has neglected the company of the ungodly and embraced Christ, meditates on the law of the Lord day and night, so that he is prepared to suffer all things and die for Christ. In this sense Christ spoke when he said in Matthew 16[:25], "The one who desired to keep his own soul safe" in the present life, having condemned me, "will lose it" in this next age, "but the one who lost his soul," that is, his present life, "on account of me, will find it," namely in the next age.

Therefore, the one who, out of love for this present life, neglects Christ and his work, has a wrong view to himself, and that with eternal consequence; by contrast, the one who prefers to lose this life, rather than to desert Christ and his work, looks out for his life best, and that for eternity. Certainly in this sense Epaphroditus cannot be said to have a view for his life poorly, but rather in the best way, since he preferred to condemn his body's well-being and this present life rather than to neglect Christ in the Apostle and let his work be done negligently and poorly. So, in a divided sense, Epaphroditus looked to his soul both poorly and well.

Here it must be observed that not only are martyrs of Christ those who pour out their life and blood for Christ and his church, such as Paul, but they are also those who have determined in their heart to suffer anything—even death itself—than to abandon Christ and perform the work to which they were called in bad faith and in a negligent way. Among such a kind of martyr was Epaphroditus. For in order to carry out the work of Christ—that is, to not only bring the alms to Paul from such a faraway land with such difficult and troublesome sailing, but also to faithfully perform what remained of the duty to Paul enjoined upon him by the Philippian church, namely that he would serve the Apostle in chains and so diligently supply what was lacking in the Philippians' duty—all this in order that this work of Christ which the Philippians could not render fully to Paul, Epaphroditus could perform faithfully on their behalf, not valuing his own life when he fell into a grave disease, so that he drew near to the very jaws of death. For Epaphroditus this was, in the sight of the Lord, equivalent to if he had died for the work of the Lord. Therefore, he himself is also a martyr for Christ. In this number are all those who, on account of the work of Christ to which they have been called as teachers and pastors of the church, must faithfully perform it and expose themselves to various dangers, fall into various diseases, and finally prefer to suffer anything and hazard their well-being and life, than to neglect Christ, to desert their post, and to perform their office in bad faith and with an evil conscience. The church customarily calls these people *confessors*, and those who are slain for Christ by tyrants *martyrs*. But in fact, all are martyrs for Christ who are prepared to go un-spared from any evil for the confession of his name, for spreading his teaching and defending his church. That is the ὑστέρημα τῆς λειτουργίας, what was lacking in the Philippian ministry, which Epaphroditus fulfilled in their name. That was his office because he supplied alms to the Apostle, serving him in chains. For if the whole church could have, she would have gone to Rome for the purpose of serving Paul. Because she could not, she did what she could; she sent money and committed the rest, whatever needed to be done, to Epaphroditus, and he performed it diligently, so diligently in fact that he preferred to neglect his own well-being than to let the duty suffer.

This therefore is why the Apostle says παραβουλευσάμενος τῇ ψυχῇ ("to thoroughly have a view to their own life") so that he would supply τὸ ὑστέρημα τῆς λειτουργίας ὑμῶν ("what was lacking in your ministry"). For it does not bind them as if they continued to lack something, but he taught that what the Church could not supply was offered by Epaphroditus with the greatest amount of diligence. Therefore, this ὑστέρημα, what is lacking, was not a lack in the hearts of the Philippians, but in the very λειτουργίᾳ, ministry, with which they could not join, because they all desired that they also each should serve their Apostle. But in their name Epaphroditus supplied this.

Whether one can flee on account of plague

The summary of the teaching which we must gather from this verse is this: the Apostle praises Epaphroditus because on account of the work of Christ he disconnected himself from his church; that is, he neglected his own welfare so that he might diligently serve the Apostle. Therefore, those must be disapproved of who, looking out for their own welfare, neglect the work of

Christ to which they were called, preferring their own convenience, welfare, and life to the glory of Christ and the safety of the church. Certainly every person must be concerned about their own welfare, but in a lawful way and so that the work of Christ is not neglected. However, under the term "the work of Christ" we mean the office and ministry of Christ to which each [minister] has been called by Christ, and which results in the glory of Christ and the safety of the Church, as the pastor, for the sake of administering the Word and sacraments first publicly and then privately, also labors to look after the sick with some disease, and to visit them with comfort. Likewise, just as magistrates have been called to rule and care for the commonwealth, likewise fathers[4] have been called to care for their family, wife, and children. Therefore, the work of Christ for each of these is what each one must do, being called by Christ individually. But what pertains to taking care of the present life? Counted among other remedies by which one can provide for life, if a pestilence invades some house or city, is departure from an infected place. In this case you would not have company with those infected with pestilence, just as one is not accustomed to do with the leprous. Therefore, not even on account of pestilence must the work of Christ be abandoned and flight for oneself be counseled. This proposition taken most simply is the most true, but the circumstances sometimes render it quite unclear.

Therefore, regarding this present Pauline passage in which Epaphroditus is praised because, for the work of Christ, he did not hold his life of any account but drew near to death, I am moved by the occasion of our time—even as God visits some cities with pestilence—and have decided to briefly explore this question of a plague that must be fled. About this I once disputed—some eighteen years ago now—back and forth with a certain pastor from Chur, Switzerland—a learned man—and said many things. He contended that no one in any way must shun company with those suffering from pestilence, much less that one must depart from places infected with such great plague. For my part, I defended both by affirming that they should only do this with legitimate reason, that is, in this way: just as if God removed you from a duty because you should not do injury to and defraud your neighbor by neglect.

Certain letters sent to Zurich gave occasion for this question, in which the learned Heinrich Bullinger returned from visiting a certain woman

---

4. Lat. *Paterfamilias*

struggling with the pestilence himself infected with the same plague. And, now infected, he infected his family such that his wife and two children died. That pastor I disputed with was proclaiming doctor Bullinger's love, disapproving of all those who either do not go near such sick people or even who think they can flee from infected places. I too praised Dr. Bullinger, but I do not simply approve of what was done when he could have taken measures for his safety and the comfort of that sick woman by other means than the visit of such an important man to her sickbed. Did he not also have to love both his family and the church? And shouldn't he have had both in view? Why do they not establish who should perform those duties for the sick, and spare such great men, from whose death such great ills result for the Church of Christ, just as such good results from their lives? A public good must be set before a private one, and a greater one before a lesser one; nor must emperors be exposed to the highest dangers on the front line, which would not be counseled by the army.

I was also defending those who, without fraud or injury to the Commonwealth or to the Church, by withdrawing from infected places have a view towards their life and children and the future of the commonwealth. This point I publicly demonstrated as an example to my church at Chiavenna, for many remained in the town while that plague was ravaging, and very many died. However, there were others who, when they saw that they could not go outside, withdrew for a time, and nearly all survived. Afterwards the church gathered again anew. And in fact, by their absence these assisted the Commonwealth more than their counsel and assistance had they been present. So, regarding those two points which I have explained just now and have done so both in person and through letters—about shunning especially the company of the infected, and about withdrawing from infected places—has this not lightly been determined amongst ourselves? That good pastor who I disputed with, when he was seized by pestilence and dying, exclaimed, "O that I had followed Zanchi's advice!" But this had been my counsel: we should see to all the sick in such a way that we would also see to the well, ourselves, and our families—indeed even to the whole church.

Four Reasons Against the Flight of Plague

Regarding the arguments of that good and learned man, nearly all were brought forth from these points: First, that pestilence is not a contagious disease, but merely God's scourge immediately sent from heaven. This is difficult to prove with examples and the authority of the Scriptures. Chiefly it is derived from the example of the plague whereby God punished the sins of David in the whole of his kingdom. Second, that pestilence is from the providence of God, whom none can resist; that those whom he willed in that number to endure it endured it, and those whom he did not will to endure it did not, so that no one could escape. Third, from love which does not seek its own but that of Christ and one's neighbor. Fourth, from the office of ministers. Regarding these especially did this question arise: whether it belongs to ministers to look after those that are sick, however long they are unwell, and whoever is struggling with the disease, even with risk to their own life. He brought forward the example of Isaiah the prophet who came to the sickbed of King Hezekiah who was struggling with the pestilence, and so forth.

Responses to the four arguments

But to the first argument I respond in this way: that one nourished by experience would confess that the pestilence is contagious. For even if it were God's scourge it still does not then follow that it is not a contagious disease. Was not leprosy also God's scourge among the people of God, and still is now? Are not also scabies, leprosy, and other diseases? If, however, by the law of God it is licit to shun leprosy and other similar contagious diseases, why not also the plague?

To the second argument I respond that the providence of God, which is the first cause of those things that happen here, does not destroy second causes. Indeed, it establishes them, because God customarily commands for the execution of the eternal decree through second causes. Therefore, even if he decreed whom he willed and whom he did not will to endure pestilence, yet then it does not follow that there is nothing for people to do for the sake of shunning the plague, and therefore also (if it could be done lawfully, in good conscience, and without any injury) one must depart for a time, not so much for their own sake as for the sake of others and the commonwealth. Also, when he inflicts famine or stirs up war, does he not know whom he wills to endure famine and sword, and whom he does not? Therefore, why is it not licit for people also to guard themselves with a sword against their enemies, drive off a famine with the purchase of food, and to preserve themselves in life? Indeed, these are the means by which

God customarily keeps in life those whom he does not will to perish, just as the examples of the Scriptures and daily experience teaches. How did God preserve Jacob and his family from famine? By stirring them up to go to Egypt for the purchase of grain.

But the example of Paul in Acts is clear and neat. He had from a revelation that none of those on the ship with him would perish. Therefore, when the ship was in danger, so that the sailors secretly thought to leave, did he remain silent and do nothing? Indeed, he said to the centurion, "If those men were to depart, you will all perish at the same time" (Acts 27[:31]). For even if he had known no one would perish, yet he was not ignorant that the ordinary means by which the ship could be saved were that it would be manned by the sailors, just as we read was done. Therefore, the lawful remedies of secondary causes are not opposed to the providence of God. Wherefore when also there is a lawful remedy against the plague—even this, namely that you would not live with the infected, and you would withdraw from an infected place, insofar as it can be done through conscience—it follows that they do not resist the providence of God who lawfully use first other remedies and then also these, about which we are disputing.

I retort to the third argument from love that fighting back against the pestilence with true and ordinate love, one could provide for another by honest and good means, or for the one struggling with the plague. You, pastor of the church, with your access to the bedside of the sick—not only will you perish, but so will your family; and you will deprive your church of your ministry, or at least you will inflict a manifest crisis of both evils. The safety of every member must be your concern, but especially of the whole body. "And whoever does not take care of his own, and especially of his own household, has denied the faith, and is worse than an unbeliever," says the Apostle in 1 Timothy 5[:8]. And the commandment of God is, "You shall not kill." But neither do the saints when they care for these things seek their own, but what belongs to Christ and the church. Therefore, it is a preposterous love blatantly to inflict on your entire family and the whole church at the same time such a crisis, about which it has been said, that you would be present only to one such private person who is not as necessary, when by another way (as I have said), that person could be comforted. For what difference does it make that you would draw near to their sick bed, when you could comfort that one with a word farther away from the sick person and commend them to God with prayers? But indeed, why does the church not establish one or another person, or several for that matter, according to the necessity of the times, to perform this duty, who would undertake the care of all the sick? Then you would free others who are more necessary to the church from this task of visitation. For this is done in this way in many places, in Italy especially, and in Geneva.

To the fourth argument regarding the office of ministers we answer the same thing. Care must especially be taken lest the whole church be deprived of your ministry. Next, the minister must be assisted by every individual, but without manifest loss and damage to the whole church. There is an outstanding passage of Augustine, who, although he treats about another matter, namely about flight in time of persecution and war, still it is not incongruous for explaining this present question and can be adapted to it. In his Epistle to Honoratus, he sets forth many brief questions on flight and briefly explains them.[5] The summary of the epistle: Augustine was asked by the bishop Quodvultdeus how he must conduct himself in persecutions when many flee. Augustine answered that those who desired to travel to better protected places if they could must not be prohibited. And the bonds of our ministry, whereby the love of Christ obligated us not to desert the churches that we serve, must not be ruptured. Thus far for Augustine. Therefore, it was licit for someone, for the sake of avoiding persecution (and thence also the plague), to withdraw to safer places, but it was not licit for ministers to desert their churches such that they would lack the necessary ministry.

This counsel—which pertains to the role of bishops, that they must remain with the churches however few they be—did not please bishop Honoratus, for Honoratus thought that bishops must also flee, or at least that it is licit to flee, just as others, such as the plebs, do. How so? Because the Lord had said to the Apostles, "If they would persecute you in one city, flee to another" (Matt. 10:23). For he did not say this to the commoner, but to the Apostles. This is why Augustine addresses Honoratus in this Epistle 180. Augustine first responds to this passage of Christ, saying that these words must not be understood as if the Lord willed that bishops would desert their flocks for the sake of preserving their own lives. For this would deprive their flocks, whom Christ bought with his blood, of the bishop's necessary ministry, without which their flocks could not live. Note the term, by "the *necessary* ministry, without which . . ."[6] But access to the sickbed is not that necessary.

---

5. For a complete English translation, see "Augustine to Honoratus, Letter 228" in *NPNF* 1:577–81.
6. *NPNF1* 1:577

Next, Augustine says, Christ as an infant fled by means of his parents to Egypt when Herod was pursuing him (Honoratus appears to have objected to these examples to Augustine). Yet this was not in such a way that he can be said to have deserted the church, which had not yet been gathered. Also Paul, when the prefect of Damascus was searching for him, fled Damascus, but he did not deprive the church of any necessary ministry, for he left behind (thus Augustine) brethren (suitable to the ministry), through whom he fulfilled it because it was necessary. This example should be noted. Therefore, he only would look out for the church, and it is not necessary for each believer that some pastor would remain in open danger of life. And he adds that the Apostle did not freely depart but for brothers willing it so that he would save himself for the church, whom that persecutor was personally seeking. Therefore, it is the duty of the church to take care that the life of the minister is not endangered and to substitute others in his place for a time. Therefore, also in a plague, someone must tend the sick so that ordinary and extraordinary pastors are not endangered.

Third, as to how the word of Christ to "flee to another city" must be reconciled, supplying the example of Paul, Augustine teaches "therefore let the servants of Christ perform the ministry of the Word and his sacrament, which he commanded or permitted. They should absolutely flee from city to city when any of them are specifically sought by persecutors, so that by others who are not so sought after the church is not deserted, and who supply food to their fellow servants, whom they know cannot live otherwise." Therefore, Augustine intends that the saying of Christ must be understood in such a way that it is licit for ministers, for the sake of preserving their life, to travel from city to city and flee persecution when it can be done without damage to the church. However, this is done without damage to the church only if it does not lack others who perform the duty of a minister. If, therefore, in a time of pestilence one can see to it that among many pastors one is appointed to the sick, why is that not done? It is certainly both licit and expedient.

Fourth, Augustine treats the question: "What if in a persecution not just one pastor is sought out but all of them simultaneously, and so the whole church?" He responds, "If it is a general danger, those who depend on others should not be deserted by them. Think of the common people, if they lack pastors, then they should not be deserted."[7] Here also he teaches that,

---

7. Ibid.

provided the church is not plainly deserted, it is licit for some, of course with the consent of the church, to depart from place to place. He states, "therefore either all should pass to protected places together, or those who have need to remain should not be abandoned by those through whom the ecclesiastical need must be supplied, in order that they would either all equally live or equally suffer, as a father would have them."[8] Thus, Augustine.

Furthermore, Augustine adds that there are two kinds of flight: The first is allowed or commanded, about which Christ says, "if they would persecute you. . ." and about which we will not speak any further now. The second is argued against and is blameworthy, about which Christ says, "but the hireling sees the wolf coming and flees, because he is a hireling and does not care for the sheep." Afterwards, concluding when it is licit to depart or not, Augustine says, "Concerning the places in which we are under the threat of persecution, ministers of Christ ought to flee either when there are none of Christ's people present to whom one could minister, or even when the necessary ministry can be fulfilled through others who do not have the same cause to flee."[9]

Therefore, Augustine teaches that there are two occasions when it is licit for ministers to withdraw from places threatened by persecution (and let us also add plague): The first is when the entire church flees or is dispersed; about this, there is no dispute, for what would a minister do there when there is no one present to whom to minister? But the other time is when, although the church is present, the necessary ministry can be fulfilled through others (Note well the term "necessary"—certainly it is unnecessary for a minister of the Word to go to the bedside of the sick). I say the necessary ministry of the church can be fulfilled through others, for whom there is not such great necessity to flee, or such great danger of contracting contagion. This other time Augustine confirms with the example of Paul; when he departed Damascus, the brothers who were left behind performed the work of Christ. Likewise the example of Athanasius who, when he was sought by the Emperor Constantius II for death with his fellow workers, left behind who would care for the church. He counseled flight for himself and preserved himself for the church at another time.

As to the rest, as Augustine treats it, if the people should remain but all the ministers flee and the ministry is withdrawn, what can this be except

---

8. Ibid.
9. Ibid. 1:578

that damnable flight of hirelings, in which there is no care for the sheep? Likewise, from the many inconveniences which result from persecution, and the cause of those things to be shunned, many ministers departed, with the churches left behind clearly without any ministry. The speaker says, "this persecution indeed must be shunned, when they can be shunned without any ungodliness; but then they cannot be shunned without ungodliness, when the necessary ministry is withdrawn."[10] Therefore, must not a contagious poison be shunned, if it can be shunned without ungodliness? There is no ungodliness introduced if the necessary ministry is not withdrawn. Moreover, the necessary ministry is not withdrawn from a sick believer either if you, the pastor, would comfort him with the Word at a distance from his sickbed. And he confirms that same teaching was handed down previously. For when he had said that Paul did not flee the treachery of the persecutor unless he wanted to save himself for others for whom he was more necessary, he addressed it saying, "Here perhaps some would say so must the ministers of God flee from such imminent evils, that they might save themselves for the usefulness of the church in more tranquil times. This is rightly done by some, when they do not lack others through whom the ecclesiastical ministry may be fulfilled, and it is not deserted by all, which we said above that Athanasius did. For it was a benefit for the church for that man to remain in the flesh, who had defended the catholic faith against the Arian heretics with his voice and love."[11] What could be clearer on this point than this example? Therefore, it must not be permitted by churches that such outstanding men, like the learned Bullinger and other similar men, should cast themselves into manifest crises to their lives, when there is no lack of others through whom the ecclesiastical ministry which is owed to the sick can be supplied.

There are also other points in this epistle of Augustine which make the same point. This is apparent in that passage that teaches what ought to be done if in one church there are many ministers of the same level of erudition and all are prepared to remain. If that church is content with one or the other and wants to free some from such a great risk, preserving them for another time, what then would be necessary to do? Augustine counsels that they should be selected by lot who ought to remain and who to depart. That custom should be kept everywhere in time of plague.

---

10. Ibid.
11. Ibid. 1:579

But we have mentioned more than enough from this letter of Augustine, with which our opinion can be abundantly and clearly confirmed. For who cannot not see that what that man wrote about flight can be accommodated to the question of the plague? Therefore, these things must be adopted from the teaching of Augustine: First, that in general manifest dangers and imminent evils must be avoided, if they can be avoided without ungodliness. But if they cannot be avoided except by ungodliness, they must be endured and one must constantly remain in the work of Christ all the way to the point of death, according to the example of Epaphroditus.

The second duty belongs to the church. In times of persecution or pestilence, the church which has many ministers must rescue some from the manifest dangers of life and preserve them for another time. This can be done either from common consent or even by lot.

Third, the ministers who remain must be constant in their duty, but they ought not recklessly lose themselves and others, and they must only perform that necessary ministry that is sufficient. Therefore, it must be diligently sought out what is necessary and what is not. But the love which they owe, they owe not only to private persons but also to the whole church, so that I would not remain silent now about what they owe to their own wives and children, and Love will be the best mistress here. For just as Love does not seek its own, so it does not do anything wrongly.

The main point? Two rocks must be steered clear of: stupid boldness and exceedingly vicious fear. On the first, one does those things that—while we fear nothing—would often lose ourselves and others. On the second it happens that as we would look to our own life, we would desert the work of Christ. Therefore, let us fear what can happen if we fail to avoid those evils. But let us be confident in the Lord and let us remain as steadfast as possible—even to the point of death—in our calling and in the work of Christ.

9

A Godly Meditation upon Death

INTRODUCTION

"It is perhaps the most fitting comment on a Christian scholar to note that, whereas his work has been of importance to the Church down the years, the details of his life have passed into obscurity."[1] With these remarks, Christopher Burchill opens his biographical sketch of one of the greatest and least well-known of the sixteenth-century protestant reformers. Zacharius Ursinus, if he is remembered at all, is remembered primarily for his work as the author of the Heidelberg Catechism, a catechism which remains in use to this day as one of the confessional standards for Dutch and German Reformed churches and the denominations which trace their roots to them. In his own day, however, Ursinus was a leading figure of the protestant reformation, highly regarded for his deep learning and irenic spirit, whose efforts greatly contributed to the development of Reformed theology (especially its theology of the covenant) throughout Europe. It has been said of Ursinus that he "possessed the rare ability of the theologian to express in persuasive form the heart of his own conviction."[2]

A native of the important Silesian port city of Breslau, Ursinus (b. 1534) entered the university of Wittenberg at the age of sixteen, and for the next seven years he studied with Philip Melanchthon. After a short tenure at St. Elizabeth Gymnasium in Breslau, Ursinus accepted an invitation to Heidelberg where he would teach at both the university and at the seminary (Sapience College). When the city adopted a strict Lutheranism, Ursinus moved to Neustadt where he taught at the newly formed Reformed

---

1. Christopher Burchill, "On the Consolation of a Christian Scholar: Zacharias Ursinus (1534–83) and the Reformation in Heidelberg," *Journal of Ecclesiastical History* 37, no. 4 (October 1986): 565–583.
2. Ibid., 583.

academy until his death in 1583. At the request of the Elector Frederick III, Ursinus served as the principal author of a catechism "intended as a tool for teaching young people, a guide for preaching in the provincial churches, and a form of confessional unity among the several Protestant factions in the Palatinate."[3]

Ursinus' treatise included here, *A Godly Meditation Upon Death*, was most likely written in 1563 and published in 1564, "at which time plague was prowling about widespread along of the banks of the Rhine."[4] After a brief reflection on the benefits of conducting and attending funerals for the dead, Ursinus sets out to develop his final point at length, specifically that funerals "serve as an opportune occasion and ground for a Christian meditation on death, and one necessary for our salvation." A frequent meditation on death benefits believers as a reminder that death is inevitable and that "all who desire to be partakers of that eternal blessedness after this life enter into eternal life *before* they depart this life; that is, by the power of the Holy Spirit we are renewed and regenerated according to the image of God. The righteousness of Christ, which is freely given and imputed to us, we receive by faith, and are thereby engrafted into Christ." Moreover, funerals are occasions to remember the cause of death, namely human sin and

---

3. Lyle Bierma, *The Theology of the Heidelberg Catechism: A Reformation Synthesis* (Louisville: Westminster John Knox, 2013), 131.

4. Some scholars have questioned whether Ursinus is the author of the 1564 German work, *Erinnerung, wes sich ein Christ by Absterbung unnd Begrebnuss*, which is the basis for Quirinius Reuter's Latin translation in Ursinus's 1612 *Opera*, entitled *Pia Meditatio Mortis et Consolationum adversus eius horrorem, tum παρασκευῆς πρὶς εὐθανασίαν*. The English translation provided here consulted the German original and accepted Reuter's additions in the Latin translation for the 1612 *Opera*. Among those who dispute Ursinus's authorship, some favor the authorship of the Zurich pastor, Otto Werdmüller (1511–1552). The relevant circumstances are: a plague struck Heidelberg in 1563; the *Erinnerung* was published both in Heidelberg and Zurich in 1564 by different printers; both printings appear anonymously; Werdmüller died in Zurich in 1552, Ursinus was a professor of theology in Heidelberg from 1562 until 1567. Johann Mayer frequently published Ursinus's works between 1563 and 1565, such as most notably, the very first edition of the Heidelberg Catechism, which first appeared in German. In Mayer's printings of Ursinus's work, sometimes Ursinus is listed explicitly as the author, sometimes only as "a University of Heidelberg theologian" (*durch der Universitet Heydelberg Theologen*), and sometimes, as is the case here, anonymously. On Ursinus's authorship of the *Pia Meditatio*, see Melchior Adam, *Vitae Germanorum Theologorum* (Heidelberg: Johannes Georgius Geyder, 1620), 534. B. Wagner-Peterson specifically mentions Adam's remarks and also references Ursinus's relevant correspondence in *Doctrina schola vitae: Zacharias Ursinus (1534–1583) als Schriftausleger* (Gottingen: Vandenhoeck & Ruprecht, 2013), 297–98 nn43–45; Gerard den Hertog, "The Heidelberg Catechism and the Art of Dying and Living" in *The Spirituality of the Heidelberg Catechism: Papers of the International Conference on the Heidelberg Catechism held in Apeldoorn 2013*, A. Huijgen (ed.) (Gottingen: Vandenhoeck & Ruprecht, 2015), 194–205; Herman Selderhuis, "Ars Moriendi in Early Modern Calvinism" in *Preparing for Death, Remembering the Dead*, J. Ø. Flaeten and T. Rasmussen (eds.) (Gottingen: Vandenhoeck & Ruprecht, 2015), 118–20.

rebellion, against which God in his perfect righteousness and justice has promised death both temporal and eternal. "For those who do not want to sink into the abyss of eternal death," Ursinus says, "it is necessary to remove the cause of death; that is, a satisfaction of divine justice for our sins must be made, either by ourselves or by another, and we must not provoke God again by sinning. For just as, from the reckoning of righteousness and divine threat, death is the wage due for sin; so, on the contrary, according to the promise of God, perfect righteousness brings life and blessedness."

Ursinus moves from eternal death and its cause to eternal life and its source. Those who would escape the penalty due their sins must reject every false source of hope and seek assurance and comfort in the only place where it may be found, namely in the gospel of Jesus Christ, the Son of God given for sinners. He sets forth the many benefits of faith in Christ—among them reconciliation, deliverance from sin, resurrection life, the presence of God, and the example of Christ who has gone before us through suffering to glory. He writes, "And God, when he turned his angry countenance from us, now through the Holy Spirit dwells among us again and wills to grant eternal life, which abundantly confirms the Church's victory song regarding death: 'Death has been swallowed up in Victory. Where, O Death, is your victory? Where O Grave, your sting?'"

The final benefit of a godly meditation on death is that it provides the opportunity to prepare for its arrival. Of the many ways the Christian must prepare for death, Ursinus speaks first and foremost of grounding ourselves in a true and sincere faith "whereby we apprehend and apply to ourselves the promise of grace, of forgiveness of sins, and of eternal life, and at last the resurrection of the flesh to glory." What Ursinus calls conversion—that which "flows forth from the streams of faith"—is closer to what later Reformed theologians would call sanctification. He writes, "We should persevere in true conversion to God throughout our whole life, daily making progress in it and earnestly pleading that we have offended God." Lastly, Ursinus directs our attention to the chief expression of Christian faith, namely prayer. He says that "in true preparation for death and sudden calamities of every kind, ardent and devoted prayer to God holds the chief place for the confirmation of faith." And he concludes "For we ourselves certainly hold this persuasion, that God wills to lavish grace and the Holy Spirit upon those who seek from him with true groaning, and that he wills to hear all who call upon him. For Christ confirms this himself: 'If you,' he says, 'being evil, know how to give good gifts to your children, how much more will the heavenly Father give the Holy Spirit to those who ask?'"

In a day and age in which the reality of death is relegated largely to the peripheries of our daily lives and, as a consequence, of our thought-lives, Ursinus' treatise offers a critical reminder: Death is inevitable. And those who wish to live well must do so by preparing to die well. This may be done by frequently reminding ourselves of both the reality of death and its cause, as well as the hope of life and its source, namely Christ given for us. Burchill is certainly correct when he says of Ursinus, "A constant theme of all his writing, prevalent as much in his dogmatics as in a short meditation drawn up in time of plague, is that of the solace to be derived from true religion."[5] Ursinus spent his life seeking that solace and consolation for himself, and through his teaching and writing, urging others to do the same. And so it is perhaps unsurprising that the author of *A Godly Meditation upon Death* would begin his famous catechism with the question, "What is your only comfort in life and in death?" which he answers with those precious words:

> That I, with body and soul, both in life and in death, am not my own, but belong to my faithful Savior Jesus Christ, who, with His precious blood has fully satisfied for all my sins, and delivered me from all the power of the Devil; and so preserves me, that without the will of my Father in heaven not a hair can fall from my head; yea, that all things must work together for my salvation. Wherefore, by His Holy Spirit, He also assures me of eternal life, and makes me heartily willing and ready from now on to live unto Him.[6]

Zacharias Ursinus, "Pia Meditatio Mortis et Consolationum adversus eius horrorem, tum παρασκευῆς πρὶς εὐθανασίαν" *Opera Theologica* (Frankfurt, 1612), 1:910–923. Cf. Anonymous, *Erinnerung, wes sich ein Christ ben der absterbung unnd begrebnüss seiner Mitbrüder trösten unnd wie er sich selbst seeliglich zusterben bereitten soll: zu jeder zeit, sonderlich aber in*

---

5. Burchill, "On the Consolation of a Christian Scholar," 583.
6. *Heidelberg Catechism, or; Method of Instruction in the Christian Religion* (Carlisle: The Banner of Truth, 2014), 9.

Sterbens läuffen tröstlich und nützlich (Heidelberg: Johann Mayer, 1564). This translation consults primarily the Latin text as found in the *Opera* of Ursinus, but also the 1564 German edition.

A Godly Meditation upon Death
Comforts against its Horror, and then a Preparation for a Noble Death, a Useful and Necessary Treatise

Zacharias Ursinus
Translated by Todd M. Rester

Written in the German language in the year 1564, at which time plague was prowling about widespread along the banks of the Rhine, now for the first time translated into Latin.

In all ages from the very first beginnings of the world, initially among the people of God and then among the heathen, by a certain instinct and leading of nature, it was received, solemnized, and became customary that the bodies of the dead would not be brought out, conducted, duly committed for burial, and interred without a procession.

THE REASON FOR CONDUCTING FUNERALS:

But the reasons for conducting funerals, why it was done previously and should still be done now, deserve to be pondered by Christians. For among us this custom should not be kept as if in the manner of gentiles and unbelievers, among whom death snatches away all hope. Instead let us not be immeasurably troubled on account of the dead, either so that we pray for them or else do something that we think will accrue to their advantage after death. Since from the Word of God it is certain for us that the time to pursue divine grace is clearly now in this life, after which unbelievers and the ungodly will be conveyed to eternal punishments, but believers and the converted to eternal life. Thus, our works and prayers on behalf of the latter are certainly and plainly unnecessary, and those on behalf of the former could bring them nothing useful at all. But for these reasons we should frequent the burial of our brothers with an honorable funeral procession and testimony of our grief:

Of first priority is that we may witness to our faith. Our bodies were not created with life only for the grave, but rather so that they would be God's holy temples and dwelling places eternally. Thus, when they will be resurrected on the last day and clothed with immortality and heavenly glory, God will be worshipped for all eternity in them.

Next, because in doing so we will demonstrate a Christian and brotherly love[7] to our neighbors. This is not because their life with us has ceased or likewise has been extinguished from our hearts the moment they breathed their last, but because they will go from us to continue in eternal life, wherein that love will then overflow and be perfected from every foul and worldly sin. Then we also show a common grief and sympathy towards others because we lack and are deprived of the works and assistance of friends and brothers, especially of those endowed with exceptional gifts for spreading the glory of the divine name in this life and for promoting their use and advantage for ourselves and others—at least until we should meet anew in the heavenly homeland.

Third, for this reason we come together for a funeral: so that we call upon God not only within our private homes but also publicly in the congregation, for God requires both. We do so with one voice, with thanksgiving for the innumerable and indescribable benefits to the departed, because he called our departed brethren to the knowledge of Christ, made them vessels of his mercy, and happily called them back to himself into a blessed life. He also led us into the fellowship of his son Jesus Christ, in which fellowship he kindly preserves us. We thank him because he converted death into an entrance and entryway into life and poured into our hearts a sure comfort both in life and in death. And let us ask with prayers poured out from the depths of our hearts, that in place of those now dead, God would even now equip and supply us with other faithful ministers in this life. But may he keep us in a true preparation for death until such a time when he would take us to himself in a blessed exit from this life.

Fourth, the presence of death and the sight or viewing of the burial of our brethren must serve as an opportune occasion and ground for a Christian meditation on death, and one necessary for our salvation. This is the concern of these four chapters. First, so that we may continuously ponder how much danger of death we are in. Second, what the true cause of death is. Third, in what ways, whether in our own death or that of our families,

---

7. Gk. φιλαδελφία

we may be correctly comforted and raised up. Finally, how we must prepare ourselves for a blessed departure from this earthly life.

The First Reason: Death is inevitable

First of all, it is confessed and evident to us all that, just as there is nothing more uncertain than the hour of death, so there is nothing at all more certain than death itself. For we are taught by experience that—as many dangers surround us in every single moment, how various, unforeseen, and (specifically) minor things could finish off a person's life, and how one should not trust in youth, strength, health, or anything else—it is not licit to promise oneself a long life. Even if we do lead the longest possible life of many years, yet it remains the briefest course. As Moses teaches in Psalm 90:10, the days of our life are seventy years or, if many, eighty; their strength is spent in perversity and iniquity; and it recedes quickly and we fly away. In death not only are soul and body separated with the greatest pain—indeed, the body falls to be devoured by worms, and it returns to the dust from which it was made—but there is something else, and that is the greater danger to which no evil at all can be compared. For a person does not expire like beasts and livestock, but is endowed with an immortal soul, and was created by God in this way so that we may live either in eternal holiness and blessedness with God or, if one offends God by their falling away and their sins, they are not reconciled to God through and on account of the perfect satisfaction of the only mediator Jesus Christ, but are afflicted with eternal punishments to both their body and soul.

Moreover, there is the eternal decree of God, and his will most clearly revealed in his Word, that all who desire to be partakers of that eternal blessedness after this life enter into eternal life *before* they depart this life; that is, by the power of the Holy Spirit we are renewed and regenerated according to the image of God. The righteousness of Christ, which is freely given and imputed to us, we receive by true faith, and are thereby engrafted into Christ. These rightly confess God, enjoy his fellowship, and, endowed with filial love and fear, set their lives according to all his commandments, endeavoring to keep them with the greatest zeal, just as Scripture teaches in 2 Corinthians 5:2–3.[8] Let us be revealed to be clothed in this, that we expire

---

8. "For in this tent we groan, longing to put on our heavenly dwelling, if indeed by putting it on we may not be found to be naked" (2 Cor. 5:2–3, ESV).

with prayers seeking our home which is in heaven, if indeed we have been so dressed, and are not revealed to be naked.

Therefore, death is such a temporal struggle, so perilous and doubtful, that anyone in it will either obtain the palm and crown of eternal life or will succumb and fall, and then collide and fall headlong into eternal death. In fact, there is no room left for an intermediate position, nor a third one. Either perpetual blessedness or perpetual condemnation immediately follows and succeeds this life. And so, in this present life it is necessary for us to be converted and obtain the grace of God, if we do not want to perpetually perish. If doubtless the unseen hand of God calls us from this place, let it not catch us in carnal security and impenitence, as it is said in Hebrews 9:27, "It is appointed for man to die once but afterwards the judgment."

Indeed, that foe and most heartless enemy to the human race, Satan, correctly knows and maintains which people in this life he would entangle in his snares, in which they can do entirely nothing against his strength and cunning. But no anguish or weakness of man is greater than when he is placed in the agony of death; therefore—although he would circle round us our whole life, like a roaring lion whom he would devour[9]—he seeks with every kind of dart and temptation to violently assail and horribly harass those wrestling with death. Next, he attempts and tries with all his might, effort, strength, and skill to seek to cast a person headlong into hopelessness and blasphemy. And as if that sworn enemy of ours did not make this fight difficult enough, as well as horrible and formidable, each person's conscience would do more than enough of the work itself. For it convicts of all these things: that the human race was created for immortality; humanity has as its judge God, who does not leave any lawlessness nor any sin unpunished; and when we all offend God with countless sins, and we would earn his wrath and blows, there is nothing else for us to expect except eternal punishments. It is necessary for all of us to sense this horror of divine judgment and eternal death in this life, if not soon and quickly, at least by the last moment of life. And unless everyone accepts this comfort by true faith in Christ and are converted, it is necessary that they would despair, no less than Cain or Judas.[10] That sense of the wrath of God in the heart and conscience is the beginning of eternal death and infernal tortures, of those about to be endured eternally in their very body and soul,

---

9. 1 Pet. 5:8
10. Gen. 4:13–14; Matt. 27:3–5

according to those words, "they will be cast into outer darkness, where there will be weeping and gnashing of teeth, whose worm will not die and the fire will not be quenched" (cf. Matt. 8:12; 22:13; 25:30).

For there is no one who can fall to the point of such profanity and barbarity, or who can so numb the sting of a bad conscience, that the thought of the termination and final ruin of his life would never enter his mind. And when the wrath of God becomes heavier, so that the weight of his sins increases more and more, it certainly occurs, with the testimony of experience itself, that for a long time the ungodly persevere in their hardness and hold God and his Word in contempt and scorn; then, when the flame of God's wrath violently burns, and they are finally afflicted with a terrible thunderbolt of divine fury, they are laid low and trampled. Indeed, the more certain atheists and the ungodly come to despise the divine will, the more they are shaken, and the more vehemently they abhor death; most are punished by God with an ultimate blindness such that they do not repent, but they devote their soul to their sins and perish eternally. Thus he threatens in Psalm 50:16–22, where the Lord says to the wicked man,

> What right have you to tell of my statutes
>   so that you take my covenant upon your lips,
> When you have hated discipline,
>   and have cast my words behind you?
> If you should see a thief, you are pleased with him
>   and with adulterers is your lot
> Your mouth, you apply to evil,
>   and your tongue frames deceit,
> Sitting, you rail against your brother,
>   against your mother's son, you utter slander
> While doing these things, because I remained silent
>   you thought that I was like you.
> I rebuke and charge you before your eyes.
>   Now attend to this, you who forget God,
>   lest I should rend and there be none to rescue.

So also in Hosea 13:6–8,

> Just like their pasture, they were filled,
>   As they were filled, their soul was lifted up,

> And then, they forgot me
> And I have been to them like an aged lion
> > I am like a panther watching on the path.
> I have fallen upon them like a bear robbed [of its cubs]
> > I have opened their chests, and
> I will devour them
> > like an enormous lion
> > like a savage beast ripping them.

Therefore, so that we do not set ourselves against him, we must recognize that certainly there is nothing more terrible than death, at least for those who are outside of Christ, nor is death to be despised boldly and carelessly, like certain ungodly persons blinded by the devil who falsely persuade themselves that they are able to excise the prick of conscience and somehow sedate its gnawing worm.

The Second Reason

In the second place, we must inquire into the true cause of that misery—certainly of the temporal death as well as the eternal one—if in fact we want to fortify ourselves rightly against those dangers. Paul shows us in Romans 5:12 that "by one man sin entered into the world, and through sin death, and so death passed to all men, in whom all sinned." So the matter stands: sin is the well-spring of this death and the eternal one, and of all the ills to which human life is exposed. This is plainly and clearly explained and confirmed in Genesis 3.

For since the majesty of God is infinite and inscrutable, and God himself threatened death to man on the day in which he would transgress the divine command, certainly his immutable justice and truth demanded that man, together with all his posterity—due to his willing apostasy, being deprived of God's grace and Spirit—be sentenced to eternal punishments. With this charge we must take heed not to sharpen a bold tongue against our Creator and murmur against him as if he were unjust and unmerciful. But rather, casting ourselves down as supplicants in view of divine majesty, let us confess that due to our fault we have drawn this death and every kind of ill upon ourselves, and let us not try to attribute to God any injustice, however many of the whole human race he has left to their own destruction, and however many he shall freely call. Next, at this point we must learn that if we do not want to sink into the abyss of eternal death, it is necessary to remove the cause of death; that is, a satisfaction of divine justice for our sins must be made, either by ourselves or by another, and we must not provoke God again by sinning. For just as, from the reckoning of righteousness and the divine threat, death is the wage due for sin; so, on the contrary, according to the promise of God, perfect righteousness brings life and blessedness. Now, however, all are convicted and accused, not only by the Word of God but also by what they bear inside; by the power of their conscience, due to its innate malice and depravity, they could not even avoid a temporal death in the divine judgment, much less escape and avoid the separation of eternal death. But our conscience convicts us because we cannot make satisfaction through ourselves except by paying eternal punishments, nor can the severe justice of God punish in another [kind of] creature those iniquities which a human being perpetrated. Therefore, it is clear that neither gold, silver, friends, power, erudition, dignity, nor indeed much less worldly desires, can strengthen us or confer anything to sustain, comfort, or deliver us in this exceedingly difficult struggle of death.

And from what has been said, this also must not be passed by in silence, that not without a just and grave cause are all the ungodly, hypocrites, and impenitent left without a solid comfort against death, which God provided in the Gospel. They even journey their whole life in the sheer horrors and terrors of death, to such an extent that true happiness does not ever rise up in their hearts, as they shudder at the slightest mention of death. Or, if they try at all to despise death with a magnanimous and lofty mind, it is not a mind well-armed and equipped with a living comfort as they affect, but rather it ought to be considered a proof and mark of blind and brazen audacity, or insanity, and thus these dangle more profoundly over the abyss of destruction, to the extent that they do not believe and take heed.

The Third Reason
After we have acknowledged that we are liable to temporal and eternal death because of our sins, and we have pulled our hearts away from every vain comfort that people either concoct for themselves or are promised by others; then only that proof, criterion, or certain mark whereby the godly are distinguished from the ungodly is urgently needed, so that we may rightly obtain what comfort we must use in our temporal death and in that of our brethren.

1. The Primary Comfort is God's Reconciliation

But the highest, primary, and most effective comfort, and the foundation of all others is the forgiveness of sins and redemption from eternal death brought about by Christ on the cross. For when the human race cast itself headlong into sin—and hence into the chasm of eternal death, and there was not any way of emerging out of it or any hope of life for the human race—God, according to his own singular mercy, promised from a sign to our first parents the seed of the woman, that he would crush the head of that ancient serpent. And the same promise—frequently repeated to the patriarchs and David, and then restricted to David's posterity—was declared again and again through the prophets, until at last in the fullness of time God sent into the world his son, who, when he had assumed from the virgin Mary a true human nature, in the same fulfilled the law with perfect obedience, sustained and overcame the wrath of God due for our sins with his suffering and death, resurrected from the dead on the third day by virtue of his divinity, ascended to heaven, reigns there powerfully at the right hand of God as the Lord of heaven and the head of the Church, and triumphs, so that all who believe in him shall not perish but have eternal life. This redemption from sin and death he offers through the preaching of the Gospel to all, earnestly admonishing us to embrace it by true faith, and to be persuaded to certainty of it in our hearts. And we are promised that God—because he made us heirs of eternal life on account of Christ and adopted us as beloved children—will be a kind and eternal Father to us. Likewise, he promises to all believers, out of pure grace, that he will impute and give the perfect satisfaction of Christ, righteousness, and obedience to them so that all their sins, weaknesses, and the rest of their defects will be covered thereafter as if they themselves had satisfied for their own sins and fulfilled the law of God. And since the sting of sin is death, and the law is the power or strength of sin—because we are exempt through Christ from the curse of sin and the law, which remained upon us, it necessarily follows from the promise of God that death has no power over us, but it has been broken and utterly destroyed. And God, when he turned his angry countenance from us, now through the Holy Spirit dwells among us again and wills to grant eternal life, which abundantly confirms the Church's victory song regarding death: "Death has been swallowed up in Victory. Where, O Death, is your victory? Where, O Grave, your sting?"[11]

---

11. 1 Cor. 15:54b–55

But we worship God with a sincere heart and confidence, however languid and weak our faith may be, in order that we would believe more clearly that he will constantly fulfill all that he has promised to us. Not only does he most abundantly repeat that promise in his Word, but he also confirmed it with the introduction of an oath in Ezekiel 18: "As I live, I do not desire the death of a sinner, but that he would be converted and live."[12] Indeed, so Christ the Savior instituted the sacraments—that is, Baptism and the Holy Supper—as signs, seals, and pledges of divine grace, so that everyone who believes and is baptized likewise comes to the table of the Lord. In their lawful use—like certain seals that God, as it were, shows from heaven in the sight of his holy ones, both angels and men—each believer considers himself certain and confirmed; not only of someone else in general, but he considers himself personally, distinctly, individually[13] cleansed from his sins by the blood and spirit of Christ, and also considers that the body of the Lord was broken on the cross for him, and his blood was poured out, and it is eaten and drank by partaking of these signs for eternal life; that is, the forgiveness of sins on account of the death and suffering of Christ. And each believer receives the Holy Spirit, by whose strength and work he is united to Christ as a member to the head, and he is confirmed with righteousness and holiness, and washed as certainly and truly as is done by the external symbol of water, and as Christ is eaten and drank when given to him externally with the broken bread and the outpoured cup.

Therefore, if we do not wickedly reject the grace of God offered, and do not stubbornly resist the divine command to believe in Christ the Son of God, there is no reason why we should fear later. Certainly our soul is not without sorrow, but it is separated from the body for a brief time. But in fact, these especially must be feared in death, namely: the death of the soul, the wrath of God against sin, and eternal torment (which also has been transferred from us to Christ). To which I say: Christ has conquered, expiated, and suffered all things so that we must neither fear nor dread them. On the contrary, life and blessedness with God and the angels in heaven forever has been gifted to us; of which certainly in the present, through a living comfort of faith, and a true knowledge of God, we taste the first fruits, until after this life we receive and possess them fully. Of this topic, Christ warned in John 5[:24], "Truly, truly, I say to you whoever hears my

---

12. Ezek. 18:23, 32
13. Gk. ἰδέως

word and believes in him who sent me, has eternal life and will not come into condemnation, but has passed from death to life." And in John 8[:51], "Truly, truly I say to you, if anyone will have kept my word, forever he will not see death." And in John 11[:25–26], "I am the resurrection and the life. He who believes in me, even if he would die, will live, and whoever lives and believes in me, will not die forever." Likewise, Paul says in Romans 8[:10], "If Christ is in us, certainly the body is dead due to sin, but the Spirit is life due to righteousness."

2. Final Deliverance

From this first and chief comfort another flows, namely, a final deliverance from the remnants of sins, and a full redemption[14] from all the miseries of this life. For because true Christians are averse to nothing more than sin, because these offend their heavenly Father; and it is clear that God does not destroy the depravity of our nature in one moment, but daily more and more, and he mortifies it in us; likewise, eternal life begins in this life; therefore, throughout our entire life we must fight against our sins and flesh, and calamities of every kind in this valley of miseries must be endured to the end, so that we would grow incrementally, day by day, in the awareness of sin in us, and our conversion would be increased by indefatigable zeal. For this reason, however many are godly desire with ardent prayers to do as much as they can. At last God calls the godly from this unhappy life and unclean world, stained with the filth of sins, and from this ocean of miseries to the shore of eternal life, even to the heavenly fellowship of our Lord and Savior, and of the saints, angels, and elect souls, where they are vindicated from every sin, ignorance, and doubt into the most blessed state. There they praise and worship God in true knowledge, perfect righteousness, holiness, and glory. Certainly, that blessedness no eye has seen nor ear has heard, nor in fact, at any time has it ever come into or occurred to the mind of any person. So let us sincerely congratulate our brethren with respect to a redemption from all the miseries of this fallen life and an eternal rest into which they have entered before us—provided we follow after them with a sincere love and we steadfastly aspire to the same gate of happiness—rather than greatly mourn because of their exit from this life. Nor should we desire, if we could, to drag them back into this life. Thus, Paul exclaims in Romans 7[:24], "O wretched man that I am! Who will deliver me from

---

14. Gk. ἀπολύτρωσις

this body of death?" And in 2 Corinthians 5[:1], truly for all Christians; after he has departed from this body, he did not make a full journey to a purgatorial fire (which the Antichrist dreamed up) due to their masses and vigils for the dead, but he fully portrays heavenly joys and eternal rest, when he speaks in this way: "We know that if the tabernacle of this earthly house should be destroyed, we will have a building from God, a home I say not made by a human hand, but an eternal one in heaven." For in this we should hope, seeking our home that is in heaven, abundantly clothed, if in fact we also would be revealed to be clothed and not naked. For we who are in this tabernacle groan as those burdened; in which we do not desire to be stripped bare but abundantly clothed, so that mortality might be engulfed by life. Furthermore, God is the one who created us for himself, who also gave us the down payment of the Spirit. Therefore we are always confident, even knowing that we are strangers in this body; away from our homeland when we are absent from the Lord. For we advance by faith, not by sight. But we are full of confidence and demonstrate that it is preferable to leave the body and go to the Lord, our dwelling place. In like manner Isaiah says in chapter 57:1-2,[15] "The righteous man dies, and no one takes note that before the coming of evil itself, the just man is taken; he enters into his peace; they rest on their bed, everyone who walks in their uprightness."

3. The Blessed Resurrection

But despite seeing the tabernacle of our body destroyed and returned to dust, let us oppose to this trial the third point of comfort that the joyful article of the Creed[16] supplies regarding the glorious resurrection of the dead. From this we know that not only are our souls taken from this life into the bosom of Abraham and paradise—that is, that rest of all believers—but also this flesh of ours, which we bear now and carry about, is not for this reason set aside and remanded to the earth to remain in this divorce and state of separation, but will outlast mortality, and in the last judgment be revived and united to the soul once more, adorned and bedecked with immortality, heavenly brilliance, and glory for singing praises to God for eternity. How outstandingly Paul depicts the blessed condition of our flesh after this life in 1 Corinthians 15:42. Our body is sown liable to corruption and is raised incorruptible. It is sown in shame and raised in glory. It is

---

15. Cf. Isa. 56:13.
16. I.e. the Apostles' Creed

sown weak and raised up powerful. It is sown an animal body and raised a spiritual one. It is an animal body and a spiritual body. It is necessary that that which is liable to corruption put on an incorruptible nature, and this mortal one to put on immortality. And in 15:50, "Moreover I say this to you, flesh and blood cannot inherit the kingdom of God." And Christ says in Matthew 13[:43], "Then the righteous will shine like the sun in the kingdom of their Father."

For when Christ came into the world for this purpose, so that he might redeem not only souls but also our flesh, it could not happen unless our bodies likewise enjoy the eternal life and glory of their head, Christ. This Christ affirms in John 6[:39] when he says this is the will of the Father, that of whatever the Father gave him he will lose none, but he will raise it up at the last day to eternal life. Just as Paul also says in Romans 8[:11]: "If his Spirit, which raised Jesus up from the dead, dwells in us; the one that raised Christ from the dead, will also make your mortal bodies alive through the indwelling of his Spirit in us." And in Philippians 3[:20–21], "Our citizenship[17] is in heaven, from where we look for our Savior the Lord," that is, the one who will transform our lowly bodies to become like his glorious body, according to that efficacy whereby he can subject all things to himself."

So then everywhere God in his Word compares the temporal death of believers to sleep, and their graves to κοιμητηρία or *dormitoria*, that is, sleeping chambers, in which their bodies rest until they are raised up to eternal glory. Thus, in Isaiah 26[:20] he speaks to the people in this way, "Come, my people, enter your chambers and shut the doors behind you, hide yourselves as for a little moment, until the fury has passed you by."

And Job, renowned for his godliness and patience, even when he looked more like a dead man than a living one, still comforted himself in this way: "Surely I know my Redeemer lives, and in the end he will stand upon the earth. And after worms have eaten my flesh, when awakened, then in my flesh will I see God. I, and not another will see him for myself, and my eyes will look upon him."[18]

4. The Presence of God

But in fact, lest the pains of bodily death, the temptations of the devil (with which even the elect are very frequently and usually attacked), and the

---

17. Gk. πολίτευμα
18. Job 19:25–26

great weakness of our flesh terrify us, in the fourth place, this outstanding comfort for us—namely the very present help of God, his fatherly providence, and the steadfast protection of our Lord Jesus and the Holy Spirit—stands foremost against all other perils and terrors. "For not one of us," testifies Paul in Romans 14:8, "lives to ourselves or dies to ourselves. For if we live, we live to the Lord, and if we die, we die to the Lord. Therefore, whether we live or die, we are the Lord's." Therefore, Christ has certainly bought us as his own with his precious blood. There is no doubt that both in life and death he watches over our salvation so that there can be no power or fury so eternally great that it could snatch us from his hands.

And when the most merciful God loved us so zealously that he delivered his only begotten son over to death for us—whereby we have been reconciled while we were still enemies—how much more will we be saved as reconciled in his life. And just as he made a promise in Psalm 91[:13-15], "You will tread on the ferocious lion and the adder, you will trample the young lion and the dragon. Because he holds fast to me in love, I will deliver him, I will shelter him, because he knows my name, and likewise he will call upon me, and I will hear him, in trouble I will be with him, I will rescue him and I will honor him." So he promises no less with us (1 Cor. 10[:13]); that he will not allow us to be tempted beyond our strength, but with the temptation he will provide a way of escape so that we can endure it.

5. The Deliverance from Sin

Furthermore, because God, who is at the same time our redeemer and creator, ought to be obeyed in all that he demands of us, there in fact seemed to him no other way to purge us entirely from the filth of our sins than through the death of the body; and to lead us from this death to eternal life as if through a final test to examine our faith and obedience, as is befitting our office; so that at last in someway or somehow, God would not order us to withdraw from our post in this life, or that we would exhibit signs of any impatience. Much less that we would defect from God and, doubting his trustworthiness and goodness, we would finally despair. Instead, because he supplies the material for exercising the owed obedience, let us exult and rejoice from our heart, namely in imitation of Job, saying, "if we would receive good things from God, why will we not endure evil ones?"[19]

19. Job 2:10

6. The Example of our Lord

Finally, this is the constant and perpetual will of God: that all the members of Christ would be conformed to him as to their head, both in this life and the next. For a disciple is not above his master. Wherefore, just as Christ had to enter into glory through suffering, so we must enter into the kingdom of heaven through various tribulations. And if we strive to enjoy eternal joy and reign with Christ forevermore, it should not seem in the least hard, difficult, or arduous to meet death in this age. For it is a faithful saying, says Paul in 2 Timothy 2[:11-12], "if we have died with Christ, then we will also live with him. If we should suffer, then we will also reign with him."

The Fourth Argument

As this comfort, however, is not set forth to us apart from the enjoyment of the Word of God, in the right and healthy meditation on death, in the fourth and final place—how we ought to prepare ourselves for death so that this comfort would take root in our hearts, and we would genuinely experience it—we must studiously pay attention to:

1. Faith

This preparation for death is especially grounded in a true and sincere faith, whereby we apprehend and apply to ourselves the promise of grace, of forgiveness of sins, and of eternal life, and at last the resurrection of the flesh to glory. Just as it is written, "the just shall live by faith."[20] And just as the Lord frequently says in the Gospel, "Your faith has saved you."[21] And here, first of all, comes what must be observed: that our salvation is not supported by the magnitude or strength of our faith, but by the mercy of God, which does not spurn weak faith[22] at all. And as often as we acknowledge and deplore our infirmities, turning away from our lack of faith,[23] and in true affection of heart beg God to increase our faith, so often are we strengthened as with a certain pledge; from the singular mercy of God the Holy Spirit has already begun to work faith in us, and we certainly pledge ourselves to augment that faith in accordance with the promise. To the one who has, more will be given. And such people persevere as constant in faith

---

20. Hab. 2:4
21. For example, Luke 7:50
22. Gk. ὀλιγοπιστίαν
23. Gk. ἀπιστίαν

according to Paul's exhortation in 1 Corinthians 16:13,[24] Be watchful in faith; be strengthened, and you shall be strong.

2. Conversion

Necessary for this preparation, it is likewise required, and flows forth from the streams of faith, that we should persevere in true conversion to God throughout our whole life, daily making progress in it and earnestly pleading that we have offended God. Hence we detest our sins; but instead, we rejoice because God has been propitiated to us through Christ. And let us not desire to have it said that we are pleasing to God through our continued obedience and because we walk in the paths of the divine precepts. On that account these fruits of faith must reveal themselves, because faith deprived of them does not at all deserve the name of true and living faith. Without these things, we would boast in vain about a firm comfort against death, as it is said in 1 John 3[:14] that those who do not love their brother remain in death.

3. Self-denial

Yet these things alone are insufficient for the art of dying well. From the command of Christ in Matthew 16[:24–25], a true preparation must be joined with our self-denial: "the one who desires to follow me should deny himself and take up his cross and follow me. For anyone who wants to save his soul will lose it. But anyone who loses their soul for my sake, will find it." Certainly that self-denial is divided into these parts so that, renouncing our sinful flesh and lusts, we would earnestly love and worship God; so that with a ready mind we would desert or abandon all that is dear to us in this world, even life itself; and that only for this reason, that by rendering due obedience to the divine will we would worship God eternally. Certainly then it would happen at last that if we felt and genuinely realized in our hearts God the Father's indescribable and infinite love—whereby he gave his only begotten son, that same love of the son who endured that most shameful death and extreme sufferings for us—then there would be no comparison or proportion between the treasures and desires of this age and the joys of the kingdom of heaven; and thus how suddenly all that has been crucified—the calamities of this world and its tribulations—would be scant trifles compared to hell, and they would vanish like smoke. Hence,

---

24. The original reads "1 Corinthians 15:13," but 16:13 is meant.

a trepidation of death arises—among not a few people—that places the delights of this age before Christ. Certainly, the Lord has declared openly that these people are not worthy of him (Matt. 10[:37]; Luke 14[:25]), saying "the one who loves his father and mother more than me is not worthy of me." On the contrary, among those who entirely consecrate and offer themselves to God, there is nothing more preferable, nothing more excellent than that—insofar as it can be done for them as quickly as possible—they would fly to Christ. Yet they are not unwilling to bear the cross patiently, insofar as it seems good to God of course, so that they would live on this earth and wander like exiles for the spread of the divine name and the building up of their neighbors. Therefore, they live and die in the company of that godly old man Simeon, possessing a good conscience in peace and tranquil hearts fortified to the utmost with comforts. And assuredly among this kind, Paul, whom we know is set before us to imitate, excels in an amazing way, and he spoke in this way in Philippians 1:20–26, "I expect and hope, and that with all courage,[25] just as always, so now also Christ will be magnified in my body, either through my life or my death. For, to me, to live is Christ, and to die is gain. But whether or not it is better for me to live in the body, and what I should choose, I do not know. For I am hard pressed between the two, desiring to leave and be with Christ—for that is far better—but to remain in the flesh is more necessary for your sake."

4. Vigilance

It is no less necessary that we, who begin in a mature way that preparation throughout the entire course of our life, should continue in a meditation upon the sins and miseries of this present life, and in a timely way we should diligently reflect upon those things of which God approves, both those which pertain to our comfort and duty, and those things which result in a noble death.[26] What else is there? Our entire life is nothing else than a gymnasium in which, through meticulous attention to and meditation upon the divine Word, we learn the art of dying well and blessedly, of which there can be nothing more useful and wholesome. For daily we see with how much difficulty those take true comfort in death who, as long as they lived, did not prepare for it with indefatigable zeal and did not impress it upon their hearts in a timely fashion so that in the last necessity they

---

25. Gk. παῤῥησία
26. Gk. εὐθανασία

would not be compelled to fetch and summon it from afar, but that comfort would be fixed in their memory, in their heart, and ready at a moment's notice. And this is what the Word of God everywhere teaches, that we are to be on guard; that is, that we would thoroughly excise any negligence and lethargy in working out and promoting our salvation, lest we fall in temptation and are called out of this life by the Lord unprepared and suddenly, at great hazard to our salvation.

5. Prayers

Lastly, in true preparation for death and sudden calamities of every kind, ardent and devoted prayer to God holds the chief place for the confirmation of faith. Instead of leaving us wavering in dangers of temptations, it daily confirms those on whom the gifts of the Holy Spirit have been generously outpoured, until at last through a blessed departure from this life, he transfers us to himself into heavenly joys and eternal glory. For we ourselves certainly hold this persuasion, that God wills to lavish grace and the Holy Spirit upon those who seek from him with true groaning, and that he wills to hear all who call upon him. For Christ confirms this himself: "If you," he says, "being evil, know how to give good gifts to your children, how much more will the heavenly Father give the Holy Spirit to those who ask" (Matt. 7:11; Luke 11:13).

An Exhortation

Therefore, because we are not ignorant of how our life is exposed to many dangers of death, nor of in what way and path we fall into dangers, especially through sins, then also knowing how we are freed from them, namely through the only Mediator—and we know this because we can rise up from the plague of sins by the grace of Christ alone, which we gain in no other way but by embracing the promised and offered grace in Christ with true faith with a true and sincere conversion to God—let us structure our life according to the norm of God's law and the rule of his commandments; let us deny our sins and the world; let us despise the world; let us seek the things above; and let us savor heavenly things. Hence let us rightly seize this occasion to examine ourselves and see whether we stand in true faith. Let us thirst for and take hold of the grace of Christ, and let us do it with each and every moment, lest by sinning against conscience we weigh ourselves down with a deadly burden. Instead, deploring the remnants of our sins, in consideration of the divine word, let us exercise ourselves daily for the hope of heavenly life, being mindful of what Christ said in Mark 13[:33, 35–37], "Be vigilant, because you do not know at what hour the Lord will come—evening, midnight, noon, or morning. May he not come suddenly and find you sleeping! Moreover, what I say to you, I say to all: Be watchful!"

But in fact this certainly is true and indubitable—it is as certain as possible—that, if the hand of God should seize us in faithlessness,[27] impenitence, and persisting carelessly in other sins, we would make the most immediate shipwreck of our faith, and our condition would not be better than that of the worthless servant of whom the master disapproved in Matthew 24[:48–51], "because the servant had said in his heart, 'My master delays on a journey,' and he began to beat his fellow servants,[28] moreover he ate and drank with drunkards. The master when he comes on a day when the servant does not expect, discharges him and assigned him a portion with the hypocrites, where there is wailing and gnashing of teeth." And the same thing applies regarding the five fatuous virgins who did not have oil in their lamps; would Christ the groom pass sentence on us with, "I do not know you?" (Matt. 25[:12]) And are we about to hear the same word as the rich man in Luke 12[:20–21], whose land was abundant: "Fool, this night your soul they will gather from you; and then to whom will belong what you have prepared? For so it happens to those," says Christ, "who accrue treasures for themselves, but are poor towards God."

But if in fact we gird up our loins and are clothed with the breastplate of righteousness and the shield of faith—that is, endowed with a true faith and a good conscience, should God strike—when at last we must depart, whether we expect death or not, nevertheless we hold it certain and are persuaded that we will be with the prudent virgins, who advanced with burning lamps in the train of the Bridegroom, and with the good and faithful servant who did the commandments of the Lord. Let us then enter from this wretched life into eternal joys with the Bridegroom, and let us gain the heavenly treasuries from the Lord.

Moreover, although by nature we are all lame and weak and as fragile as vases, even as our most hostile enemy prowls about day and night like a roaring lion seeking whom he may devour, yet it is the merciful will of

---

27. Gk. ἀπιστία
28. Gk. συνδούλους

God that we both ask for the grace of the Holy Spirit with diligent prayers and gain it according to his promises. Certainly this necessity demands that as long as the days of our life continue, before we arrive at their predetermined end, we ought to seek this grace from God with continuous and devout prayers, which this next formula of prayer attempts to do.

A Prayer

We give thanks to you, almighty, eternal, and merciful God and Father, because on account of your inexhaustible mercy among us, you have gathered the Church to yourself through the Word and Spirit, and you have revealed to us that only and solid comfort in your Word, which we all know—we who breathe our last in true faith and with the invocation of your name. We give thanks not only because you granted to us the use of this life, and up to this point have kindly preserved us, but because you have also begun that spiritual and eternal life in us, and you embraced us in such great love that on our behalf you delivered up your only begotten son to death, so that all who would believe in him should not perish but have eternal life. And you have called us to that blessed fellowship[29] of your son, and by the work of your Holy Spirit you have kindled true faith in us, and you have mercifully protected us up to this day against the force and attack of the Devil. You have guarded us in the truth known. And finally, you have fortified our hearts with this steadfast comfort, that temporal death is our entrance into eternal life. We ask, O eternal God, that you would cause the pure and sincere teaching of the Gospel to enlighten us and our posterity forevermore, for the sake of the glory of your name and our salvation. Always raise up faithful ministers in place of those who have passed on, and send out many into your harvest. Also strengthen and protect the good work that you have begun in us. Forgive us our sins, and deliver us from eternal death, through our Lord Jesus Christ. Likewise, daily mortify our corrupt nature until at last we lay down the burden of sins, under which we frequently grow weary in this life. Cause that we are comforted with a firm faith in the blessed resurrection of our flesh to eternal glory. Guard us against the temptations of Satan. Be at hand and help us especially when we must leave this life. Cause us to be rendered compliant, ready, and thankful to your divine will in our life and death, and let us rejoice in pain and suffering, because we are being

---

29. Gk. κοινωνίαν

conformed to our head, Christ. Grant constancy to us, increase of faith, and holiness of life. Cause that we deny ourselves and seek things above, where Christ is, and let us not seek our joy in the desires of this world but in meditation upon your Word. And finally, pour out in our hearts the spirit of grace and prayer so that we may always be vigilant, and let us pray that we would not fall into temptation but be ready, so that whenever it would please you, we would pass to you through a blessed, noble death,[30] and bring us boldly to the tribunal of your son. All this, what you would most mercifully lavish upon us, through and on account of your son, our Lord Jesus Christ, who reigns with you forevermore, Amen.

---

30. Gk. εὐθανασίαν

10

On Flight in Persecution or Plague

Introduction

George Abbot's parents converted to the protestant faith under the reign of Edward VI (r. 1547–1553) only to suffer persecution under the reign of Mary Tudor (r. 1553–1558). It seems that George (b. 1562), the fourth of six boys, embraced both the faith and the tenacity of his parents early on as he would spend his life defending and promoting the protestant cause against countless critics and detractors. Under the auspices of generous patrons Abbot attended Balliol college, Oxford where he would later teach and serve as master of University college. His entrance onto the national stage, however, came with his three appointments as vice-chancellor of the university in the academic years 1601–1602, 1603–1604, and 1605–1606. At Oxford, Abbot distinguished himself not only as an adept theologian and biblical scholar, but also as an immensely competent ecclesiastical dignitary, all of which led to his acquiring increasingly prominent preferments.

Nevertheless, for many, Abbot's lack of local parish ministry experience combined with his evident puritan sympathies disqualified him as a viable option for the archbishopric. Thus, his appointment to the office by James I in 1611 was met with a great deal of surprise and, in some quarters, outrage. James's unexpected attraction to Abbot was, at least according to one historian, due to a "combination of his theological learning and the conciliatory and skillful statesmanlike behavior he showed in Scotland."[1] She goes on to note, however, that "if James believed that Abbot would be subservient, he was mistaken, for where loyalty to the king clashed with Abbot's conscience and his sense of his godly duty, there was not doubt

---

1. On behalf of James I, Abbot played a prominent pacifying role in restoring diocesan episcopacy in presbyterian Scotland. S. M. Holland, "George Abbot: 'The Wanted Archbishop,'" *Church History* 56, (1987): 186.

which would prevail."[2] Abbot served as archbishop until his death in 1633 (though from 1625 he exercised little influence due to his differences with Charles I on, among other things, the divine right of kings). Lamenting the low esteem with which Abbot was held by posterity, Arthur Fox anticipated a time in which Abbot would "rise to his true place in the history of his Church, and he will be found to have been a strong, true-hearted and noble-minded man."[3] Fox's explanation for Abbot's tepid reception is a fitting tribute to the man's character and convictions:

> His rugged manners were ill-calculated to gain him the affections of those whose appetite for flattery was as gross as it was insatiable. But he remained true to himself in the face of strong temptations, and as such he must be known and honoured for all time.... In fine, he has left behind him the memory of a just and righteous man, who according to his lights faithfully discharged the duties of every station in life which he occupied, and that, too, with a temperate spirit of moderation, which his successor would have done well to have imitated in his more turbulent primacy.[4]

Abbot's treatise, *On Flight in Persecution or Plague*, is one of six theses he defended in public disputations for his doctoral degree in theology at Oxford in 1597. The disputations were published initially in Oxford, England (1598) and again in Frankfurt, Germany (1616).[5] The second publication, promoted by the Reformed theologian and Old Testament professor at Heidelberg, Abraham Scultetus (1566–1625), reached a broader Reformed audience and garnered an impressive amount of interest on the continent, especially as Abbot was the archbishop of Canterbury and concurrently the chancellor of Trinity College Dublin.[6]

---

2. Ibid.
3. Arthur William Fox, *Book of Bachelors* (New York: E. P. Dutton, 1900), 202.
4. Ibid.
5. George Abbot, *Georgii Abbatis Quaestiones sex, totidem praelectionibus in schola theologica, Oxoniae, pro forma, habitis, discussae, et disceptatae* (Oxford: Joseph Barnes, 1598); idem, *Georgii Abbatti Reverendissimi Archiepiscopi Cantavariensis Explicatio sex illustrium quaestionum . . . Oxoniae anno 1597 in schola theologica proposita, ibidem edita, et nuncprimum in Germania recusa* (Frankfurt: Jonah Rosa, 1616). Both works have been consulted, compared, and utilized for this translation.
6. Hoornbeeck reports that Abraham Scultetus was instrumental in the second printing. Hoornbeeck et al., *Variorum Tractatus Theologici de peste* (Leiden: Johannes Elsevir, 1655), 300. See page 146 in this volume.

Abbot takes as his starting point the account of the apostle Paul's flight from Damascus recorded in Acts 9:23–25, and on the basis of this he considers the principles by which Christians, and especially ministers of the gospel, may, must, or must not flee persecution and plague. "God has" says Abbot, "ingenerated every human being with a certain natural love of life, which constantly functions for their own preservation, and thus no one freely dashes into danger." To knowingly and willing expose oneself to danger and death *without good cause* is in effect to violate the sixth commandment, "Thou shalt not murder." Against Tertullian, who maintained that flight is always illicit, Abbot cites an impressive array of church fathers and contemporary theologians who maintained the contrary, and concludes, "So the ancients, and recent theologians, everywhere and absolutely thought that flight was not interdicted for the Christian."

On account of his special office, however, the pastor's calling is markedly different. Abbot writes,

> If [pastors] should withdraw into flight in a raging pestilence, who will supply the necessary duties of the church? Who will preach a sermon to the well? Who will share comfort with the sick? Indeed, there are countless things which call him to daily use and cannot be rightly transacted if the spiritual leader who applies that counsel is absent. Therefore, I believe that a priest (that is, the pastor of a congregation), lest he become a mercenary, must not depart from his particular calling—a calling which takes away the liberty that is granted and permitted to others.

Though the greater portion of his treatise is taken up with a discussion of flight from persecution, Abbot concludes by highlighting the salient connections with the related issue of flight during times of plague. There are, of course, important similarities. In both seasons of persecution and seasons of plague believers are obligated to protect their own life and the life of their neighbor. This is most naturally, obviously, and effectively accomplished by fleeing to places of greater safety; and so, they are obligated to do so. Also, in both persecution and plague the pastor's calling and duty require him to remain in harm's way for the purpose of caring for Christ's flock. To do otherwise, for Abbot, would reveal a mercenary rather than a Christlike spirit.

There are also, however, important differences that, while not changing *what* the pastor is called to do, may alter *how* the pastor is called do it, especially in light of his obligation to serve the healthy as well as the sick. For example, regarding the pastor's obligation to visit the sick and the dying, Abbot writes, "Yet because in a private and secret death the divine glory is not so manifest as in an open martyrdom, for the sake of a good conscience, and since there are many duties that must be rendered to the whole congregation and equally even to the sick, I do not think there is a necessity incumbent upon a minister to enter into the dwellings and bedchambers of the sick, because that cannot be done without manifest danger to life." The archbishop's advice for ministering in times of plague, as relevant today as it was over four hundred years ago, displays the enviable mixture of theological sophistication with practical and pastoral sensibilities.

"De Fuga Ministri in persecutione aut peste" in George Abbot, *Explicatio sex quaestionum . . . Oxoniae anno 1597 in schola Theologica proposita, ibidem edita et nuncprimum in Germania recusa* (Frankfurt: Jonas Rosa, 1616), 129–51. Cf. idem, *Quaestiones sex ... in schola theologica Oxoniae ... discussae et disceptate, anno 1597 per Gerogium Abbatem* (Oxford: Joseph, Barnes, 1598). The following selection is the fifth of the six questions in Abbot's disputations defended *pro gradu*, for his doctorate of theology at Oxford in 1597.

On Flight in Persecution or Plague
George Abbot
Translated by Todd M. Rester

"But when the days were fulfilled, at the same time the council of the Jews took counsel to kill Saul. But their treachery was understood by Saul, but they kept watch over the gates day and night so that they might kill him. Therefore, the disciples took him at night and set him over the wall, lowered down in a basket." (Acts 9:23–25)

§§1–3 *The causes impelling Paul to flee; §§4–7 it is licit for a layman to flee in persecution; §8 but not for the minister of a congregation; §11 examples and reasons for a pastor's flight are brought forward and resolved; §17 it is licit for a layman in time of plague to turn aside; §19 but a minister must remain.*[7]

---

7. Rather than a Table of Contents, this series indicates, in the convention of the time, the high points of the argument (hence the gaps in section numbers), the implication being that there are further specifications of detail in the sections not cited.

§1. That comment of John the Baptist is very true, that God can raise up children of Abraham from stones (Matt. 3:9). For even the one who converts to faith in Christ those whose hearts are like flint, harder than stone, and sharper than even the jagged rocks themselves (with respect to what concerns godliness), rightly raises up children from stones like believing Abraham. In another way, if, as happened in the case of the apostle Paul, someone is placed in danger who breathes out slaughter and blood against all who profess the Savior, and at his request with letters received from the high priest, sets out for Damascus to menace everyone in his path, arresting them and binding them in chains to abduct them to Jerusalem to be imprisoned and accused, is, with a distinct light from heaven like a lightning bolt, blinded in his eyes and a voice from heaven strikes his heart, God has suddenly stripped away the wolf and clothed him a lamb. And thoroughly changed in his heart, after having a conversation with a certain Ananias—by whose hand he had received his sight and been cleansed[8] by the holy waters of baptism—he burst into the proclamation of Christ in a singular display of his glory. Thus it happened through the conspicuous mercy of God to the one who was once deceived by Satan; who like a lion and rapacious tiger believed he was sent out against believers in Christ; who perpetrated butchery against men, women, and everyone; who, with gusto, would have pulled up the Church of the saints from its very roots, and collapsed its very foundations into a heaping mass; who truly gave himself as an adversary of Christ, and a kind of war-chief, a renowned standard bearer, the like of which I do not know if even among so many throngs in the whole world scarcely anyone could match him. In fact, with his malign fury laid aside, he began to proclaim publicly that Jesus Christ is the only begotten of the great God, and publicly and privately he held Christ in front of himself, by demonstrating the truth with arguments and convincing the stubborn Jews by the very force of the Scriptures.

§2. With that unexpected success, as the brethren were exulting for joy, so Satan grew indignant and his troops began to roar. For when Satan saw the one whom he hoped would lead countless souls into his traps and snares now driving off herds and preventing him from taking rich plunder; can we not see how he sets cruel means in motion, he who ardently desires the destruction of the human race? Therefore, Satan roused the servants and slaves of darkness, and the sons of malice, who from ambush might try to

---

8. Lat. *expiatus fuerat*

intercept and kill him. The one who by force previously sought out others is now himself sought out by force; the assailant is being assailed; the slayer is being slain; the killer is sought to be killed. Thus, as soon as a person gains a name for godliness and sincere religion, there will be no shortage of people who curse with poisoned tongues, who slay with satirical teeth,[9] who attack to kill with a bloody hand. Every Isaac will have his Ishmael, every Abel his brother Cain, every David a Doeg (2 Chr. 6:14). What agreement will there be between light and darkness, believers and unbelievers, between the holiest servants of Christ and his avowed enemies? Therefore, despite the proof that Christ demonstrated both to his countrymen and his compatriots, the Jews, that the son of Mary was the true Messiah and the redeemer of Israel, they despised him and held him in contempt; indeed they crucified in a shameful and disgraceful way him who will be the judge of the living and the dead. Then the Jews who traveled to Damascus took counsel to shut believers' mouths, not by imposing silence, but by thoroughly crushing out their light and life. In order to accomplish their goal without hinderance, they set guards at the gates of the city who might suddenly accost Paul as he passes through. Nothing, except his life, could satisfy their savage rage.

§3. But God—who as a sign of his omniscience is accustomed both to count every hair and to mark even the least sparrow, and who reins in rabid lions as with a muzzle—mercifully checked the malice of the malign. He revealed the plans of the plotting enemies to the brethren who embraced Paul in love, who were unwilling for the blood of an innocent man to be shed; indeed, especially one in the flower of youth, with such great talents, with such studied erudition, so much sweetness of eloquence, such brilliant expertise in the Scriptures, who could afterwards promote the honor of God to such great an extent and spread the faith of Christ. For these reasons they brought him help and, as much as they could, kept him safe from the edge of the sword. Therefore, when he could not pass through in public, they suffered him to go into hiding in secret places, so that when the occasion permitted, at last at night in cover of darkness, they approached the walls of the city and, whether by an opening in the wall or an opening made, they lowered him down in a basket suspended by a rope. So Paul took flight by hastening and speeding his steps, having escaped death. And in saving himself for better times for the church, he afterwards became an

---

9. Lat. *Theoninino dente*: lit. "with Theonine teeth," referencing the satirical poet Theon.

instrument and organ for the manifestation of divine praise throughout all quarters of the earth.

What should we take as our rule? And, lest we fail to speak about those sufferings, shouldn't it be investigated further whether other people should follow in Paul's footsteps? And shouldn't we also investigate whether it is licit for them to flee in secret from the fury of tyrants? Since sometimes the congregation of the faithful is mangled by the sword of Domitians and Diocletians, and evil people rage such that the ships of the church seem to be lost to the waves and storms in the ocean of the world, even though the spirit is willing and ready, the flesh could be weak. Therefore, while one who is thoroughly embarrassed[10] by Christ and his confession ought to be remanded to hell, it is necessary to trace out whether it is licit for one who cherishes godliness to flee in persecution. And this is especially necessary in the case of a minister of the gospel, who functions with the duty of a governor, and who will give an account no less for other souls as for his own. Therefore, since there is not much difference between this topic and another—namely, flight during a severe time of ravaging plague—due to the similarity of the circumstances today, with God guiding us, this disputation will handle both.

§4. God has ingenerated every human being with a certain natural love of life, which constantly functions for their own preservation, and thus no one freely dashes into danger. And, as has been rightly observed, God endowed this desire so that, when seized by some fleeting occasion of melancholy, envy, or fear, one would not lay violent hands on themselves and kill themselves. Without which it would happen that, scattered and swept away, the human race would be destroyed in a brief amount of time. So then the most prudent builder of this workmanship gave to everyone this desire to safeguard and cherish their own life. And the remembrance of this feeling for the Christian person can apply a spur to the doubtful, so that he would avoid injury by withdrawing himself from the midst of it. For as God supplied us equally with feet, whereby we are able to flee, and with hands to fight, and a back to bear and endure all kinds of things, so it bears to reason that sometimes one must employ the benefit of one's feet, especially when there is no testimony of Holy Scripture prohibiting it. So it is also the case that no one in possession of their own strength can be so self-conscious

---

10. Lat. *rubore suffunditur*: lit. "one is drenched with redness", that is, thoroughly blushing with embarrassment.

that he does not also acknowledge his own weakness in bearing a cross. In fact, would someone made of flesh and blood presume to avow such great patience for themselves that, when they could safely leave in advance, they would not shudder, waver in speech, and vacillate in mind surrounded by the teeth of wild beasts, fire, sword, rack, and the most thorough tortures? "For a corruptible body will weigh down the soul" (Wis. 9:15), and although by itself the spirit is ready, it is attached to a weak and feeble flesh. "Let anyone who appears to himself to stand, let him see that he does not fall" (1 Cor. 10:12). "Do not ever be haughty, but rather fear" (Rom. 11:20). There was one who appeared to have carried himself with such great spirits, as if everyone else would desert Christ, but he would not; and if he were about to die, he would not renounce him to escape. But when he would arrive at the very point of removing his head, in the hall of the chief priest, trembling and fearful, he denied his Lord. Therefore, if the Lord has offered an opportunity to cut off and diminish all occasion for what follows by departing into exile, whether by retiring to a desert, cave, or wood, will it do to obtrude oneself by speciously and audaciously coming into danger, and to show such reluctance in the conflict itself, and miserably to collapse, so that faith and Christian profession come into opprobrium among those strangers and enemies of God? Because if among what must be fled, would it surprise anyone if first divine assistance must be implored with prayers, so that one wishes to add strength and confidence in order to confess his name, even to the point of death? But more of that after everything has been tested.

§5. The godly who survived gales and deeps directed their ships into a given port instead of another. When Saul was treacherous toward David and sought him daily both on his own and through others so that he might be slain (1 Sam. 21:1, 22:1, 27:1), David saved his life by departing to foreign nations like a wanderer and by hiding himself in mountains, forests, and caverns (2 Sam. 15:14). And did he not also withdraw himself from Absalom's fury? After the slaughter of Stephen, all of the faithful, with the apostles alone exempted (Acts 8:1), stole away by flight. Those who are celebrated in the Epistle to the Hebrews with such praises and testimonies that it would be said that the world was unworthy of their company, are said to have wandered around in the skins of sheep and goats, and that they lived in deserts, mountains, caves, and hollows of the ground.[11] And

---

11. Heb. 11:32-38

for what other reason than that they did not want to give themselves into the hands and evil threats of tyrants? In the time after Christ ascended, persecution grew hot from all sides, and the flock of the faithful was miserably rent to pieces and mangled for three hundred years. Up to the time of Constantine they wandered from place to place, and the faithful were frequently compelled to retreat to safer places, as Eusebius mentions in his *Ecclesiastical History*.[12] And thus they decreed consideration both for divine glory and for their safety. Meanwhile, several who seem to themselves quite strong, forgetting the danger, and who wanted to experience the last things, failed under the burden and offered incense on the altars to idols. In doing so they caused scandal to the church and their consciences and gave an opportunity to Novatus to cause a schism, in which he disputed the full admission of them to the Eucharist. How different it would have been if, when they should have considered their own weakness, they would have turned aside for a short time? Very many people from our own country did just that in the times of Mary. And many in our age, in France and the Netherlands, have fled in great number from those savage tempests at home. As ours fled into other parts of the world, so they have fled to our England for some asylum. And that in a reasonable and godly manner. Indeed thus far no one is testing the Lord, who has granted them liberty to depart. Surely he wanted us, wonderfully, to minister help to them in their straits, and to free them from their vexations, rather than to yield to the constancy of their suffering and dying, even though he offered other means of departing, which must not be rashly and rigorously repudiated.

§6. Therefore, the opinion of Tertullian in his book, *On flight in persecution*,[13] if not exploded, due to the honor of such a great man, nevertheless must be rejected and repudiated in that he taught one must stand alone, confess, and that to the point of death, and one must never turn back. Christians, at that time severely afflicted, withdrew themselves from imminent dangers only by turning aside or by secretly fleeing to their friends, and some of them bought their peace by paying their own money, that is, by paying more than the tribute and excise tax to the emperor's purse. Thus they placated the prefects and proconsuls, not so much by their secret gifts and bribes as by an open registration; they relied on that testimony of

---

12. Eusebius, *Ecclesiastical History*, bk. 6, §35.
13. Cf. Tertullian, *De Fuga in Persecutione*; idem, *On Flight in Persecution* in ANF 4:116–25.

the Savior, "Make for yourselves friends from mammon" (Luke 16:9). As should not be done for any reason, Tertullian disapproves of this, alleging that in no circumstance may someone flee. Interpreting that statement of Christ, "when they will have persecuted you in one city, flee to another" (Mark 10:23), as a temporary commandment given for the apostles and not for others, he says "I say it was only for the apostles because, with them slain, the gospel would not be preached, but would be thoroughly extinguished." Thus he concludes it must not be fled. But it is a weak foundation on which his whole structure depends, because in fact nothing touches us except with God disposing it, and there is neither any persecution except from his special omnipotent will nor any apart from his good pleasure. But he certainly confesses nothing can be done except with God willing. But who knows the time when God wills that a life will be taken away? He permits an enemy to pursue, and for you to flee. In both his glory will be preeminent. He leads the same person into temptation, and frees them from it. He allows evil to be intended, and he delivers from evil. The one who wills this to happen also prolongs your life and also supplies the means of doing so through withdrawal. Then David wrongly withdrew himself from Saul's sight, if he ought not to have shunned that treachery, even though these things could not be intended apart from God willing. Therefore, Jerome thinks that Tertullian's book was written specifically against the Church, just as others also think of it;[14] and therefore Tertullian's opinion should be discarded. We do not doubt that it is licit for a layman to remove himself, if done, not by a reckless motion, but with a sober and prudent conscience. And when the divine Spirit, who presides over even the thoughts of his servants, will order this one's death to be stayed and that one to be killed instead when this one was considered, if affairs and circumstances bear out, it must be addressed with a confident heart.

§7. What contrary arguments brought forward are more trivial than those which delay the course of progressing to more difficult ones. The one who desires to read more should consult Peter Martyr in his theological epistles, for both what has been cited as opposed and what has been learnedly refuted.[15] Meanwhile I add nothing besides the judgment of the purer

---

14. *De Scriptoribus Ecclesiasticis*: This work is sometimes entitled Jerome, *De viribus illustribus* in PL 23:663–4 idem, *Lives of Illustrious Men* in NPNF2 3:373.

15. See Classis Tertia, Loc. XII "De Cruce et Afflictionibus perferendis, ubi etiam de fuga et exilio" in Peter Martyr Vermigli, *Loci Communes*, (Zurich: Christopher Froschouer, 1580), fols. 344v–348v.

and more ancient church on this matter. Hear Clement of Alexandria, "If he who kills a man of God sins against God, he also who presents himself before the judgement seat becomes guilty of his death. And such is also the case with one who does not avoid persecution, but out of daring presents himself for capture."[16] Hear Origen on John:

> It is certainly right, if one should fall into a struggle for confessing Christ, not to shun the confession nor to hesitate to encounter death for the truth. But no less than this, it is right that one does not give an occasion to such and so great a temptation, but in every way to shun it; not only because the outcome of such a great matter is uncertain to us, but also so that we might not become the occasion for those who have at least not yet become guilty of having shed our blood to become greater sinners and more ungodly.[17]

Hear Cyprian, who, although he suffered the palm of the martyr later,[18] nevertheless persuaded the people of flight in such a way that he considered them martyrs for Christ if they were taken among those about to die by famine, the teeth of beasts, butchers, or events of this sort. These are his words, "He is not alone to whom Christ is his companion in flight; he is not alone who, serving the temple of God wherever he will be, is not without God. And if a robber has overwhelmed a fugitive in solitude or in the mountains, if he is attacked by a beast, afflicted by hunger, thirst, or cold, or when storms have submerged him traveling by sea on a precipitous journey, Christ everywhere looks upon his soldier who fights."[19] So the ancients, and recent theologians, everywhere and absolutely thought that flight was not interdicted for the Christian.

§8. But regarding the pastor of the congregation and the herald of the Gospel, from his special office and calling there is another determination: whether in fact he must render care not only for his own body but for the

---

16. Clement of Alexandria, *Stromata, or Miscellanies*, bk. 4, ch. 10 in *ANF* 2:423.
17. Origen, *Super Ioannem*, 28.18 in *PG* 14:727–28; Origen, *Commentary on the Gospel according to John, Books 13–32*, trans. R. Heine in The Fathers of the Church Series (Washington D.C.: CUA Press, 1993), 28:193–4; cf. Origen, *Comm. Matth.*, 10.23 in *PG* 3:897.
18. The palm branch, signifying victory, peace, and eternal life, became associated in the Christian tradition with the triumph of the spirit over the flesh (cf. Rev. 7:9).
19. *Cypriani lib. 4 Epist. ad Thybaritas*: see "58 Cyprian to the People of Thibaris" in Cyprian, *Letters (1–81)*, trans. R. B. Donna, in *The Fathers of the Church* series (Washington, D.C.: The Catholic University of America Press, Inc., 1964, 1981), 165–6.

souls of others. Upon his mouth the people depend like an infant upon its mother's breast. And in his counsel, assistance, and example he must be steadfast, and remain in his confession. And as the Roman bishop Leo said at some point, "Who would steer the ship among the waves of the sea if the helmsman should leave? Who will guard the sheep from the treachery of the wolves if the care of the shepherd is not vigilant? And finally, who will withstand the brigands and thieves if the lookouts leave their post due for a little rest and love of quiet?"[20] A person to teach and to comfort is a perpetual need for the people; how much more so then when with each day new crises arise, and there is never any chance for any tranquility? It is pernicious for a captain to desert the ship in the midst of calm—how much more in high seas? What a fearful and dreadful thing it is if those languishing without infant baptism, without the eucharistic sacrament, or without the pardon for the excommunicant should depart from the living! What great scandals to be borne by the weak! Indeed, how much of your congregation will begin to wander from the truth of the Gospel and its teaching, which you have taught with certainty, if your congregation should see you, who have taken flight, not willing to persevere and guard it? What else will they think is licit for you, for the congregation, and for themselves? You then, with your feet and silence, in a kind of way, have denied Christ; others will deny with their tongue and hand, by recalling the opinion and then subscribing to the conceived words of enemies. Therefore, one must take heed, lest by his own example the minister plunges the souls of the weak into perpetual ruin; lest Christ himself, the chief shepherd, require their blood from him with a severe examination.[21] By confessing and being confident, the tardiness of others must be cast out, souls be stirred up, and spirits be raised up, whereby the glory of the revered Christ would more fully shine. With the leader advancing, the soldiers follow. With a bold ram, the rest of the flock follows. The people will not fear, either to seal the truth of the Savior with their own blood or to endure a fiery test, when they will look upon their priest immolated on the altar of suffering. Therefore it is incumbent upon him, due to his peculiar office, what is not incumbent upon others.

§9. There cannot be encountered one who would define and determine this offering as a wiser, more faithful, truer, and more just judge than Christ

---

20. *Leo Papa Epistola 70 in conciliis*: Leo, Ep. 157 in *PL* 54:1201.
21. Gk. ἀρχιποίμην

our Redeemer. Christ demonstrates the difference between a good shepherd and a hired hand. He teaches from his own example what a good shepherd is: one who lays down his life for his sheep, who intervenes and interposes himself between them and arising dangers, and who by his own life purchases their safety. "A hireling," he says, "and one who is not the shepherd, and one who does not own the sheep, sees the wolf coming and abandons the sheep and flees, and then the wolf ravages and scatters the flock" (John 10:11). Behold, it is none other than a mercenary who deserts their flock when the destroyer rushes upon them. And under the name of mercenary is meant an unfaithful steward, a negligent traitor, one unworthy to be trusted with such a great care. How many steps—or miles rather—of difference do we think there are between a faithful steward and an unfaithful one? Hence, at some point Novatus turned to this vice because, when he was a presbyter (as Eusebius refers to Cornelius the Roman bishop), in the face of a storm of persecution and fury that approached church, not only did he entirely desert the common people who were then left behind destitute and mired in dangers, but also he entirely deserted his calling by renouncing the priesthood and by denying the office of a presbyter.[22] At that time he was a hireling and deserter of the flock, just as afterwards he was a heretic. He ought rather to have expressed that love and affection towards believers, of which kind the apostle John mentioned, "By this we know the love of God, because he laid down his life for us; therefore we ought to lay down our lives for the brethren" (1 John 3:16). So that the prerogative of dying would not seem to concern Christ alone, who is described as the Good Shepherd, it adds, "we ought to lay down our lives for the brethren." Because it is also not difficult to gather from other words of Christ; indeed when he had said, "greater love has no one than this, that someone would lay down his life for his friends" (John 15:13), he immediately subjoins, "you will be my friend, if you shall do what I command to you," as if to remind them that blood must be shed for the safety of the flock, if necessity should require.

§10. Those who thrived in the primeval Church, the holy priests and bishops, both retained it [Christ's reminder] in their memory and rendered it in their passion. So then Peter was fixed to a cross upside down.[23] James and Paul were killed with the sword (Acts 12:2).[24] There was not nearly any

---

22. Eusebius, *Eccl. Hist.* bk. 6, ch. 43 §11 in *NPNF2* 1:289.
23. Lat. *calcibus in coelum obversis*: Eusebius, bk. 3 ch. 1 §2 in *NPNF2* 1:132–3.
24. Ibid., bk. 2 ch. 24 in *NPNF2* 1:128.

one of the apostles who did not suffer a violent and bloody death. They most earnestly desired to lay down their life for their brethren,[25] for which reason a great number of the Christians became seed, for "the blood of the martyrs is the seed of the Gospel." So it happened that Ignatius, who—if anyone were most desirous of another martyr—both from love of Christ and confirmation of the brethren, condemned the cross, flame, the teeth of beasts, and the rack.[26] That most godly man, Polycarp, who was not ashamed to bear witness to the truth of the Gospel before a tyrant, underwent similar sufferings. So Justin Martyr, and thus the refined Cyprian. Being the most faithful sort of pastors, they had more care for their flocks than for themselves. Our most recent times were not unfruitful, sterile, or lacking good men either. There were many very learned, holy, and constant men who lost their life under Gardner and Bonner, and who did not abandon their congregations until the point of death. Indeed, the most renowned bishops—Ridley, Latimer, Hooper, Ferrarius, and archbishop Cranmer—gave their bodies to the flames, so that they demonstrated from the heart that they loved their own country and those who believe in Christ. When many ways to flee had been offered, when exhortations were repeated, so that even at last after their capture they could have removed themselves, they did not want to desert their people like mercenaries; but esteeming their death as profitable, provided that they would light the way for other weaker believers in the way of salvation, they steadfastly suffered the cruelest things. These all were certainly considered foolish and unwise in the highest degree—the apostles, the fathers, bishops, ministers—if with the obedience to Christ and care owed to the congregation, they took to flight. But they knew that staying and remaining was their office. If this should seem like a hard opinion, it is Christ's viewpoint. Just as he commanded everyone to be circumspect and consider whether they wanted to leave behind friends, father, mother, wife, indeed even life itself for Christ (Luke 14:26); so, undoubtedly, he reminds ministers of the gospel that with great judgment and careful consideration they should enter into this charge. Does not the one who will build a house sit and begin to reason whether he has enough to finish? And these things follow.

§11. But there are not lacking those who want to lower their sail out of timidity, and who would cite the reasoning and examples of faithful

---

25. Ibid., bk. 2, ch.1 §8. in *NPNF2* 1:104.
26. Ibid., bk. 3, ch. 30 in *NPNF2* 1:161–2.

people who did likewise. The weakness of our flesh is such that we could rightly fear that, overcome with torments, we would succumb in the midst of temptations. Therefore, one is ready to flee away rather than bring infamy to one's religion and blasphemy to the divine name. But at the same time see that you who teach others to put Christ first—to despise friends, parents, spouses, possessions, the world, indeed even blood itself, and to vilify the use of this light and the delights of the present age—see that you should prefer the knowledge of the Savior. You rightly know that all things must be abandoned for Christ. Therefore, although the flesh may seem weak and impotent, if the Lord would be solicitous to us by prayer and invocation, he may bless those who, due to their circumstances, are bound to patience; and he will administer strength, so that those things which are grave will seem trivial; and in the midst of the flames he will send down dew, by which they could be revived in the difficulties and tortures which affect their bodies. Or if he does not will at this point to give such great constancy, he will give other occasions of comfort, either by softening the hearts of the persecutors, or by delaying the time until they will be snatched from the very jaws themselves. God is faithful and will not ever tempt or place a burden on someone beyond what they can bear. He knows exactly our ability, and what we are strong enough to sustain, and what we are not. Therefore, he deals with us in a gentle and friendly way with his singular clemency and prudence, so that we may acknowledge him in the direst straits. If, secondarily, it happens that one flees today but returns later, when it will be more necessary, then Christ will be present again. But beware lest it would present an opportunity for the Lord in which he defends his truth. Now the Lord summons and must be obeyed. Evil must not be done in order that good would follow. Now the lion roars and growls, now therefore it is necessary for a guardian to be present. Now the enemy fights and so the warrior must oppose him, like a wall for the house of the Lord.

§12. But is it also licit for us since it is licit for others? Holy men in the Scriptures (indeed the Savior himself) frequently fled, yet not so that they would become deserters of his flock. Moses fled from Pharaoh (Ex. 2:15); Elijah from Jezebel (1 Kgs. 19:3), Uriah the prophet was sought by king Jehoiakim and fled to Egypt (Jer. 26:21). And those prophets were the watchmen of Israel. Did not Christ go down to Egypt with Joseph and Mary as an infant (Matt. 2:13–15)? Afterwards when the greatest storm threatened so that he would soon be stoned, did he not withdraw from the middle of the crowd and avoid the sight of the furious multitude (John 8:59)? And whose footsteps must be followed besides Christ's, our leader and Lord? Indeed, he enjoined them with a special command to the apostles, so that when people persecute them in one city they might flee to another (Matt. 10:23). Afterwards the benefit of that command or tolerance they enjoyed. But is whatever can be held clearer or more undebatable than what Paul did, who in that very circumstance which this passage discusses, was lowered down in a basket by a rope, and thus by fleeing saved his life (Acts. 9:21)? Bishop Athanasius of Alexandria also, when Emperor Constantius II himself was searching for him to punish him either with chains or death, by running away at various times, withdrew by fleeing, hiding himself from the madness and tyranny of his pursuers.[27] And when certain persons of his enemies—chiefly Arians—turned their plots toward him, because by hiding he did not fear the divine will, he wrote his *Apology* or defense in favor of his flight in which he abundantly demonstrated that he had use of that same liberty which the Scriptures granted and the deeds of the saints confirm. So, seeming to be surrounded by so great a crowd of witnesses of the prophets, apostles, the bishop Athanasius, and Christ our redeemer, who thinks that flight is granted to a minister and a pastor?

§13. But by the circumstances of those actions, if we want to handle them as carefully as is fitting, there will be no hindrance to determining as we have above that one must not flee. First, therefore, regarding the departure of Moses: that is not something we should fear, since he was not yet endowed with a prophetic spirit when he first departed from Pharaoh. In fact, the Lord had stated that by his hand, after miracles were to be performed of which there has not been any equal since, Moses was thoroughly taught with a special inspiration so that he may prophesy and withdraw himself. This evidently touches upon Elijah, for with an express edict of an angel he was commanded to make a forty-day journey (1 Kgs. 19:5). Other things were done that are preserved [in Scripture] whereby the Lord willed to preserve Elijah. And the decree of the Most High was that he would not die a death, but would be brought to heaven in a fiery chariot. So too with Christ who, when an infant, had to undergo many things before the time had come for teaching, healing, and performing miracles, whereupon he

---

27. *Socrat. Hist. Eccl.* 13 : See Socrates Scholasticus, *Historia Ecclesiastica*, bk. 2, ch. 11 in *NPNF2* 2:40–1.

would be offered up on the altar of the cross; for his hour had not yet come. And from the power of the divinity, before whose eyes all things past and future are open, this was known as thoroughly as possible. Moreover, all these have most brazenly invited these dangers on their own heads when the occasion of standing and remaining rushes upon them. Did not Moses intrepidly go to Pharaoh each day, to declare in his presence the thoughts of his heart (Ex. 5:1)? Did not Elijah, who was known on sight, reproach Ahab of his idolatry and impiety to his face? So also Christ publicly rebuked the scribes and Pharisees, taught in the temple, and opposed Jerusalem, and that nearly every day; and at last he stood for trial, was arrested, accused, beaten, and crucified, being subject to the harshest judgment of death. Therefore, when our times have nothing comparable to these, one must not take to flight from such things but steadfastly remain. For the fear of death did not oppress them, nor did the face of their enemies terrify them, whom they often went before to oppose. And they were also preserved in other greater tests and exercises, and that was revealed by God from his certain foreknowledge, none of which is common to us. And if we turn our backs, languishing and trembling before the fear of death, who would be persuaded that greater things remain for us in the hereafter? We cannot offer more illustrious service to God than, in the storms of persecutions, to show ourselves immoveable and immutable. And we who once have been shackled in leg irons may often and perhaps always be shackled. And if it happens that there might be greater hardships and difficulties to be endured, how will that [counsel] occur? From what oracle or divine speech? None at all. Therefore, [that one must flee] is a carnal imagination, not a suggestion of the divine spirit and counsel; human infirmity, not Christian prudence.

§14. Because the apostles fled, and that with the Savior commanding, it might appear to be similar with us as with them; but in fact it is nowhere close. For the apostles at that time were not appointed to any certain congregation in order that they might preach the Gospel everywhere. By them he grew the grainfields. The increase of the word of God was not expected in one city more than another, so Christ did not restrict them to Jerusalem, Nazareth, Cana, or Capernaum; but rather, when in Judea, or in Galilee, or in the Decapolis, they went from village to village and town to town, sowing the seed of the kingdom. The province of the apostles was similar after the ascension of Christ, who generally taught proclaiming to the Gentiles to such an extent that the care of *all* the churches was weighing upon Paul (2 Cor. 11:28). Therefore, the goal and end of their calling was not in vain or void when they went from place to place; everywhere they labored to gather believers into one. Indeed, it must be believed regarding the labor, that the Lord sometimes stirred up the crowds and storms, so that leaving from one region they might teach godliness in another. But after the preaching of God was spread, church polity was established in a different way. In every congregation, all presbyters had to be ordained by Titus (Tit. 1:5), and in certain assemblies their own particular pastors were designated in the apostolic custom (Acts 14:23), which continues in use today. Now since it has been established, it is known that those [ordained] are entrusted with both feeding and instructing us. This belongs to your rule, that each and every one ought to be diligent in their station and watch-post. So then diocese and parishes are distinguished by their own certain limits and boundaries and in Christian states[28] where these ought to be established for each [minister], and this is understood in holy matters. And among those, the bishop in his province and the minister among his people are engaged in the office commended by Christ. Upon his mouth souls depend, and the minister's mouth depends upon God; therefore each shares his nourishment. Who will lighten their burdens, if in the greatest crisis their patron and father departs? God, the greatest *paterfamilias*, has committed his children to a minister, and will demand them back from him. Therefore, when a wolf or tyrant arrives, a minister by no means must flee. The one who is free to exercise his own choice is one who is not bound to certain persons; he may depart if he wills since he does not abandon his station. I think it is this very point why, in the case of our country after the happy times of Edward VI, of blessed memory, very many bishops and ministers ultimately experienced the ravages of fire and sword; namely, they were certain pastors of certain flocks. But others, especially in the universities of Oxford and Cambridge, left to parts across the sea. God had not fixed them to any people before whom they would go in or out but, like the sons of the prophets in the schools of the prophets, they were freely supported, so that when God might call they would be ready. Because they were fellows of colleges, they were not involved in pastoral care; the Lord had them in mind so that by fleeing they might

---

28. Lat. *Rebuspublicis Christianis*

serve as a seedbed[29] for the English Church in more tranquil times. But this has no bearing on the rest who are so bound, just as there is no difference with the apostles and with Christ, who did not preside over some specific place, and as Paul demonstrated when he left Damascus lowered in a basket.

§15. But there is also another point, because in the person of Paul an exception is opened. The persecution, which arose in Damascus, was not yet against all Christ's faithful or instituted against all pastors but was maliciously focused upon Paul; against him and his head only, and he would smart for it, since he had so forcefully proclaimed Christ. Therefore, those bloodthirsty men raved against him and desired to plot against his life. The rest were living safely enough and sound, and Ananias stood firm in Damascus, who, because he had been endowed with such grace as to comfort Saul and was able to heal him, undoubtedly could minister the Word in season to those who remained who professed Christ. But they could also preside over other disciples, so that by Paul's departure the church would not lack a needed minister. Although perhaps they did not teach, as the previous one did, with such ability, eloquence, or power; nevertheless they did teach. Therefore, because that was a specific persecution and personal to someone, that person could flee. This point must be observed regarding Uriah in retreating to Egypt so that he might shun the fury of King Jehoiakim. In fact, Jeremiah the prophet remained in Jerusalem at that time and, according to the need of the time, made known the divine will to the king and the people. And the case of Athanasius was no different, for whom such great hatred was kindled by the Arians with Constantius II that they plotted against his life. Just as when the rest of the priests remained at Constantinople after John Chrysostom alone—and him only—was sent into exile,[30] and every madness was brought out against him; so the rest of the clerics in Alexandria remained when Athanasius alone had churned the stomach of the emperor. It is evident from this: once, when he was about to preach at the church, it was surrounded by soldiers who intended to arrest the bishop, but the deacons surrounded him and compelled the

---

29. Lat. *Seminarium*: lit. "a seedbed" or nursery held in reserve for the sake of replanting another crop. Abbot seems to be referring to the phenomenon of English exile congregations in the Netherlands, Geneva, and the German Palatinate during the reign of Queen Mary I (r. 1553–58).

30. Sozomen, *Ecclesiastical History*, bk. 8, ch. 27 in *NPNF2* 2:416.

unwilling and reluctant [bishop] to withdraw, although he rather had it in mind to tarry in the church. There were also others of the clergy who so surrounded him while he was departing that, as if God blinded the eyes of his enemies, he was not recognized by the soldiers among the others.[31] Therefore, because the practice of the sacraments and sermons as well as the service of godliness did not depart with him, it was licit for Athansius to flee. Therefore it is also licit for pastors in our time to flee, if there is not a general but a specific persecution, and there would remain those who are installed [in the office].

§16. The judgment of Augustine regarding the departure of Athanasius and of others is the godliest and most solid in his Epistle to Honoratus, which is another source one may consult if anyone wants to know more on these things. In fact, there, from his design, the most learned father treats the present question and asserts that the necessary ministry of the church in no way must be abandoned under danger to one's soul. "Far be it," he says, "that this great ship of ours should slacken" (that is, that the church should become so worthless) "that the sailors, and especially its helmsman, must abandon it in trials, even if one could escape by leaping into a rowboat or by swimming."[32] He also sets forth the misery of a congregation so abandoned and widowed by the name of mercenary, and of the charge of what tends toward the mercenary, that these should terrify a pastor who is ready to flee. Yet in a personal persecution, of which sort one calls the persecution of Athanasius, he affirms that it is licit to retreat when others are present to function as supply. Such as when there might be a crazed leader who was either against all the pious or all ministers, then one must employ prudence and faithfulness. If the people should perish,

---

31. Cf. Athanasius, *Apologia de Fuga* in *NPNF2* 4:255–65; here, *NPNF2* 4:263–4: "But the commander having now made a forcible entry, and the soldiers having surrounded the sanctuary for the purpose of arresting us, the clergy and those of the laity who were still there, cried out, and demanded that we too should withdraw. But I refused, declaring that I would not do so, until they had retired one and all. Accordingly I stood up, and having requested prayer, I then made my request of them, that all should depart before me, saying that it was better that my safety should be endangered, than that any of them should be harmed. So when the greater part had gone forth, and the rest were following, the monks who were there with us and certain of the clergy came up and dragged us away. And thus—truth is my witness—while some of the soldiers stood about the sanctuary, and others were patrolling around the church, we passed through them, under the Lord's guidance, and with His protection we withdrew without notice, greatly glorifying God that we had not betrayed the people, but had first sent them away, and then had been able to save ourselves, and to escape the hands of them that sought us."

32. *Augustin. Epistola 180 ad Honoratum*: See Augustine, *Epistle to Honoratus* CCXXVIII in *NPNF1* 1:577–81.

so also should the priest offer up himself, like a leader to heaven. But if all the people flee so that there are none remaining to whom teaching is necessary, then also the minister may depart. But if there would be peace among the laity, the priest should take heed in what way he retires, because these would be abandoned without a leader, and among some of them there are hiding places where one might hide for the sake of God's promise. When a tyrant rages against pastors only, if there are very many and numerous ministers found in the same flock, they ought to meet amongst themselves to decide who must remain so that they may shine forth before the people, and then the rest must depart so that they might be set aside as a seedbed for the church. Yet, lest someone be compelled to remain that is unwilling, or another, being exceedingly presumptuous, chooses to remain out of his own strength, the matter should be decided by lots or the casting of lots.

Nothing is more learned, nothing more holy, nothing more prudent than Augustine here, which since that time the church regards as the orthodox position, as far as I know. But we also add a small addendum. As a summary, which embraces everything that has been said, as it is licit for a layman to flee in persecution, so also for a woman or a youth, because they will not render an account for other souls. But a minister must be expected to remain if he were to have a pastoral care, and against his own person there is not instituted a persecution when there are many pastors. But if this be so, then he can transfer the common care to the rest of the ministers and leave for a time. Thus far, the first issue.

§17. At the beginning I had promised that I would add something, due to the similarity of the argument, regarding a ravaging plague. The substance of the matter, although it is not so directly related to our passage, could be resolved from the Pauline example; nevertheless from Christ's sermon in John 10:12 it could be resolved more directly, where under the name of "wolf" is understood to be everything dangerous and devastating. To speak briefly here: just as there were those who argued that no Christian can flee in a persecution—among whom was Tertullian, as is clear above—so a great number of people, as well as not a few in the capital city of our kingdom, but especially those of an inferior sort, stubbornly affirm that a Christian must not depart from a prowling pestilence. I say this from experience. And they assign this reason—perhaps a somewhat fine-looking one for themselves: that a disease and contagion is a divine visitation, from which it is illicit for any person to withdraw. And because for every person their own lifetime is assigned, with the result that in no way can it be lengthened or shortened, so neither can [a disease] be contracted, averted, or anticipated. But surely how futile these points are should be prudently inspected. For if something is illicit for me to do according to my choosing—because certain times of dying are fixed in advance, and there is a period of life, and the hour of expiration would not come sooner, then I would die regardless—what next? Should I toss myself into the sea, or leap headlong off a cliff, or as Satan had suggested to Christ (Matt. 4:6), should I hurl myself from the pinnacle of the temple? The Savior shows that this is to tempt the Lord, which is precisely forbidden (Matt. 4:7). The Most High God, just as he has ordained for us limits, so he has ordained means, and these we must in every way diligently seek out. The means of preserving life are for me to eat, to sleep, and to retreat from ills and imminent dangers; and it is necessary to do these things. But what pertains to a divine visitation certainly shall be the rod of God, and if it were to strike you, it must be patiently born. But what is not necessary you shall not bring upon yourself recklessly, so that it seems you laid violent hands upon yourself and thus are guilty of homicide. God counts not only pestilence and disease in the number of his scourges—and among the harshest ones at that—but also the sword, famine, the teeth of harmful beasts, and other things that are plainly of the same sort (Deut. 28:59–61, Ezek. 14:21). Why then, in those cases, do you not embrace the chastisement of God equally as you do in the case of plague? When Saul hurled his spear at David and thought to peg him to the wall (1 Sam. 19:10), why ever did David flee? When a great famine oppressed Jacob and the patriarchs, why, for the sake of grain, did Jacob send them down to Egypt and not rather perish from fasting? Because it was a divine chastisement? Surely such people behave more piously and wisely than Jacob and David ever did.

§18. Everyone must flee opportunities to perish. It is a specific command (Ex. 20:13) regarding shunning murder; and if of a foreigner, certainly of ourselves, if in fact charity begins from ourselves, and others must be loved no differently that we do ourselves (Matt. 22:39). If therefore it is not licit for us in any way to inflict a death, then neither is it also to enter upon a path that leads to death, nor to approach the means which are joined to it. And as that is true in other cases, so it is in the case of plague, which is certainly a slayer (Ps. 21:6, 2 Sam. 14:15), and destroys so very quickly by the thousands. Again, God even threatened all his plagues, both terrible and to be feared, and therefore to be avoided body and soul. Among these is pestilence. Additionally, because God had in view the well-being of his people, he abundantly treated of leprosy in the law: that it must be recognized, how it is to be discerned, and in what respects to care for it. But he also wanted the leprous to be distinguished in their clothing and to cry out, "I am unclean, I am unclean!" (Lev. 15:45). And he commanded them to live outside the camp or city, separately and apart (Lev. 15:46, Num. 5:2) so that they would not infect others with their fetid contamination. If God did not want his people defiled with a lesser disease which truly infects but does not slay like the plague does, how much more does he want us to depart quickly from one of the most formidable contagions? The Turks, then, do that when they rush into pestilential and contagious places without distinction; but Christians check themselves. Nor should troublesome people cause quarrels with their complaining about their brethren who withdraw themselves, their children, and their family for necessary times. God has granted to them opportunity for the issue; they may employ means in good conscience. But even in their absence let them not abandon their languishing and now miserable brethren, but let them help, guide, and comfort them with counsel, aid, and with whatever means they can. This is the sympathy and compassion of Christians.

§19. But regarding the minister of the Gospel and pastor of a congregation, I think differently. And the reasons considered above regarding their people's souls entrusted to their care, from which one should not depart in persecution, also have place here. If he should withdraw into flight in a raging pestilence, who will supply the necessary duties of the church? Who will preach a sermon to the well? Who will share comfort with the sick? Indeed, there are countless things which call him to daily use and cannot be rightly transacted if the spiritual leader who applies that counsel is absent. Therefore, I believe that a priest (that is, the pastor of a congregation), lest he become a mercenary, must not depart from his particular calling—a calling which takes away the liberty that is granted and permitted to others. Yet because in a private and secret death the divine glory is not so manifest as in an open martyrdom, for the sake of a good conscience, and since there are many duties that must be rendered to the whole congregation and equally even to the sick, I do not think there is a necessity incumbent upon a minister to enter into the dwellings and bedchambers of the sick, because that cannot be done without manifest danger to life. Therefore the middle way must be taken, so that the minister should neither flee nor intermix himself with contagion with excessive confidence. Where occasion permits exhortation in writing, and preaching by shouting from a distance; by these, and deliberating on the good of others and that even excessively, he would avoid bringing evils upon himself. But if some extraordinary cause, very evidently working for the divine glory or for conspicuous usefulness of the Church, forcefully urges that he should be present to someone, I do not dare to remove his ability to do so; but only after he is moved by earnest and heart-felt prayer and the impulse of his conscience—and that prudently, soberly, and with the highest amount of judgment (in fact I attribute much to the sober impulse of a prudent man; and the minister of the Gospel must be the most prudent kind). But just as medical doctors fortify themselves in such great tempests with fumigations, vapors, and medicines, so a minister may use a cure of the body as much as he can. But by praying humbly, let him deny any presumptuous arrogance before the Almighty, and let him entrust his soul to God for any outcome. Regarding the pastor's assembling the people in churches when the plague prowls about—so that it must be worthily feared that by coming together they would increase the languor and infection amongst themselves even more—I will prescribe nothing. But the circumstances of assembling or remaining in private homes, I leave to the circumspect and vigilant judgment of the magistrate, minister, and to the godly in the congregation to whom such care [for the congregation] belongs, so that all things are conducted in a holy, friendly, prudent way with the least amount of inconvenience possible. Nor must anyone here be either wise beyond sobriety or stubborn beyond modesty, but humbly seek advice in common. Thus you have the judgment of my heart on flight, first in persecution and then in plague.

O Eternal God, turn aside these evils from us and our church, and grant favor that throughout all ages until the coming of your son that our England peacefully embraces the Gospel to the glory of your son, to whom with you and with the Holy Spirit be honor and immortality forever. Amen.

11

A Letter to my Mother

INTRODUCTION

The Great Plague of London (1665–1666) was the last major outbreak of the bubonic plague to occur in England. It is estimated that in just eighteen months the plague killed 100,000 people, almost a quarter of London's population. At the time John Rawlet (b. 1642) was serving as the tutor and chaplain in the house of John Pynsent, the protonotary of the court of common pleas in London, and laboring under the near certainty that he would at any moment contract the deadly virus (not an unreasonable fear given the circumstances). This apprehension of dying from the plague compelled Rawlet to write his mother the consolatory letter reprinted here. Thankfully, Rawlet's life was spared and the letter, never sent, was discovered a half-century later.

Rawlet is by no means a major figure in church history and the details of his life are, by comparison with others featured in this volume, quite sparse. He was baptized at St. Editha's church in Tamworth on March 27, 1642. His father died in the civil war the following year, and he was provided with what he describes as a "pious education" from his mother. Rawlet began studies at Pembroke College, Cambridge but did not finish due to financial hardships and, perhaps, reasons of conscience. After London, Rawlet ministered at Hulcote in Bedfordshire. He then served as curate first of Dunton in Buckinghamshire, and then at Wigan in Lancashire. In 1673 he became minister of St. Stephen's in Kirkby Stephen, Westmorland, and in 1679 was appointed to the lectureship of St. Nicholas in Newcastle upon Tyne.

A few years after this last appointment, Rawlet was assigned to the chapel of St. Anne's in Sandgate, a depressed area of Newcastle, and he was given responsibility of instructing and catechizing the children. This Rawlet apparently did to great effect with the result that he became much loved and admired by the people he served, and his biographer could say of him that "he may be justly thought, to have been the happy instrument of gaining more souls to God, by his plain, pathetic [i.e., sensitive], and practical preaching, and by an uncommon exemplariness in life and conversation, than most others in the days he lived in."[1] Unsurprisingly, Rawlet's publications are notable for their ability to present complex theological issues with a simplicity and clarity appropriate to their design to evangelize and to minister to the poor and uneducated. These include *A Treatise of Sacramental Covenanting with Christ* (1667); *An Explication of the Creed, the Ten Commandments, and the Lord's Prayer* (1672); *A Dialogue betwixt Two Protestants, in Answer to a Popish Catechism* (1685); and *The Christian Monitor* (1686).

Rawlet's letter to his mother is of particular interest because it sets on display the faith and fortitude of an ordinary Christian minister as he faces the prospect of an illness which would almost certainly result in a painful and premature death. The reader is struck by the fact that its author seems far less concerned about the danger of contracting the plague, or about securing the available means of preserving his life, than he is about his mother's spiritual wellbeing in the aftermath of his death. Rawlet states his purpose at the outset: "to beseech you with all earnestness not to be immoderately afflicted with the providence of our heavenly Father in my removal out of this world."

To this end, he reminds his mother of several gospel truths and commends to her certain points for reflection in her grief. First, he encourages his mother to remember that God's hard providences "proceed from infinite wisdom and goodness." Second, that God is himself the believer's greatest portion and delight; and though she may suffer loss, he writes, "you have God to direct, quicken, and comfort you; and God has his choice of means whereby to convey these benefits to you; so that in this regard, at the most there is but a bucket broke, but you still have the fountain." Third, Rawlet reminds his mother that even God's beloved children are not exempt from death, and that death is the necessary doorway to eternal life. To this point, he asks rhetorically, "Yea, did not our Lord himself for our sakes tread this way before us? And that not only to make satisfaction for us, but to perfume the grave, and by his example to render death less

---

1. Thomas Bray, 'A brief account of the life of the Reverend Mr John Rawlet,' in G. Carleton and T. Bray, *Two select and exemplary lives, of two parochial ministers* (W. Roberts, 1728)

terrible? And shall we grudge that ourselves or friends go any way which Christ has gone before us?" Fourth, he says that the loss of him would be used to her advantage in allowing her to "discover [her] own heart," that is, to have greater insight into the ultimate source of her happiness and hope.

Importantly, Rawlet never proscribes the mourning, grief, sadness, or tears that naturally attend the loss of a loved one. But at every point he insists that his mother's grief be mixed with gratitude to God for the many years they have had together, and her sorrow be mixed with joy in the knowledge that they will one day see each other again in an estate so glorious and everlasting that it is, at present, incomprehensible to the human mind. Recalling the words of his late father, Rawlet writes, "Remember the expression of my dear, though unknown father, with whom I hope shortly to meet in heaven, in his last letter you ever received from him, that he was gone but a little before, and shortly you will follow after. What a little while will it be before we whose ways may now part, shall all meet at our journey's end, ever in the presence of the great *Jehovah*, the bosom of our dear Lord Jesus?"

In addition to a minister of the Church of England, theologian, and author, readers will not be surprised to learn that Rawlet was a minor poet. His letter not only overflows with robust theology, practically and powerfully applied, but it does so in a prose that often borders on the poetic. This, of course, is fitting. Those who have apprehended something of the tragedy of human life under the curse of sin and the glory of a future blessedness secured by a Savior who died for their sins wish ardently to express both realities in a form fitting their content. Rawlet does this masterfully.

"A Consolatory Letter of that Reverend and Pious Man, Mr. Rowlett, the Author of *The Christian Monitor*, to his Mother, upon his Apprehension of Dying by the Plague." in Rawlet, *A Brief Account of the Life of the Reverend Mr. John Rawlet, Author of* The Christian Monitor. *Together, With a Valuable Remain of His, never before Printed,* viz. His Consolatory Letter *to his Mother, Written on Occasion of his Apprehension of Dying by the Great Plague, 1665.* (London: W. Roberts, 1728), 1–24.

A Letter to my Mother
John Rawlet

Dear Mother,

Considering the mortality that is now abroad, which calls upon us to expect and prepare for death, with more than ordinary seriousness and care to get everything done that we would have finished before our dying hour, which may suddenly surprise us; I was therefore willing to have this letter by me, that if it should please God to remove me hence before I have leisure to give you notice of my sickness, I might do something towards the abating of your sorrow by this farewell letter. Probably it may but aggravate your grief to stand much in the acknowledgement of all that tender love, which I have received from you ever since you brought me into the world: and though this be the effect of nature yet does it call for our owning and thankfulness.

I desire in the first place to bless God for you, and then to return you my humblest thanks for all the love you have manifested both to my soul and body. I bless and praise my God, who so graciously consulted my happiness that I should be born of a Christian parent, of a true believer, and that he made me a new member, not only of the visible church but of the mystical body of Christ. This I really take for a greater happiness than to have been born of the most honorable lady, queen, or empress in the world; and from my heart I trust, I have often returned thanks to God that he so disposed of my birth, that I was not heir to honor or riches, the usual snares of souls, but that I had the happy advantage of a pious education. And as for that means, I desire to be sincerely thankful to you, who under God have been the chief instrument of bringing me not only into the world of *nature*, but of *grace*. To your prayers, your instructions, your example, as the means appointed and blessed by God, I chiefly owe it that ever I had any sense of the concernments of my immortal soul. You prayed for me when I was yet in the womb, and ever after followed me with precepts, and God with petitions, even travailing again in birth of me, till Jesus Christ should be formed in my heart; or never ceasing till you had some hopes your desires were accomplished. And I account myself moreover bound to acknowledge the goodness of God, and your care and kindness in doing your utmost to give me an ingenuous education in knowledge and learning, that so I might be better fitted to serve my God in some public employment; and to the ministry it was you designed me, which had it pleased my God to have accomplished me for, and then employed me therein, I know nothing next to his love in Christ to my soul, that would have more rejoiced my heart; but these things now I cannot stand on. I know you have long since forgiven any stubbornness or undutifulness which ever I have been guilty of, for which I earnestly beg pardon both of God and you, and that I have done no more in a way of duty and gratitude for all that dear and constant love which you have followed me with.

But that which is the chief design of this writing is, to beseech you with all earnestness not to be immoderately afflicted with the providence of our heavenly Father in my removal out of this world. And here I will for clearness sake, reduce the reasons I shall give in for your moderation and comfort, to some heads which I shall briefly hint to your thoughts, and desire you to enlarge upon them, and deliberately to ponder and digest them. And consider,

First, the author of this dispensation, the wise, the gracious God; and is not here enough to calm and quiet your spirit? Nature no doubt will have its work, but by that time the first transports of grief are over, and you shall have reduced yourself, but to the serious consideration of this, that it is God who has thus ordered things, surely this cannot but mightily prevail with you to submit with a great deal of patience to his will. Oh! how many sheets of paper might I spend in enlarging upon this, but because I shall have but one to confine my letter to, I shall only touch upon things cursorily. Consider, did not this providence as dark and sad as it seems, proceed from infinite wisdom and goodness, and can you then quarrel within? Could you have ordered things better? You will not say so, let not your discontent practically speak as much. And has not that God who has thus disposed of me, power to do with us what he will? Can his creature limit his will or authority? Must we give him laws or set him bounds, and are we not altogether his own? Can he possibly wrong us by any of his dealings? And surely none should ever complain, but those who are wronged, who gave us our breath, who has continued it us hitherto? May not he who has done so, withdraw it when he pleases? Are not all creatures in the world subject to his power? And would we be from under his government?

Secondly, remember 'tis this God from whom you have received all that mercy which you have had so full and frequent experience of all your days, and can you think hardly of any providences of that God who has ever manifested himself so good to you? Shall one lash make you forget all his love? This would be very disingenuous. Oh! show yourself even now more thankful for former mercies than disquieted with the present affliction. Is it not for this that God has tried you himself, and is not this enough for your support? Bethink yourself solemnly that even while you are reading these lines, the Great Majesty of Heaven and Earth stands over you; knows with what a frame of heart you are possessed, and how you demean yourself under his hand, and how you entertain these directions, and may argue you of undutifulness or impatience. And think well within yourself how the ever blessed God can take it from you, that you cannot see enough in him to satisfy you, and to make up the loss of a relation? When he is yet still willing to be your God and portion! Oh! get but more practically and experimentally acquainted with God, and you will find his love is an all-sufficient treasure. In him is all we want or are deprived of. In him are riches, honors, health, children, friends, and everything that is good. Our strangeness to him makes us so fond of other things. For these being near us and so suited to our natures, as we consist of flesh, as well as spirit, our converse with them is sensible and delightful, and we know not well how to get that practical knowledge of God, and clear communion with him that may supply the want of creatures. But would we earnestly press after it, we should really find that whatever made our friends dear to us, is to be met with in God with infinite advantage; he is nearly related to us, he loves us better, he can do us more good, he is always with us, and will never leave us. Make not this then any ground for your complaints, that in my removal you have lost any help, and advantage to your soul, for still you have God to direct, quicken, and comfort you; and God has his choice of means whereby to convey these benefits to you; so that in this regard, at the most there is but a bucket broke, but still you have the fountain.

Thirdly, consider it is but death that has befallen me, which since the fall is appointed for all men: and as for the kind of death, I hope you will not lay it more to heart, supposing I do die by the plague, which is now spread abroad. I must confess, I can not as to the particular persons that it seizes, look upon it more a judgment than any other disease, supposing we are prepared to die. This was the sickness good Hezekiah was seized withal, as is commonly thought; and of this died the precious servant of Christ Mr. B—hs, besides thousands of others, God's dearest children no doubt. I know the dreadfulness of it is, that our friends run away from us, and dare not come to us; but yet one comfort is that we are quickly past needing them, or their help. Wherefore do not disquiet yourself needlessly with fearing that I had not what was good for me, nor because you were not with me, either to have looked to me, or to have taken your last farewell of me. Alas, that is but a mere formality, for you could neither have done me, or yourself any good thereby. Yet I have oft known persons torture themselves with such vain imaginations wherefore I caution you against them. And withal remember never any of God's servants got to heaven any other way than by death, except Enoch and Elijah, and they no doubt had something equivalent to death passed upon them. You would not sure have me exempted from the lot of all, and of God's own children. Yea, did not our Lord himself for our sakes tread this way before us? And that not only to make satisfaction for us, but to perfume the grave, and by his example to render death less terrible? And shall we grudge that ourselves or friends go any way which Christ has gone before us?

Fourthly, I shall speak something relating to ourselves, that may tend to your good I suppose. I know you will be apt to say, that had you but died first, the parting with me would not have been grievous to you, which I believe indeed; and no reason that it should, for when you were to go to God and Christ, 'tis not imaginable you should be loath to leave the dearest of your mortal sinful frail relations. But consider what I hinted before, who must have the disposal of us, but our Creator who is our Owner and Ruler? Do you think it was for want of wisdom to know which was best, or for want of love and pity to you that God has thus done? You have no reason to think either one or the other. If you say you used to please yourself with hopes that I should survive you, give me leave to tell you it was not prudently done. For what promise had you to fix those hopes upon? And you cannot think such ungrounded hopes should lay any engagement upon God to satisfy them; and I do not think, that when at first you prepared for a child, you desired one upon condition that God would let him outlive you. But then further consider, has not God been wonderfully gracious to you and preserving me alive with you thus long? And in giving us so much comfort from each other? All which we owe to his mere mercy and undeserved goodness. And to stir you up to more thankfulness to God, and submission to his will, I may add, I hope without vanity, that my life has been so much your joy, that it is not fit my death should be much your sorrow; and if you think this may be an aggravation of your grief, I am sure it calls upon you more to bless God for former mercies, and to acquiesce in his present pleasure. Moreover through the blessing of God, I hope, this Providence may be very much to your advantage. Hereby you will have more opportunity and help to discover your own heart, how great your love was to any creature, how much of your comfort came purely from God, and what mistakes of carnality there were in it, and what strength your faith is of now it comes to the trial. I have oft thought it was worth parting with every creature and the comfort thereof, to know clearly the state of our own souls, and to see what God alone, and the hopes of glory alone could do with us; whether this would bear us up when everything else failed. Certainly this is very profitable for us, for the time is coming, when we shall have none of these bladders to swim upon; and we had better they went from under us in the shallow water, where the loss of them will not do us much hurt, than in the deep ocean where we can get no help, but must drown. If God alone be not enough for us, what shall we do at death, and in the other world? And then this may have an happy influence upon you, to draw your heart nearer to God. Oh! How well will it be for you, when all the love that I had is placed upon him that deserves a thousand times more than all, and who alone should be loved in all, since all their goodness and loveliness is derived from him. And as God's essential goodness is not less when any conduct pipes are cut off, by which it was conveyed, no more than the light of the sun is diminished, when our chamber windows are shut up: so no more should our love be lessened to him when any of the comforts he lent us are withdrawn.

Nor need our joy be diminished any more than our love, since still we may see that in himself which he lent to any creature for use. And by your loving God more, and depending on him, more immediately for your comfort, you shall enjoy much more of him, and feel more the plenty of the communications of his goodness to your soul. And was there ever a true believer in the world who had tasted the sweets of God's special love, that would not heartily cry out, Lord strip me of food, raiment, health, liberty, friends, life, everything, so I may but enjoy more of thyself. Is he a Christian who would not part with all these for the full enjoyment of God in heaven? And is there not the same reason we should part with any of them for more of God upon earth? And then this Providence may more effectually loosen your heart from every other comfort under the sun, and make you more willing and desirous to leave this sinful miserable world: I mean not that you should in Jonah's pet for the withering of a gourd, be angry and discontented even to the death, desiring to leave the world, only because there's trouble in it, but from experience of the vanity and frailty of all things here below, you may be profitably taught to moderate your love to, and delight in them, and retire your soul to God, and long to be at your rest, filled with those joys which leave no emptiness, nor vexation, nor thirst in the soul; which joys God derives from himself into the spirit of just men, made perfect, and fitted for the receiving of the same.

'Tis not well that our enjoying of the gifts of God, should at all estrange our hearts from him: Nay, 'tis very sad and disingenuous, but alas how common! But yet it is well if the removal of them draw us nearer to him, and make us more desirous after him? Oh! the gracious nature of the ever blessed God, that will accept of our love after we have been lavishing it upon vanity, and will give us rest with himself after we have been wearied in our wanderings from him. And then consider what a little while it is before all this will be forgotten and over, and as to any trouble, as if it had never been. This consideration has many a time kept me from being much affected with any of the saddest and most dreadful occurrences that ever amaze the world, so that I have feared sometimes I was gone into the other extreme of insensibility. We ought I know to be very sensible of the hand of God in all his dealings with us, so far as we can make any advantage of his Providences, and so far as our grief may be to any good purpose; but surely no farther; for why should we torment ourselves with what we cannot help, and when our vexing will do no good? And I know not of any more effectual remedy for the allaying of all immoderate passions upon any account whatsoever, than a due regard of things with their reference to eternity. And then alas, what are *wars*, and *plagues*, and *famines*, they do but kill a many at once, who would at length all have died.

And in a very little time where are the tokens and remembrance of them? I confess, I know nothing worth a sad or serious thought, but the matters of *salvation* and *damnation*. These are overwhelming, astonishing things! What will it be to you within these very few years, it may be a very few days, that I was thus taken away, or what difference will there be then, whether you or I died first? 'Tis now nothing to *Jacob* that his *Joseph* and *Benjamin* were once in such danger of being both lost, which then did so sadly affect him.[2] The poor *Shunamite* that was in such a sad taking for the death of her only son, and ran with so much eagerness to the prophet, has lost those affections and cares long ago.[3] 'Tis a long time since *David* ceased his bitter outcries, Oh! *Absalom* my son, my son.[4] And every day there are multitudes upon the stage of the world, some acting a merry, others a sad

2. Gen. 37; Gen. 43
3. 2 Kgs. 4:8–37
4. 2 Sam. 19:1–8

part; but by the time they have taken a few turns, off they go, and still more succeed them, who though they thought they seem all as serious as may be while their part is acting, presently it appears that all was but a show; and such are all the things of life save, as they refer to eternity. Where are all the aching hearts and weeping eyes, to go no farther, that our late civil wars made? Where are now all those complaints which were poured out, some for a husband, some for a child, or brother, or friend? Are not your days of mourning for my father long since ended, and yet once, how hearty was your grief? Now let the consideration of what in a little time, death has upon all, have speedily the same effect upon you. And was not your mourning or sighs as the wind, or spilt not you your tears on the ground? For the wind will carry away those, and the dust will mingle with these, and all will presently vanish and be forgot, when as you might so husband your sorrow as it may redound to your infinite advantage. But however, I must acknowledge the apprehensions of this makes me at present to be less moved with pity for you, because I know your eyes will soon be dried and though you go mourning to the grave, yet then you will cease: and when you are in glory, I am sure you will have something else to do than complain, that I was taken out of the world so young, and before you. Remember the expression of my dear, though unknown father, with whom I hope shortly to meet in heaven, in his last letter you ever received from him, that he was gone but a little before, and shortly you will follow after. What a little while will it be before we whose ways may now part, shall all meet at our journey's end, ever in the presence of the great *Jehovah*, the bosom of our dear Lord Jesus? Methinks you should be as well content that I was in another world, as an hundred miles from you, as I have for some while been; you cannot hear from me, it is true, but you will quickly see me, and is not that better? Had not you rather be without a letter for an year, and have my company ten or twenty years, if we might live so long together, than all that while only to hear from me? Why, this is the case; could not you be content that I should go to possess the crown of *France*, supposing crowns and kingdoms, and such like very trifles were as fine things in your eyes, as in their blind admirers, though you were left behind and should never hear of me more; but especially if I would shortly send for you over there to spend all your days, and do you not really prize heaven at a higher rate than any low spirited wretch does a kingdom? And do you not strongly hope that we shall meet in glory?

As for yourself, I believe you have comfortable evidences for heaven, and if there were any darkness therein, this is a matter more deserves your thoughts than the loss of me? Who would stand troubling himself for the loss of sixpence, that believes, without present care and diligence, he shall lose his whole estate? And when to your own sense your title to happiness is cleared up surely the joy that arises from such hopes, may well swallow up all other sorrow. And as for my own particular, it is my great and confident hope, through the infinite mercies of my God in Christ, that I shall by death be translated to everlasting life. Oh! what does my soul hope to feel by that time that these lines are got into your hand? What words shall I hear, what sights shall I see, what ravishing wonders of love shall I feel? And could you be so uncharitable as to wish me thence? Have you any thing greater to desire for me than his glory? And can you be grieved that at length your prayers and hopes are all fully accomplished for me? Say not you would have had me stayed to have done God good service here on earth, for surely he knows best what to do, and how to dispose of his servant? I wonder not much indeed, that yourself did long to be first partaker of this; but yet I say, since God has otherwise ordered it, envy me not, much less grieve for me.

There is no need I should now stand to give you any large account of my life, or the reason of my hope, I have been always well known to you. A vile wretch, I acknowledge I have been! And have walked very unsuitably to that love with which the Lord has followed me all my days! And good reason I have to be ashamed, and confounded and blush in my appearance before the most holy God, but into the hands of the great reconciler I commend myself and all my affairs, through whom I hope to be presented into the Father's presence without spot or wrinkle, or any such thing. I bless God, I fear not death so far as I can judge myself at the distance, I yet stand from it; nay, with a submission to his will I earnestly desire it, for I am exceedingly afraid of decaying and declining in my love to God, and longing after him, and I am even tired out with a base carnal treacherous unconstant heart. I am weary of my ignorance, especially of my strange unsuitable conceptions of God, Christ, and heaven. I groan under these remnants of sin that even weigh me down. And can you choose but rejoice that I am delivered from such a load? Surely, dear mother, you loved me so well, that you cannot but prefer my gain before your own loss, and joy more that I am with God and my dear Savior, than mourn that I am not with you and the rest of my friends here on earth. The time was that I felt a loathness to die out of a desire to prevent that sorrow, which would thereby be occasioned to you. But now I cannot be moved by this consideration, which is not of less love to you, but I hope out of more to God. I was thinking to tell you something of God's way in working upon my soul, which it may be, I never fully manifested to you. In brief then, from about twelve or thirteen years as I remember, I had by fits, convictions upon my conscience, but they made no very deep impression. About a year or two after when I was at Moseley,[5] I thought my apprehensions in religion were somewhat more repined, and my resolutions for holiness confirmed, and I thought I received much light from Mr. Shaw's sermon, concerning the covenants, which he preached in order to the sacrament, and which I then began to understand the nature of, and did then first celebrate the same. I thought with a sincere resolution to devote myself to God, with a desire to receive more of his grace for my conduct through the many snares and temptations of life; but alas, I was still seized with much vanity of mind, and lived much estranged from God, though I kept on a tract of duties. After my return from Cambridge, being left at my Cozen *Woods* alone, having then more opportunity for private thoughts, I began more practically to discern the nothingness of the world, and withal saw that there was no way for true peace and serenity of mind, but by a thorough strong resolution and strict watch against every sin, and an indifferency of affection to every creature, and regarding them no farther than as subservient to our eternal interest. Being called out of this pleasant solitariness to *London*, I was very fearful of the prejudice I might sustain through the greater temptations of that place, but here God was pleased to reveal himself to me in a more powerful affecting manner than ever; and making me almost without my design, the happy instrument, I trust of awakening some in our family to an apprehension of their eternal concernments, by this means did bring them closer to my own soul, and they made upon my thoughts deeper impressions than ever. Oh blessed! and for ever praised be infinite and Almighty Love which thus followed a poor creature with such gracious design for, and importunate tenders of an everlasting happiness! Vile wretch that I should once withstand this motion! Good God, that would ever tender it a second, yea, innumerable times! You may find amongst my papers if they come safe to your hands, some meditations upon Heb. 11:27, and also upon the 13th verse of that chapter, both of which I chiefly designed for you. If either of

---

5. A district south of Birmingham where Rawlet had followed his teacher and mentor Samuel Shaw who had been appointed curate of chapelry at Moseley.

them be finished when you find them (as yet they are not) communicate them to Mr. *Shaw* or Mr. *Langley*, and if they think fit, let either of them be put to the press. I hope this motion proceeds not from a vain ambition of what I shall not live to enjoy, but I know I have many friends whose love to me may make something of mine acceptable, especially when I am taken from them; and methinks it would much please me if I might after my departure be in any capacity of doing the least good. Let me I beseech you be commended with all heartiness to everyone to whom I stand engaged for their love to me, and for their Remembrance of me, whether my relations or Christian acquaintance; but should I go to particularize them, I should straiten myself of what I have more to say, and scarce keep within the bounds I confine my letter to. Present my duty to my father, with many thanks for his kindness to me. My humble and earnest request to him is, that he would beware of those many temptations and snares his employments and converse in the world expose him to, and to give all diligent heed to adorn the gospel by his conversation, as remembering the world he is hasting to. My counsel in general to all my friends is, in the words of the apostle, 1 Cor. 15, the last verse and of 1 Pet. 1:31.[6]

Now once again, let me renew to you my first great request, that you let not your grief exceed the bounds of a Christian mourning, for the departure of a relation from a troublesome sinful world to the land of holiness, peace, and bliss, whither you expect shortly to follow. Where would you have me, but where you shall ever be in company with me? Is it so great a matter whether our whole way lies together, so long as we shall meet so soon, and be so long e'er we part? Say not you fear you shall not particularly know, and therefore not rejoice in me in the next world; for be certain, such a particular knowledge as may conduce any thing to our joy we shall then have, and none shall there complain that they know not how to find out and renew their acquaintance with their former friends. What the converse of those blessed spirits is, I am yet utterly to seek, but through the infinitely free grace of God in Christ, I hope experimentally to know by that time these have wrought your hands; and whilst you are bedewing these lines with you tears (which I wish may proceed from as great a mixture of joy

---

6. "Therefore, my beloved brothers, be steadfast, immovable, always abounding in the work of the Lord, knowing that in the Lord you labor is not in vain" (1 Cor. 15:58, ESV). The reference to 1 Peter 1:31 is either a mistake on the part of the author or the printer. It is possible that 1 Peter 1:13 was meant: "Therefore, preparing your minds for action, and being sober-minded, set your hope fully on the grace that will be brought to you at the revelation of Jesus Christ." (ESV)

as sorrow) I hope to be received into that place of joy and triumph, where all tears shall be wiped away from our eyes. Alas, what will it be then to me, what any of the poor world I leave behind me are doing, whether they cry or laugh in those dreams out of which they'll soon be awaked, and the memory of them presently vanished? O then shall all the busy anxious doubtings and conjectures of my soul be resolved; then shall all my fears and jealousies be banished; then shall the desires and longings of my soul be fully satisfied. I can now find my heart but little warm or raised by the most serious forethoughts this blessed state; and that even makes me more earnestly breathe after it, since I here can attain to so very little foretastes, and can meet with nothing else that will afford me anything like contentment. Oh! who that is persuaded that his happiness consists in his nearness to God, can ever be much satisfied at such a distance from him. Now I hope he will take pity on my poor bewildered desolate soul, and put an end to all her wanderings, and finish her labors, receiving her to that everlasting rest which remains for his people. In the midst of all the present deadness, darkness, and distemperedness of my soul, this is my great comfort that I shall leave all these with my body behind me. They shall no longer haunt and torment me in my attendance upon God, but with the greatest freedom, cheerfulness, raisedness, and vigor of mind, shall I be employed in sounding forth the everlasting praises of the most high God. Oh! the difference betwixt my prayers and those praises, my meditations of God, and my fruition of him, my following after, and being filled with him! Oh! the difference betwixt hearing or reading of, and beholding God, betwixt celebrating the memorial of Christ's undertaking, and enjoying the full fruits of it, betwixt the receiving of a sacrament, and seeing and conversing with Christ himself, and sitting down at his table in his kingdom! Betwixt a communion of imperfect saints, and the society of glorious angels, and the perfect spirits of the just! In a word, for I must have done; how vast will be the difference betwixt the present dark fore-thoughts of these great things, and my attainment of them! Oh let then the consideration of this glory my soul has entered upon, silence and allay your sorrow for my departure, and quicken and raise your own earnest expectations of this blessed state! Let the believing views and rational hopes of it cheer now your own soul, and intently fix your affections and thoughts there. And live in the practice of the excellent duty of meditation, especially on the future happiness. I believe it is but a very little while before we that now part with some sadness for those we leave behind, shall all meet in the general assembly of saints, and be for ever with the Lord and with one another; wherefore be comforted with these words. Now the God of mercy through the son of his love, bless, protect and keep you, and all my surviving friends, conducting you by his grace through this vale of tears, giving us all boldness in the great day of Christ's appearance, and a joyful admission into the everlasting kingdom. These are the sincere desires of him who gives you this his last farewell, desiring to manifest himself to have been,

Your dutiful son,
John Rawlet

Appendixes

++++

Appendix A

On Mortality

Introduction

In addition to meditating on Psalms 91 and 103, Romans 8, and Hebrews 12 for spiritual remedies against life's afflictions, Gisbertus Voetius recommends the reading of what he calls "that golden sermon of Cyprian, *On Mortality*." Similarly, Rivet says of Cyprian's "exquisite work," "I would desire that little book frequently set in the hand, day and night, of those who in this current situation are excessively anxious and worried." Cyprian, bishop of Carthage—born sometime between 200 and 210 and martyred in 258—is admittedly an unexpected feature in a collection of writings by protestant reformers. However, his brief treatise *On Mortality* (*De Mortalitate*) exercised such a considerable influence on Reformed pastors and theologians who ministered in the time of plague—including many featured in this volume—that the editors thought it would be of value to include as an appendix.

As the unspeakable horrors of the Decian persecution began to abate, a new horror in the form of a plague swept through Carthage. This plague has come to bear the name of Cyprian himself on account of his vivid description of the disease's effects on the human body:

> . . . the bowels, relaxed into a constant flux, discharge the bodily strength; that a fire originated in the marrow ferments into wounds of the fauces; that the intestines are shaken with a continual vomiting; that the eyes are on fire with the injected blood; that in some cases the feet or some parts of the limbs are taken off by the contagion of diseased putrefaction; that from the weakness arising by the maiming and loss of the body, either the gait is enfeebled, or the hearing is obstructed, or the sight darkened.

While Cyprian describes the effect of the disease on the human body, his devoted student and biographer Pontius describes the effect of the disease on the city of Carthage:

> Afterwards there broke out a dreadful plague, and excessive destruction of a hateful disease invaded every house in succession of the trembling populace, carrying off day by day with abrupt attack numberless people, every one from his own house. All were shuddering, fleeing, shunning the contagion, impiously exposing their own friends, as if with the exclusion of the person who was sure to die of the plague, one could exclude death itself also. There lay about the meanwhile over the whole city, no longer bodies, but the carcasses of many, and, by the contemplation of a lot which in their turn would be theirs, demanded the pity of the passersby for themselves. No one regarded anything besides his cruel games. No one trembled at the remembrance of a similar event. No one did to another what he himself wished to experience.[1]

Cyprian wrote *On Mortality* to remind the beleaguered and bewildered Carthaginian Christians, surrounded as they were by death and the inhumanity and fear that accompanies it, that their trials are not outside of God's control. Jesus himself, in fact, had promised that "wars, and famines, and earthquakes, and pestilences" would arise, and yet these would be signs of the coming of a kingdom that can never be shaken, the kingdom of God and of his Christ. Such trials, therefore, serve Christians as an ever-present reminder that this world is not their home and that as they endure the sorrows and hardships of life with faith and fortitude, they bear witness to their heavenly citizenship and their hope in the world to come.

Cyprian acknowledges that the believer's heavenly citizenship does not make sufferings disappear (in fact it adds to them considerably since the Christian "must struggle more with the attacks of the devil"), yet he rehearses the many ways God uses such trials for the benefit of his children. Trials serve the Christian in revealing the true object of one's faith and the true source of one's hope. Thus Cyprian puts the question somewhat

---

1. ANF 5:270

pointedly, "What room is there here for anxiety and solicitude? Who, in the midst of these things, is trembling and sad, except he who is without hope and faith? For is it for him to fear death who is not willing to go to Christ." Furthermore, trials serve to reveal something of the Christian's character. He writes,

> And further, beloved brethren, what is it, what a great thing is it, how pertinent, how necessary, that pestilence and plague which seems horrible and deadly, searches out the righteousness of each one, and examines the minds of the human race, to see whether they who are in health tend the sick; whether relations affectionately love their kindred; whether masters pity their languishing servants; whether physicians do not forsake the beseeching patients; whether the fierce suppress their violence; whether the rapacious can quench the ever insatiable ardor of their raging avarice even by the fear of death; whether the haughty bend their neck; whether the wicked soften their boldness; whether, when their dear ones perish, the rich, even then bestow anything, and give, when they are to die without heirs.

Perhaps most importantly, however, the Christian's faithful endurance of suffering displays their association with a Savior who suffered and who trod the path of great sorrow before entering his glory. Thus Cyprian calls on believers to "embrace the benefit of the occasion; that in thus bravely showing forth our faith, and by suffering endured, going forward to Christ by the narrow way that Christ trod, we may receive the reward of His life and faith according to His own judgment!" Just as Jesus, "who for the joy that was set before him endured the cross, despising the shame," (Heb. 12:2, ESV) so too the one who follows Christ, says Cyprian, must "show forth his strength in the struggle, since all the injury inflicted by present troubles is to be despised in the assurance of future blessings."

At heart, Cyprian desires all Christians to view all their sufferings through the lens of faith—faith in God, in his Son, and in his Word—and to look with eager expectation for faith to produce its fruit, namely hope, joy, and assurance. The afflictions that are, for the unbeliever, sad presages of an eternal death are not so for the believer. Rather, as Cyprian puts it, "These are trainings for us, not deaths: they give the mind the glory of fortitude; by contempt of death they prepare for the crown."

Cyprian, "On Mortality," trans. Ernest Wallis, *The Ante-Nicene Fathers*, vol. 5, ed. Alexander Roberts and James Donaldson (Buffalo, NY: Christian Literature Company, 1886), 469–475. The following is a slightly revised and updated republication. Footnotes from the original translation, mostly identifying text critical issues, have been omitted, though references for direct biblical and deutero-canonical quotations have been preserved in text. Indirect quotations and allusions are identified in footnotes.

On Mortality

Cyprian of Carthage

1. Although in very many of you, dearly beloved brethren, there is a steadfast mind and a firm faith, and a devoted spirit that is not disturbed at the frequency of this present mortality,[2] but, like a strong and stable rock, rather shatters the turbulent onsets of the world and the raging waves of time, while it is not itself shattered, and is not overcome but tried by these temptations; yet because I observe that among the people some—either through weakness of mind, or through decay of faith, or through the sweetness of this worldly life, or through the softness of their sex, or what is of still greater account, through error from the truth—are standing less steadily, and are not exerting the divine and unvanquished vigor of their heart, the matter may not be disguised nor kept in silence, but as far as my feeble powers suffice with my full strength, and with a discourse gathered from the Lord's lessons, the slothfulness of a luxurious disposition must be restrained, and he who has begun to be already a man of God and of Christ, must be found worthy of God and of Christ.

2. For he who wars for God, dearest brethren, ought to acknowledge himself as one who, placed in the heavenly camp, already hopes for divine things, so that we may have no trembling at the storms and whirlwinds of the world, and no disturbance, since the Lord had foretold that these would come. With the exhortation of his foreseeing word, instructing, teaching,

---

2. "The word *mortalitas* is found only rarely in classical Latin, where it has the meaning of death (Cicero, *De natura deorum* 1.10.26). In this treatise Cyprian uses it in a new sense to indicate the plague (*Mort.* 8.15-17). However, it here denotes the death rate . . . " Cyprian, *Saint Cyprian: Treatises*, trans. Roy Deferarri (Washington, D.C.: Catholic University of America Press, 1958), 199, n. 1.

preparing, and strengthening the people of his Church for all endurance of things to come, he predicted and said that wars, famines, earthquakes, and pestilences would arise in each place; and lest an unexpected and new dread of mischiefs should shake us, he previously warned us that adversity would increase more and more in the last times. Behold, the very things occur which were spoken; and since those occur which were foretold before, whatever things were promised will also follow, as the Lord himself promises, saying, "But when you see all these things come to pass, know that the kingdom of God is at hand" (Luke 21:31). The kingdom of God, beloved brethren, is beginning to be at hand; the reward of life, and the rejoicing of eternal salvation, and the perpetual gladness and possession lately lost of paradise, are now coming, with the passing away of the world; already heavenly things are taking the place of earthly, and great things of small, and eternal things of things that fade away. What room is there here for anxiety and solicitude? Who, in the midst of these things, is trembling and sad, except he who is without hope and faith? For it is for him to fear death who is not willing to go to Christ. It is for him to be unwilling to go to Christ who does not believe that he is about to reign with Christ.

3. For it is written, "the just lives by faith" (Hab. 2:4; Rom. 1:17b). If you are just and live by faith, if you truly believe in Christ, why, since you are about to be with Christ and are secure of the Lord's promise, do you not embrace the assurance that you are called to Christ and rejoice that you are freed from the devil? Certainly Simeon, that just man, who was truly just, who kept God's commands with a full faith, when it had been pledged him from heaven that he should not die before he had seen the Christ, and Christ had come an infant into the temple with his mother, acknowledged in spirit that Christ was now born, concerning whom it had before been foretold to him; and when he had seen him, he knew that he should soon die. Therefore, rejoicing concerning his now approaching death, and secure of his immediate summons, he received the child into his arms and, blessing the Lord, he exclaimed and said, "Now let your servant depart in peace, according to your word; for mine eyes have seen your salvation" (Luke 2:29–30); assuredly proving and bearing witness that the servants of God then have peace, then free, then tranquil repose when, withdrawn from these whirlwinds of the world, we attain the harbor of our home and eternal security when, having accomplished this death, we come to immortality. For that is our peace; that our faithful tranquility; that our steadfast, abiding, and perpetual security.

4. But for the rest, what else in the world than a battle against the devil is daily carried on, a struggle against his darts and weapons in constant conflicts? Our warfare is with avarice, with immodesty, with anger, with ambition; our diligent and toilsome wrestle is with carnal vices, with enticements of the world. The mind of man besieged, and in every quarter invested with the onsets of the devil, scarcely in each point meets the attack, scarcely resists it. If avarice is prostrated, lust springs up. If lust is overcome, ambition takes its place. If ambition is despised, anger exasperates, pride puffs up, wine-bibbing entices, envy breaks concord, jealousy cuts friendship; you are constrained to curse, which the divine law forbids; you are compelled to swear, which is not lawful.

5. So many persecutions the soul suffers daily, with so many risks is the heart wearied, and yet it delights to abide here long among the devil's weapons, although it should rather be our craving and wish to hasten to Christ by the aid of a quicker death; as he himself instructs us, and says, "Truly, truly, I say to you, that you shall weep and lament, but the world shall rejoice; and you shall be sorrowful, but your sorrow shall be turned into joy" (John 16:20). Who would not desire to be without sadness? Who would not hasten to attain to joy? But when our sadness shall be turned into joy, the Lord himself again declares, when he says, "I will see you again, and your heart shall rejoice; and your joy no man shall take from you" (John 16:22). Since, therefore, to see Christ is to rejoice, and we cannot have joy unless when we shall see Christ, what blindness of mind or what folly is it to love the world's afflictions, and punishments, and tears, and not rather to hasten to the joy which can never be taken away!

6. But, beloved brethren, this is so because faith is lacking, because no one believes that the things which God promises are true, although he is true, whose word to believers is eternal and unchangeable. If a grave and praiseworthy man should promise you anything, you would assuredly have faith in the promiser, and would not think that you should be cheated and deceived by him whom you knew to be steadfast in his words and his deeds. Now God is speaking with you; and do you faithlessly waver in your unbelieving mind? God promises to you, on your departure from this world, immortality and eternity; and do you doubt? This is not to know God at all. This is to offend Christ, the Teacher of believers, with the sin of incredulity; this is for one established in the Church not to have faith in the house of faith.

7. How great is the advantage of going out of the world, Christ himself, the Teacher of our salvation and of our good works, shows to us, who,

when his disciples were saddened that he said that he was soon to depart, spoke to them, and said, "If you loved me, you would surely rejoice because I go to the Father" (John 14:28); teaching thereby, and manifesting that when the dear ones whom we love depart from the world, we should rather rejoice than grieve. Remembering this truth, the blessed Apostle Paul in his epistle lays it down, saying, "To me to live is Christ, and to die is gain" (Phil. 1:21); counting it the greatest gain no longer to be held by the snares of this world, no longer to be liable to the sins and vices of the flesh, but, taken away from smarting troubles, and freed from the envenomed fangs of the devil, to go at the call of Christ to the joy of eternal salvation.

8. But nevertheless it disturbs some that the power of this Disease attacks our people equally with the heathens, as if the Christian believed for this purpose, that he might have the enjoyment of the world and this life free from the contact of ills; and not as one who undergoes all adverse things here and is reserved for future joy. It disturbs some that this mortality is common to us with others; and yet what is there in this world which is not common to us with others, so long as this flesh of ours still remains, according to the law of our first birth, common to us with them? So long as we are here in the world, we are associated with the human race in fleshly equality, but are separated in spirit. Therefore until this corruptible shall put on incorruption, and this mortal receive immortality, and the Spirit lead us to God the Father, whatsoever are the disadvantages of the flesh are common to us with the human race.[3] Thus, when the earth is barren with an unproductive harvest, famine makes no distinction; thus, when with the invasion of an enemy any city is taken, captivity at once desolates all; when the serene clouds withhold the rain, the drought is alike to all; when the jagged rocks rend the ship, the shipwreck is common without exception to all that sail in her; and the disease of the eyes, the attack of fevers, and the feebleness of all the limbs is common to us with others, so long as this common flesh of ours is borne by us in the world.

9. Moreover, if the Christian know and keep fast under what condition and what law he has believed, he will be aware that he must suffer more than others in the world, since he must struggle more with the attacks of the devil. Holy Scripture teaches and forewarns, saying, "My son, when you come to the service of God, stand in righteousness and fear, and prepare your soul for temptation" (Ecclus. 2:1). And again: "In pain endure, and in

---

3. Cf. 1 Cor. 15:50–56

your humility have patience; for gold and silver are tried in fire, but acceptable men in the furnace of humiliation." (Ecclus. 2:4–5).

10. Thus Job, after the loss of his wealth, after the death of his children, grievously afflicted, moreover, with sores and worms, was not overcome, but proved; since in his very struggles and anguish, showing forth the patience of a religious mind, he says, "Naked came I out of my mother's womb, naked also I shall go under the earth: the Lord gave, the Lord has taken away; as it seemed good to the Lord, so it has been done. Blessed be the name of the Lord" (Job 1:21).[4] And when his wife also urged him, in his impatience at the acuteness of his pain, to speak something against God with a complaining and envious voice, he answered and said, "'You speak as one of the foolish women. If we have received good from the hand of the Lord, why shall we not suffer evil?' In all these things which befell him, Job sinned not with his lips in the sight of the Lord" (Job 2:10). Therefore the Lord God gives him a testimony, saying, "Have you considered my servant Job? For there is none like him in all the earth, a man without complaint, a true worshipper of God" (Job 1:8). And Tobias, after his excellent works, after the many and glorious illustrations of his merciful spirit, having suffered the loss of his sight, fearing and blessing God in his adversity, by his very bodily affliction increased in praise; and even him also his wife tried to pervert, saying, "Where are your righteous deeds? Behold what you are suffering!" (Tob. 2:14) But he, steadfast and firm in respect of the fear of God and armed by the faith of his religion to all endurance of suffering, yielded not to the temptation of his weak wife in his trouble, but rather deserved better from God by his greater patience; and afterwards Raphael the angel praises him, saying, "It is honorable to show forth and to confess the works of God. For when you prayed, and Sara your daughter-in-law, I offered the remembrance of your prayer in the presence of the glory of God. And when you buried the dead in singleness of heart, and because you did not delay to rise up and leave your dinner, and went and buried the dead, I was sent to make proof of you. And God again has sent me to heal you and Sara your daughter-in-law. For I am Raphael, one of the seven holy angels, who are present and go in and out before the glory of God" (Tob. 12:11–15).

11. Righteous men have ever possessed this endurance. The apostles maintained this discipline from the law of the Lord, not to murmur in

---

4. "as it seemed good to the Lord" follows LXX and derived versions.

adversity, but to accept bravely and patiently whatever things happen in the world; since the people of the Jews in this matter always offended, that they constantly murmured against God, as the Lord God bears witness in the book of Numbers, saying, "Let their murmuring cease from me, and they shall not die" (Num. 17:10). We must not murmur in adversity, beloved brethren, but we must bear with patience and courage whatever happens, since it is written, "The sacrifice to God is a broken spirit; a contrite and humbled heart God does not despise" (Ps. 51:17); since also in Deuteronomy the Holy Spirit warns by Moses and says, "The Lord your God will vex you, and will bring hunger upon you; and it shall be known in your heart if you have well kept his commandments or not" (Deut. 8:2). And again: "The Lord your God proves you, that he may know whether you love the Lord your God with all your heart, and with all your soul" (Deut. 13:3).

12. Thus Abraham pleased God, who, that he might please God, did not shrink even from losing his son, or from doing an act of parricide.[5] You, who cannot endure to lose your son by the law and lot of mortality, what would you do if you were bidden to slay your son? The fear and faith of God ought to make you prepared for everything, although it should be the loss of private estate, although the constant and cruel harassment of your limbs by agonizing disorders, although the deadly and mournful wrench from wife, from children, from departing dear ones; let not these things be offences to you, but battles; nor let them weaken nor break the Christian's faith, but rather show forth his strength in the struggle, since all the injury inflicted by present troubles is to be despised in the assurance of future blessings. Unless the battle has preceded, there cannot be a victory; when there shall have been, in the onset of battle, the victory, then also the crown is given to the victors. For the helmsman is recognized in the tempest; in warfare the soldier is proved. It is a wanton display when there is no danger. Struggle in adversity is the trial of the truth. The tree which is deeply founded in its root is not moved by the onset of winds, and the ship which is compacted of solid timbers is beaten by the waves and is not shattered; and when the threshing-floor brings out the corn, the strong and robust grains despise the winds, while the empty chaff is carried away by the blast that falls upon it.

13. Thus, moreover, the Apostle Paul, after shipwrecks, after scourgings, after many and grievous tortures of the flesh and body, says that he is

---

5. Cf. Gen. 22:1ff

not grieved, but benefited by his adversity, in order that while he is sorely afflicted he might more truly be proved. "There was given to me," he says, "a thorn in the flesh, the messenger of Satan to buffet me, that I should not be lifted up. For which thing I besought the Lord thrice, that it might depart from me, and he said to me, 'My grace is sufficient for you, for strength is made perfect in weakness'" (2 Cor. 12:7–9). When, therefore, weakness and inefficiency and any destruction seize us, then our strength is made perfect; then our faith, if it shall stand fast when tried, is crowned; as it is written, "The furnace tries the vessels of the potter, and the trial of tribulation just men" (Ecclus. 27:5). This, in short, is the difference between us and others who know not God, that in misfortune they complain and murmur, while adversity does not call us away from the truth of virtue and faith, but strengthens us by its suffering.

14. This trial—that now the bowels, relaxed into a constant flux, discharge the bodily strength; that a fire originated in the marrow ferments into wounds of the fauces; that the intestines are shaken with a continual vomiting; that the eyes are on fire with the injected blood; that in some cases the feet or some parts of the limbs are taken off by the contagion of diseased putrefaction; that from the weakness arising by the maiming and loss of the body, either the gait is enfeebled, or the hearing is obstructed, or the sight darkened—is profitable as a proof of faith. What a grandeur of spirit it is to struggle with all the powers of an unshaken mind against so many onsets of devastation and death! What sublimity, to stand erect amid the desolation of the human race, and not to lie prostrate with those who have no hope in God; but rather to rejoice, and to embrace the benefit of the occasion; that in thus bravely showing forth our faith, and by suffering endured, going forward to Christ by the narrow way that Christ trod, we may receive the reward of his life and faith according to his own judgment! Assuredly he may fear to die who, not being regenerated of water and the Spirit, is delivered over to the fires of Gehenna; he may fear to die who is not enrolled in the cross and passion of Christ; he may fear to die who from this death shall pass over to a second death; he may fear to die who, on his departure from this world, eternal flame shall torment with never-ending punishments; he may fear to die who has this advantage in a lengthened delay, that in the meanwhile his groanings and his anguish are being postponed.

15. Many of our people die in this mortality; that is, many of our people are liberated from this world. This mortality, just as it is a plague to

Jews and Gentiles, and enemies of Christ, so it is a departure to salvation to God's servants. The fact that, without any difference made between one and another, the righteous die as well as the unrighteous, is no reason for you to suppose that it is a common death for the good and evil alike. The righteous are called to their place of refreshing, the unrighteous are snatched away to punishment; safety is the more speedily given to the faithful, penalty to the unbelieving. We are thoughtless and ungrateful, beloved brethren, for the divine benefits, and do not acknowledge what is conferred upon us. Lo, virgins depart in peace, safe with their glory, not fearing the threats of the coming Antichrist and his corruptions and his brothels. Boys escape the peril of their unstable age, and in happiness attain the reward of continence and innocence. Now the delicate matron does not fear the tortures; for she has escaped by a rapid death the fear of persecution, and the hands and the torments of the executioner. By the dread of the mortality and of the time the lukewarm are inflamed, the slack are nerved up, the slothful are stimulated, the deserters are compelled to return, the heathens are constrained to believe, the ancient congregation of the faithful is called to rest, and the new and abundant army is gathered to the battle with a braver vigor to fight without fear of death when the battle shall come, because it comes to the warfare in the time of the mortality.

16. And further, beloved brethren, what is it, what a great thing is it, how pertinent, how necessary, that pestilence and plague which seem horrible and deadly search out the righteousness of each one and examine the minds of the human race, to see whether they who are in health tend the sick; whether relations affectionately love their kindred; whether masters pity their languishing servants; whether physicians do not forsake the beseeching patients; whether the fierce suppress their violence; whether the rapacious can quench the ever insatiable ardor of their raging avarice even by the fear of death; whether the haughty bend their neck; whether the wicked soften their boldness; whether, when their dear ones perish, the rich even then bestow anything and give, when they are to die without heirs. Even although this mortality conferred nothing else, it has done this benefit to Christians and to God's servants, that we begin gladly to desire martyrdom as we learn not to fear death. These are trainings for us, not deaths: they give the mind the glory of fortitude; by contempt of death they prepare for the crown.

17. But perchance someone may object and say, "It is this, then, that saddens me in the present mortality, that I, who had been prepared for

confession, and had devoted myself to the endurance of suffering with my whole heart and with abundant courage, am deprived of martyrdom, in that I am anticipated by death." In the first place, martyrdom is not in your power, but in the condescension of God; neither can you say that you have lost what you do not know whether you would deserve to receive. Then, besides, God the searcher of the reins and heart, and the investigator and knower of secret things, sees you, and he praises and approves you; and he who sees that your virtue was ready in you will give you a reward for your virtue. Had Cain, when he offered his gift to God, already slain his brother? And yet God, foreseeing the fratricide conceived in his mind, anticipated its condemnation.[6] As in that case the evil thought and mischievous intention were foreseen by a foreseeing God, so also in God's servants, among whom confession is purposed and martyrdom conceived in the mind, the intention dedicated to good is crowned by God the judge. It is one thing for the spirit to be wanting for martyrdom, and another for martyrdom to have been wanting for the spirit. Such as the Lord finds you when he calls you, such also he judges you; since he himself bears witness and says, "And all the churches shall know that I am the searcher of the reins and heart" (Rev. 2:23). For God does not ask for our blood, but for our faith. For neither Abraham, nor Isaac, nor Jacob were slain; and yet, being honored by the deserts of faith and righteousness, they deserved to be first among the patriarchs, to whose feast is collected every one that is found faithful, righteous, and praiseworthy.

18. We ought to remember that we should do not our own will, but God's, in accordance with what our Lord has bidden us daily to pray. How preposterous and absurd it is, that while we ask that the will of God should be done, yet when God calls and summons us from this world, we should not at once obey the command of his will! We struggle and resist, and after the manner of froward servants we are dragged to the presence of the Lord with sadness and grief, departing hence under the bondage of necessity, not with the obedience of free will; and we wish to be honored with heavenly rewards by him to whom we come unwillingly. Why, then, do we pray and ask that the kingdom of heaven may come, if the captivity of earth delights us? Why with frequently repeated prayers do we entreat and beg that the day of his kingdom may hasten, if our greater desires and stronger wishes are to obey the devil here, rather than to reign with Christ?

6. Cf. Gen. 4:3–12

19. Besides—that the indications of the divine providence may be more evidently manifest, proving that the Lord, prescient of the future, takes counsel for the true salvation of his people—when one of our colleagues and fellow-priests, wearied out with infirmity and anxious about the present approach of death, prayed for a respite to himself, there stood by him as he prayed (and when he was now at the point of death) a youth, venerable in honor and majesty, lofty in stature and shining in aspect, and on whom, as he stood by him, the human glance could scarcely look with fleshly eyes, except that he who was about to depart from the world could already behold such a one. And he, not without a certain indignation of mind and voice, rebuked him and said, "You fear to suffer, you do not wish to depart; what shall I do to you?" It was the word of one rebuking and warning, one who, when men are anxious about persecution, and indifferent concerning their summons, consents not to their present desire, but consults for the future. Our dying brother and colleague heard what he was to say to others. For he who heard when he was dying, heard for the very purpose that he might tell it; he heard not for himself, but for us. For what could he, who was already on the eve of departure, learn for himself? Yea, doubtless, he learnt it for us who remain, in order that, when we find the priest who sought for delay rebuked, we might acknowledge what is beneficial for all.

20. To myself also, the very least and last, how often has it been revealed, how frequently and manifestly has it been commanded by the condescension of God, that I should diligently bear witness and publicly declare that our brethren who are freed from this world by the Lord's summons are not to be lamented, since we know that they are not lost, but sent before; that, departing from us, they precede us as travelers, as navigators are accustomed to do; that they should be desired, but not bewailed; that the black garments should not be taken upon us here, when they have already taken upon them white raiment there; that occasion should not be given to the Gentiles for them deservedly and rightly to reprehend us, that we mourn for those, who, we say, are alive with God, as if they were extinct and lost; and that we do not approve with the testimony of the heart and breast the faith which we express with speech and word. We are prevaricators of our hope and faith: what we say appears to be simulated, feigned, counterfeit. There is no advantage in setting forth virtue by our words and destroying the truth by our deeds.

21. Finally, the Apostle Paul reproaches, rebukes, and blames any who are in sorrow at the departure of their friends. "I would not," says he, "have

you ignorant, brethren, concerning those who are asleep, that you do not grieve even as others which have no hope. For if we believe that Jesus died and rose again, even so God will bring with him those which are asleep in Jesus" (1 Thess. 4:13–14). He says that those have sorrow in the departure of their friends who have no hope. But we who live in hope, and believe in God, and trust that Christ suffered for us and rose again, abiding in Christ, and through him and in him rising again, why either are we ourselves unwilling to depart hence from this life, or do we bewail and grieve for our friends when they depart as if they were lost, when Christ himself, our Lord and God, encourages us and says, "I am the resurrection and the life: he that believes in me, though he die, yet shall he live; and whosoever lives and believes in me shall not die eternally?" (John 11:25–26). If we believe in Christ, let us have faith in his words and promises; and since we shall not die eternally, let us come with a glad security unto Christ, with whom we are both to conquer and to reign forever.

22. That as we die, we are passing over to immortality by death; nor can eternal life follow, unless it should befall us to depart from this life. That is not an ending, but a transit, and, this journey of time being traversed, a passage to eternity. Who would not hasten to better things? Who would not crave to be changed and renewed into the likeness of Christ, and to arrive more quickly to the dignity of heavenly glory, since Paul the apostle announces and says, "For our conversation is in heaven, from whence also we look for the Lord Jesus Christ; who shall change the body of our humiliation, and conform it to the body of his glory?" (Phil. 3:20–21). Christ the Lord also promises that we shall be such when, that we may be with him, and that we may live with him in eternal mansions and may rejoice in heavenly kingdoms, he prays to the Father for us, saying, "Father, I will that they also, whom you have given me, may be with me where I am, and may see the glory which you have given me before the world was made." (John 17:24). He who is to attain to the throne of Christ, to the glory of the heavenly kingdoms, ought not to mourn nor lament but rather, in accordance with the Lord's promise, in accordance with his faith in the truth, to rejoice in this his departure and translation.

23. Thus, moreover, we find that Enoch also was translated, who pleased God, as in Genesis the Holy Scripture bears witness and says, "And Enoch pleased God; and afterwards he was not found, because God translated him" (Gen. 5:24). To have been pleasing in the sight of God was thus to have merited to be translated from this contagion of the world. Moreover,

the Holy Spirit teaches by Solomon that they who please God are more early taken hence, and are more quickly set free, lest while they are delaying longer in this world they should be polluted with the contagions of the world. "He was taken away," says he, "lest wickedness should change his understanding. For his soul was pleasing to God; wherefore he hastened to take him away from the midst of wickedness." (Wisd. of Sol. 4:11). So also in the Psalms, the soul that is devoted to its God in spiritual faith hastens to the Lord, saying, "How amiable are thy dwellings, O God of hosts! My soul longs, and hastens unto the courts of God" (Ps. 84:1).

24. It is for him to wish to remain long in the world whom the world delights, whom this life, flattering and deceiving, invites by the enticements of earthly pleasure. Again, since the world hates the Christian, why do you love that which hates you? And why do you not rather follow Christ, who both redeemed you and loves you? John in his epistle cries and says—exhorting that we should not follow carnal desires and love the world—"Love not the world," says he, "neither the things which are in the world. If any man love the world, the love of the Father is not in him. For all that is in the world is the lust of the flesh, and the lust of the eyes, and the pride of life, which is not of the Father, but of the lust of the world. And the world shall pass away, and the lust thereof; but he who does the will of God abides forever, even as God abides forever" (1 John 2:15–17). Rather, beloved brethren, with a sound mind, with a firm faith, with a robust virtue, let us be prepared for the whole will of God: laying aside the fear of death, let us think on the immortality which follows. By this let us show ourselves to be what we believe, that we do not grieve over the departure of those dear to us, and that when the day of our summons shall arrive, we come without delay and without resistance to the Lord when he himself calls us.

25. And this, as it ought always to be done by God's servants, much more ought to be done now—now that the world is collapsing and is oppressed with the tempests of mischievous ills; in order that we who see that terrible things have begun, and know that still more terrible things are imminent, may regard it as the greatest advantage to depart from it as quickly as possible. If in your dwelling the walls were shaking with age, the roofs above you were trembling, and the house, now worn out and wearied, were threatening an immediate destruction to its structure crumbling with age, would you not with all speed depart? If, when you were on a voyage, an angry and raging tempest, by the waves violently aroused, foretold the coming shipwreck, would you not quickly seek the harbor? Lo, the world

is changing and passing away, and witnesses to its ruin not now by its age, but by the end of things. And do you not give God thanks, do you not congratulate yourself, that by an earlier departure you are taken away and delivered from the shipwrecks and disasters that are imminent?

26. We should consider, dearly beloved brethren—we should ever and anon reflect that we have renounced the world and are in the meantime living here as guests and strangers. Let us greet the day which assigns each of us to his own home, which snatches us hence, which sets us free from the snares of the world, and restores us to paradise and the kingdom. Who that has been placed in foreign lands would not hasten to return to his own country? Who that is hastening to return to his friends would not eagerly desire a prosperous gale, that he might the sooner embrace those dear to him? We regard paradise as our country—we already begin to consider the patriarchs as our parents: why do we not hasten and run, that we may behold our country, that we may greet our parents? There a great number of our dear ones is awaiting us, and a dense crowd of parents, brothers, children, is longing for us, already assured of their own safety and still solicitous for our salvation. To attain to their presence and their embrace, what a gladness both for them and for us in common! What a pleasure is there in the heavenly kingdom, without fear of death; and how lofty and perpetual a happiness with eternity of living! There the glorious company of the apostles; there the host of the rejoicing prophets; there the innumerable multitude of martyrs, crowned for the victory of their struggle and passion; there the triumphant virgins, who subdued the lust of the flesh and of the body by the strength of their continency; there are merciful men rewarded, who by feeding and helping the poor have done the works of righteousness—who, keeping the Lord's precepts, have transferred their earthly patrimonies to the heavenly treasuries. To these, beloved brethren, let us hasten with an eager desire; let us crave quickly to be with them, and quickly to come to Christ. May God behold this our eager desire; may the Lord Christ look upon this purpose of our mind and faith, he who will give the larger rewards of his glory to those whose desires in respect of himself were greater!

Appendix B

Prayer and Thanksgiving from the Book of Common Prayer, 1662

Prayer
"In the time of any common Plague or Sickness."

O Almighty God, who in thy wrath didst send a plague upon thine own people in the wilderness, for their obstinate rebellion against Moses and Aaron; and also in the time of King David, didst slay with the plague of Pestilence threescore and ten thousand; and yet remembering thy mercy didst save the rest; Have pity upon us miserable sinners, who now are visited with great sickness and mortality; that like as thou didst then accept of an atonement, and didst command the destroying Angel to cease from punishing, so it may now please thee to withdraw from us this plague and grievous sickness, through Jesus Christ our Lord. *Amen.*

Thanksgiving
"For Deliverance from the Plague, or other common Sickness."

O Lord God, who has wounded us for our sins, and consumed us for our transgressions, by thy late heavy and dreadful visitation; and now in the midst of judgment remembering mercy, hast redeemed our souls from the jaws of death; We offer unto thy fatherly goodness ourselves, our souls and bodies, which thou hast delivered, to be a living sacrifice unto thee, always praising and magnifying thy mercies in the midst of thy Church, through Jesus Christ our Lord. *Amen.*

Or this.

We humbly acknowledge before thee, O most merciful Father, that all the punishments which are threatened in thy law, might justly have fallen upon us, by reason of our manifold transgressions and hardness of heart. Yet seeing it hath pleased thee of thy tender mercy, upon our weak and unworthy humiliation, to assuage the contagious sickness wherewith we lately have been sore afflicted, and to restore the voice of joy and health into our dwellings; we offer unto thy Divine Majesty the sacrifice of praise and thanksgiving, lauding and magnifying thy preservation and providence over us, through Jesus Christ our Lord. *Amen.*

Bibliography

Abbot, George. *Explicatio Sex Illustrium Quaestionum*. Frankfurt: Rosa, 1616.

———. *Quaestiones Sex Totidem Praelectionibus in Schola Theologica Oxoniae*. Oxford: Joseph Barnes. 1598.

Adam, Melchior. *Vitae Germanorum Theologorum*. Frankfurt: Jonah Rosa, 1563.

Alciato, Andrea. *Paradoxorum ad Pratum, Libri Sex, Dispunctionum, Lib. IIII, de Eo quod Interest, Liber Unus, in Tres Libros Codicis, Lib. III, Praetermissorum, Lib. II, Declamatio, Una, de Stip. Diuisionib. Commmentariolus*. Lyon: Sebastianus Gryphius, 1543.

Alpini, Prospero. *De Medicina Aegyptorum Libri Quatuor*. Venice: Franciscus de Franciscis Senensem, 1591.

Alsted, Johann Heinrich. *Summa Casuum Conscientiae Nova Methodo Elaborata*. Frankfurt: Paulus Jacobus, 1628.

———. *Theologia Casuum exhibens Anatomen Conscientiae et Scholam tentationum*. Hanover: Conrad Eifridus, 1630.

Althusius, Johannes. *Dicaeologica Libri Tres, Totum et Universum Jus, quo Utimur Methodice Complectentes*. Frankfurt: Christophorus Corvinus, 1649.

Ambrose of Milan. *Ambrose of Milan: Political Letters and Speeches*. Translated by J. H. W. G. Liebeschuetz and C. Hill. Liverpool: Liverpool University Press, 2005.

Ames, William. *Conscience With the Power and Cases Thereof*. [London]: 1639.

———. *De Conscientia, et Ejus Jure, vel Casibus, Libri Quinque*. Amsterdam: Joannes Janssonius, 1631.

———. *Von Dem Recht Dess Gewissens und Desselben Begebenden Fallen in V Büchern Verfasset*. Nuremberg: Wolfgang dess Jüng & Johan Andreas Endter, 1654.

———. *Vyf Boecken Vande Conscientie En Haar Regt of Gevallen*. Translated by C. V. Wallendal. Amsterdam: Jan Pieterse Kuypen, 1660.

Amicus, Diomedes. *Tractatus Tres Exactissimi*. Venice: Haeredes F. de Franciscis, 1599.

Anonymous. *Erinnerung, Wes Sich Ein Christ Ben der Absterbung Unnd Begrebnüss Seiner Mitbrüder Trösten Unnd Wie Er Sich Selbst Seeliglich*

Zusterben Bereitten Soll: Zu Jeder Zeit, Sonderlich Aber in Sterbens Läuffen Tröstlich und Nützlich. Heidelberg: Johann Mayer, 1564.

———. *Het Leven van Den H. Rochus, S. Ioseps, Ende Den H. Hubertus Patroonen Teghen de Peste.* Antwerp: 1645.

Apostolicarum Constitutionum et Catholicae Doctrinae Clementis Romani Libri VIII. Antwerp: Christophorus Plantin, 1578.

Arcolani, Giovanni. "Signa Pestilentiae Aeris." In *De Febribus ... in Avicennae Quarti Canonis Fen Primam Dilucida Atque Optima Expositio*. Venice: Iunta, 1552.

Aretius, Benedictus. "Locus CXLV Fascinatio." In *S. S. Theologiae Problemata, Hoc Est Loci Communes Christianae Religionis Methodice Explicati*. [Lausanne]: Isayas le Preux, 1617.

D'Aubigné, Merle. *History of the Reformation*. Edinburgh: Oliver & Boyd, 1853.

Aymon, Jean et al., eds. *Actes Ecclesiastiques et Civils de Tous les Synodes Nationaux des Eglises Reformées de France*. 2 vols. Charles Delo, 1710.

Azor, S.J., Juan. *Institutiones Morales*. Cologne: Antonius Hierat, 1608-1618.

Baer, Ludwig. *Ludovicus Berus ... ad Quaestionem Ei Propositam, utrum Uidelicet Tempore Pestis, vel ex Alia Causa, ad Uitandam Mortem, seu Mortis Periculum, Fugere interdum Liceat, nec ne? et si Quando Liceat, an tunc Praestet, non Fugere?* Basel: Joanes Oporinus, 1551.

di Bagnolo, Francesco Accorso. "De Episcopis et Clericis." In *Codex Dn. Iustiniani Sacratissimi Principis Accursii commentariis*. Paris: Merlin, Desboys, & Nivellius, 1559.

Baile, S.J., Guillaume. *Catechisme et Abbregé des Controverses de Nostre Temps, Touchant la Religion*. 2nd ed. Lyon: Pierre Rigaud, 1625.

———. *Catechismus seu Epitome Complectens Tractatus IV Capita*. Translated by Henri Lamormain. Lyon: Matthaeus Formica, 1626.

———. *Controversiarum Catechismus, das is Kurtzer Bericht Auff 124 Strittige Religionspuncten*. Munich: Cornelius Leyserius, 1642.

Balduin, Friedrich. *Tractatus Luculentus Posthumus ... Casibus Nimirum Conscientiae*. Frankfurt: Caspar Wachtler, 1654.

Bakhtiar, L., ed. *The Canon of Medicine (Qanun Fi Al-Tibb: The Law of Natural Healing): Volume 4: Systemic Diseases, Orthopedics and Cosmetics*. 5 vols. Great Books of the Islamic World, Inc., 2014.

Bãnez, O.P., Domingo. *Scholastica Commentaria in Secundam Secundae S. Thomae*. Douai: Petrus Borremans, 1615.

Baronio, Cesare. "367 ad §xxxii." In *Annales Ecclesiastici*. 12 Vols. Venice: Laurentius Basilius and Antonius Tivanius, 1705-1712.

———. *Martyrologium Romanum*. Ioannes Gymnicus, 1603.

———. "De Parabolanis Rescriptum Imperatoris." In *Annales Ecclesiastici*. 12 vols. Venice: Laurentius Basilius and Antonius Tivanius, 1705-1712.

Bauer, Georg. *De Peste Libri Tres*. Giessen: Caspar Chemlin, 1611.

Becanus, S.J., Martin. *Summa Theologiae Scholasticae*. 6 vols. Lyon: Nicolai Gay, 1644-1645.

———. *Theologiae Scholasticae Pars Secunda ... Tomus Prior*. Mainz: Joannes Albinus, 1619.

Bellarmine, Robert. *De Scriptoribus Ecclesiasticis cum Adjunctis Indicibus*. Brussels: Jean Leonard, 1719.

———. *Opera*. Paris: L. Vivès, 1870-1891.

Benzoni, Rutilio. *Speculum Episcoporum et Curatorum in quo de Fuga in Peste, Fame, et Bello Per Tres Libros*. Venice: Minima Societas, 1595.

Bernard of Clairvaux. *Sancti Bernardi Opera*. 9 Vols. Turnhout: Brepols, 1957-1998.

———. *St. Bernard's Sermons on the Canticle of Canticles*. 2 vols. Dublin: Browne & Nolan, 1920.

Beza, Theodore. *De Peste Quaestiones Duae Explicatae, Una Sitne Contagiosa, Altera an et Quatenus Sit Christianis per Secessionem Vitanda*. Geneva: Eustache Vignon, 1579.

———. *De Peste Ubi Quaestiones Explicatae Una Sitne Contagiosa, Altera an et Quatenus Sit Christianis per Secessionem Vitanda*. Geneva: Eustache Vignon, 1580.

———. "De Peste..." In *Variorum Tractus Theologici de Peste*, Leiden: Johannes Elsevir, 1655.

———. *A Shorte Learned and Pithie Treatize of the Plague*. Translated by John Stockwood. London: Thomas Dawson, 1580.

Biel, Gabriel. *Sermones Dominicales ... Hyemales Estivales de Tempore ... Sermones Medicinales [Con]tra Pestem Epidimie*. 2nd ed. Hannau: Henricus Gran, 1510.

Bonacina, Martino. "Summae Moralis Theologiae sive Tractatuum de Casibus Conscientiae." In *Opera Omnia Moralia*. 3 vols. 2nd ed. Lyon: Gabriel Boissat & Laurence Anisson, 1639.

———. *Tractatus Tres de Legibus, de Peccatis, et de Praeceptis Decalogi*. Brescia: Joannes Baptista Bozzola, 1622.

Bonaventure. "Commentaria in Quatuor Libros Sententiarum." In *Opera*, Quaracchi, 1882.
Boretius, A. and V. Krause, eds. *Capitularia Regum Francorum*. 2 vols. Hannover: Bibliopolis Hahniana, 1883-1897.
Bradford, John. *The Writings of John Bradford*. 2 vols. Cambridge: Cambridge University Press, 1848-1853.
Briard, Jean. *Quaestiones Quodlibeticae*. Theodorus Martinus, 1518.
Brun, C.G. et al. *Fontes Juris Romani Antiqui*. 2 vols. 6th ed. Freiburg: 1893.
de'Buoni, C.R.S.P, Omobono. *Commentarii Resolutorii de Examine Ecclesiastico et Disquisitionibus Moralis ac Practicae Theologiae Christianae Philosophiae et Casuum Conscientiae*. 3 vols. Bologna: Nicolò Tebaldini, 1623.
Busaeus, S.J., Joannes. *Viridarium Christianarum Virtutum ex Sacrosanctae Scripturae*. Mainz: Joannes Albinus, 1610.
de Busbecq, Ogier Ghiselin. *Legationis Turcicae Epistolae IV*. Monaco: 1620.
Buxtorf, Johannes. *Synagoga Judaica, Auscpiciis Authoris iam olim Latinitate Donata*. Basel: Ludwig König, 1641.
———. *Synagoga Judaica, das Ist Jüden Schul, Darinnen der Gantz Jüdische Glaub und Blaubens Ubung*. Basel: Sebastian Henricpetrus, 1603.
Calvin, John. "Ep. 247." In *Epistolae et Responsa*. 3rd ed. Hanover: Guilielmus Antonius, 1597.
Cardano, Girolamo. *De Rerum Varietate Libri XVII*. 2nd ed. Avignon: Matthieu Vincent, 1558.
———. *The de Subtilitate of Girolamo Cardano Volume 1*. Arizona Center for Medieval and Renaissance Studies, 2013.
———. *De Subtilitate Libri XXI*. Lyon: Guilelmus Rouillius, 1559.
———. *De Venenis Libri Tres*. Padua: Paolo Frambotti, 1653.
Carpzovius, Benedictus. *Jurispendentia Ecclesiastica seu Consistorialis Rerum et Queastionum ... Definitiones*. Leipzig: Timothy Ritzsch, 1655.
de Clemanges, Nicolaus. Ep. 27, "On a Certain General Pestilence and Its Causes According to the Doctors as Much as to the Divine Scriptures." In *Opera Omnia*. Leiden: Johannes Balduinus, 1613.
Copernicus, Nicolas. *De Revolutionibus Orbium Coelestium Libri VI*. Petreius, 1543.

Curtis, H.R., and B.T.G. Mayes, eds. *Theological Commonplaces: On the Ministry II*. Translated by R. J. Dinda. St. Louis: Concordia Publishing House, 2012.

Darawche, R., M. Mouty, and M.R. Sbeinati. "The Historical Earthquakes of Syria: An Analysis of Large and Moderate Earthquakes from 1365 B.C. To 1900 A.D." *Annals of Geophysics* 48, no. 3 (2005): 385.

Demaitre, Luke. *Leprosy in Premodern Medicine: A Malady of the Whole Body*. Baltimore: Johns Hopkins University Press, 2007.

Dindorf, Wilhelm, ed. *Onomasticon*. 5 vols in 6. Leipzig: Libraria Kuehniana, 1824.

Dubray, Charles. "Claude D'espence." In *the Catholic Encyclopedia*. New York: R. Appleton Co., 1909.

Durandus of Pourçain. *In Quatuor Libros Sententiarum Quaestionum Resolutiones*. Lyon: Gulielmus Rouillius, 1563.

Durante, Jean-Etienne. "De coemeteriis." In *De Ritibus Ecclesiae Catholicae Libri Tres*, Paris: Denis Moreau, 1644.

Eckhard, Melchior Sylvester. *Pastor Conscientiousus, Hoc Est: Variae Quaestiones, de Casibus & Rebus Dubiis, Ministri Personam Proplus Tangentibus*. Ulm: Balthasar Kuhnen, 1651.

d'Espence, Claude. *In Priorem D. Pauli Apostoli ad Timotheum Epistolam, Commentarii et Digressiones*. Paris: Michaelis Vascosanus, 1561.

———. "De Fuga in Tempore ac Periculo Pestis." In *Opera Omnia*, Paris: Claude Morelle, 1619.

———. *Traité contre l'erreur Vieil et Renouvelé des Prédestinés*. Lyon: 1548.

Evagrius Scholasticus. *The Ecclesiastical History of Evagrius Scholasticus*. Liverpool: Liverpool University Press, 2000.

Feltoe, C. L., ed. *The Letters and Other Remains of Dionysius of Alexandria*. Cambridge: Cambridge University Press, 1904.

Follinus, Hermannus. *Amuletum Antonianum seu Luis Pesterae Fugae*. Antwerp: Hieronymus Verdussius, 1618.

Forster, E. S., ed. *The Turkish Letters of Ogier Ghiselin de Busbecq*. Baton Rouge: Louisiana State University Press, 2005.

Foxe, John. *The Ecclesiastical Historie, Containing the Acts and Monument of Martyrs*. 3 Vols. London: 1641.

———. *Fox's Book of Martyrs: The Acts and Monuments of the Church*. 3 Vols. London: George Virtue, 1851.

Fracastoro, Girolamo. "De Signis Contagiosum." In *De Sympathia et Antipathia Rerum Liber Unus ... de Contagione et Contagiosis Morbis et Curatione, Libri III.* Venice: 1546.

Galen of Pergamum. "De Simplicium Medicamentorum Temperamentis ac Facultatibus." In *Galeni Opera Omnia.* Leipzig: C. G. Kühn, 1821.

Gerhard, Johann. "De Ecclesiastico Ministerio." In *Theologici Loci.* 9 vols. Frankfurt & Hamburg: Zacharias Hertelius, 1657.

Gesner, Conrad. *Epitome Bibliothecae Conradi Gesneri.* Zurich: Christopher Froschouer, 1555.

Gesner, Conrad et al. *Bibliotheca Instituta et Collecta a Conrado Gesnero, deinde in Epitomen Redecta ... Tertio Recognita ... per Iosiam Simlerum ... Postremo ... per Iohannem Iacobum Frisium.* Zurich: Christopher Froschouer, 1583.

Giovo, Paulo. *Historiarum sui Temporis.* 2 vols. Florence: Lorenzo Torrentini, 1550.

Giraldi, Gregorio Giglio. *De Sepultura ac Vario Sepeliendi Ritu Libellus.* Basil: Michael Ising, 1589.

Gonzaga, Francisco. *De Origine Seraphicae Religionis Franciscanae.* 3 Vols. Venice: 1603.

Grataroli, Gulielmo. *Pestis Descriptio, Causae, Signa Omnigena, et Praeservatio.* Paris: Federicus Morellus, 1561.

———. "Pestis Descriptio, Causae, Signa Omnigena, et Praeservatio." In *Opus non minus Luculentum quam Iucundum Lectu.* Cologne: Petrus Horst, 1571.

Gratian. "Decretum." In *Corpus Iuris Canonici*, Graz: Akademische Druck- u. Verlagsanstalt, 1959.

Gregory I. *Dialogues.* Translated by O. J. Zimmerman O.S.B. New York: 1959.

———. "Bk. 11, Ep. 2." In *the Letters of Gregory the Great.* 3 vols. Pontifical Institute of Medieval Studies, 2004.

———. "Registrum Epistularum." In *Opera.* 5 vols. 2nd ed. Rome: Typographia Camerae Apostolicae, 1613.

Gregory of Nazianzus. *D. Gregorii Nazianzeni Orationes XXX.* Edited by Willibald Pirckheimer. Basil: Officina Frobeniana, 1531.

———. *Selected Poems of Gregory of Nazianzus: I.2.17; II.1.10, 19, 32: A Critical Edition With Introduction and Commentary.* Göttingen: Vandenhoeck & Ruprecht, 2009.

Gregory of Nazianzus et al. *Julian the Emperor: Containing Gregory Nazianzen's Two Invectives and Libanius' Monody with Julian's Extant Theosophical Works*. Translated by C. W. King. London: George Bell & Sons, 1888.

Gregory of Tours. "Gregorii Episcopi Turonensis Libri Historiarum X." In *Monumenta Germaniae Historica*. 2nd ed. Edited by B. Krusch and W. Levinson. Hanover: 1951.

———. *The History of the Franks*. Translated by L. Thorpe. London: Penguin UK, 1974.

Gregory Thaumaturgus et al. *St. Gregory Thaumaturgus Life and Works*. Translated by M. Slusser. Washington, D.C.: Catholic University of America Press, 1998.

de Grentemesnil, Julien Le Paulmier. *De Morbis Contagiosis Libri Semptem*. Paris: Dionysius Du-Val, 1578.

Grillot, S.J., Jean. *Lyon Affligé de Contagion ou Recit de ce qui s'est Passe de Plus Memorable en Cette Ville, Depuis le Mois d'aoust de l'an 1628 jusques au Mois d'octobre de l'an 1629*. Lyon: François de La Bottiere, 1649.

Hahn, Philip. *Consilia sive Iudicia Theologica et Requisita Ministerii Totius Ecclesiae, New Verbessert und Vollständig Kirchen Buch*. 3 vols. Braunschweig: Andreas Duncker, 1647.

Hall, Joseph. Dec. 4, Ep. 9, "to Mr. E. A., Ep. IX, a Discourse of Fleeing or Staying in the Time of Pestilence, Whether Lawfull for Minister or People." In *Epistles containing two decades*. 3 vols. London: E. Edgar, 1608-1611.

Hefele, C. J. *A History of the Councils of the Church*. 5 vols. Edinburgh: T. & T. Clark, 1876.

Hercules of Saxony. "Whether Sorcery Could be the Cause of Lice?" In *De Plica quam Poloni Gwozdziec, Roxolani Koltunum Vocant*. Laurentius Pasquatus, 1600.

Hoornbeek, Johannes. *Dissertatio de Peste Theologica in Variorum Tractatus Theologici de Peste*. Leiden: Johannes Elsevirius, 1655.

Hurtado, O.P., Tomás. *Resolutiones Orthodoxo-Morales, Scholasticae, Historicae de Vero, Unico, Proprio et Catholico Martyrio Fidei, Sanguine Sanctorum Violenter Effuso, Rubricato adversus Quorundam Καινολογίαν de Proprio Martyrio Charitatis et Misericordiae*. Cologne: Cornelius ab Egmond et Socios, 1655.

Ingrassia, Giovanni Filippo. *Informatione del Pestifero et Contagioso Morbo*. Edited by L. Ingaliso. FrancoAngeli, 2005.

———. *Informatione del Pestifero et Contagioso Morbo Ilquale Affligge et Have Afflitto Questa Citta di Palermo, et Molte Altre Citta, e Terre di Questo Regnodi Sicilia Nell' Anno 1575 et 1576*. Giovan Mattheo Mayda, 1576.

Jerome. *St. Jérôme Chronique: Continuation de la Chronique d'eusèbe*. Translated by Benoît Jeanjean and Bertrand Lançon. Rennes: Presses Universitaires de Rennes, 2004.

du Jon, François. "De Ministerio Ecclesiastico." In *Opera*. 2 vols. Geneva: Pierre et Jacques Chouet, 1613.

Junius, F., F. Gomarus, A. Walaeus, G. Coddaeus, and J. Bruno. *Compendium Theologiae Thesibus in Academia Lugduno-Bat. Ordine ... ab Anno 1598 Usq[ue] ad Annum 1605 Concinnatum*. Hanover: Antonius, 1611.

Junius, Franciscus. *Omnia Opera Theologica*. 2nd ed. Geneva: Samuel Crispin, 1613.

Junius, Franciscus (praes.), and Daniel Couppé. *Theses Theologicae de Vita Christiana*. Leiden: J. Patius, 1599.

Kalwitz, Seth. *Opus Chronologicum ubi Tempus Astronomicum per Motus et Eclipses*. 4th ed. Frankfurt: Anthonius Hummius, 1650.

Karoli Magni et Ludovici Pii Christianiss... Regum et Impp. Francorum Capitula sive Leges Ecclesiasticae et Civiles ab Ansegiso Abbate et Benedicto Levita Collectae Libris Septem. Paris: Guilelmus Pelé, 1640.

Kis, István Szegedi. *Theologiae Sincerae Loci Communes de Deo et Homine*. Basil: Officina Pernea, 1585.

à Lapide, Cornelius. *Commentaria in Acta Apostolorum, Epistolas Canonicas, et Apocalypsin*. Paris: George Josse, 1648.

———. *Commentaria in Duodecim Prophetas Minores*. Venice: Hieronymus Albrizzi, 1703.

———. *Commentaria in Pentateuchum Mosis*. Antwerp: Jacobus Meursius, 1659.

Lavater, Ludwig. "Homilia XVI." In *Propheta Ezechiel ... Homilis seu Commentariis Expositus*. Geneva: Jean Crespin, 1571.

———. *In Libros Paralipomenon sive Chronicorum Commentarius*. Zurich: Christophorus Froschouerus, 1573.

———. *De Pestilentia concio Lvdovici Lavateri, in qua ostenditur, unde sit et quare immitatur: item, quo pacto se gerere debeant, qui illo morbo corripiuntur*. Translated by Joannes Pontisella. Zurich: Froschen, 1586.

———. *Van de Peste, Een Seer Christelijcke Onderrichtinghe*. Deventer: Jan E. Cloppenburch, 1599.

———. *Von der Pestilentz, Zwo Predginen: die Ein Vom Ursprung der Pestilentz, Wohar die Sye, Item Warumb Sy Regiere Unnd Wie Man Sich Darinnen Halten Sölle. Beschriben Durch Ludwigen Lavater, Dienern der Kirchen Zuo Zürych*. Zurich: Christoffel Forschower, 1564.

Lea, Henry Charles. *Histoire de l'inquisition au Moyen Age*. 3 vols. Translated by S. Reinach. Paris: Société Nouvelle de Librairie et d'Édition, 1902.

Lemnius, Levinus. *Occulta Naturae Miracula Libri IIII*. [Amsterdam]: Officina Paltheniana, [1598].

Lindsay, W. M., ed. *Nonius Marcellus' Dictionary of Republican Latin*. 3 vols. Oxford: 1901-1903.

de Locre, Ferry. *Maria Augusta Virgo Deipara in Septem Libros Tributa*. Aras: R. Maudhuy, 1608.

de Lorca, O. Cist., Pedro. *Commentaria et Disputationes in Secundam Secundae Diui Thomae Tomus Iste Tres Continet Sectiones, Primam de Fide, Alteram de Spe, Tertiam de Charitate*. Madrid: Luis Sanchez, 1614.

de Lorin, S.J., Jean. *Commentarius in Sapientiam*. Lyon: Horace Cardon, 1607.

Luther, Martin. *Ob man fur dem sterben flieben muge*. Wittenberg: 1527.

Marchini, Filiberto. *Belli Divini, sive Pestilentis Temporis Accurata et Luculenta Sepculatio Theologica, Canonica, Civilis, Politica, Historica, Philosophica*. Florence: Sermartelliana, 1633.

———. *Philosophica de Pestilentia Problemata*. Florence: Sermartelliana, 1633.

Marcquis, Gulielmus. *Decas Pestifuga seu Decem Questiones Problematicae de Peste*. Antwerp: Caesar Ioachim Trognaesius, 1627.

Marti, Benedict. *SS. Theologiae Problemata hoc est, Loci Communes Christianae Religionis Methodice Explicati*. Geneva: Isayas le Preux, 1617.

Melanchthon, Philip. *Consilia sive Iudicia Theologica itemque Responsiones*. 2 vols. Neustadt: Wilhelm Harnisius, 1600.

———. *Epistolae*. 2 vols. London: 1570-1574.

Mercuriale, Girolamo. "How Contagion Acts in a Healthy Body." In *De Peste in Universum, Preasertim vero de Veneta et Patauina*. Venice: Paulus Meietus, 1577.

Meyer, P.M., and T. Mommsen, eds. *Theodosiani Libri XVI cum Constitutionibus Sirmondianis et Leges Novellae ad Theodosianum*. 2 vols. Berlin: Weidmann, 1905.

Möller, Heinrich. *Enarrationis Psalmorum Davidis ... Novissima Editio*. Geneva: Pierre et Jacques Chouet, 1610.

———. *Enarratio Psalmorum Davidis ex praelectionibus Henrici Molleri*. 8th printing. Geneva: Samuel Chouët, 1660. Navarra, Petrus. *De Restitutione in Foro Conscientiae*. 2 vols. Toledo: Pedro Rodrigo, 1595-1597.

Nicholas of Lyra. *Biblia Sacra cum Glossis, Interlineari et Ordinaria, Nicolai Lyrani Postilla et Moralitatibus*. 7 vols. Lyon: 1545.

Nuñez, Luis. *Hispania*. Antwerp: Hieronymus Verdussen, 1607.

Oecolapadius, Johannes. *Ioannis Oecolampadii ... Commentarorum in Prophetas*. 2 vols in 1. Geneva: Jean Crispin & Nicolaus Barbier, 1558.

Oomius, Simon. *Des Heeren Verderflicke Pyl, ofte Twee Boeken van de Pest*. Amsterdam: Willem van Beaumont, 1665.

de Palude, O.P., Pierre. *Scriptum in Quartum Sententiarum Petri Lombardi*. Venice: 1493.

de Paméle, Jacques. *Liturgica Latinorum Iacobi Pamelii ... Duobus Tomis Digesta*. Cologne: Gervinus Calenius, 1557.

Paolini, Fabio. *Praelectiones Marciae sive Commentaria in Thucydidis Historiam seu Narrationem de Peste Atheniensium*. Venice: Juntae, 1603.

Paraeus, David. *Exercitationum Philosophicarum et Theologicarum Libri IV*. Heidelberg: Lancelotus, 1610.

———. "Exercitatio XlVI: Paraphrasis Exegetica Historiae de Pestis Cohibitione et Aversione 1 Par. 21 et 2 Sam. 24." In *Exercitationvm Philosophicarvm and Theologicarum Libri IV*, Heidelberg: Johannes Lancellotus, 1610.

———. "Exercitatio XlV: de Electione Pestis Prae Bello et Fame 2 Sam. 24 et 1 Chron. 21." In *Exercitationvm Philosophicarvm and Theologicarum Libri IV*. Heidelberg: Johannes Lancellotus, 1610.

von Pastor, Ludwig. *The History of the Popes: From the Close of the Middle Ages*. 40 vols. Translated by R. F. Kerr. London: Paul, Trench, Trübner and Co., 1910.

Paul the Deacon. *History of the Langobards*. Translated by W. D. Foulke. Philadelphia: Dept. of History, University of Pennsylvania, 1907.

———. "Historia Langobardorum." In *Monumenta Germaniae Historica Saec. VI–IX*. Edited by G. Waitz. Hannover: Bibliopolis Hahniana, 1878.

Paulinus, Fabius. *Praelectiones Marciae sive Commentaria in Thucydidis Historiam seu Narrationem de Peste Atheniensium*. Venice: Juntae, 1603.

Pelgrom, Simon. *Sylva Synonymorum*. Amsterdam: Henricus Laurentius, 1635.

Jaroslav Jan Pelikan, Hilton C. Oswald, and Helmut T. Lehmann, eds. *Luther's Works* Philadelphia: Fortress Press, 1999.

Pereira, S.J., Benito. *Selectae Disputationes in Sacram Scripturam*. 5 vols. 3rd ed. Lyon: Horatius Cardon, 1607-1610.

Perkins, William. *The Workes of That Famous and Worthy Minister of Christ in the Universitie of Cambridge Mr. William Perkins*. 3 vols. London: John Legatt, 1626.

Pierre Grégoire of Toulouse. "Cap. 11 de Maleficiis et Incantationibus Homines, Animalia Aliasque Res Interimentibus, vel iisdem Nocentibus." In *Syntagma Iuris Universi, atque Legum Pene Omnium Gentium, et Rerum Publicarum Praecipuarum in Tres Partes Digestum in quo Divini et Humani Juris Totius Naturali*, Frankfurt: Officina Paltheniana, 1599.

von Polansdorf, Amandus Polanus. "De Sancta Vita et Beato Obitu Oecolampadii." In *Analysis Libelli Prophetae Malachae ... Adiunctae sunt Orationes Quatuor*, Basil: Conrad Waldkirch, 1597.

Porto, Francesco. *Ad Petri Carpentarii Causidici Virulentam Epistolam, Responsio Francisci Porti Cretensis, pro Causariorum quos Vocat, Innocentia*. Geneva: 1573.

Possidius. *Sancti Augustini Vita*. Translated by H. T. Weiskotten. Princeton: Princeton University Press, 1919.

Praevidellus, Hieronymus. "De Peste et Eius Privilegiis." In *Tractatus universi iuris*. 22 vols. Venice: Franciscus Zilettus, 1584-1586.

de Pretere, S.J., Guillaume. *Catechismus*. Antwerp: 1623.

———. *Gheesteliicke Remedien Teghen de Haestige Sieckte, Ter Oorsaecek Vande Devotie die Binnen Antwerpen Betoont Wordt Besonderlijck in Het Aen Roepen van de H. Moeder Godts Ende Andere Heyligen Patroonen Ot Marschalcken Teghen de Haetighe Sieckte*. Antwerp: Jan Gnobbaert, 1624.

al-Qashsh, E., and A. Zay'ūr, eds. *Al-Qānūn fī l-tibb*. 4 vols. Beirut: 1413 A.H./1993 A.D.

Raynaud, S.J., Theophilé. *De Martyrio per Pestem*. Lyon: Jacques Cardon, 1630.

———. *Index Librorum Prohibitorum*. Rome: the Vatican, 1946.

———. *Omnia Opera*. Lyon: Boissat & Remues, 1665-1669.

Rhegius, Urbanus. August 1, 1540, In *Omnis Generis Afflictionibus, in Persecutionum Procellis, in Pestis*, Aliisque Morbis. Frankfurt: Petrus Brubachius, 1545.

———. *Opera Vrbani Regii Latine Edita*. Nürnberg: vom Berg und Neuber, 1562.

Rivet, André. *Andreae Riveti … Operum Theologicorum*. 2 vols. Rotterdam: Arnoldus Leers, 1652.

Rivet, André et al. *Variorum Tractatus Theologici de Peste*. Leiden: Johannes Elsevirius, 1655.

Rufinus of Aquileia. *The History of the Church*. Translated by P. R. Amidon. Washington D.C.: Catholic University of America Press, 2016.

Rutgers, F. L., ed. *Acta van de Nederlandsche Synoden der Zestiende Eeuw*. Utrecht: Kemink & Zoon, 1889.

Sánchez, S.J., Tomás. *Opus Morale in Praecepta Decalogi*. Antwerp: Joannes Meursius, 1614.

de Salas, S.J., Juan. *Tractatus de Legibus in Primam Secundae S. Thomae*. Lyon: Jean de Gabian, 1611.

Salmeron, S.J., Alphonso. "Tractatus 16 de Fuga in Persecutione." In *Commentarii in Evangelicam Historiam et in Acta Apostolorum*. 16 vols. Cologne: Hierat & Gymnicus, 1612-1615.

di San Nazzaro, Gianfrancesco Riva. *Tractatus de Peste*. Leipzig: Jacob Apelius, 1598.

Sarazin, Jean-Antoine. *De Peste Commentarius*. Lyon: Louis Cloquemin, 1572.

Sennert, Daniel. *Epitome Institutionum Medicinae, et Libr. de Febribus*. Amsterdam: Jodocus Janssonius, 1655.

Scaliger, Julius Caesar. *Exotericarum Exercitationum Liber XV, de Subtilitate*. 1557.

Scultetus, Abraham. *Idea Concionum in Jesaiam Prophetam ad Populum Haidelbergensem Habitarum*. Geneva: Pierre Aubert, 1618.

de Serres, Jean. *Commentarii de Statu Religionis e Reipublicae in Regno Galliae*. 5 vols. Geneva: 1571-1590.

Settala, Ludovico. *In Aristotelis Problemata Commentaria*. 3 Vols. Lyon: Claude Landry, 1632.

ibn Siman as-Simani, Yusuf et al., eds. *Ephraemi Syri Opera Omnia quae Exstant Graece, Syriace, Latine*. 6 vols. Rome: Johannes Mariae Henrici Salvioni, 1737-1746.

Simler, Josiah. *Vita Clarissimi Philosophi et Medici Excellentissimi Conradi Gesneri Tigurini*. Tigurinus: Froschouerus, 1566.
Sirmond, Jacques. "Concilium Nannetense (658)." In *Concilia Antiqua Galliae Tres in Tomos*. Paris: Sebastian Cramoisy, 1629.
Sylvius, Franciscus. "Commentarii in Totam Secundam Secundae S. Thomae Aquinatis." In *Opera Omnia*. 6 vols. Antwerp: Joannes Baptista Verdussen, 1697-1698.
Sohn, Georg. *Operum Georgii Sohnii Sacrae Theologiae Doctoris … Continens Scripta Auctoris Methodica*. 2nd ed. Nassau-Siegen: Christopher Corvinus, 1598.
———. "XV de Causis et Curatione Pestis." In *Theses de Plerisque Locis Theologicis*, Siegen: Christophor Corvinus, 1598.
Stengel, O.S.B., Karl. *Commentarius Rerum Augustanarum ab Urbe Condita ad Nostra usque Tempora*. Ingolstadt: Gregory Haelin, 1647.
Suarez, S.J., Francisco. *Tractatus de Legibus ac Deo Legislatore in Decem Libros Distributus*. Lyon: Horace Cardon, 1619.
Tarnow, Paul. *De Sacrosancto Ministerio, Libri Tres in Quibus de Ministerii Evangelici in Ecclesiis Lutheranis Veritate et Efficacia … et Praeter Theoreticas Quaestiones Complures, Pleraeq; Omnes Practicae*. Rostock: Johannes Hallervordius, 1624.
Terilli, Domenico. *De Causis Mortis Repentinae Distinctiss … Tractatio*. Venice: Damian Zenarius, 1615.
Theophanes the Confessor. *The Chronicle of Theophanes: an English Translation of Anni Mundi*. 2 vols. Translated by H. Turtledove. Philadelphia: University of Pennsylvania Press, 1982.
de Thou, Jacques-Auguste. *Histoire Universelle*. 16 vols. Translated by. Le Beau. London: 1734.
———. *Historiae sui Temporis*. 6 vols. Paris: Ambrose et Jerome Drouart, 1606-1614.
———. *Jac. Augusti Thuani Historiarum sui Temporis*. 7 vols. London: Samuel Buckley, 1733.
———. *Monsieur de Thou's History of His Own Time*. Translated by B. Wilson. London: 1730.
Thwaites, G. et al. "The English Sweating Sickness, 1485–1551." *The New England Journal of Medicine* 336 (1997): 580–82.
Tostado, Alfonso. *Opera Omnia*. 27 vols. Venice: Balleoniana, 1728.
———. *Commentaria in Genesim: Mendis nunc sanè quam Plurimis Diligenter Expurgate*. Venice: Sessa, 1596.

Trelcat Jr., Lucas. "Antidotum Pestis, seu Tractatus Christanus de Causis et Remediis Eiusdem." In *Opuscula Theologica Omnia*, Leiden: Johannes Orlers & Johannes Maire, 1614; Amsterdam: Henricus Laurentius, 1614.

———. *Remèdes contre le Mal-Reiglé Mespris, l'oubliance, et la Trop Grande Apprehension de la Mort, Cueillis au Jardin de Vie*. Geneva: Jacques Chouet, 1604.

Tutino, S. *Uncertainty in Post-Reformation Catholicism: A History of Probabilism*. Oxford: Oxford University Press, 2018.

Ursinus, Zacharias. "Pia Meditatio Mortis et Consolationum adversus Eius Horrorem, tum Παρασκευῆς Πρὶς Εὐθανασίαν." In *Opera Theologica*. Frankfurt: 1612.

———. *Zachariae Vrsini, Vratislaviensis Scholasticarum in Materiis Theologicis Exercitationum*. 2 vols. Neustadt: Matthaeus Harnisch, 1589.

Vallés, Francisco. *Sacra Philosophia*. 6th ed. Lyon: Jean-Antoine Huguetan & Marc-Antoine Ravaud, 1652.

Vázquez, Gabriel. *Commentaria ac Disputationes in Tertiam Partem S. Thomae*. 2 vols. Ingolstadt: Officina Typographica Ederiana, 1612.

Vermeulen, Jan. *Theologiae Practicae Compendium*. Cologne: Birckman, 1590.

Vermigli, Peter Martyr. *In Samuelis Prophetae Libros Duos...Commentarii*. 2nd ed. Zurich: Christophorus Froschouerus, 1564.

———. *Loci Communes*. 11th ed. Geneva: Pierre Aubert, 1624.

Vignier, Nicolas. *Theatre de l'antechrist, Auquel est Respondu au Cardinal Bellarmin, au Sieur de Remond, a Pererius, Ribera, Viegas, Sanderus et Autres qui Par Leurs Escrits Condamnent la Doctrine des Eglises Reformes sur ce Subjet*. Geneva: Philippe Albert, 1613.

Voetius, G. *Desperata Causa Papatus*. Amsterdam: Joannes Jansson, 1635.

———. *Dissertatio Epistolica, de Termino Vitae ad ... Johannem Beverovicium*. 2nd ed. Utrecht: Esdras Wilhelmus, 1641.

———. *Politicae Ecclesiasticae*. Amsterdam: Joanne à Waesberg, 1663.

———. "Section IV de Titulo Alexipharmaci et Magia Papatus." In *Desperata Cavsa Papatvs. Præmissa etiam Velitatione de Magia, Aliisque Abominationibvs Papatvs*, Amsterdam: Joannes Jansson, 1635.

———. *Selectarum Disputationum Theologiacarum*, vols. 1–4, Utrecht: Johannes Waesberg, 1648–1667; vol. 5, Utrecht: Antonius Smytegelt, 1669.

———. "Tractatus de Peste, seu Pestis Antidoto Spirituali." In *Variorum Tractatus Theologici de Peste*, Leiden: Johannes Elsevirius, 1655.

de Voragine, Jacobus. *The Golden Legend: Readings on the Saints*. 2 vols. Translated by W.G. Ryan. Princeton: Princeton University Press, 1993.

Vossius, Gerardus, ed. *Operum Omnium Sancti Ephraem Syri*. 3 vols. Rome: Jacopo Torneri, 1589-1598.

Wigand, Johann. *De Persecutione Piorum*. Frankfurt: Werdestein, 1553.

Zanchi, Girolamo. *In D. Pauli Apostoli Epistolas ad Philippenses, Colossenses, Thessalonicenses Commentarii*. Neustadt: Matthaeus Harnisius, 1595.

Zepper, Wilhelm. *Auszführlicher Bericht von Sterbensläuften*. Herborn: Christoff Raben, 1607.

Zwinger, Theodor. *Theatrum Humanae Vitae*. Basil: Eusebius, 1586.

Zwingli, Huldreich. "A Christian Song Written by Huldreich Zwingli When He Was Attacked by the Pestilence." In *Huldreich Zwingli: The Reformer of German Switzerland 1484-1531*. 2nd revised ed. New York: G. P. Putnam's Sons, 1903.

Index of Subjects and Names

A

Aa, A. J. van der, 123:n
Aaron, 71, 97
Abel, 276
Abbot, George, *On Flight in Persecution or Plague*, 274–94; xix, xxxii, 42, 103, 107, 146, 271–74
Abimelech, 145
Abraham, 24, 44, 198, 209, 275, 321
Absalom, David's son, 22, 303
Adam, Melchior, 85, 248:n
Adrian VI (pope), 88
Aeschines, 20:n
Aesculapius, 89
Agabus, 17
Agatho (pope), 110
Agricola, Georgius, 77
Ahab, 145, 230, 287
AIDS, xviii
Alciato, 160–61
Alexander, Archibald, 31
Alexandria, 25, 163
Alpini, Prospero, 121
Alsted, Johann Heinrich, 101
Althusius, Johannes, 118
Ambrose, bishop of Milan, 105, 218:n
Ames, William, 100, 176, 178
Amicus, Diomedes, 78
Amsdorf, Nikolaus von, 192
Anabaptists, 124–25, 218
Ananias (of Damascus), 289
Anaxagoras, 6
Andel, H. A. van, 120:n
angels, 15
Anhalt, George, Prince, 222:n
Antonine Plague, xviii
Apostles' Creed, 261:n

Aquinas, 175
    Summa Theologica, 170, 177
Aramaic, 72:n
Arethusius, Marcus the Stylite, 145
Aretius, 118
Arianism, 142, 145, 286, 289–90
Armed Forces Epidemiological Board, xi
Arminius, 67
Asa (king of Judah), 10
Assyrians, 17, 129
astrology, 14
Athanasius, 22, 142–46, 198, 244, 245, 286, 289–90
Athens, Plague of, xvii, 76–79
Augustine, 17, 32, 62, 84:n, 104, 105, 137, 145, 147, 148, 152, 158, 159–60, 175
    Epistle to Honoratus, 242–46, 290–91
    The Morals of the Catholic Church, 52
    On Friendship, 105
Aurelius, Marcus, 136

B

Bächtold, Hans Ulrich, 211:n
Backus, Irena, 211:n
Baer, Ludovicus (Ludwig), 49, 50
Bagnolo, Francesco Accorso di, 160
Baile, Guillaume, 90
Balduin, Friederich, 47, 103, 106:n, 178
Bañez, Domingo, 112, 174
Baronio, Cesare, 59:n, 92, 162, 166:n
Baruch, 25
Baschera, Luca, 211:n

Bavinck, Herman, 125
Becanus, Martinus, 105
    Summary of Scholastic Theology, 176
Beeke, Joel, I, 67, 68
Belgic Confession, xxvi
Bellarmine, Robert, 150
Benedict VIII (pope), 76, 104
Benjamin, Jacob's son, 303
Benno of Hildesheim, 92
Benzoni, Rutilio, 112
Berckhusen, Antonius von, 43
Bernard of Clairvaux, 83, 92, 114
Beza, Theodore, *A Learned Treatise on the Plague*, 6–29; xix, xxvi–xxxii, xxvi–xxxii, 3, 14:n, 3, 37, 47, 61:n, 70, 85, 100, 103, 128, 132, 150–51
    Confession of the Christian Faith, 3
    he had the plague, 28
    ministry during plague, xxvii–xxxi
    prayer, "Upon eternal death," 4
    regarding Augustine 17:n
Bibliander, Theodor, 85, 212
Biel, Gabriel, 49, 104–105, 112
Bierma, Lyle, 248:n
Bilney, Thomas, 106
black death, xii, xviii, 35:n
Bonacina, Martino, 112
Bonaventure, 93, 174
Book of Common Prayer, "Prayer and Thanksgiving from the Book of Common Prayer, 1662," 329–30; xix, xxxii
Borrhaus, Martin, 85
Borromeus, Carolus, 94, 104
Boulin, Jean, 48
Bradford, John, 137
Bradley, James, 7:n
Bray, Thomas, 296:n
Breda, Orange College of, 31
Breslau, 191, 194, 208, 247
Briard, Jean, 118
Bruges, 48
Bucer, Martin, 231
Bugenhagen, Johann, 191–92
Bullinger, Heinrich, xix, 211–12, 231–32, 238, 239, 245
    contracted plague during pastoral visit, 47
Buoni, Omobono de, 112
Burchard of Worms, 59
Burchill, Christopher, 247, 250
burials of victims, 53–61, 165, 181, 209, 251–52
    statistics regarding, 126
Busaeus, Joannes, 104
Busbecq, Ogier Ghiselin de, 121
Buxtorf, Johannes, 90

C
Cain, 254, 276, 324
Calvin, John, xxvi, xvii, xxix, 3, 29, 70
    Institutes, 18:n
    letter to Jerome Zanchi, 231
    On the Visitation of the Sick, xix
    on fleeing the plague, 36–37, 103
Calvinism, Calvinist, 67, 80
causation, 129
    contingent, 17, 18
    natural, 14, 18, 19
    primary, 68
    secondary, xxviii, 4, 9–12, 15, 32, 34, 39, 68, 97, 101, 241
CDC, National Vaccine Advisory Committee on Immunization Practices, xi
Chaldeans, 25
Charan, Jean, 48
Cambridge University, 288, 306
    Pembroke College, 295

Campi, Emidio, 186:n
Canterbury, archbishop of, 42, 146, 272
Capito, Wolfang Fabritius, 85
Cardano, Girolamo, 71, 76, 77:n, 110, 116, 118
Carpzovius, Benedictus, 179
Carthage, plague in, xviii, xxxii, 35:fn, 313–14
Casas, Juan de las, 151
Catholicism, xviii, xxxi, 49:n, 88:n, 49, 91–92, 118, 123, 125, 150
  hospitals, 3
  Masses, 94
  martyrs, 77:n
  morals of, 52
  prayers of exorcism, 93
  rites of, 58
Charlemagne, 58–59, 161
Christians, xv, xxiii–xxxii, 3–6, 18, 25, 42, 43, 55, 57, 58, 59, 60, 63, 80, 98, 102, 120, 142, 163, 165, 175, 176, 193, 195, 222, 233, 251, 260, 261, 273, 279, 284, 293, 314. 315, 323
Christopher, 92, 93
Chrysostom, 63, 136, 168, 289
Cicero, 17:n, 40:n, 56, 171
  De Lebigbus, 56:n,
  De natura deorum, 316:n
  Pro Milone, 40:n
  Tusculan Disputations, 171
"Cito, Longe, Tarde," "flee quickly, go far, and return slowly," xxi, 26:n, 41:n, 44, 98, 116, 117
Clark, R. Scott, 67
Claudius, Tiberius, 17, 78:n
Clemanges, Nicolaus de, 105, 156–57,
Clement VI, pope, 94
Clement of Alexandria, 130, 131:n, 280–81

College of St. Thomas, Strasbourg, 231
Colloquy of Poissy, 150
Constantine, Emperor, 127, 279
Constantinople, 76, 128, 289 [search?]
Constantius II, 244, 286, 289
councils
  Braga (Spain), 59
  Nantes, 58, 60
  Trent, 50, 93:fn
  Vaison, 58
COVID-19, xi, xvii, xviii, xxv, xi
Coleman, Stephen M., xii, xx, xxxii
Copernicus, 6, 7:n
Cranmer, Thomas, 284
Curtis, Daniel R., 126:n
Cyprian, bishop of Carthage, *On Mortality*, 316–28; xviii, xxxii, 35:n, 79, 80, 81, 100, 104, 105, 128, 136, 213, 281, 284, 313–16

D

Daniel, 137, 220:n, 228
D'Aubigné, J. H. Merle, 187:n
David, 10, 22, 24, 39, 42, 56, 97, 111, 127, 129, 130:n, 141, 145, 160, 198, 214–22, 224, 226, 227, 228, 229, 230, 240, 258, 276, 278, 280, 292, 303, 329
decree of God, 9, 16, 17, 18, 25, 33, 39, 40, 134, 201, 205, 240, 253, 279, 286
  immutability of it, 16, 20, 21, 26
Defense Health Board, xi
Defferarri, Roy, 316:n
Demaitre, Luke, 11:n
Dene, Tilo, 191
D'Espence, Claude, 93, 148–50, 153, 180
  Commentary on 1 Timothy, 50, 112, 148–153
Diocletian, Emperor, 56:n, 277

Dionysius of Alexandria, 25:n, 100
   Alexandrian plague and, 163–65, 168–69
Doeg, 276
Domitian, 277
Durandus of Pourçain, 174
Durante, Jean Etienne, 58, 59
Dutch Reformed, 102, 120:n, 123, 125, 247
Dutch Further (Second) Reformation, 67, 125

E
Ebola, xviii
Eckert, Edward A., xxiv, xxv
Eckhard, Melchior Sylvester, 103, 179
Edward VI, king of England, 271, 288
Egypt, Egyptians, 11, 13, 40, 121, 198, 215, 222, 225, 241, 243, 285, 289
   death of firstborn, 72
   famine, 16–17, 42, 198
Elijah, 141, 145, 198, 285, 286–87, 301
   fiery chariot, 87
   fled from Jezebel, 22, 44, 285
Elisha, 141
England, Church of, 297
Enoch, 301, 326
Epaphroditus, 38–39, 232–237, 246
Ephrem the Syrian, 127
epidemic, 5, 123, 130, 169, 170, 201, 205
Erpenius, Thomas, 85
Esau, 144, 198
Eucharist, see Lord's Supper
Eusebius of Caesarea, *Ecclesiastical History*, 25, 47, 76, 100, 141, 163, 164:n, 165:n, 166, 279, 283
Evagrius Scholasticus, 75, 77
Ezekiel, 216

F
Fabritius, Thomas, 70

famine, xi, xvii 14, 15, 16, 17, 23, 24, 25, 40, 41, 42, 71, 72, 74, 79, 110, 111, 134, 149, 174, 198, 214, 216, 219, 220, 224, 226, 228, 240, 241, 281, 292, 303, 314, 317, 319
Farel, Guillaume, xxvii
FDA, Vaccines and Related Biologic Products Advisory Committee, xi
Ficino, Marsilio, *Antidote of Epidemics*, 53, 80:n
Follinus, Hermannus, 73, 80
Forest, Michael, 48
flu, xviii
   Asian, xi
   Bird, xviii
   H1N1, xi
   Hong Kong, xi
   Spanish, xviii
   Swine, xviii
Fox, Arthur, 272
Fracastoro, Girolamo, *On Contagion*, 110, 117
France, xix, xxiv, xxxi, 31:n, 48:n, 64, 72:n, 77:n, 80, 92, 98, 103:n, 120, 151, 279, 304
Frederick III, Elector of Saxony, 248
Funerals, 51, 69, 82, 248
   reason for conducting them, 251–57

G
Galen of Pergamum, xii, 8, 11:n, 41:n, 153:n
Gamze, Rabbi, 131
Gardner, E. G., 60:n
Geneva, xix, xxvii, xxxi, 37, 45, 289:n
   academy of, 3, 103:n
   care for sick in, xxix–xxxi, 47, 103, 157, 242
   church of, 103
   plague and xxvii, xxviii
Gerartsen, Jan, 91

Gerhard, Johann, 46, 103, 178, 179,
German Reformed, 247
Germany, xviii, xxiv, 122, 123, 146, 272
Gesner, Conrad, 37, 85
Ghent, 48, 92
Giovo, Paulo, 88
Giraldi, Gregorio Giglio, 56:n, 57–58
Giuntini, Francesco, *On the Plague*, 116
Gomarus, Franciscus, 67, 86
Gonzaga, Francisco, 91
Good Samaritan, xviii, 99
Gordon, Bruce, 211:n
Grataroli, Gulielmo, 98
Greeks, 8, 92, 93:n, 161, 182
Grégoire, Pierre, 49, 118
Gregory I (the Great, pope), 60, 102, 104, 111, 128
Gregory XIII (pope), 70:n
Gregory of Nazianzus, 87, 128, 145–46
Gregory of Nyssa, 79, 110, 111:n
Gregory of Tours, 128
Gregory Thaumaturgus, (the Wonderworker), 79:57, 110–11
Grillot, Jean, 80
Grindal, Edmund, xix
Guido, Alfani, xxiv, 116
Gwalther, Rudolf, 212

H
Haag, Emile, 31:n
Haag, Eugène, 31:n
Hague, The, 65
Hahn, Philip, 103
Hall, Joseph, 101–104
Harderwijk University, 123
Hebrews (the people), 8
Heidelberg, xix, 48, 75, 85
    plague in, 248:n
    Catechism, xix–xx, 247, 248:n, 250:n
    University of, 41, 232, 247, 272

Helvetic Confession, 102
Herculanus, Joannes, 117
Herod, 18, 145, 243
Hertog, Gerard den, 248:n
Hess, Johann, xii, 191, 192, 194
Heurnius, Justus, 125
Hezekiah, king of Judah, 15, 17, 22, 25, 129:n, 134, 240, 300
Hippocrates, 8, 41:n
Holy Scripture, 10, 13, 15, 20, 21, 22, 24, 48, 55, 127, 129, 145, 150, 198, 215, 235, 319, 326
Holland, S. M., 271:n
Homer, *The Iliad*, 71
Hooper, John, xix, 284
Hoornbeeck, Johannes, *Theological Dissertation on the Plague*, 126–182; xii, xix, xxxii, 123–26, 127:n, 272:n
hospitals, xiii, xvi, xviii, xxvii, 38, 154–56, 161, 200, 225
Hottomanus, 161
Huguenots (French Reformed), xxxi, 31
Huijgen, A., 248:n
Hurtado, Tomás of Toledo, 167, 169–71.

I
Ingrassia, Giovanni Filippo, 116
Isaac, 24, 44, 198, 276, 324
Italy, xxiv, 49, 80, 88:n, 92, 94, 98, 107, 117, 231, 233, 242
Itterzon, G. P. van, 31:n

J
Jackson, Samuel Macauley, 187
Jacob, 22, 24, 44, 144, 198, 241, 292, 303, 324
James I, King of England, 271
Jehoiakim, 198, 285, 289
Jeremiah, 25, 289
Jerome, 60, 84, 105, 127, 142, 280:n
    on Micah 7, 105

Jewel, John, 212
Jews, 17, 41, 52, 90, 119, 124, 137, 145, 159, 182, 209, 229, 275–76, 321, 323
    should Christians use Jewish physicians, 120–21, 218
Jezebel, 22, 145, 198, 285
Job, 72, 262, 263, 320
John the Baptist, 137, 275
Jonah, 43, 96, 137, 228, 302
Jongeneel, Jan A. B., 120:n
Joseph, Mary's husband, 285
Joseph, Jacob's son, 17, 303
Josephus, 129
Joshua, 97
Jouanna, Arlette, xxxi
Judas (Iscariot), 13, 254
Junius, Franciscus, xxvi, 85, 86, 128, 148, 155, 180–81,
Justin Martyr, xviii, 284
Justinian I, Byzantine emperor, xviii 111, 160, 162

K

Kalwitz, Seth, 76
Kimedoncius, Jacobus, 85
Kingdon, Robert, xxxi
Kuyper, Abraham, 125

L

La Trémoille, Duke of, 31
Lactantius, 105
Lapide, Cornelius à, 71, 80, 92, 166, 175
Last Judgment, 209, 261
Latimer, Hugh, 284
Lausanne, 3, 28, 212
    plague in, xxvi,
Lavater, Hans Rudolph, 211:n, 213
Lavater, Ludwig, *The Merciful Hands of the Lord: Commentary and a Brief Excursus on Plague from 1 Chronicles 21:9–15*, 214–230; xix, xxxii, 43, 70, 89:n, 95, 100, 111, 122, 211–14,
Le Paulmier, Julien, 73, 78, 116
Leiden, xxvi,
    academy in, 148,
    University of, 31, 67, 123, 124, 128:n
Lemnius, Levinius, 113
leprosy, 11, 12, 39, 41, 42, 97, 108, 240, 193
Licinius, Petreius, 89
Lillback, Peter A., xvii:n
Lindberg, Carter, xvii:n
Lipsius, Justus, 94
Livy, 55:n, 56:n, 89,
Locre, Ferry de, 94
Lodensteyn, Jodocus van, 125
London, 306
    plagues in, xviii, xix, xxv, xxvi, 295
Lorca, Pedro de, 174, 175:n
Lord's Prayer, 83, 199, 296
Lord's Supper, 46, 79, 231
Lorin, Jean de, 91
Lorraine, Cardinal Charles de, 150
Lot, 134, 215
Lucretius, 76, 77
Luther, Hans (Martin's son), 191
Luther, Martin, *Whether One May Flee from A Deadly Plague*, 194–210; xii, xix, xxxii, 103, 191–94, 104:n
Lutherans, 37, 46:n, 47:n, 103, 231–32, 233, 247
Lydius, Johannes, 106
Lyra, Nicholas of, 72

M

magistrate, 27–29, 35–37, 45–46, 54, 63, 83, 98, 114, 172–73, 218, 228, 294
Manetsch, Scott M., xxvi, 3:n

Index of Subjects and Names

Mansi, Govanni Dominico, 59:n, 60:n
Marcellus, Nonius, 222:n
Marchini, Filiberto, 70, 72, 73, 75, 80, 90, 91, 92, 94
    On the Plague, 101, 104, 105, 106, 107, 110, 112, 115, 116, 118, 119, 120, 166-69, 174
Marcquis, Gulielmus, 73, 74, 113, 118
Marot, Clément, 3
Martin, Craig, 14:n
Mary (mother of Jesus), 72:n, 90-94, 258, 276, 285
Mary Tudor, Queen of England, 137, 271, 279
Mastricht, Petrus van, 123
Mathesius, Johann, 148
Maximus, Valerius, 89, 176
Mayer, Johann, 248:n
Mayo Clinic, xi, xx
Melanchthon, Philip, 148, 221-22, 231, 247
Mercuriale, Girolamo, 114, 115
MERS, xviii
Modestinus, Herennius, 163
Möller, Heinrich, 70
monasticism, xviii, 91, 114:n, 119, 149
Monstrolio, Johannes de, 156
Moriendi, Ars, 248:n
Moser, Christian, 211:n
Moses, 15, 71, 97, 145, 198, 215, 229, 253, 285, 286
Moulin, Louis du, xxvi

N
Nanninck, Pieter, 145
Naphy, William G., xxvii
nature, laws of, 11, 15, 28, 113:n, 114
Navarra, Petrus, 174
Naucratis, Julius Pollux of, 161:n
Netherlands, xix, 54, 64, 67, 86, 109, 122-26, 279

Nicephorus, 77, 100, 116
Noah, 134, 215
Novatus, 279, 283
Nuñez, Luis, 92:n

O
Obadiah, 145
Oecolampadius, Johannes, 85-86
Oosterom, Johannes, 125
Orestes, 162
Origen, on Gospel of John, 281
Orosius, Paulus, 51
Osler, Sir William, xi:n
Owen, John, 67
Oxford University, 288
    Balliol College, 271

P
Paolini, Fabio, 117
parabolani (ancient care givers), 160-63
Pareus, David, 75, 85, 101, 111
Paul, apostle, 10, 17, 21, 44, 157, 195, 196, 209, 241, 243, 265, 319, 321-22, 325
    flight from Damascus, 145, 273, 289
Paul the Deacon (ancient historian), 110
Paludanus, 174
Paulmier, Julien le, 73, 78, 116
Pelgrom, Simon, 11:n
Pellikan, Konrad, 212
Pereira, Benito, 71
Perkins, William, 41, 100, 101
Peter, apostle, 135, 195, 283
Peter of Alexandria, 143
Petrarch, xvii
Pharoah, 145, 285, 286
plague
    avoiding it, 138-56
    bubonic, xii

burial of its victims, 181–82
cause of, Galenic theory (miasma), xi, xxvii, 18, 36, 37, 80
Christian response to, xxiii–xxiv, 134–38
"diseased wind," 47
duties to those with it, 156–63
etymology of the word, xii
fleeing infected locations, xxvii–xxviii, 3, 7, 40–45, 132–34, 192–93, 237–39
martyrdom and, 163–179
questions about it unresolved, 120–21
Reformation era, xxiv
severity of it varies, xxiv–xxv
should infected goods be burned, 119–20
shutdowns caused by, 1500–1720, xxv
theologians who died of it, 85–86
Plato, *Gorgias*, 20
Plutarch, 79, 89, 90
Poissy, Colloquy of, 3, 150
Poland, Gregory A., xv, xx
Polansdorf, Amandus Polanus von, 85–86
Polycarp of Smyrna, 141, 284
Pontisella, Johannes, 70:n, 95, 100:n, 213:n
Porto, Francesco (of Crete), 103
Possidius, 158, 159:n, 160:n
Poynter, F. N. L., xxvi
Praevidello, Jerome, 70
Pretere, Guillaume de, 91, 101
Procopius, 76, 77, 111
Puritanism, xix, 67, 271
Pynsent, John, 295

Q

Quodvultdeus, a bishop, 242

R

Ramirez, King, 59
Rawlet, John, *A Letter to my Mother*, 298–309; xix, xxxii, 295–97, 306:n, 309
    died of the plague, 300
Raynaud, Theophilé, 77, 101, 112, 118, 166–69
Reformed, the, xii, xiii, xxviii, xxix, xxxii, 32, 48, 67, 69, 106, 109, 122, 123, 125, 211, 233, 247, 249, 272, 313
Rester, Todd M., xii, xx, xxxii, xv:n, xx:n
    translator 34, 70, 126, 214, 234, 251, 274
Rhegius, Urbanus, 43, 44
Ridley, Nicholas, 284
Ripa, Gianfrancesco, 70
Rivet, André, *A Letter to a Friend*, 34–65; xix, xxix, xxxii, 31–34, 55:n, 70, 71, 128, 148, 182, 313
    died of the plague, 32–33
Rovellus, Protasius, 76
Rufinus of Aquileia, 100

S

Salas, Juan de, 112
Salmeron, Alfonso, 148
Sánchez, Tomás, 112
Saravia, Adrianus, 125
Sarazin, Jean-Antoine, 73, 76, 78, 98, 114–15
SARS, xviii
Saul, king of Israel, 22, 42, 145, 198, 230, 292
Scaliger, J. C., 74–76
Schindler, Carl J., 194
Scott, S. P., 56:n
Scultetus, Abraham, 146, 272:n
Sebastian, 91–92
Selderhuis, Herman, 248:n
Seneca (the younger), 65, 77
Senensis, Bernardinus, 104

Sennacherib, 129
Sennert, Daniel, 74–75, 77, 80, 89:n, 97, 115, 116, 119
Serapion, 47
Serres, Jean de, 151:n
Settala, Ludovico, 96
Shaw, Samuel, 306:n
Siculus, Diodorus, 53
Simler, Josias (Josiah), 85, 212
Sirmond, Jacques, 58
Slack, Paul, xiii:n
Socinians, 67, 124, 125
Socrates Scholasticus, (of Constantinople), 286:n
Sohn, Georg, 41, 44, 100, 103
Sozomen, 136:n, 289:n
Spaans, Joke, 126:n
Spain, xxiv, xxv, 49, 59, 72:n, 92, 110:n
Spartan, Demetrius, 88
Stengel, Karl, 93
Stockwood, John, 6
Stoic philosophy, 15, 17, 135
Strassburg, 103, 212
Stucki, Johann Wilhelm, 211, 213
Suarez, Francisco, 112
Sulpitius, Titus, 89
Switzerland, xxiv, xxvii, 38, 118, 122, 212, 213, 238
Sylvester, Melchior, 103, 179
Sylvius, Franciscus, 175
Synod of Dort, 67, 102
Synod of Vitré, 31, 48
Synod of Trebur, 58, 60
Syrianus, 142

T

Talmud, 90, 120:n, 122
Tarnow, Paul, 37, 46, 103
Teelinck, Willem, 125
Ten Commandments, 70, 225, 230
    sixth, murder, 27

Terilli, Domenico, 76
Tertullian, 22, 136, 141–42, 273, 279–280, 291
Theodosian Code, 160, 162
Theon, poet, 276:n
Theophanes the Confessor, 137:n, 216:
Thomson, George, 94
Thou, Jacques-Auguste de, 151
Thucydides, 76, 77, 78, 117, 153:n
Tostado, Alfonso, 72, 105, 111
Trelcat, Lucas (the younger), 70, 100
Trinity College, Dublin, 272
Trueman, Carl R., 67:n
Turks, 42, 55, 121, 122, 198, 292, 293
Tylenda, Joseph, 231, 232:n

U

Udemans, Godefridus, 125
Urban VIII (pope), 120
Ursinus, Zacharias, *A Godly Meditation upon Death*, 251–70; xix, xxxii, 48, 100, 101, 232, 247–50
Utrecht, 101, 151
Utrecht University, 68, 123, 124

V

Valentinian I, Roman emperor, 127
Valerian, historian, 166
Vallés, Francisco, 110
Vázquez, Gabriel, 112, 169
Vermeulen, Jan, 104
Vermigli, Peter Martyr, 111, 147:n, 176, 212, 220, 231, 280
Vespasian, Roman emperor, 76
Vignier, Nicolas, 94
Vincent, Thomas, xix
Viret, Pierre, 28
Voetius, Gisbertus, *A Treatise on the Plague, or a Spiritual Antidote for the Plague*, 70–122; xii, xix, xxxii, 67–70, 158:n, 123, 125, 128, 313

Vos, Gerhardus, 125
Vossius, Gerard Johann, 85, 127

W
Wagner-Peterson, Boris, 248:n
Watt, Gideon van der, 120:n
Werdmüller, Otto, 248:n
White, Thomas, xix
Wigand, Johann, 103
will of God, 17, 18, 20, 22, 23, 142, 182, 223, 229, 233, 264, 299, 324, 327
Winsheim, Veit, 153
Wittenberg, xix, 194, 209, 210
    Academy, 153, 155
    plague in, 191, 207
    University of, 191, 247
Wolf, Johann, 212
Wright, Shawn D., xxvi, 5:n
Wyß, Georg von, 211:n

Y
yellow fever, xviii

Z
Zanchi, Jerome (Girolamo), *The Work of Christ and the Christian's Duty an Excerpt from an Exposition of Philippians 2:30*, 234–46; xii, xix, xxix–xxx, 38–40, 46, 47, 48, 64, 70, 101, 102, 185, 186, 231–33, 234, 239
Zepper, Wilhelm, 128
Zika virus, xviii
Zurich, xix, xxvi, 43, 47, 185, 186, 211, 212, 213, 248n
Zwinger, Theodor, 76
Zwingli, Huldrych, *Plague Song ("Pestlied")*, 187–89; xix, xxvi, xxxii, 185–87, 211, 212

Index of Scripture References

Genesis
3	256
4:3–12	324:n
4:13–14	254:n
5:24	326
6:13	72
12:10–16	42:n
14	105
22:1ff	321:n
25:9	56
27	22:n
32	60
37	303:n
40–47	198
41:46–57	17:n
42	42:n
43	303:n
47	55:n

Exodus
2:15	285
3	87
3:7	227
5:1	287
5:2–3	129
8:15	135
8:16–32	13:n
8:19	73
9	70, 75, 79, 80
9:3	71
9:3, 15	72
9:13–35	13:n
9:34	135
12	72:n, 79
12:29–32	222
17:3	20
20:4–6	230:n
20:13	292
32:31–32	229:n

Leviticus
13	xvii
13–14	11:n, 119, 206
15:45	293
15:46	293
26	71
26:25	50–51, 129

Numbers
5	119
5:2	293
17:10	321
14:11–12	51
25:1–9	xvii

Deuteronomy
8:2	321
8:3	136
13:3	321
27:21–22	129
28	71
28:15–68	42:n
28:21	51
28:59–61	292
32:24	72

Judges
7:22–23	12:n

1 Samuel
2	83
2:2	83
3:18	136
9:9	214
18:33	173
19:1–10	42:n
19:10	292
19:21	22:n
21:1	278
22:1	278
24	70
24:10–17	xvii
27:1	278

2 Samuel
14:15	292
15	22:n
15:14	278
16	83
19:1–8	303:n
21	216
24	10, 39, 79, 111, 230
24:11	214
24:13, 15	129
24:14	130:n
24:15–16	129
24:16	72
24:17	24:n
24:21	72

1 Kings
8	51
19	22:n
19:3	198, 285
19:5	286
19:13, 21	87
22:19–23	13:n

2 Kings
4:8–37	303:n
19:20–37	222:n

19:35	129	**Psalms**		103–104	69, 84
19:35–37	13:n	6	214	103:11–13	220
		6:2	137	104	84
1 Chronicles		17:14	10, 87	106	69, 84
9–15	100:n	18	185	106:30–31	72
9:15–17	226	21:6	292	115:18	61
12:32	127	22:12	86	119:71	136
21	10, 13, 70, 100, 111, 122, 213	23	85	139	225
		23:1–4	86	139:7	152
21:9–12	214	24:1	136	139:8–9	98
21:9–17	100:n	27:9–10	86		
21:13	217	28	10	**Proverbs**	
21:14–15	100:n, 221	30	227	5	217
21:15	43	31	10:fn	23:34–35	135
21:15–16	72	33	227:n		
21:17	24:n	37:26	87	**Song of Solomon**	
		38	10	2:6	86
2 Chronicles		39	83		
6	51	41:1	82	**Isaiah**	
6:14	276	41:1–3	99, 202	1:5	52, 135
7:14	136	41:3–4	86	5	70
16:12	10:fn	50:16–22	255	12:16	72
22:10	72	51:17	321	13:11	72
32	79	76:10	xix	14	70
32:21	72	77:49	72	22:12–14	52:n
36:13	135	78:18	20	26:20	262
		84:1	327	28:15	51
Esther		86	227	36–37	17:n
4:13–14	159	88	13	37:21–38	222:n
		90:10	253	37:36–38	13:n
Job		91	10, 24, 70, 81, 96, 99, 100, 117, 128, 313	38	25:n
1	83			38:9–20	22:n
1:8	320	91:5	72	42:15	86
1:13–19	13:n	91:6	19, 42, 72	42:24–25	135
1:21	136, 137, 320	91:7	45, 179	43:1–2	152
2:10	263:n, 320	91:11–13	203	45:7	129
7:1	135	91:13–15	263	49	227
13:7	131	91:15	86	54:6–7	86
14:1	135	94:9	227	56:13	261:n
19:25–26	262:n	103	81, 84, 219, 227, 313	57:1–2	261
38:1	87			58:3–10	82

58:7	99	**Daniel**		7:11	267	
58:7–12	82	4:37	136	7:12	56, 99, 201	
65	96	5:22	136	8:12	255	
		9	228	10	96	
Jeremiah				10:23	22, 242, 286	
5:3	135	**Hosea**		10:28, 33	196	
7:11	61	13	87	10:29–30	16:n, 129	
14	71	13:6–8	255	10:30	179	
17:17	86	13:14	72, 86	10:30–31	82	
18	217			10:37	266	
21	71	**Joel**		10:40	235	
24	71	2:12	82	13:43	262	
24:10	51	2:12–15	84	15	215	
26:21	285			15:5	108	
27	71	**Amos**		16:3	127	
29	71, 79	3	215, 225	16:24–25	265	
32	71	3:6	11:n, 23:n, 71, 129,	16:25	236	
34	71	4	79	16:26	172	
37:12	25	4:10	129	17	83	
38	71			22	99, 149	
		Micah		22:13	255	
Lamentations		7	105	22:37–39	172	
3:37–38	129			22:39	204, 292	
3:39–43	82	**Zephaniah**		24	221	
		2:1–2	82	24:7	72	
Ezekiel				24:46	159	
5	71	**Habakkuk**		24:48–51	268	
5:14	79	2:4	264:n, 317	25	217	
5:17	72	3	227	25:12	268	
14	71, 79, 100:n	3:3–5	51	25:30	255	
14:21	292			25:36, 43	99	
6	71	**Matthew**		25:40	204, 235	
6:12	51	2:13–15	285	25:41–46	193, 197	
9	13	3:9	275	25:42	44	
14	79, 100	4:6	292	25:43	200	
14:21	129, 292	4:7	42, 292	26	228	
16:49	200	5:7, 25, 36, 43	99	26:40	86	
18	229	6:25	198	27:3–5	254:n	
18:23, 32	259	6:33	135			
23	217	7:2	203	**Mark**		
28:23	51	7:6	207	2:17	61	

5:2, 14	56	15:13	173, 283	11:25–27	120		
8	83	16:20	318	13:1	83		
10:23	280	16:22	318	13:1–2	83:n		
13:33, 35–37	268	17:24	326	13:4	196		
16:18	19, 195			14:5	155		
		Acts		14:7	209		
Luke		8:1	278	14:8	263		
1:74	138	9:3	21:n	15:1	195		
2:29–30	317	9:21	286				
4:28–30	17:n	9:23–25	273, 274	**1 Corinthians**			
7:12	56, 209	9:25	196	1:10	195		
7:50	264:n	11:27–30	17:n	2:30–32	82		
10	99	12:2	283	5	155		
11:13	267	13:36	127	10:6–13	xvii		
12:16	72	14:23	288	10:12	278		
12:20–21	268	19:30	196	10:13	138, 263		
13:11	72	20:20	102	11:30	79		
14	83	20:24	100	11:30–31	52		
14:25	266	21:13–14	100	12:21–26	197		
14:26	284	25:11	22	12:22	195		
16:9	280	27	40	13:5, 7	99		
18	228	27:21–23	17:n	15	87, 307		
21:31	317	27:14, 31	21	15:30	157		
22:3	13:n	27:31	40, 241	15:42	261		
		28:5	19	15:50	262		
John				15:50–56	319:n		
2:3, 31	56	**Romans**		15:54, 57	87		
3:16	173, 178	1:17	135, 317	15:54b–55	258:n		
5:24	259	1:31	20:n, 99	15:55–56	86		
6:15	17:n	5:2–3	136	15:57	307:n1		
6:39	262	5:7	173	6:13	171, 265		
7:30	17:n	5:12	256				
8:12	85	7:24	85, 260	**2 Corinthians**			
8:44	199	8	69, 81, 84, 155	1:3–5	xxiii, xxx		
8:51	260	8:1	130	1:11	22		
8:59	286	8:10	260	3	85		
10:11	44, 102, 196, 283	8:11	262	4:7	102		
		8:28	82	5	69, 84		
10:12	291	8:28–30	xiv, xix, 131	5:1	261		
10:11–12, 15	102	8:37–39	131	5:1–2	87		
11:25–26	85, 260, 326	9:3	21	5:2–3	253		
14:28	319	11:20	278	5:4–8	85		

7:3	102	6:12	137	**1 John**	
7:12	82			2:15–17	327
11:26	157	**2 Timothy**		3	149
11:28	288	2:11–12	264	3:14	265
12:7–9	322	4:2	102	3:15, 17	200
13:5	135	4:7	137	3:16	99, 102, 167, 175, 176, 178, 201, 283
13:11	195	4:7–8	87		
		5:8	196	3:16–17	99
Galatians					
6:10	173	**Titus**		**Jude**	
		1:5	288	23	82
Ephesians					
5	85	**Hebrews**		**Revelation**	
5–6	99	2:14–15	138	2:10	13, 152
5:15	114	9	180	6:8	14
5:29	197	9:27	254	9:1	14
6:16	135	10:34	136	16	222:n
		11:13, 27	306	16:2	13:n
		11:32–38	278:n	22:9	228:n
Philippians		12	81		
1:20–26	266	12:6–8	135	*Apocrypha*	
1:21	319	12:7–8	87		
1:23	85	12:10	135	**Tobit**	
2	70, 102	12:22	315	2:14	320
2:2	195	13:1, 13, 16	99	12:11–15	320
2:3	100	13:5	179		
2:30	xxix, 38, 234, 262, 326	13:9	81	**Wisdom of Solomon**	
3:20–21				4:11	327
4:11–12	136	**James**		9:15	278
4:12	186	1:2	136	18:19	91
		1:4	135	11:15–16	221:n
Colossians		1:5	135		
3	85	1:27	82	**Ecclesiasticus (Sirach)**	
3:5–7	136:n, 168:n	2:13	99	2	227
		2:13–14	82	2:1	319
1 Thessalonians		4:10	136	2:4–5	320
4:13–14	326			3:26	205
		1 Peter		27:5	322
1 Timothy		1:6	135		
4:8	202	1:31	307		
5	149	5:6	136		
5:4, 8	99	5:8	254:n		
5:8	196, 10:n, 241				

Westminster Seminary Press (WSP) was founded in 2011 by Westminster Theological Seminary in Philadelphia, Pennsylvania. WSP is a uniquely Reformed academic publisher dedicated to enriching the church, the academy, and the Christian through the printed word. WSP collaborates widely—including with faculty, staff, and students at Westminster—to publish new and classic books that foster faith in and obedience to Jesus Christ from an orthodox, Reformed perspective. For more information, visit www.westminsterseminarypress.com, email wsp@wts.edu, or write to us at 2960 Church Road, Glenside, Pennsylvania 19038.

FRAMEWORK
PUBLIC THEOLOGY
from WESTMINSTER

Framework: Public Theology from Westminster exists to equip pastors and church leaders by deploying a biblically faithful theological framework to engage the challenging moral, civic, and cultural issues the church faces in society. Learn more at www.framework.wts.edu.